Writing DR DOS® Batch Files

Ronny Richardson

Windcrest®/McGraw-Hill

FIRST EDITION
FIRST PRINTING

© 1993 by **Windcrest Books**, an imprint of TAB Books.
TAB Books is a division of McGraw-Hill, Inc.
The name ''Windcrest'' is a registered trademark of TAB Books.

Library of Congress Cataloging-in-Publication Data

Richardson, Ronny.
    Writing DR DOS batch files / by Ronny Richardson.
       p,   cm.
    ISBN 0-8306-4244-7 (P)
    1. Electronic data processing—Batch processing. 2. DR DOS.
 I. Title.
    QA76.76.063R44 1992
    005.4'46—dc20   92-25964
                                         CIP

Acquisitions Editor: Ron Powers
Book Editor: David M. McCandless
Book Design: Jaclyn J. Boone
Cover: Sandra Blair Design
  and Brent Blair Photography, Harrisburg, Pa.   WR1

Contents

_____ PART THREE _____
Intermediate batch file topics

_____PART FOUR_____

Advanced batch file topics

_____PART FIVE_____

Improving batch files with software

_____ **PART SIX** _____

Batch file applications

APPENDICES

Other Books

MS DOS Batch File Programming, 1st-3rd Ed.
MS DOS Batch File Utilities
Batch Files To Go
Dr. Batch File's Ultimate Batch File Collection
Builder Lite: Developing Dynamic Batch Files

Acknowledgments

I want to thank the folks at Hyperkinetix. Chris Bascom (the president) agreed to let one of his programmers, Doug Amaral, write Batcmd and BatScreen especially for my batch books. Doug did a wonderful job on those custom programs, and I appreciate all his work. I think you will find BatCmd and BatScreen to both be wonderful programs. Best of all, you get full-use unrestricted copies of both programs when you buy this book.

I also want to thank Keith Ledbetter for allowing me to include a copy of his Dual Boot Utility. This nice utility allows you to boot your computer off either DR DOS 6 or MS DOS 5 just by running a batch file and without having to use floppy disks. This benefits anyone who isn't sure whether or not they want to switch to DR DOS 6 or anyone who has to write batch files that will end up running on both MS and DR DOS machines.

Personally, I want to thank my wife Cicinda, my son Tevin, and my daughter Dawna for their support and patience. Because I have only a limited pool of time available, some of the time I spent writing this book had to come from the time I would have spent with my family. They were all very understanding and supportive.

Introduction

Your local bookstore has many books intended to introduce you to PC-compatible computers and the DR DOS operating system. All of these books spend a lot of time explaining DR DOS. Then they usually spend about one chapter explaining the basics of batch file programs. One chapter is enough to convince you that batch files are powerful tools; however, it isn't enough to teach you how to use batch files effectively, much less how to write them.

Who this book is for

This book will help you learn to utilize the power of batch files. In writing this book, I'm assuming you have a general understanding of DR DOS. You don't have to be a computer whiz, but you should know how to boot the computer, format a disk, and how to erase and rename files. If you have a hard disk, you should know how to make, delete, and change directories. In general, you should feel comfortable performing simple tasks from the command line prompt. If this isn't the case, you should start with a general book first.

How this book is structured

This book covers one topic per chapter. Sometimes, the topic involves one command, and other times it involves several commands. Most chapters include one or more example batch files.

The first time you read this book, you'll get much more from it if you're in front of a computer. As you read about each new topic, you should enter and run the batch file or run the batch file from the disk that comes with this book. This is also an excellent time to experiment; you'll retain the information much longer if you try to modify it to your own needs. As you read about the various batch files, try to think if you could modify them to better suit your needs or perform some similar task that interests you. This is the best way to learn new material.

Special Notes

The book has a number of brief portions of text broken from the rest of the text and marked with icons. These items are very important. Even if you are only "skimming" a chapter, you should read these. You will find different types of messages:

Note   This is a general point of interest you should be aware of.

Remember   These are important points that can cause minor problems if you forget them.

Notice   This is information on how DR DOS batch files work with other programs. If you don't have that particular program, you may choose to ignore the information.

Warning   These are important points that can cause you significant problems or loss of data if you are not careful.

Hardware and software

Writing a computer book is difficult. I never know what type of hardware and software you have; I don't even know what version of the operating system you are using. In writing about batch files, I'm more fortunate than many writers. Most batch files will run on any hardware configuration, and most of the batch files in this book will run on DR DOS 5.0 or higher. I've indicated where this is not true. So I have much less to worry about in terms of compatibility, and you can be sure that most of the batch files in this book will work on your system.

   For most of the examples in this book, I assume that the files supporting DR DOS external commands like FORMAT and BACKUP are either in the current subdirectory or in the path when an example batch file requires one of these programs. I also assume that the few utilities programs included with the disk that comes with this book are either in the current subdirectory or in a subdirectory that's in your path.

Writing the book

I wrote this book using a Northgate Super Micro 386/20 and an HP Laserjet III. The word processor I used for everything except the batch files and tables was Microsoft Word 5.5. I edited batch files and other ASCII files with the extremely nice editor that's built into DR DOS 5 and 6. Finally, I created all the tables using Word for Windows. While too slow for general writing, it has the best table-editing engine I've ever seen.

   All of the batch files were tested on an Apple Macintosh IIcx running SoftPC. SoftPC simulates an 8088 computer on the Macintosh. SoftPC treats each simulated 8088 computer as a single document, much like a word processor treats your letters. I was able to set up multiple 8088 computers on my Macintosh and then install different operating systems on each one. I had DR DOS 5, DR DOS 6, MS DOS 3.3, MS DOS 4.0, and MS DOS 5 all running on the same Macintosh! While each had their own boot drive (C drive), I configured them all to attach to the same D drive. By copying my batch files and utilities to this drive, I was then able to easily switch between operating systems to test them under all five operating systems. Try this with a PC and you're stuck booting off floppy disks! All of the problems I encountered were confirmed by Novell, who recently purchased Digital Research, as operating system bugs. Not one problem was due to running DR DOS on the Macintosh.

Conventions

You should keep a few important pieces of information in mind when reading this book:

- The numbered function keys on the keyboard are shown as F1 through F12. Most older keyboards have ten function keys on the left side of the keyboard, labeled from F1 to F10. Newer keyboards have twelve function keys, F1 to F12, along the top of the keyboard.
- Enter stands for the Enter or Return key, which can also be represented on the keyboard as Rtrn or a bent arrow. Most other named keys, like Del or Tab, are also referred to by their name. The directional keys are simply up, down, right, and left arrow.
- Information you type into the computer and pieces of programs broken out from the regular text is in an alternate typeface. The names of keys you hit, like F6 or Enter, and explanatory text is in regular type.
- The caret symbol, ^, generally means that you hold down the Control, or Ctrl, key and then tap the following key. So ^Z means hold down the Ctrl key and press the Z key. This type of key combination is shown as Ctrl-Z.
- Any command inside brackets, [ ], is optional. Brackets are generally used when I'm giving the syntax for a command. In the following, for example,

    DIR [/P]

    the /P switch is optional. It causes the listing to pause each time the screen is full. Pressing any key restarts the listing.

- Most of the commands in this book are shown in uppercase when shown on a command line. For the most part, the computer doesn't care. Entering DIR, dir, or DiR are all the same to the computer. About the only time it matters is when you're using the equal sign to compare two strings.

Last notes

If this book causes you to develop a nice batch hint or raises a batch-related question not currently answered in the book, write to me in care of TAB Books and let me know. While I can't respond to individual letters, your hint or question just might show up in the next edition of this book. The address is

Ronny Richardson
c/o TAB Books
P.O. Box 40
Blue Ridge Summit, PA 17294

If you are active in the on-line community, you can reach me on CompuServe, where my address is 70322,3100 or on PC-Link or America On-Line where my address is PC Ronny.

I tested all the batch files in this book on DR DOS 5 and 6. They were not tested on earlier versions of DR DOS. TAB Books and I have done everything possible to ensure that the programs and batch files included with this book and on the disk either run under both DR DOS 5 and 6 or are clearly labeled as to which version they require. We have also done our best to make sure that every program and batch file does exactly what we claim it will do. Neither TAB Books or I make any warranty of any type, expressed or implied, regarding the programs, batch files, and documentation included in this book and on the included disk. In addition, we aren't liable for incidental or consequential damages in connection with, or arising from, the performance of these programs and batch files.

PART ONE
Batch file introduction

Before you begin to learn to write batch files, these first three chapters will help you understand more global issues relating to batch files.

Chapter 1: Batch files are just DR DOS commands. Some of your most useful batch files can be created by simply writing down the DR DOS commands you use to perform a particular task and then storing that command or those commands in a batch file. This chapter explains that concept in more detail.

Chapter 2: Creating your own batch files. DR DOS users have three general ways to write batch files: the COPY command, the editor included with DR DOS or some other editor. This chapter explains the advantages and disadvantages of each of these approaches.

Chapter 3: Batch file construction. This chapter explains naming conventions and layout considerations you need to understand when you begin to write batch files.

When you finish these three chapters, you will be able to consolidate one or more DR DOS commands you would normally enter from the command line prompt into a batch file.

1
Batch files are just
DR DOS commands

The basic idea of a batch file is really very ingenious. When you want the computer to perform a given task more than once, why not have the computer store the details of that task? A batch file is DR DOS's way of doing that. When you tell the computer to execute a batch file, DR DOS reads and follows that batch file just like an actor reads and follows a script. In fact, the concept of the computer following a script is an excellent mental image of a batch file for you to use throughout this book.

What is a batch file good for?

Think of this section as a batch file "sales pitch" where I try to convince you that batch files are worth using! As we will see, batch files have four major functions:

- keystroke reduction
- new command construction
- consistency
- safety

We'll look at each of these in more detail.

Keystrokes reduction

Let's think about an example. When I sat down to begin writing this chapter, I had to enter some commands first:

- C:. I had been doing some "housecleaning" on my D drive. My word processing software is on my C drive, however, so the first thing I did was change to the appropriate drive.
- CD\WORD. My word processor is stored in the CD WORD subdirectory, so I then changed to that subdirectory.
- WORD. You start my word processor with the command WORD, so I issued that command.

Counting the return needed at the end of each line, I had to type sixteen keystrokes to start my word processor. As we will see, a computerized script (in other words, a batch file) can easily reduce this to as few as two keystrokes. So the first advantage of a batch file is keystroke reduction.

☑ **Remember** Batch files can save you a lot of keystrokes.

I'll offer an example to prove this and give you your first experience with batch files. The command to get a directory from the A drive is

DIR A:*/P

We can shorten this command. Without worrying about what you're typing, enter the following at the command line prompt. Just remember that Enter means press the Enter key (which might also be labeled as Rtrn or Return), and F6 means press the F6 function key and *not* type "F6" from the keyboard:

COPY CON A.BAT   Enter
DIR A:/P   F6   Enter

You should see the message "1 File(s) copied." Now put a disk in drive A and type

A   Enter

If everything goes well, you'll now see a directory of the A drive. You might be thinking to yourself, "So what? I can simply type DIR A:/P when I want a directory." The advantage of A.BAT is that you can get a directory with two keystrokes instead of nine. I use a similar batch file to start my word processor with two keystrokes rather than the sixteen described.

New command construction

When I first started using computers, I had a great deal of difficulty remembering the command to check a disk. Instead of trying to force myself to remember CHKDSK (CHecK DiSK), I wrote a batch file called CHECK.BAT, containing the single command CHKDSK. Typing CHECK instead of CHKDSK saves one keystroke, but that isn't the primary purpose of CHECK.BAT: I can remember the word "check" much easier than I can remember the nonword "CHKDSK."

☑ **Remember** Batch files can create new commands or change the name of existing commands.

Of course, I could have renamed CHKDSK.COM to CHECK.COM and achieved the same thing, but then no one else would have been able to check a disk on my computer. Writing a batch file allowed me to use the name I wanted without interfering with normal operations.

In this simple example, "new command construction" is a very fancy name for making a command accessible under another name, much like calling a garbage collector a sanitation engineer or a salesman a purchase consultant. However, as we will see later, long series of commands can be connected to form fairly intelligent sets of commands.

Consistency

Now it's time for a simple one-question test. Put away your DR DOS manual and don't look at the next figure in this book. What's the solution to the following problem?

We all know how important it is to back up your hard disk. You should be making frequent full backups, say weekly or monthly, and daily incremental backups. So write down the proper syntax of an incremental backup using the DR DOS program BACKUP .COM.

☑ *Remember* A batch file can remember complex syntax for you.

Most of you probably didn't do well on this test. Computer software often uses complex commands on the command line that are difficult for the user to remember. Happily, you don't have to. Figure out the command syntax once, and then put it into a batch file and forget it. That way, you'll never have to remember.

By the way, in case you still haven't figured it out, the syntax to make an incremental backup with DR DOS is

```
BACKUP C:\*.* A: /S /M
```

but you could easily store this in a batch file called I.BAT and just have to remember "I"—which is short for "incremental." If you can't remember that, you can pick another name. With batch files, *you* get to decide.

I can see you mentally waving a flag. You're asking "Hey, isn't this just another example of new command construction?" The answer is both yes and no. True, we have created a new command called "I" that is easier to remember than the string of switches previously listed, just as Check is easier to remember than CHKDSK. That statement can be made about almost every batch file we will construct in this book. However, the real purpose of this batch file was to always perform the backup consistently—without having to remember the syntax.

Most of the batch files we've looked at so far have one thing in common—they each do only one thing. They don't need to be limited to one activity, though. DR DOS keeps track of its location in a batch file even while it's doing something else. Let's do away with that one-command constraint right now. Consider this simple two-line batch file:

```
CHKDSK
DIR
```

First, it runs CHKDSK. While CHKDSK is running, DR DOS maintains its place in the batch file. Think of yourself putting your finger in a book so that you won't lose your place while answering the phone. After your phone conversation is over, you can pick up reading just where you left off.

When CHKDSK finishes, DR DOS reads the next command in the batch file and runs Dir. Although CHKDSK takes only a few seconds to run, it could have been a word-processing program that runs indefinitely. It doesn't matter. DR DOS remembers and picks up the batch file whenever the program finishes.

☑ *Remember*   Batch files run programs consistently.

In this past example, the batch file established a standard script to be followed each time it is run. While this is not important in this example, consider the next one:

```
C:
CD\WORD
WORD
CD\
MENU
```

This batch file automates loading my word processor, using the steps I have just described. The first three lines are identically the commands I discussed using above when I manually start my word processor. The last two lines reload my menu program once my word processor has finished. This way, my word processor starts and terminates consistently—always starting on the same drive and in the same subdirectory and always terminating in the root directory of the C drive.

Safety

A final reason for using batch files is safety. Some of the DR DOS commands are pretty dangerous. Digital Research has made their operating system safer than the other guys, but any operating system is inherently dangerous. Anything that gives you the power to format disks and erase files has the potential for accidents!

Typing "format" instead of "format A:" can destroy the data on your hard disk. Sure, Digital Research has built-in unformatting to help you recover from such an accident, but do you really want to even take the chance of a mishap? Additionally, "erase *.DOC" instead of "erase *.BAK" can erase all your documents. Without Delwatch active, you'll need the Norton Utilities (or a similar program) and some luck to get your files back. Batch files can form a strong line of defense against the indiscriminate use of these powerful commands.

☑ *Remember*   Batch files make dangerous commands safer.

You can prevent accidental formatting of a hard disk by first renaming FORMAT .COM to XYZ.COM and then creating FORMAT.BAT with the single command @XYZ A:. The @ sign will be examined later, but I'll reveal now that it keeps the XYZ from showing on the screen. If you saw the name, you might be tempted to bypass the batch file. We'll find out later how to construct more complex batch files to help prevent erasing our .DOC files.

☑ *Remember*   Batch files are the easiest programming language to learn!

When most computer users think of programming, they think of spending months to learn languages such as Pascal or C. Like programs created with Pascal or C, DR DOS batch files are programs. Unlike other programming languages, however, batch file commands are made up of mostly DR DOS commands, most of which are already familiar to most of you. Therefore, you already know most of the commands you need to write a batch program. Batch files have only a handful of special commands; the vast majority of batch file commands are the regular DR DOS commands you use every day. If you know how to use DR DOS, you know most of what you need to know in order to write effective batch files.

When you learn to program in most computer languages, you must learn a great deal before you're able to write even the simplest program. This isn't true with batch files, though. As you'll soon see, you can write some very powerful batch files with standard DR DOS commands and just a few special batch commands.

Although batch files are easy to write, this ease comes at a price: batch files are limited in what they can do. One of your most common thoughts as you study this book will be "If only..." You'll see many situations where you could really automate things if only batch files had specific commands. That is the real drawback to batch files: They're easy to learn and easy to write, but they always seem to stop just short of having enough power.

One way to overcome many of the limitations of DR DOS batch files is with the many batch utilities available in the public domain as shareware and commercial programs. Many of these are described in my book *MS DOS Batch File Utilities*, also available from Windcrest. Additionally, this book includes a copy of Batch Commander, a special batch file utility kit written especially for my batch file books by Doug Amaral, chief programmer at hyperkinetix.

Summary

In summary, batch files have four major functions:

- They can reduce the number of keystrokes needed to execute a command.
- They allow you to combine one or more existing commands into your own specialized commands.
- They allow you to store the proper syntax of command sequence in a script file so you do not have to remember this information.
- They can protect you from dangerous DR DOS commands.

Batch files are the easiest programs to write because they consist of mostly DR DOS commands with just a few special batch file commands thrown in.

2

Creating your own batch files

As we will see, creating batch files is easy. You can create simple batch files batch files using nothing more than the COPY command. For more complex batch files, DR DOS has a very nice built-in editor that does a fantastic job. For even more complex batch files (and there are very few this complex), chances are the word processor you currently use will edit batch files as well. However, before we get into the mechanics of creating the batch files, we need to explore a couple of other issues.

Picking a name

The easy part of picking a name is picking an extension. DR DOS gives you no choice except for .BAT. I know of no way to avoid this limit.

When picking a name, you want to choose one that describes the function of the batch file as well as possible, given the constraints of the eight-character limitation DR DOS places on filenames. If you're naming your word processor documents, a specific extension and eight characters for the name is probably the only limitation you face. However, batch file authors face other limitations.

Internal DR DOS commands

DR DOS will accept four kinds of commands: internal commands, .EXE programs, .COM programs, and batch files. Every time DR DOS receives a command, it first checks to see if that command is internal, like ERASE. If so, then it executes that command.

Internal commands are commands so important that they're built directly into DR DOS. Internal commands represent a trade-off. If DR DOS had every possible command built-in, then it would take up so much room that there would be no room left for application programs. If no programs were built into DR DOS, however, every system disk would require numerous programs to perform every simple task. This would waste a lot of space. The trade-off made by DR DOS is that the most important commands are built-in, while the remaining commands are external programs that require an .EXE or .COM file to run.

The names for internal commands are part of DR DOS, which is why you can't name your batch file the same name as an internal command. If you do, there's no way to execute your program. If you created a file named COPY.BAT and tried to run it with the command:

```
COPY
```

then DR DOS would automatically go to the built-in DR DOS COPY command, and try to copy nothing to nothing. If you tried to run it using

```
COPY.BAT
```

then DR DOS would try to copy a file named .BAT to nothing and thus would return an error message.

🖅 **Remember** If you give your batch file the same name as a DR DOS internal command, you will be unable to run your batch file.

Table 2-1 lists the commands that are so important that DR DOS makes them internal commands. Remember that these words cannot be used as the name of a batch file.

Table 2-1   DR DOS internal commands.

BREAK	DIR	MD	RMDIR
CALL	ECHO	MKDIR	SET
CD	ERA	MORE	SHIFT
CHCP	ERAQ	PATH	SWITCH
CHDIR	ERASE	PAUSE	TIME
CLS	EXIT	PROMPT	TYPE
COPY	FASTOPEN	REM	VER
CTTY	FOR	REN	VERIFY
DATE	GOSUB	RENAME	VOL
DEL	GOTO	RETURN	
DELQ	HILOAD	RD	

External commands

If a DR DOS command is not an internal command built into the operating system itself, then it is an external command that exists as a .COM or .EXE program in your DR DOS subdirectory. You don't want a situation where the same name is used for a .COM and .BAT file or an .EXE and a .BAT file. Table 2-2 lists the DR DOS external commands.

While you don't want to use the same name for a batch file that is already in use for a program, external commands are not nearly as intractable as internal commands. With an internal command, the only way to change the command is to modify the contents of the DR DOS operating system files—a topic too advanced for this book.

However, it is easy to alter external commands. Just rename FORMAT.COM to XYZ.COM, and the name of the command changes. Now, create a batch file called FORMAT.BAT and you will have no conflict. As you'll see later on in this book, you sometimes have very good reasons for doing this.

Table 2-2 DR DOS external commands.

APPEND	EDITOR	MEMMAX	SID
ASSIGN	EXE2BIN	MODE	SUPERPCK
ATTRIB	FASTOPEN	MOVE	SYS
BACKUP	FC	NLSFUNC	TASKMAX
CHKDSK	FDISK	PASSWORD	TOUCH
COMMAND	FILELINK	PRINT	TREE
COMP	FIND	RECOVER	UNDELETE
CURSOR	FORMAT	RENDIR	UNFORMAT
DELPURGE	GRAFTABL	REPLACE	UNINSTALL
DELWATCH	GRAPHICS	RESTORE	VIEWMAX
DISKCOMP	JOIN	SCRIPT	XCOPY
DISKCOPY	KEYB	SETUP	XDEL
DISKMAP	LABEL	SHARE	XDIR
DISKOPT	LOCK	SORT	
DOSBOOK	MEM	SUBST	

☑ *Remember*   If you give your batch file the same name as a DR DOS external command or any other .EXE or .COM program, the batch file will conflict with that program. When that happens, the batch file or the program might run in response to the command—depending on which subdirectory you are in.

So, my point with external commands is to simply avoid any name conflicts. You'll want to avoid the same conflicts with all your other software as well. If the file that runs your word processor is WP.EXE, then you'll want to avoid creating WP.BAT because you'll end up running WP.EXE under some conditions and WP.BAT under others. While it's been said that consistency is the hobgoblin of small minds, it seems reasonable to me that you would always want the WP command to do the same thing on your system.

How DR DOS decides which command to run

Because the issue has come up, let's take some time and look at the process DR DOS goes through in deciding what to run when you give it a command. When you issue a command, DR DOS first checks to see if that command is an internal command. If it finds the command as an internal command, then it runs it.

This explains why COPY.BAT (just mentioned) never runs: DR DOS never checks the drive because it finds Copy in its internal list of commands.

If the command isn't an internal command, DR DOS next checks the current subdirectory for a .COM file by that name, then an .EXE file, and finally a .BAT file. If DR DOS finds a program with the correct name, it executes that program. If DR DOS doesn't find a file with the correct name in the current directory, then it searches the PATH subdirectory by subdirectory, looking for a .COM, .EXE, or .BAT file (in that order) in each subdirectory. If DR DOS finds a program in the PATH with the correct name, it executes that program. Otherwise, it returns the "Bad command or file name" error message. Table 2-3 illustrates this.

Table 2-3 Hierarchy of DR DOS commands.

When The Path Is C:\FIRST;C:\SECOND;C:\THIRD

1. An internal command.
2. A .COM file in the current subdirectory.
3. A .EXE file in the current subdirectory.
4. A .BAT file in the current subdirectory.
5. A .COM file in the C:\FIRST subdirectory.
6. A .EXE file in the C:\FIRST subdirectory.
7. A .BAT file in the C:\FIRST subdirectory.
8. A .COM file in the C:\SECOND subdirectory.
9. A .EXE file in the C:\SECOND subdirectory.
10. A .BAT file in the C:\SECOND subdirectory.
11. A .COM file in the C:\THIRD subdirectory.
12. A .EXE file in the C:\THIRD subdirectory.
13. A .BAT file in the C:\THIRD subdirectory.

Let's look back at our earlier example of WP.EXE and WP.BAT. Assume that WP.EXE is in the C:\WP subdirectory and that WP.BAT is in the C:\BAT subdirectory. If the path is C:\;C:\DRDOS;C:\BAT;C:\WP, then WP.BAT will usually be run in response to the WP command because its subdirectory comes earlier in the path. However, if you look at lines 2-4 in Table 2-3, when the user is in the C:\WP subdirectory, then WP.EXE is run instead of WP.BAT in response to the WP command.

This uncertainty about whether WP.EXE or WP.BAT will run is why you should avoid naming conflicts. In this example, if the purpose of WP.BAT is to run WP.EXE in a particular fashion, then WP.EXE could be renamed and the new name built into WP.BAT to avoid this conflict.

Where to put batch files

Batch files are designed to help you automate everyday processes, which means that you must be able to run your batch files at any time in any location. Thus, they must be in a subdirectory in your path. You could put them in your DR DOS subdirectory, but batch files like FORMAT.BAT might get erased when the operating system gets upgraded. Besides, that subdirectory has sixty or more files just from having DR DOS there, so why make things even more crowded?

I recommend that you give your batch files their own subdirectory called \BAT. Regardless of what you end up naming it, you're going to want that subdirectory to be listed near the front of your path.

Remember Batch files belong in the C:\BAT subdirectory, and that subdirectory belongs in your path.

As a general rule, you want the subdirectories in your path listed in order of frequency of use. Subdirectories with commands you use a lot should be listed first, while subdirectories with less frequently used commands can be listed last. Many users will want their DR DOS subdirectory first and their batch subdirectory second.

Creating batch files

You can create batch files in three main ways:

- Use the COPY command
- Use the editor that comes with DR DOS
- Use your own word processor

Each of these approaches has advantages and disadvantages. We'll look at each one in turn.

The COPY command

One of the most basic DR DOS commands is the COPY command. You've probably used this command to copy files in the past. For example,

```
COPY A:*.* B
```

copies between two DR DOS logical devices, both of which happen to be files. The COPY command can be used to copy between any DR DOS logical devices. In addition to files, there are other logical devices:

CON   Depending on the usage, this is either the screen or the keyboard. When used as the target, it's the screen. (After all, you can't copy to the keyboard!) When used as the source, CON is the keyboard.

PRN   The PRN specification refers to your printer.

NUL   This is DR DOS's version of a black hole. Anything that's copied to NUL is gone. I'll show you later how to send unwanted messages to NUL.

You can copy between files and any of these DR DOS logical devices or between the logical devices. (Not all combinations make sense—for example, copying from NUL or PRN.) You can view your CONFIG.SYS file on the screen by typing the following:

```
COPY C:  CONFIG.SYS CON
```

This command copies the file to the screen. You can turn your printer into a simple typewriter with the command:

```
COPY CON PRN
```

When you're finished typing, press the F6 function key, followed by Enter, and what you've typed will be sent to the printer. All the combinations that work with COPY, however, don't work with XCOPY. Unlike COPY, XCOPY can only copy between files.

Remember   XCOPY cannot be used to create batch files from the console the way that COPY can.

You can create simple batch files by copying from the keyboard (CON) to a file. To create a simple batch file called EXAMPLE1.BAT, enter the following command:

```
COPY CON EXAMPLE1.BAT
```

What you're telling DR DOS with this command is to copy from the console to a file called EXAMPLE1.BAT. Note that the command line prompt doesn't return when you press Enter. Now enter

```
DIR *.*
```

then press the F6 function key and Enter. You should see the message "1 File(s) copied." That's it: you've created the file. If you issue a DIR command, you'll see EXAMPLE1.BAT listed among your other files.

📝 **Remember**   You can use the COPY command to create short batch files or other short ASCII files.

You can use this method to create batch files of any length. In fact, you can use this method to write a file containing a letter or anything for which you'd use a word processor. You could, but you probably wouldn't want to. Once you press Enter, there's no way to go back and edit that line. And once you create a file, there's no way to edit it. If you make a mistake, you must start over! In spite of the fact that editing is limited to the current line, COPY CON is an effective way to create short batch files.

Editor

For anything other than a one- or two-line quickie, using COPY is clearly not the best approach. Happily, DR DOS includes a very good editor called (amazingly!) Editor. Your DR DOS manual includes detailed information on using Editor, so I won't go into that much detail here. What I will do is give you the information you need to use Editor to create new batch files or edit existing ones. In addition, Table 2-4 is a very-quick-reference chart showing just those commands you will need frequently while editing batch files.

Here's one appropriate note about Editor use. I've used the same syntax for commands that you see on the Editor help screen and in the DR DOS manual. When you see a caret (^) before a letter (e.g., ^A), it means to hold down the Ctrl key while pressing the key. When you see a caret preceding two letters (e.g. ^KD), it means to hold down the Ctrl key while pressing the first key. It is not necessary to hold down the Control key for both letters although it usually does not hurt. Of course, if you see something like ^P^A, then holding down the Ctrl key for both letters is required.

📝 **Remember**   The Editor uses a subset of the Wordstar keystrokes.

Wordstar users will feel right at home with Editor because all of the keystrokes are Wordstar keystrokes. Although not all the Wordstar commands are supported. Non-Wordstar users might find the keystrokes a little confusing. Fortunately, you only need to know a few keystrokes in order to edit batch file.

Table 2-4 Editor quick reference.

Keystrokes needed to edit batch files

^A	Moves the cursor one word to the left.
^F	Moves the cursor one word to the right.
^J	Calls help.
^KD	Saves the current file and removes it from memory but stays in Editor.
^KQ	Stops editing the current file without saving the changes.
^KR	Imports the contents of another file into the current file.
^KS	Saves your work and continues editing.
^KX	Saves the current file and exits Editor.
^P	What follows this is a control character for the file and not an Editor command.
^QD	Moves to the end of a line.
^QS	Moves to the beginning of a line.
^T	Deletes the word under and to the right of the cursor.
^Y	Deletes the current line.
BkSp	Deletes characters to the left of the cursor.
Del	Deletes the character under the cursor.
End	Jumps to the end of the file.
F1	Calls help.
Home	Jumps to the beginning of the file.
Ins	Toggles between insert and overstrike modes.

Starting the Editor   You can start Editor with the command Editor by itself or followed by the name of a file to edit. If you start it without supplying the name of a file to edit, it immediately prompts you for one, so save time and just give it a name on the command line. If the file exists, the Editor loads it into memory. Figure 2-1 shows the editor with my AUTOEXEC.BAT loaded for editing.

```
c:\utility\autoexec.bat   chr=77 col=42                          ins. ^J=help
@ECHO OFF
REM NAME:      START.BAT
REM PURPOSE:   This Is My AUTOEXEC.BAT File
REM VERSION:   4.00
REM DATE:      November 15, 1991

ECHO Setting Prompt and Environment
CALL C:\BAT\NICEPROM.BAT
CLS

CALL C:\BAT\SETS
CALL C:\BAT\SETPATH

REM Delete the .TMP Files That Seem to Keep Appearing In My Word Subdirectory
IF EXIST C:\WORD\*.TMP DEL C:\WORD\*.TMP

REM Run utility to reduce printer retries from 20 to 1
NOWAIT-1     Uses LPT1
NOWAIT-2     Uses LPT2

REM Run utility to turn off screen print
NOPRTSCR

REM Loading CD ROM Driver
```

2-1   The DR DOS Editor with a file loaded for editing.

Entering text   To enter text into Editor, just type. Like most editors, Editor doesn't have wordwrap (i.e., long lines don't automatically move down to the next line at the right margin to form a paragraph); you must press the Enter key at the end of each line. You don't want wordwrap in a batch file editor because long command lines must remain on a single line in your batch file in order to work.

As you work, the top of Editor displays some useful information, such as the name of the file you are working on, the path to that file, the cursor position, an indicator of the status of the editor (overtype or insert mode) and a reminder that pressing ^J brings up the help screen.

The default mode of operation for Editor is insert mode. With insert on, if you enter text in the middle of a file, the existing text is shifted to make room for that text. You can switch to overstrike mode by pressing the Ins (Insert) key; in overstrike mode, any text you type in the middle of a file replaces existing text. The Insert key acts as a toggle key; whenever you press Ins, it switches you out of the mode you are currently using and into the other mode. You can change modes as often as you like.

Sometimes you can save typing by reading in the contents of another file and deleting the parts that you don't want. For example, as we'll see later, I place a form at the top of each batch file and then put certain information into that form. To save typing, I have a file containing nothing but that form, and I bring it into the top of each new batch file I create. Bringing in text from one file to another like this is called *importing*.

To import text into Editor, press ^KR. Editor then prompts you for the name of the file to import. The contents of that file are copied into Editor without affecting the original file on the disk. Any changes you make to the text in this file are *not* reflected in the file you imported the text from; it's still sitting safely on your disk.

Deleting text   To delete the text the cursor is sitting under, press the Del key. To delete the character to the left of the cursor, press the Backspace cursor. Pressing ^T while the cursor is under the first character of a word deletes the entire word. If the cursor is in the middle of a word, it deletes the remainder of the word to the right of the cursor. Pressing ^Y deletes the entire line the cursor is on.

Moving the cursor   You can move the cursor up, down, right, and left one space/line at a time using the arrow keys. The Home key takes you to the top of the file, while the End key takes you to the end of the file. To move left and right quicker, ^A moves to the left one word at a time, while ^F moves to the right one word at a time. To go even faster, ^QS moves to the beginning of a line and ^QD moves to the end of a line.

Entering control characters   Most batch files do not need control characters, except for two special occasions. The first occasion is for when you want a batch file to control a printer; most printers use control codes to set things like the default font and line spacing. Additionally, if your batch files are going to use ANSI.SYS to gain extra control over the screen appearance, then the files must be able to enter control characters.

Because all of Editor's commands are control characters, you cannot enter a control character like ^Z directly. Instead, you must type a ^P first. That tells Editor that the following control character is intended for the file and not for the editor. So, once again, to enter a ^Z in your text, type ^P^Z.

Saving your work   After you have begun making changes and feel like it's time to save your work, press ^KS to save and then continue editing. You should take the time to save your work after you've done enough work that you wouldn't want to go back and redo it if there was a power failure or other problem. Once you have finished with a file, if you want to edit another file, press ^KD to save the current file and stay in Editor. If you are finished with Editor, press ^KX to save the file and return to DR DOS. If you decide your changes to the current file were wrong, you can press ^KQ to stop editing this file without saving the changes. Editor will ask you if you really want to do this.

Help! If you are editing a file and forget what to do, you can get on-line help quickly. Just press ^J or the F1 function key and Editor will display several screens of useful information. At the end of these screens, it will give you the option of using the top part of the Editor screen to display a quick reference display. Figure 2-2 shows Editor with this quick reference display. Until you become familiar with Editor, this quick reference display is a handy thing to keep on the screen.

```
c:\utility\autoexec.bat  chr=929 col=1                              ins. ^J=help
          TO MOVE THE CURSOR              TO DELETE TEXT        TO FINISH EDITING
^Qr  Top of file      ^Qc Bottom of file   ^H  char left    ^Ks save text & resume
^R   Previous page    ^C  Next page        ^G  char         ^Kd save text & edit new
^E   Previous line    ^X  Next line        ^T  word         ^Kx save text & exit
^A   Previous word    ^F  Next word        ^Y  line         ^Kq don't save, edit new
^S   Previous char    ^D  Next character
ECHO Saving Hard Disk Information and Making Final Configurations
IMAGE C: /SAVE
IMAGE D: /SAVE
IMAGE E: /SAVE
LOCKEYS N:OFF
CD\
LOADHIGH FASTCONS
CD\SYSLIB
LOADHIGH DOSKEY /BUFSIZE=2500
CD\
IF EXIST \WINDOWS\*.SWP DEL \WINDOWS\*.SWP > NUL
CALL C:\BAT\ASSIGNME
SCREEN1
```

2-2 The DR DOS Editor can leave a quick-reference chart at the top of the screen while you are working.

☑ *Remember* If you ever forget what the appropriate keystrokes are while using Editor, just press F1 for instant help.

Last words on Editor For the vast majority of your batch file work, Editor is the perfect solution. The file is small enough to fit on either a floppy disk or the most crowded hard disk, and the program is fast and reasonably powerful. Most of the rest of your work will be with tiny batch files that you handle quickly with COPY, as described earlier. For the remaining small percent of your batch files, you'll need to use a word processor.

Using a different editor on batch files

Occasionally, you are going to want to use your word processor to edit your batch files instead of Editor. Editor does such a nice job that those occasions will be rare. However, I usually run my finished batch files through the spell checker in my word processor. In addition, I load batch files into my word processor when I want to insert boxes because my word processor has a box-drawing command that can insert the high-ordered ASCII characters very easily.

Most full-featured word processors, like Wordstar or Microsoft Word, can be used to edit batch files. Normally, Wordstar doesn't produce ASCII files. If you copy a Wordstar file to the screen, you'll see that the last letter of most words looks funny. To produce ASCII text with Wordstar, you must open your document in what Wordstar calls the nondocument mode. This means that you can't open your batch file at the same time you start Wordstar, using this shortcut:

WS BATCH.BAT

Wordstar lets you specify the filename when you start the program and thus avoid the opening menu. But this method automatically puts you in document mode, and you won't get an ASCII file. Even in nondocument mode, Wordstar won't produce an ASCII file if you use the paragraph reformat command, ^B. However, if you follow these few precautions, Wordstar will work well as a batch file editor.

With Microsoft Word, you can easily produce ASCII files as well. If you load an existing ASCII file into Word, it automatically treats it as straight ASCII. To create a new ASCII file within Word, just save the file using the "Save as" option and select the "Text only" option. Word has difficulty with ASCII files with long lines, however. While it saves them properly without the wordwrap, it cannot display them without wordwrap. That can make looking at the lines on the screen very confusing.

Most other word processors will produce ASCII files. However, ASCII probably won't be the default mode. It might be a separate mode, which will usually have wordwrap turned off, or you might need to translate your document into ASCII format. A simple word processor might work similar to a typewriter with limited editing ability. If you're in doubt, create a small document and then copy it to the screen. If you see exactly what you typed, then it's ASCII.

Summary

Batch files should not have the same name as an internal command.

It's generally not a good idea to give batch files the same name as an existing .COM or .EXE program.

When deciding which programs to run, DR DOS first looks for internal commands. If the command is not an internal command, then DR DOS looks for a .COM program, an .EXE program, or a batch file in the current subdirectory, in that order. If the command is not an internal command, a program, or a batch file in the current subdirectory, then DR DOS looks for a .COM program, an .EXE program, or a batch file in each subdirectory on the path, in the order listed in the path.

Batch files are best located in their own subdirectory, generally called \BAT. This subdirectory should be in the path.

Simple batch files can be created quickly with COPY.

More complex batch files can be created with the DR DOS Editor program.

In addition, most word processors have the ability to edit batch files, although you generally have to use a special unformatted or programming mode.

3
Batch file construction

So far, you have been introduced to some good reasons to use batch files and you've seen how to use the nice editor that's included with DR DOS. Now, it time to begin writing your own batch files. But before that, we'll spend a few minutes talking about how to structure them.

What is a batch file?

A batch file script is a special file containing one or more DR DOS commands and a few batch sub-commands, with each command on a separate line. That's it—nothing more and nothing less. This is illustrated with the following:

First command
Second command
Third command
Fourth command
Fifth command
(and so on)

You run a batch file by entering its name at the command line prompt. You can enter the .BAT extension, but you don't have to. For example, to run a batch file named FRED.BAT, you would enter

FRED

Some batch files require additional information, which you must enter after the batch file name. The batch file name and each separate piece of information must be separated by either a space or a comma; for example,

FRED Yes,1,*.BAK No

Remember Replaceable parameters are data you enter on the command line after the name of the batch file.

Batch file formatting

DR DOS doesn't require batch files to have any special form of formatting. The computer doesn't care either: it will successfully execute any properly written batch file, no matter how it is formatted. The only reason to format batch files in any special way is for human readability.

What follows is the scheme I've developed for use with my batch files. It makes the batch files easily readable, while using the limited formatting the DR DOS allows. If you develop a different system that works better for you, feel free to use it.

Capitalization

I use ALL CAPITAL LETTERS in both the batch files and the messages they display to draw attention to particularly important elements. In general, I use capitalization in the following fashion:

- I use all capital letters for DR DOS commands and program names in the batch files.
- I capitalize the first letter of each word in most messages and remarks.
- When a message tells you what to enter on the command line, I capitalize the command line.
- When a message is very important, I capitalize the entire message; for example, "WARNING: THIS TAKES AN HOUR."

Spacing

In a long program, it can be difficult to see the different sections if you enter text on each line. To visually break the program up into different sections, I leave one or more blank lines between each section. These blank lines don't affect the operation of the batch because DR DOS ignores them, but they do make it much easier to read.

While the batch files in this book do have blank lines between the sections, I've left those blank lines out of the table listing I use for the longer batch files. I've found that, while blank lines enhance the readable of programs, they don't enhance the tables.

Indenting sections

I've also found that it can be useful to indent the lines of a section between the beginning and ending label of the section. If you do that, a batch file segment might looks like this:

```
:HELP
        ECHO This Runs Your Backup Program
        ECHO You Must Start It With Either An F or I
        ECHO On The Command Line
        ECHO The F Is For A Full Backup
```

```
ECHO The I Is For An Incremental Backup
GOTO END
```

As you can see, this clarifies which statements belong in this section, something that's especially useful in longer programs.

Message length

You will notice that most of the messages in my programs have fairly short lines. For longer messages, I use multiple lines. It's been my experience that shorter lines are easier to read on the screen than longer ones. It's a lot like printing your documents in multi-column format, except the batch files only use the left column.

Line-length limit

Commands entered from the command line are limited to 127 characters. (Technically, the limit is 128 characters, but the last character must be the return you must press to send the command to DR DOS.) Batch files are limited to this same limitation: No batch file command can exceed 127 characters. As we will see later in this book, DR DOS treats some lines in your batch file as being longer than their physical length. That can sometimes make it difficult to gauge the actual length of the line, but the line must still be 127 characters or less after DR DOS expands it to its final length.

If a line exceeds this limit, one of two things are likely to happen. Either the computer will lock up, or DR DOS will truncate the command after the 127th character. In either case, the batch file will not perform as you expected.

Fortunately, you'll rarely encounter this problem. However, it's a good idea to keep this limit in the back of your mind in case you ever find yourself typing in a very long line.

Let's write a batch file

So far in this book, I've have not introduced a single batch file command. I'm not going to introduce any until the next chapter. Yet, you can still write some useful batch files. You have already seen a couple of useful batch files: I.BAT, which performs an incremental backup, and CHECK.BAT, which runs the DR DOS Chkdsk program. Now, let's look at two more situations where batch files are useful.

The problem

When I work in Windows, I sometimes run COMMAND.COM to shell out to DR DOS to copy and erase files because Windows does a very poor job handling file management. A couple of times, I've been called away from the computer while running DR DOS. When I returned, I forgot that Windows was already running in the background and thus loaded it again. Needless to say, that second copy did not run too well.

The solution

You want to make it plain that you are shelled out of Windows while running DR DOS under Windows but Windows will not do that by itself. Yet if you start Windows with a batch file, it's easy to do that. Take the following steps:

- Change to the drive containing Windows.
- Change to the subdirectory containing Windows.
- Change the prompt from the my usual PG to a reminder that Windows is running. I can't see this prompt in Windows; but if I shell out of Windows, it uses the same prompt that was present when Windows started, so I'll see my reminder.
- Start Windows.
- Once Windows terminates and my batch file have taken back over, reset the prompt.

None of these steps requires a batch file command, so you already know enough to write this batch file. If you have Windows on your system, you might even want to put this book down and fire up Editor and give it a shot. Go ahead; the rest of us will wait.

The resulting batch file requires five lines, one for each of the things we just listed:

```
C:
CD\WINDOWS
PROMPT Type EXIT To Return To Window $P$G
WIN
PROMPT $P$G
```

With the "Type EXIT To Return To Window C:\ >" showing, it will be hard for me to accidentally run a second copy of Windows.

By the way, this solution is not limited to Windows. Microsoft Word, WordPerfect, Lotus 1-2-3, and many other fine program give you the option of shelling out to DR DOS to run a quick command. When you shell out from any of these programs, you can easily forget that the original program is still running. Luckily, this same batch-file-based solution works equally well for all these programs.

A second problem

I like to perform an incremental backup at the end of every day using the XCOPY command. However, there are certain files that get modified every day that I don't need to backup. These are

- IMAGE.*. These three files (.BAK, .DAT, and .IDX) are files that are updated by the Norton Utilities every time I boot. They contain information about my file allocation table that Norton uses to unformat the hard disk and unerase files. (DR DOS also has similar programs, but I've always used Norton.)
- TREEINFO.NCD. This file stores my subdirectory structure for quick directory changes using the Norton NCD program. It's updated every time the directory structure changes.
- 386SPART.PAR. This is my Windows permanent swap file and is modified each time I run Windows.

I need a backup file that first uses the Norton Utilities FA program (short for File Attribute) program to remove the archive setting for these files and then performs the incremental backup.

The solution

The first two steps are to make sure the computer is in the root directory of the C drive. After that, using the Norton FA program and wildcards, it takes three lines to remove these archive settings and one more line to perform the incremental backup using XCOPY. This six-line batch file is shown next:

```
C:
CD\
FA IMAGE.* /A-
FA TREEINFO.NCD /A-
FA 386SPART.PAR /A-
XCOPY *.* A: /S /M
```

Once again, this batch file is nothing more than the same commands you would enter at the command line to perform this same task. However, once you've figured out how to do it once, you can record those commands in a batch file and forget about it because the batch file remembers everything for you. Additionally, entering the name of the batch file take far fewer keystrokes each afternoon than entering all these commands.

Summary

Batch files can be nothing more than a series of DR DOS commands identical to the commands you would enter on the command line.

Batch files can be created by writing down the commands you used at the command line prompt and then entering them into a batch file.

Proper formatting can make batch files more readable to humans without affecting the computer's ability to execute them.

Consistent capitalization, blank lines between parts of the batch file, and indenting the commands within a section all contribute to a readable batch file.

Very useful batch files can be written without using a single batch command.

PART TWO
Simple batch file topics

Now that you've seen how to name, write, and structure batch files, it's time to look at some of the simpler batch subcommands. A batch subcommand is a DR DOS command designed to run inside a batch file. However, most of them will also work from the command line if you have a use for that.

Chapter 4: REM Documentation: "Why in the world did I do that?" The batch language only has a few commands of its own but it can also run any program you own. As a result, some batch files tend to become very long. Using the REM command to document those longer batch files can make following their logic easier when you have to modify them in the future. This chapter explains how to do that.

Chapter 5: Let's keep it quiet. The default mode of operation for a batch file is to have command echoing on, which means that commands are displayed on the screen before they are executed. By turning command echoing off, your screens will look much neater. This chapter explains how to do that.

Chapter 6: Talking to the user. Batch files frequently need to "talk" to the user to display information, ask questions or provide warnings. The ECHO command provides the method for doing this. This chapter explains how to use the ECHO command effectively.

Chapter 7: Using high-ordered ASCII characters. Your batch files can be made much more attractive by using some of the high-ordered ASCII characters available through DR DOS. This chapter explains how to use these characters.

Chapter 8: Hold that batch file! Sometimes you need for the batch file to wait for the user to catch up. Maybe it has put a lot of information on the screen for the user to read or the user needs a chance to press Ctrl-Break and halt the batch file. This chapter explains how to use the PAUSE command in a batch file to suspend its operation until a key is pressed.

Chapter 9: Applications and problems. Before moving on to the intermediate batch subcommands, you should understand the commands and concepts covered so far. This chapter is a quick test. Pass it, and you're ready to move on.

4

REM documentation: "Why in the world did I do that?"

One of the worst possible feelings a programmer can have is going back to an old program and not understanding how it works. Basic programmers even have a name for the type of code most likely to cause this condition: *spaghetti code*, because it twists and turns like cooked spaghetti.

In any programming language, it's important to document your work—both written documentation and documentation inside the program. If you look at the source code for any well written program in any language, you'll see lots of documentation, shown as comments. *Comments* are lines of text inside the program that have nothing to do with the actual program. They're simply intended to help you understand the surrounding code, especially when you haven't seen the program for six months.

Internal documentation for a batch file consists of the remark line, started with the REM command. If you start a line with REM followed by a space, you can enter almost anything you want to. The only thing you can't use are the DR DOS redirection characters. The computer will skip the remark line, so the information on that line are simply comments for anyone who has to go back to modify the code.

Take a look at the sample batch file in Fig. 4-1. This example includes some commands you haven't learned yet, but they're not the important part. The important thing is that %1 takes the place of a filename while the batch file is running. Given that, do you

```
:START
ERASE %1.BAK
COPY %1.DOC B:
COPY C:\WORD\NORMAL\%1.STY B:
ERASE C:\WORD\NORMAL\%1.BAK
COPY \WORD\%1.CMP B:
SHIFT
IF /%1==/ GOTO END
GOTO START
:END
```

4-1 A batch file that has no internal documentation. Can you tell what it does?

know what the file is doing? Probably not. Now consider the same batch file, properly documented, as shown in Fig. 4-2. It's the same batch file; none of the working commands are any different. But now you can probably understand the batch file without my explaining the commands I haven't yet covered.

```
REM YESDOC.BAT
REM Batch file to copy new files to floppy
REM disk. Name top of loop
:START
REM Erase the backup file
ERASE %1.BAK
REM Copy the document file to floppy disk
COPY %1.DOC B:
REM Copy the associated style sheet to
REM floppy disk
COPY C:\WORD\NORMAL\%1.STY B:
REM Erase backup copy of style sheet
ERASE C:\WORD\NORMAL\%1.BAK
REM Copy document dictionary to floppy disk
COPY \WORD\%1.CMP B:
REM Get next name
SHIFT
REM Test for next name existing and go to
REM bottom if does not exist
IF (%1)==() GOTO END
REM Go to top since there is another file
GOTO START
:END
REM Finished copy
```

4-2 The batch file segment from Fig. 4-1, this time with proper documentation.

This isn't a made-up example. Figure 4-1 is an actual working batch file that's used every day. The author of the batch file could probably modify it, but it isn't likely that anyone else could. The point is that batch files aren't so simple that you can skip documentation. No one ever suffered from too much documentation.

☑ *Remember* Use the REM command inside your batch files to document the logic of the batch file.

All the remark command does, therefore, is allow you to add comments to your batch file. The syntax is "REM", followed by a space, and then your comments. Remember, the line length must be 127-characters or less. In the next chapter, we will see how to keep remark lines from showing when you run your batch files.

Written documentation

You can also use written documentation, one example of this being the tables in this book that list the batch files. The code is on the left, and a detailed explanation is on the right. Of course, you probably won't need to document your batch files in this level of detail but might find it adequate to simply print out a listing and write margins in the notes. While the DR DOS Editor cannot print, you can quickly get a printout from DR DOS directly with the command

```
COPY FILE.BAT LPT1
```

where FILE.BAT is the batch or other ASCII file to print out and LPT1 is the LPT port your printer is attached to.

☑ **Remember**   If your batch files are used by others, written documentation can help them use those batch files more effectively.

A third form of documentation is a printed user's manual. All you need is a brief explanation of how each batch file works and the inputs it expects. If you use a lot of batch files on your system, you might find it useful to keep a similar listing of your own programs. You might also find it useful to keep this sort of documentation on the utility programs you add to your system.

Even more documentation

Over the course of the years, I've written six books for TAB dealing with batch files. While working on all these batch file books, I've written and debugged over 700 batch files! In addition, I've looked at and debugged countless batch files written by others. Because of my diverse experience with batch files, I've developed some ideas on what they should look like.

Self-documentation

DR DOS 6 has added a nifty new feature to most of its commands. If you're not sure what they do or how to use them, you can start them with a /? switch and get a screen of helpful information. This makes it quick and easy for the user to find out what a program does or what inputs it needs. I expect that, over time, this feature will be added to most programs.

Implementing it in a batch file is fairly easy. A section of code near the top of each of the script tests to see if the user entered a /?. If it is, the script displays a help screen and exits to DR DOS. I use the /? switch to be consistent with DR DOS. In Chapter 18, after covering some more basics, we'll see the details of how to add this to batch files.

Special information at the top

Some information is important enough that every batch file must have it. The importance of this information suggests that we put it at the top of each program:

- *Name.* The first line of the program gives the name of the batch file. This isn't extremely critical because you know the name from the DR DOS filename; however, it *is* useful information—especially if your editor does not display the name of the file you are editing. In addition, some of the batch files later in this book will use this information.

- *Purpose*. The second line of the program gives the purpose of the batch file. In this book's sample programs, I've kept the purpose line fairly short and used multiple lines for a longer purpose in order to make the tables look good. For reasons we'll see later in the book, you should use as descriptive a purpose statement as possible but still keep the entire line below 80 characters long. This is not absolutely necessary, but some batch files shown later in the book use this information and work better with line lengths below 80.
- *Version*. The first version of a program is 1.00. A tiny change would make it 1.01, a larger change would make it 1.10, and a major change would make it 2.00. Because programs tend to evolve over time, this line is a good indicator of how long a batch file has been in use.

    You might notice that many of the batch files in this book are version 1.0. This isn't because I write perfect programs each time but rather because my programs undergo extensive beta testing before they are added to my book. As is common with many software vendors, I begin numbering my beta copies at 0.00 and only mark them as 1.00 after they have finished this extensive beta testing. As a result, they don't get a number higher than 1.00 unless I enhance them, fix a bug after beta testing, or go back and figure out a better way to do something.
- *Date*. This is the date of the last modification to the program. A program that has not been updated for a very long time is either very stable or not used very often.

Following this scheme, the top of a typical program will look something like this:

```
REM NAME:     I.BAT
REM PURPOSE: Perform An Incremental Backup
REM VERSION:  1.00
REM DATE:      February 15, 1992
```

☑ *Remember*   Adding the name, purpose, version number and date created/modified to the top of each batch file is an excellent form of documentation.

   If you study the sample programs that come with this book, you will see that almost all of them follow this documentation scheme.

Tricky documentation

While I don't recommend it, you can use two tricky ways to add documentation to your batch files—both of which will speed up your batch file execution slightly. Because the operating system processes a batch file line-by-line, both tricks involve working around this line-by-line processing of the Rem commands:

Using labels as remarks

When a line begins with a colon, the operating system knows that line is a label; thus, it only needs to process labels when processing a GOTO command. When the batch file is not processing a GOTO command, it skips any line that begins with a colon. (GOTO is examined in detail in Chapter 12.) One way to do this is just to start each documentation line with a colon, like this:

```
:Name:     BATCH.BAT
:PURPOSE: Show Using Colon To Mark Documentation
:VERSION: 1.00
:DATE:     May 28, 1992
:None Of These Lines Will Execute Or Show On The Screen
:So They Function Similarly To Rem Commands
```

However, this can cause problems later on if you plan on using a label like :NONE that conflicts with one of your documentation lines. The colon is also hard to see in printouts, so you might not notice these as comments right away. A partial solution is to combine the colon with a character that is invalid in a label, like an asterisk. That way, it's more visible and has no chance of conflicting with a label. The resulting batch file segment would look like this:

```
:* Name:     BATCH.BAT
:* PURPOSE: Show Using Colon To Mark Documentation
:* VERSION: 1.00
:* DATE:     May 28, 1992
:* None Of These Lines Will Execute Or Show On The Screen
:* So They Function Similarly To Rem Commands
```

Bypassing the comments

The GOTO command and labels are detailed in Chapter 12. The GOTO command causes the batch file to jump over lines to a line beginning with a colon and the label specified after the GOTO command. For example, GOTO START would cause a batch file to jump to the line containing :START. Because jumping over lines is quicker than processing those lines, a batch file segment like this

```
GOTO START
REM Name:     BATCH.BAT
REM PURPOSE: Show Using Colon To Mark Documentation
REM VERSION: 1.00
REM DATE:     May 28, 1992
REM None Of These Lines Will Execute Or Show On The Screen
REM So They Function Similarly To Rem Commands
:START
```

would run quicker than the same batch file segment without the GOTO command. In fact, because the remark lines are jumped over and never executed, the REM command isn't needed, so this batch file could be written as

```
GOTO START
Name:     BATCH.BAT
PURPOSE: Show Using Colon To Mark Documentation
VERSION: 1.00
DATE:     May 28, 1992
None Of These Lines Will Execute Or Show On The Screen
```

So The Function Similarly To Rem Commands
:START

Conclusion

Either of these tricks will give your batch file a slight speed boost; the more remarks you have grouped together and the slower your computer, the greater the speed boost. However, they are both nonstandard and make your batch files harder to understand. For that reason, I don't recommend either approach.

Summary

Remark lines starting with the REM command make your batch files much easier to understand and follow.

Written documentation is important to both the users of your batch files and anyone who later wants to modify the batch file.

Batch files should be able to explain their purpose to a user who starts them with a /? switch on the command line. How to do this is covered later in the book.

Adding some standard information to the top of each batch file is a good way to begin documenting your batch files and will allow batch files introduced later in this book to access that information in a useful fashion.

You can trick the operating system into skipping over documentation remarks quicker than with the REM command by preceding the remarks with a :* rather than the REM command.

You can trick the operating system into skipping over documentation remarks quicker than with the REM command using a GOTO command to jump over the remarks.

5

Let's keep it quiet

Let's take a moment to recreate the batch file called A.BAT we wrote earlier that performed a directory of the A drive. This time, let's use what we learned in the last chapter to include some documentation at the top of that batch file. Your resulting batch file might look like this:

```
REM NAME:    A.BAT
REM PURPOSE: Directory Of A Drive
REM VERSION: 1.00
REM DATE:    May 8, 1992
DIR A:
```

Now, run that batch file. While the batch file will run properly and you will get the information you want, the screen will be very unattractive. As the batch file runs, every command in the batch file shows up on the screen—even when the user doesn't need or want this information.

Back in Chapter 1, I introduced the concept of a batch file being a script followed by the computer. Well, the computer has a bad habit of reading everything on the script. Take the following text, for example:

Billy   Sally, you can't leave me. I need you.
Sally   I'm leaving you. [Opens door and walks out]

While the writer expects Sally to open the door and walk out, he expects her to do it quietly. You also expect the computer to do what you tell it. But while running a tax program, you don't expect to see

```
Line Input A$
SalesTax = Income * .04 − (State * 2.3)
```

When you use a word processor or spreadsheet, you never see the code running. Why should a batch file be any different?

Command echoing

The process of showing commands on the screen while they're being executed is called *echoing*. When this echoing is on, you see commands as they execute. When echoing is off, you don't see commands as they execute. With DR DOS, every batch file starts with echoing turned *on*.

You can turn off echoing in two different ways, and each method has its own uses. Normal, you can add an ECHO OFF command at the top of the batch file, which turns command echoing off for the entire batch file and any batch file this batch file runs (a process examined later in the book), although not for any other batch files that execute after it terminates. So, as a general rule, you need an ECHO OFF command at the top of each batch file.

The ECHO OFF command turns off just command echoing but *doesn't* turn off DR DOS messages. If you copy a file in a batch file, you'll see the "1 File(s) copied" DR DOS message. If you use a batch file to start a program, you'll still see that program on the screen. All ECHO OFF affects is the display of batch file commands while that specific batch file is running.

☑ *Remember* The ECHO OFF command keeps the screens produced by your batch files cleaner.

The second way to turn off command echoing only affects a single line. When a line in a batch file is preceded by an ampersand (@), that single line executes without being echoed to the screen, even if command echoing is on. Most users combine these two methods and add the command @ECHO OFF as the first line of their batch files.

We can now modify A.BAT to present a much clearer screen:

```
@ECHO OFF
REM NAME:      A.BAT
REM PURPOSE: Directory Of A Drive
REM VERSION:  1.00
REM DATE:      May 8, 1992
DIR A:
```

Only the first line has changed. With command echoing off, the screen is much clear, as Fig. 5-2 shows.

☑ *Remember* Adding an ampersand in front of a command turns off command echoing for that command, even if command echoing is on for the entire batch file.

For almost all batch files, you can safely add an @ECHO OFF command to the top and forget about it. As we'll see in the next chapter, we can communicate with the user in spite of command echoing being off. Additionally, important DR DOS messages find their way to the screen in spite of command echoing being off. However, when we start working with ANSI in Chapter 21, some of the batch files we work with will need to have command echoing on in particular portions of the batch file. Once command echoing is turned off, it can be turned back on with the ECHO ON command.

```
D:\>a

D:\>REM NAME:    A.BAT

D:\>REM PURPOSE: Directory Of ADrive

D:\>REM VERSION: 1.00

D:\>REM DATE:    May 8, 1992

D:\>DIR A:

 Volume in drive A has no label
 Directory of A:\

TO        BAT       133 06-02-91   6:57p
INT10     COM      6040 09-14-90   1:07a
SPR       DOC      4294 09-14-90   1:07a
PMREAD    ME       1612 07-22-91   3:46p
        4 file(s)        12079 bytes
                       1444352 bytes free

 D:\>
```

5-1 In batch default mode, every command in the batch file shows on the screen as it executes.

```
D:\>a

 Volume in drive A has no label
 Directory of A:\

TO        BAT       133 06-02-91   6:57p
INT10     COM      6040 09-14-90   1:07a
SPR       DOC      4294 09-14-90   1:07a
PMREAD    ME       1612 07-22-91   3:46p
        4 file(s)        12079 bytes
                       1444352 bytes free

 D:\>
```

5-2 With command echoing off, the screen is much clearer when A.BAT executes.

Summary

The normal state of batch files is command echoing on, where commands are displayed on the screen before being executed.

ECHO OFF turns off command echoing for an entire batch file and any other batch files that it runs.

Preceding a batch file command with an ampersand prevents command echoing for that command, regardless of the status of command echoing.

Most users start each batch file with an @ECHO OFF command.

On the rare occasion when you need command echoing on in a portion of a batch file, command echoing can be turned back on with ECHO ON.

32 *Simple batch file topics*

6
Talking to the user

Some DR DOS commands are multi-modal: they perform two or more different functions depending on how they are used. Some commands are bi-modal, meaning they perform two different functions, depending on how they are used. For example, the command

    SET

displays the contents of the environment, while the command

    SET VARIABLE=VALUE

stores a value to an environmental variable. (If the value is missing, it deletes the environment variable—meaning that it stores a nul value in it.)

While SET is bi-modal, the PATH command is tri-modal because it has three different functions. The command

    PATH

displays the contents of the path, the command

    PATH=C:\;C:\WORD;C:\123

stores a value to the path and the command

    PATH;

resets the path to nul.

☑ *Remember* Some DR DOS commands perform several different functions depending on how they are used.

Like the PATH command, the ECHO command is tri-modal. In the last chapter, we saw that when it is combined with an ON or OFF, the ECHO command can be used to changes the status of command echoing. This is only one use for the ECHO command. When used by itself, the ECHO command displays the status of command echoing.

Displaying messages

While the ECHO command can turn command echoing on or off and can display the status of command echoing, the ECHO command has another even more important function: You can use it to communicate with the user. When ECHO is followed by a space and then a message, that message is displayed on the screen.

When command echoing is on, the message is actually displayed twice. It gets displayed once when the command is executed (echoing) and a second time when the command is carried out. When command echoing is off, the message is displayed only once.

Let's stop for a moment and look at a simple example. Key in this brief batch file segment and then run it:

```
@ECHO OFF
CLS
ECHO Hello World
ECHO I Am A Brand New Batch File!
```

When you run the file, the screen clears and the two messages are displayed, one per line.

You have several good reasons to echo messages in a batch file, many of which I'll mention here.

Telling the user what is going on

Anytime a batch file is doing something for the user, you should let the user know what is going on—especially if the process takes a long time. Messages like

```
Defragmenting The Hard Disk: This Takes Two Hours
Backing Up To Tape Drive: This Take Twenty Minutes
Attempting To Log Onto Network: Please Wait
```

can go a long way to comfort the user when the computer doesn't immediately respond. After all, you don't want the user rebooting because he or she thinks that the computer has locked up.

Keeping the user informed

Not all commands take a very long time to run, but it's still nice to keep the user informed. For example, my AUTOEXEC.BAT file takes about a minute to run, but I've still got several messages in it to remind me what is going on. As an example, here's the file:

```
@ECHO OFF
REM NAME:    AUTOEXEC.BAT
REM VERSION: 4.00
REM DATE:    November 15, 1991
```

```
ECHO Setting Prompt and Environment
CALL C:\BAT\NICEPROM.BAT
CLS

CALL C:\BAT\SETS
CALL C:\BAT\SETPATH

ECHO Delete the .TMP Files In My Word Subdirectory
IF EXIST C:\WORD\*.TMP DEL C:\WORD\*.TMP

ECHO Run Utility To Reduce Printer Retries From 20 To 1
NOWAIT-1        Uses LPT1
NOWAIT-2        Uses LPT2

ECHO Run Utility To Turn Off Screen Print
NOPRTSCR

ECHO Loading CD ROM Driver
C:\CDROM\MSCDEX /D:MSCD210 /M:4 /L:F /V
C:\CDROM\MSCDINFO

ECHO Saving Hard Disk Information
IMAGE C:   /SAVE
IMAGE D:   /SAVE
IMAGE E:   /SAVE

ECHO Turning NumLock Off
LOCKEYS N:OFF

ECHO Loading TSR Software
CD\
LOADHIGH FASTCONS
CD\SYSLIB
LOADHIGH DOSKEY /BUFSIZE=2500
CD\

SCREEN1
```

Most of the commands run software utilities. The lines beginning with CALL run other batch files. However, none of that is really important; what *is* important is all the ECHO commands. Some of these commands execute very quickly, while others take ten to fifteen seconds. Regardless, you can always look at the screen and know what the computer is doing at that moment.

Giving the user instructions

Sometimes, the computer needs for the user to either physically do something or provide some information. Messages displayed from within the batch file are an excellent way to provide the user with additional information on what to do.

An example will help you understand. The following batch file is an improved version of I.BAT for performing incremental backups:

```
@ECHO OFF
REM NAME:     I.BAT
REM PURPOSE: Perform Incremental Backups
REM VERSION:  2.00
REM DATE:     May 9, 1992

ECHO This Batch File Performs An Incremental Backup
ECHO Using The XCOPY Command
ECHO Insert A Freshly Formatted Disk In The A Drive
ECHO And Then Press Any Key When Ready
ECHO Note: If The Disk Fills Up, The XCOPY Command Will Abort
ECHO Without Finishing
ECHO If That Happens, Run The Batch File Over With
ECHO Another Freshly Formatted Disk To Copy The Files
ECHO That Were Missed The First Time

PAUSE

XCOPY C:\ *.* /S /M A:
```

With the extra information provided by the ECHO commands, even someone who has never performed an incremental backup would know what to do.

Remember   The ECHO command lets you display text on the screen to give instructions and keep the user informed.

A DR DOS 5 bug

In a batch file, you can display the status of command echoing with ECHO by itself. When command echoing is on, you get an "ECHO = on" message; when it's off, you get an "ECHO = off". However, under DR DOS 5, when an ECHO is used by itself in a batch file, it simply repeats the last statement displayed by the ECHO command. Thus, the following batch file segment would display "Hello" twice:

```
ECHO Hello
ECHO
```

Note   Due to a bug in DR DOS 5, when used by itself without being followed by a space, the ECHO command doesn't function properly. Instead of displaying the status of command echoing, it repeats the last ECHO message.

This isn't a major problem because this bug has been fixed in DR DOS 6 and because you rarely need to display the status of command echoing in a batch file. You can still easily circumvent the problem, though: If you put a single space after the ECHO command in DR DOS 5, the status of command echoing will be displayed properly.

Making your messages attractive

Probably the single most important aspect of writing attractive messages is to make sure the message you echo to the screen is no wider than the screen. When a message is too long for the screen, it goes to 80 columns and then wraps to the next line without regard for words. If the break occurs in the middle of a word, then the line is broken in the middle of a word.

In addition to avoiding messages longer than 80 characters, I also tend to avoid long messages in general. It has been my experience that messages of 40 or fewer characters across are much easier for the user to read than messages that go all the way across the screen.

You can center titles by putting additional spaces between ECHO and the message. When I have several screens of information, I tend to display a title first on each screen and center that title with a blank line under it.

Where appropriate, I also use subtitles. For these, I display a blank line above and below the subtitle, and I underline the subtitle by displaying a series of dashes equal in length to the subtitle. Both items help to draw attention to the subtitle, as well as breaking up the 24 lines of text you can display on the screen.

Blank lines

As I just mentioned, I often times use blank lines in my screen messages to call attention to a certain portion of the message or just to break up long messages. However, displaying a blank line is not as simple as it sounds. You might expect that putting an ECHO on a line by itself would skip a line, but as I said earlier, this displays the status of command echoing.

You can choose from five different ways to display a blank line, with the one you select depending on several different factors.

Use an almost blank line   The easiest way to display a blank line is to use commands like these:

```
ECHO !
ECHO .
```

Both of these commands display a printable character that is fairly inconspicuous. Most users will either not notice or else ignore the single inconspicuous character. This approach is the easiest but is also the least attractive.

Use a DR DOS undocumented trick   You can easily display a blank line in DR DOS 6 using the command

```
ECHO.
```

where there is no space between the ECHO and the period. This is quick and easy, but it relies on an undocumented quirk in ECHO that might not be supported in future versions. This is best reserved for quick-and-easy batch files that are not likely to be used for too long.

Use a high-ordered ASCII character   High-ordered ASCII characters are special characters supported by the computer but not shown on the keyboard. I'll explain more about them in Chapter 7. However, one of them is perfect for displaying blank lines. The high-ordered ASCII character with a value of 255 looks like a space on the screen, even though it isn't, so it's treated like any other character. Thus, if I represent this character with a <HO255>, the command

```
ECHO <HO255>
```

will display a blank line on the screen.

To create this high-ordered ASCII character, hold down the Alt key and enter 255 from the keypad with NumLock on. Note that using the numbers at the top of the keyboard won't work. Because of the way you enter these characters, they are usually represented as Alt-#, or Alt-255 for this character. This is the notation I will use for the remainder of this book.

Some editors and word processors either do not accept high-ordered ASCII characters at all or make the process of entering them difficult. There's an easy solution to this problem. From the command line, enter the command

```
COPY CON 255
Alt-255^Z
```

to include an Alt-255 and nothing else in a file called 255. Now, import that into your word processor and paste it wherever you need it in the file.

The DR DOS Editor has an unusual approach to working with Alt-255. When you enter Alt-255 in Editor, it internally converts it to a space. You can use the trick above and ^KR to import a file with an Alt-255 or else leave it as a space. As explained below, an ECHO followed by two spaces displays a blank line under DR DOS.

While the Editor's unique handling of Alt-255 won't cause a problem with the ECHO command, it can cause other significant problems. If you create a subdirectory with an Alt-255 in its name, for example, you will not be able to use the editor to write a batch file to change to that subdirectory. Both files and subdirectories can have one or more Alt-255's included in their name. You will be unable to write a batch file with Editor to work with any of these files or subdirectories.

Warning   When entering an Alt-255 high-ordered ASCII character with Editor, it is internally converted to a space. While this doesn't cause a problem with the ECHO command, it can cause serious problems with the COPY, MD, CD, RD, XCOPY, piping, and other commands that work with files.

Use two spaces   When the ECHO is followed by no spaces or a single space, DR DOS displays the "Echo = on/off" message just as MS DOS does. However, when ECHO is followed by two or more spaces, DR DOS displays a blank line. For this reason, typing ECHO followed by a space and Alt-255 with the Editor produces a blank line under DR DOS. The Alt-255 gets converted to a space, and the two spaces after the ECHO results in a blank line.

MS DOS doesn't display a blank line when the ECHO is followed by two spaces. Therefore any batch file designed to run under both MS and DR DOS should not use this approach to displaying blank lines.

Remember   While DR DOS displays a blank line when the ECHO is followed by two or more spaces, MS DOS does not.

Use a utility   One of the files on the disk that comes with this book is a batch file utility called Batch Commander, written by Doug Amaral of hyperkinetix. One function of this program is to easily display a blank line on the screen, by use of the command

    BATCMD SL

Note that you must include BATCMD.EXE in your path somewhere. Full documentation for Batch Commander is provided in Chapter 25.

What you can and can't echo

While the ECHO command is very flexible, there are a few things that you either cannot display using the ECHO command or that displaying is more difficult than displaying most characters.

DR DOS pipes

You can include the pipe symbols <, >>, >, or ¦ in an ECHO statement. However, if you do, the text to be displayed by the ECHO command is piped into a file or alternative DR DOS device rather than being displayed on the screen. Piping is examined in more detail in Chapter 15.

Warning   Extreme care should be used when including piping symbols in an ECHO command. The text is piped somewhere rather than displayed on the screen.

Percent sign

You cannot directly include a percent sign in an ECHO statement because DR DOS tries to interpret a single percent sign as a variable. If you need a percent sign in your ECHO statement, include a double percent sign (%%). DR DOS will display this as a single percent sign.

Remember   To display a single percent sign in an ECHO command, the batch file must have two percent signs.

On/Off

You can't echo any message that begins with an "on" or "off" because DR DOS interprets this as an ECHO ON or ECHO OFF command. You can solve this in two ways. The easiest way is to rewrite the message so that the words "ON" or "OFF" are not the first words in the message. If rewriting the message isn't possible, then begin the message with the Alt-255 "space" described. Because the high-ordered Alt-255 is treated as a character, the "ON" or "OFF" are no longer the first words in the message.

Warning   Make sure the ECHO command is 127 characters or shorter after everything on the command line has been expanded.

Longer and fancier messages

When you must display a lot of text or when you want fancier formatting, you have three possibilities:

- Place the text in a separate file and use the TYPE command to send it to the screen. See Chapter 20 for more detail.
- Use ANSI commands to improve the appearance of the text (examined in Chapter 21).
- Use a screen compiler to turn each screen full of text into a stand-alone program. (See Chapter 20.)

Each of these approaches is detailed later on in the book, once you have more experience with the simpler batch file commands.

Summary

Some DR DOS commands have two or more functions, depending on how they are used.

The ECHO command can turn on/off command echoing, display the status of command echoing, and display a message on the screen—all depending on how it is used.

Displaying messages to the user via the ECHO command is useful to tell the user that the batch file is running a process that takes a very long time.

Displaying messages to the user via the ECHO command is useful to tell the user what the batch file is doing.

Displaying messages to the user via the ECHO command is useful to give the user additional instructions.

Echo messages should be 80 characters or less to prevent unexpected wrapping on the screen.

Shorter echo messages are easier to read than longer messages.

Due to a bug in DR DOS 5, the ECHO command doesn't display the status of command echoing when used by itself in a batch file. The work-around is to add a single space after ECHO when used in a batch file to display the status of command echoing.

Echo messages can be centered by adding additional spaces between ECHO and the message.

Nearly blank lines can be displayed by printing a single inconspicuous character on a line.

A blank line can be displayed with the undocumented command of placing a period directly after ECHO without a space in between.

A blank-looking line can be displayed by echoing the high-ordered ASCII character Alt-255.

DR DOS will display a blank line when ECHO is followed by two or more spaces. This will not work under MS DOS.

The Batch Commander program included with this book includes the SL (skip line) option to display a blank line.

DR DOS piping symbols cannot be displayed in an ECHO command.

In order to display a single percent sign, the ECHO command must have two percent signs side-by-side.

The words "ON" and "OFF" cannot be used as the first word of an ECHO message.

7
Using high-ordered ASCII characters

DR DOS can use 256 different characters, each one having an associated ASCII value that runs from 0 to 255. Figure 7-1 shows an ASCII chart listing each value. Most users only concern themselves with the values below 128 because these are the values that can be entered by pressing a key on the keyboard. However, the values of 128 and higher offer some nice formatting tools for batch files.

Standard ASCII chart (character codes 0-127)

Code	Function	IBM character	Code	Function	IBM character
000	NUL	(none)	016	DLE	►
001	SOH	☺	017	DC1	◄
002	STX	☻	018	DC2	↕
003	ETX	♥	019	DC3	‼
004	EOT	♦	020	DC4	¶
005	ENQ	♣	021	NAK	§
006	ACK	♠	022	SYN	▬
007	BEL	•	023	ETB	↨
008	BS	◘	024	CAN	↑
009	TAB	○	025	EM	↓
010	LF	◙	026	EOF	→
011	VT	♂	027	ESC	
012	NP	♀	028	FS	∟
013	CR	♪	029	GS	↔
014	SO	♫	030	RS	▲
015	SI	☼	031	US	▼

7-1 An ASCII chart.

Standard ASCII characters

Code	Character	Code	Character
032	sp	074	J
033	!	075	K
034	"	076	L
035	#	077	M
036	$	078	N
037	%	079	O
038	&	080	P
039	'	081	Q
040	(	082	R
041	)	083	S
042	*	084	T
043	+	085	U
044	,	086	V
045	–	087	W
046	.	088	X
047	/	089	Y
048	0	090	Z
049	1	091	[
050	2	092	\
051	3	093	]
052	4	094	^
053	5	095	_
054	6	096	`
055	7	097	a
056	8	098	b
057	9	099	c
058	:	100	d
059	;	101	e
060	<	102	f
061	=	103	g
062	>	104	h
063	?	105	i
064	@	106	j
065	A	107	k
066	B	108	l
067	C	109	m
068	D	110	n
069	E	111	o
070	F	112	p
071	G	113	q
072	H	114	r
073	I	115	s

7-1 Continued.

Code	Character	Code	Character
116	t	122	z
117	u	123	{
118	v	124		
119	w	125	}
120	x	126	
121	y	127	(bs)

Extended ASCII chart (character codes 128 - 255)

Code	Character	Code	Character
128	Ç	162	ó
129	ü	163	ú
130	é	164	ñ
131	â	165	Ñ
132	ä	166	ª
133	à	167	º
134	å	168	¿
135	ç	169	⌐
136	ê	170	¬
137	ë	171	½
138	è	172	¼
139	ï	173	¡
140	î	174	«
141	ì	175	»
142	Ä	176	░
143	Å	177	▒
144	É	178	▓
145	æ	179	│
146	Æ	180	┤
147	ô	181	╡
148	ö	182	╢
149	ò	183	╖
150	û	184	╕
151	ù	185	╣
152	ÿ	186	║
153	Ö	187	╗
154	Ü	188	╝
155	¢	189	╜
156	£	190	╛
157	¥	191	┐
158	₧	192	└
159	ƒ	193	┴
160	á	194	┬
161	í	195	├

7-1 Continued.

Code	Character	Code	Character
196	—	226	Γ
197	┼	227	π
198	╞	228	Σ
199	╟	229	σ
200	╚	230	μ
201	╔	231	τ
202	╩	232	Φ
203	╦	233	Θ
204	╠	234	Ω
205	=	235	δ
206	╬	236	∞
207	╧	237	φ
208	╨	238	ε
209	╤	239	
210	╥	240	
211	╙	241	±
212	╘	242	≥
213	╒	243	≤
214	╓	244	⌠
215	╫	245	⌡
216	╪	246	÷
217	┘	247	≈
218	┌	248	°
219	█	249	•
220	▄	250	·
221	▌	251	√
222	▐	252	n
223	▀	253	2
224	α	254	■
225	β	255	(null)

7-1 Continued.

If you wanted to draw a box without the high-ordered ASCII characters, you would have to use colons for the vertical bars (remember, the | symbol is a pipe and cannot be used in Echo messages), the plus sign for the corners, and the dash for the horizontal bars. However, with the high-ordered ASCII characters, nice boxes are easy.

HI-ASCII.BAT in Fig. 7-2 illustrates this. The lines that appear to be an ECHO by itself also have an Alt-255 character to produce a blank line. A copy of HI-ASCII.BAT is on the disk, and you can run it to see how the boxes look on your screen.

Characters with an ASCII value of 128 or higher are called *high-ordered ASCII characters*. Figure 7-3 lists those high-ordered ASCII characters that are most useful in batch files.

If you ever need to quickly look up an ASCII value while running DR DOS, you don't have to look for your copy of this book. Just copy ASCII.EXE from the enclosed disk to a

```
@ECHO OFF
REM NAME:    HI-ASCII.BAT
REM PURPOSE: High-Ordered ASCII Demonstration
REM VERSION: 1.00
REM DATE:    May 10, 1992
CLS
ECHO
ECHO  ┌─────────────────────────────────────────────────┐
ECHO  │    High Order ASCII Character Demonstration      │
ECHO  └─────────────────────────────────────────────────┘
ECHO
ECHO
ECHO  ┌────┬────┬────┬────┬────┬────┬────┬────┬────┬────┐
ECHO  │    │    │    │    │    │    │    │    │    │    │
ECHO  │    │    │    │    │    │    │    │    │    │    │
ECHO  └────┴────┴────┴────┴────┴────┴────┴────┴────┴────┘
ECHO
ECHO  ╔════╦════╦════╦════╦════╦════╦════╦════╦════╦════╗
ECHO  ║    ║    ║    ║    ║    ║    ║    ║    ║    ║    ║
ECHO  ║    ║    ║    ║    ║    ║    ║    ║    ║    ║    ║
ECHO  ╚════╩════╩════╩════╩════╩════╩════╩════╩════╩════╝
ECHO
ECHO Now Don't Those Look Better Than This
ECHO
ECHO +----+----+----+----+----+----+----+----+----+----+
ECHO :    :    :    :    :    :    :    :    :    :    :
ECHO :    :    :    :    :    :    :    :    :    :    :
ECHO +----+----+----+----+----+----+----+----+----+----+
PAUSE
```

7-2 HI-ASCII.BAT shows how high-ordered ASCII characters can produce attractive boxes in a batch file.

subdirectory in your path, and then enter ASCII at the command line prompt to get a display of all the ASCII characters with values 30-255. (Values below thirty are mostly used for control functions, so most of them won't display on the screen anyway.

Entering high-ordered ASCII characters

If you are using the COPY command or Editor to create your batch files, then entering high-ordered ASCII characters is easy. Take these steps:

1. Make sure the NumLock is on.
2. Hold down the Alt key.
3. Type the three-digit code for the character using the number pad. (The numbers at the top of the keyboard *will not work.*)
4. Release the Alt key.
5. Repeats steps 2-4 for any additional characters you want to enter.

In Context

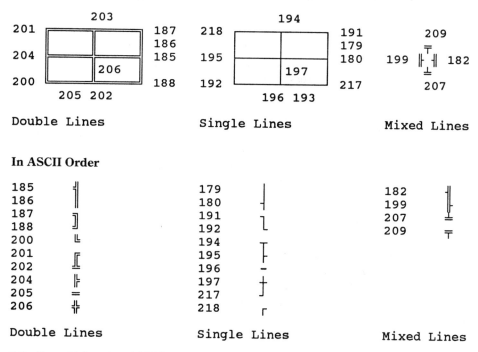

In ASCII Order

Double Lines		Single Lines		Mixed Lines	
185	╣	179	│	182	╢
186	║	180	┤	199	╟
187	╗	191	┐	207	╧
188	╝	192	└	209	╤
200	╚	194	┬		
201	╔	195	├		
202	╩	196	─		
204	╠	197	┼		
205	═	217	┘		
206	╬	218	┌		

Double Lines   Single Lines   Mixed Lines

7-3 These high-ordered ASCII characters are particularly useful in formatting batch files.

This method is not limited to just high-ordered ASCII characters; you could use Alt-68 to enter a capital D, for example. However, using the keyboard for the low-ordered ASCII characters is much easier.

☠ *Warning*   When entering an Alt-255 high-ordered ASCII character with Editor, it is internally converted to a space. While this does not cause a problem with the ECHO command, it can cause serious problems with the COPY, MD, CD, RD, XCOPY, piping, and other commands that work with files.

Some editors make it easy to enter the box-drawing characters. Microsoft Word, for example, has a line-drawing utility that draws using single- or double-lines as you move around the screen and automatically inserts the proper joint when the lines cross.

Many editors make it difficult to enter high-ordered ASCII characters. Microsoft Word, for example, uses the Alt-key to pull down its menus so you sometimes have to enter the high-ordered ASCII character several times before Word figures out you are entering a character and not requesting a menu. Some versions of Wordstar require you to enter a ^P and then the three-digit code rather than using the Alt-key combination. If the Alt-key combination doesn't work in your editor or word processor, check your manual to see what your program expects.

Entering high-ordered ASCII characters when your editor won't let you

A few editors and word processors make it difficult or impossible to enter high-ordered ASCII characters into your batch files. Even the DR DOS Editor has trouble with Alt-255, as mentioned above. There is an easy solution that works with almost every editor and word processor—including Editor. Take these steps:

1. From the command line prompt, enter the command COPY CON 255, only replace the "255" with the name of the file to use. I found it handy to create one file per character I use a lot and to use the ASCII number as the filename.
2. Hold down the Alt key and type in the ASCII code for the high-ordered ASCII character to include in the file.
3. Press F6.
4. Press Enter.

At this point, the file exists and contains the character of interest. Now, to get this character into your file, just import it into the file using the editor's / word processor's import command (^KR in Editor). If it does not have one, open this file first and copy the character to the "paste buffer" (the area where you store characters to paste into other files). If your editor or word processor cannot import a file and doesn't have a paste buffer, you might want to consider finding another editor.

Summary

High-ordered ASCII characters make it easy to draw attractive boxes inside a batch file.

ASCII.EXE on the enclosed disk displays an ASCII chart of most characters on the screen.

Many editors let you enter high-ordered ASCII characters by holding down the Alt key and entering the associated number from the number pad.

If your editor or word processor will not let you enter high-ordered ASCII characters, you can pipe them to a file using DR DOS and then read that file into your editor or word processor.

Hold that batch file!

Imagine you are running the following batch file segment:

```
@ECHO OFF
CLS
ECHO Warning: The Following Program Will Do Damage
ECHO.
ECHO            It Erases All Documents
ECHO            It Damages .EXE Programs In This Subdirectory
ECHO            And It Removes The \BAT Subdirectory
ECHO.
RUNIT
```

This batch file presents a fairly stern warning to the user but doesn't give the user the ability to do anything about it: by the time the user has read the warning, the program has already started running!

It is unlikely you would ever run such a damaging program—at least intentionally. However, the purpose of a warning is to give the user the time to read it and react to it.

Additionally, what if you had a ton of information to give to the user and that information was going to take sixty ECHOs? Using the commands we have learned so far, all you could do is put one after another in a batch file. However, unless the computer was very slow, the messages would scroll by too fast for the user to read.

Pausing the batch file

The DR DOS PAUSE command is the solution to this dilemma. When a batch file comes to a PAUSE, it stops and displays a "Strike a key when ready…" message. The batch file then waits until the user presses any printable key. Keystrokes like Alt, Shift, Ctrl, NumLock, or others that don't produce a character on the screen won't cause a batch file to resume while waiting on a PAUSE command.

If the user presses Ctrl-Break, the batch file will respond with a "Halt Batch Process (Y/N)?" message. Using this, you can build an "escape clause" into your batch files. Let's reconsider the first batch file with a PAUSE command used as an escape clause:

```
@ECHO OFF
CLS
ECHO Warning: The Following Program Will Do Damage
ECHO
ECHO          It Erases All Documents
ECHO          It Damages .EXE Programs In This Subdirectory
ECHO          And It Removes The   BAT Subdirectory
ECHO.
ECHO To Skip Running The Program, Hold Down The Control Key
ECHO And Press The Break Key
ECHO When The Computer Asks "Halt Batch Process (Y/N)?"
ECHO Respond With A Y
PAUSE
RUNIT
```

The batch file now tells the user how to abort processing and has a PAUSE and that gives the user a chance to think about the messages on the screen and decide how to respond.

☑ *Remember*   The PAUSE command stops the computer while the user reads the screen or thinks about a response. It even gives the user a chance to stop the batch file by pressing Ctrl-Break.

PAUSE is useful even if the user won't need to press Ctrl-Break; it simply gives the user time to read the messages and think about them before continuing. If you are going to display several different screens of information, then PAUSE followed on the next line by CLS is critical to ensure that the user is able to read all the information.

Aborting the batch file

As mentioned previously, the Ctrl-Break keystroke can be used to stop a batch file immediately and display a "Halt Batch Process (Y/N)?" message. If the user responds with a y, control is immediately returned to DR DOS. If the user responds with an n, control returns to the batch file.

This makes it easy for the user to abort a batch file prior to running a dangerous command. Later on, in Chapter 19, we will see a better approach to giving the user an escape clause.

'Halt Batch Process' bug

Both DR DOS 5 and 6 have a significant bug in the way they handle an n response to the "Halt Batch Process (Y/N)?" message. When the user responds with a "no," control is supposed to return to the batch file line immediately following the line being processed when Ctrl-Break was pressed. DR DOS tries to do this, but the batch file quickly aborts, often with an error message like "Filename too long" that has nothing to do with the real problem.

You can see this for yourself. Create a batch file with a series of long ECHO commands. The faster your computer, the more ECHO commands you will need because you must have time to press Ctrl-Break in the middle of the batch file. Make the ECHO commands sequential, like a row of A's, followed by B's, C's, and so on.

Once you have finished this batch file, run it and press Ctrl-Break in the middle. When you see the "Halt Batch Process (Y/N)?" message, answer "no" and watch the batch file after it resumes. Every time I've run it, the ECHO statements quickly stop without any error message. If you substitute the COPY command or some other similar command that works with the disk, the batch file will stop and then display an unusual error message, with "Filename too long" being the most common.

This bug has been reported to Digital Research; they've been able to reproduce it and have confirmed it as a bug. Hopefully, it will be fixed soon. However, this bug means you should never respond with a no to the "Halt Batch Process (Y/N)?" until you are sure you have a version of DR DOS where this bug has been corrected.

☠ *Warning*   Due to a significant bug in both DR DOS 5 and 6, you should never respond with a "no" to a "Halt Batch Process (Y/N)?" message. If you do, your batch file execution will be very erratic!

I don't have a complete solution to this problem, but I do have some hope and a partial answer. Most of the time, the user presses Ctrl-Break to stop a batch file, and the batch file stops properly. The most frequent reason for a "no" response is when the batch file is asking the user to think about stopping and the user changes her mind: for example,

```
ECHO This Takes Six Hours
ECHO Press Ctrl-Break To Abort Running The Program
PAUSE
```

To circumvent the problem, don't use PAUSE in this situation and require the user to press Ctrl-Break; instead, use a utility that is designed to ask the user a question and accept a response. I've included it on the enclosed disk; I'll explain more in Chapter 19.

Summary

PAUSE stops a batch file until the user presses any printable keystroke.

If the user presses Ctrl-Break at a PAUSE command—or any other point in the batch file—DR DOS gives the user the option to stop processing of the batch file.

DR DOS 5 and 6 have a significant bug in the way they handle a "no" response to the "Halt Batch Process (Y/N)?" message. Until this bug is fixed, users should never answer "no" to this question.

9

Applications and problems

It's time to stop and catch our breath. While it might not seem so at first, we have covered a tremendous amount of material. You now know how to use a brand new editor, and you've learned how to write simple batch files that contain a mixture of DR DOS commands and a few batch subcommands.

That's why we should take a few moments and make sure that you're up to speed before we continue. What follows are three quick problems. Take a few moments and try to work them. If you get stuck, glance back through the first few chapters. It's important that you have the skills necessary to solve these problems before you go on; otherwise, you'll find continuing difficult.

Problem 1

Write a batch file to format a floppy disk that is in the A drive. Assume that FORMAT.COM has been renamed to XYZ.COM. Use plenty of ECHO statements to tell the user what to do, and be sure to turn command echoing off so that the user won't see the XYZ command and be tempted to run the program directly. Once the disk is formatted, restart the menu program with the command MENU. You can assume that XYZ.COM is in the path. Also, you should make sure to be in the root directory of the C drive sometime prior to restarting the menu.

Problem 2

Write an AUTOEXEC.BAT file that performs the following tasks:

- Sets the path to include the following subdirectories:

  C:\
  C:\DRDOS
  C:\NORTON
  C:\123
  C:\WP
  C:\UTILITY

C:\BAT
C:\MENU

- Creates the following environmental variables:

TEMP=C:\TEMP
DOSONLY=YES
LIB=D:\BLDLITE
OBJ=D:\BLDLITE

- Runs a program called Noprtscr in the C:\UTILITY subdirectory to turn off screen printing.
- Starts a menu program in the C:\MENU subdirectory using the command MENU.

While order generally doesn't matter, remember that if the path doesn't yet point to a subdirectory, then you must change to that subdirectory before running a program; also, loading the menu program must be the last command in the batch file.

Problem 3

Your system has three accounting programs—DAILY.EXE, WEEKLY.COM and ANNU-AL.EXE—that can only be run on your computer by authorized people. Write an informational batch file called ACCTHELP.BAT to give the users information about these programs. That information should include:

- The names of the programs.
- The people authorized to run the programs.
- The fact that passwords are required.
- The name of the person to contact for help with these programs.

Finally, note how important it is to perform a backup after running one of these programs and how a copy of the backup must be sent to the appropriate department at the corporate headquarters.

For the names and numbers you need for this problem, make up any information that you don't have.

Answers

You have a number of ways to tackle each of these problems. My solutions are shown in Appendix C in the back of the book. It isn't important that you match my answers; if you developed a working solution to the problem, your solution is just as good as mine and maybe even better.

PART THREE
Intermediate batch file topics

Now that you've seen the simple batch file commands, it's time to take a look at some slightly more complex commands. As it turns out, the next seven chapters are the "meat" of the book. As you write your own batch files, you'll find that the vast majority of the batch file commands you use are either the REM or ECHO command or the commands covered in these next seven chapters. Just to be sure, there is also a eighth chapter where you can test your knowledge.

Chapter 10: Replaceable parameters. Unless you have a way to get information into a batch file, it is difficult to have the batch file perform differently each time it runs. Replaceable parameters are a method of adding additional information on the command line that the batch file then has access to. This information can be used as file names, extensions, subdirectories, commands, or just about anything you use in a batch file.

Chapter 11: Using more than nine replaceable parameters. When it first starts, the batch file only has access to its name and the first nine pieces of information you entered on the command line. This chapter shows you how to gain access to additional information.

Chapter 12: Looping and program flow. This chapter shows you how to define different execution paths through the batch file and how to create loops within a batch file.

Chapter 13: The environment. The environment is an important scratch pad for the operating system. It uses the environment to store information that all the programs need access to.

Chapter 14: ERRORLEVEL. The ERRORLEVEL is a one-byte portion of memory that programs can use to communicate to each other or with a batch file. While only a few DR DOS programs use the ERRORLEVEL, most batch file utilities use it to pass results back to the batch file that ran them. This chapter provides an overview of the ERROR-LEVEL.

Chapter 15: DR DOS punctuation. Many of the batch files you have seen so far have used varying types of DR DOS punctuation to help them perform their work. This chapter documents that punctuation as a resource to help you understand these batch files as well as write more powerful batch files of your own.

Chapter 16: Logic testing. The different paths you learned to create in Chapter 12 are useless unless you have a method of selecting different paths at different times. Additionally, the loops you learned to create in Chapter 12 are useless unless you have a way to get out of them. In both cases, logic testing is the solution. This chapter shows you how to build logic testing into your batch files. Logic testing is what turns a batch file away from being just a dumb script the computer plays back.

Chapter 17: Applications and problems. Before moving on to the advanced batch subcommands, you should understand the commands and concepts covered so far. This chapter is a quick test. Pass it, and you're ready to move on.

10
Replaceable parameters

DR DOS batch files would be useful if they did nothing more that what's been covered so far. However, one big limitation of the commands that we've looked at is that they're "written in stone." If you want to erase a file with a batch file that just uses these commands, you'll need to physically enter that filename in the batch file code. This is called *hardwiring*.

Sometimes you want to hardwire filenames. If you want to copy all your *.WK1 spreadsheet files to a floppy as backup, then hardwiring the

    COPY *.WK1 A:

command is appropriate. Other times, however, you want the flexibility to have the batch file process different files. DR DOS replaceable parameters offer just such flexibility.

You need to know two things in order to use replaceable parameters: how to give the values for the replaceable parameters to the batch file, and how to code the replaceable parameters in the batch file.

Sending replaceable parameters to a batch file

Giving the values of the replaceable parameters to the batch file is easy. Replaceable parameters are entered after the batch file name and before pressing Enter. For example, the command

    BATCH Para1 Para2 Para3 Para4

will run BATCH.BAT and pass it *Para1* through *Para4* as replaceable parameters.

Each parameter is separated by either a space, comma, or semi-colon. How many replaceable parameters does the previous line have? The obvious (and wrong) answer is four. DR DOS counts the name of the batch file as a parameter, so there are five replaceable parameters on this line. Just to make things confusing, DR DOS names them %0, %1, %2, %3, and %4 and *not* the %1 through %5 you'd expect. See Fig 10-1.

The notation DR DOS uses leaves me with a dilemma in writing this book. Do I refer to %1 as the first replaceable parameter or the second? It truly is the second; however, that

```
C>BATCH *.BAK,*.DOC,*.TMP,*.WKS,*.WK1,*.TXT,*.DBF,*.PRG,*.IN
```

%0 = BATCH
%1 = *.BAK
%2 = *.DOC
%3 = *.TMP
%4 = *.WKS
%5 = *.WK1
%6 = *.TXT
%7 = *.DBF
%8 = *.PRG
%9 = *.IN

10-1 A sample command line and the replaceable parameters seen by BATCH.BLD.

causes confusion for two reasons. First, most readers associate second with 2 and not 1, so they expect the second replaceable parameter to be %2. Second, %1 is actually the first piece of information you enter for the batch file to use, so you really intended it as the first replaceable parameter; you just had to enter the name of the batch file first in order to run it. Thus, I've decided that, throughout this book, I will refer to %1 as the first replaceable parameter, %2 as the second, %3 as the third, and so on. When I need to talk about %0, I will refer to it by the name %0.

▓▶ *Note* When describing replaceable parameters, I will refer to %1 as the first replaceable parameter, %2 as the second, and so on. When I want to talk about %0, I will refer to it by the name %0.

The general rule is that everything you enter on the command line prior to the space becomes %0, everything between the first and second spaces becomes %1, and so on. This means that the name of the batch file becomes %0. This is stored exactly as you enter it on the command line, so if you run BATCH.BAT with the command BATCH, %0 contains "Batch" with that capitalization and without the .BAT extension. If you run it with the command BATCH.BAT, then %0 contains "BATCH.BAT" with the extension—just as you entered it.

However, there is an exception to this rule of %0 containing everything you entered before the first space exactly as you entered it. Many programs expect command line parameters to be entered with a slash, like the command:

DIR/W

DR DOS doesn't care if you place a space between the DIR and the /W: it knows that DIR is the command and the /W is a parameter. DR DOS handles batch files the same way. If you run BATCH.BAT with the command

```
BATCH/H
```

then BATCH becomes %0 and /H becomes %1.

If you use DR DOS exclusively, this next part doesn't matter to you; but if you switch between MS DOS and DR DOS, you should be aware that the two operating systems handle parameters entered with a slash differently when there isn't a space between the name of the batch file and the slash. As we've seen, if you enter BATCH/H under DR DOS, BATCH becomes %0 and /H becomes %1. If you do the same under MS DOS, though, BATCH/H becomes %0 because MS DOS doesn't separate the parameter from the batch file name. We will revisit this issue when we look at logic testing.

Warning DR DOS and MS DOS handle replaceable parameters differently when the name of a batch file is followed immediately by a slash with information after the slash. DR DOS makes the slash and everything that follows %1, with the next replaceable parameter %2, and so on; for example, if you enter BATCH/? under DR DOS, BATCH becomes %0 and /? becomes %1. However, MS DOS treats everything before the first space as %0, so if you enter BATCH/? under MS DOS, BATCH/? becomes %0. This makes it very difficult to write batch files that run under both MS and DR DOS and that accept parameters with a slash.

This can be quite confusing so let's look at a couple of examples. For each of these examples, we will need a batch file. SHOWREPL.BAT is shown below and handles the job nicely:

```
@ECHO OFF
REM NAME:     SHOWREPL.BAT
REM PURPOSE: Show Replaceable Parameters PG
REM VERSION: 1.00
REM DATE:     May 12, 1992

ECHO %%0 = %0
ECHO %%1 = %1
ECHO %%2 = %2
ECHO %%3 = %3
ECHO %%4 = %4
ECHO %%5 = %5
ECHO %%6 = %6
ECHO %%7 = %7
ECHO %%8 = %8
ECHO %%9 = %9
```

Before running SHOWREPL.BAT, you should note that the ECHO commands with the %%0 are used to display a %0. In order to display a percent sign using an ECHO command, DR DOS requires the ECHO to have two percentage signs.

SHOWREPL.BAT is expanded later, and that expanded version is included on the disk. However, that expanded version works fine for these examples, so you don't need to key in the batch file. If you run SHOWREPL.BAT with the command

SHOWREPL/H/I/J One

then the replaceable parameters are

%0   SHOWREPL
%1   /H/I/J
%2   One

Note that the three switches /H/I/J are separated from the SHOWREPL but are not separated from each other. DR DOS does this consistently; the only break it forces is the one between the name of the batch file and the first slash. Also note that "One" becomes %2 even though it comes after the first space. Because /H/I/J is stripped off %0 and treated as %1, all the remaining replaceable parameters have their number increased by one.

When SHOWREPL.BAT is started with the command

SHOWREPL /H /I /J One

then the replaceable parameters are

%0   SHOWREPL
%1   /H
%2   /I
%3   /J
%4   One

just as you would expect.

If you are still confused, you might want to run SHOWREPL.BAT several times with different combinations of replaceable parameters to make sure you understand how DR DOS is translating your command lines into replaceable parameters. I placed a copy of SHOWREPL.BAT on the enclosed disk for that purpose.

Using replaceable parameters in your batch files

Replaceable parameters are global variables and are available to any command in the batch file. They can even be passed by the batch file to other batch files or to programs. However, once the batch file terminates, the values of the replaceable parameters are terminated as well.

DR DOS uses replaceable parameters as if they don't exist. That sounds like an extreme statement, but the supporting logic is solid. Everywhere *you* see a replaceable parameter, *DR DOS* sees the value of that parameter. That statement will make more sense if we look at an example.

First, we need a batch file. I've modified the SHOWREPL.BAT batch file we used earlier to include some REM commands at the bottom of the batch file along with a PAUSE command.

```
@ECHO OFF
REM NAME:      SHOWREPL.BAT
REM PURPOSE: Show Replaceable Parameters
REM VERSION:  1.00
REM DATE:      May 12, 1992

ECHO %%0 = %0
ECHO %%1 = %1
ECHO %%2 = %2
ECHO %%3 = %3
ECHO %%4 = %4
ECHO %%5 = %5
ECHO %%6 = %6
ECHO %%7 = %7
ECHO %%8 = %8
ECHO %%9 = %9
ECHO
ECHO Now, Watch These Remark Statements
ECHO After I Turn Command Echoing On
ECHO ON
REM This Batch File Shows The Values
REM For The First Ten Replaceable
REM Parameters (%0-%9) Entered On
REM The Command Line
@PAUSE
```

Before running SHOWREPL.BAT, you should note that the next to last REM line has two replaceable parameters in it. Because command echoing is on when the batch file reaches this point, we will want to notice how DR DOS treats this line.

Figure 10-2 shows the results of running SHOWREPL.BAT. Notice that, when a batch file executes with command echoing on—beginning in the middle of the batch file—each command in the batch file is preceded by the command line prompt. In other words, DR DOS treats the commands in the batch file exactly like it would if you entered them from the command line prompt. This is consistent with our idea of a batch file being a script the computer follows.

Now, notice the next to last REM line. In the batch file, it reads REM Parameters (%0-%9) Entered On. When I ran this batch file, I ran it with the command:

showrepl One 2 Three Four 5 6,7,8 Nine

so "showrepl" became %0 and "Nine" became %9. In the Rem line on the screen, you can see that DR DOS has replaced the %0-%9" in the batch file with "showrepl-Nine".

With the single exception of a %%0, everywhere there's a %0 in the batch file, DR DOS sees the value of the first replaceable parameter. Except for %%1, everywhere there's a %1 in the batch file, DR DOS sees the value of the second replaceable parameter, and so on. In facts, they are called replaceable parameters for exactly that reason. Because the values come from the command line, you can replace them with new values each time you run the batch file.

```
D:\DRDOSBAT\BAT>showrepl One 2 Three Four 5 6,7,8 Nine
%0 = showrepl
%1 = One
%2 = 2                          ┌─────────────────────────┐
%3 = Three                      │ What Was Entered        │
%4 = Four                       │ On The Command Line     │
%5 = 5                          └─────────────────────────┘
%6 = 6
%7 = 7                          ┌─────────────────────────┐
%8 = 8                          │ Compare The Text On     │
%9 = Nine                       │ This Line Against The   │
                                │ Text Shown For This     │
Now, Watch These Remark Statements  │ Line In The Batch File  │
After I Turn Command Echoing On     │ Listing                 │
                                └─────────────────────────┘
D:\DRDOSBAT\BAT>REM This Batch File Shows The Values

D:\DRDOSBAT\BAT>REM For The First Ten Replaceable

D:\DRDOSBAT\BAT>REM Parameters (showrepl-Nine) Entered On

D:\DRDOSBAT\BAT>REM The Command Line
```

10-2 A screen shot of SHOWREPL.BAT running.

Limits on the number of replaceable parameters

DR DOS does not directly place a limit on the number of replaceable parameters you can specify on the command line. However, it does place an indirect limit. A command line is limited to 127 characters, and the name of the batch file and the first replaceable parameter—as well as each set of replaceable parameters—must be separated by a space, comma or semi-colon. If you run a batch file with a single character name, like A.BAT, and you give it only single character replaceable parameters, like:

    A 1 2 3 4 5 6 7 8 9 0 A B C ...

Then you will have room for 63 replaceable parameters. However, only the replaceable parameters %0-%9 are valid in your batch file. We will see a way around this problem in Chapter 11.

Some uses for replaceable parameters

Back in Chapter 1, we looked at the following batch file segment to start Microsoft Word:

    C:
    CD\WORD
    WORD
    CD\
    MENU

At the time, we didn't give it a name, so let's call it WP.BAT.

Like many programs, Microsoft Word gives you the ability to immediately begin editing a file by specifying the name of that file on the command line. If you start Word with the command

```
WORD CHAP-10
```

you not only start Word, you cause it to load CHAP-10.DOC so that you can begin to edit it. (If CHAP-10.DOC doesn't yet exist, Word will warn you and then create the document for you.) Using replaceable parameters and the commands we have learned since Chapter 1, we can make this a much more useful batch file:

```
@ECHO OFF
REM NAME:     WP.BAT
REM PURPOSE: Run Microsoft Word
REM VERSION: 2.00
REM DATE:     May 12, 1992
C:
CD\WORD
WORD %1
CD\
MENU
```

Now, when the user starts this batch file with the command:

```
WP CHAP-10
```

the batch file both starts Word and tells Word to load the CHAP-10.DOC document. (*Note*: Word doesn't require you to enter the extension; it automatically uses .DOC.)

You might wonder what happens when you start WP.BAT without a replaceable parameter. In that case, %1 has no value. DR DOS performs an exact replacement of the value of %1, so the batch file line WORD %1 is treated by DR DOS as "WORD".

In other words, no replaceable parameter was entered so DR DOS treats that line as though the %1 does not exist. That gives you the flexibility of using the same batch file both when you want to specify a file name and when you don't.

Replaceable parameters as commands

DR DOS is extremely literal in replacing the replaceable parameters with their values and treating those values as though they were hardwired in the batch file. So literal, in fact, that replaceable parameters can even be used as commands. For example, this batch file

```
@ECHO OFF
REM NAME:     COMMANDS.BAT
REM PURPOSE: Show Using Replaceable Parameters
REM            As Commands
REM VERSION: 1.00
REM DATE:     May 12, 1992
%1
%2
%3
```

would treat the first three non-zero replaceable parameters as commands. If you ran the batch file with the command:

it would first perform a Dir, then run CHKDSK in the repair mode and finally run the menu program. Note that /F is not separated from CHKDSK because a slash is only separated from the %0 replaceable parameter.

Of course, just because this works doesn't mean it is a good idea. When you allow the user to enter the command, you lose the control the batch file was designed to provide. So, as a general rule, using replaceable parameters as commands is not a good idea.

A couple of examples

Let's create a couple of example batch files using replaceable parameters. As I introduce additional commands for working with replaceable parameters as well as general batch file commands, we will revisit these batch files to make improvements to them. They are on the disk that comes with this book—but only in their final form. So, if you want to experiment with the intermediate versions, you will need to enter them yourself.

This first batch file—A.BAT—performs a directory of the A drive. It uses a single replaceable parameter. When you run it without a replaceable parameter, it gives you all the files on the A drive. You can enter a replaceable parameter like "*.DOC" to narrow the search.

```
@ECHO OFF
REM NAME:     A.BAT
REM PURPOSE: Directory Of A Drive
REM VERSION: 1.00
REM DATE:     May 12, 1992

DIR A:%1 /P
```

This second batch file—RONNYMD.BAT or Ronny's MD command—will create a subdirectory branching off the current subdirectory and then change to that subdirectory.

```
@ECHO OFF
REM NAME:     RONNYMD.BAT
REM PURPOSE: Make And Change To A Subdirectory
REM VERSION: 1.00
REM DATE:     May 12, 1992

MD %1
CD %1
```

A.BAT runs fine if you don't enter a replaceable parameter—you just get a listing of all the files. RONNYMD.BAT has a small problem. The "MD %1" becomes "MD" when no replaceable parameter is entered—resulting in a DR DOS "Path required" error message. Without a replaceable parameter, the "CD" command just displays the current subdirectory. One of the enhancements we will be making to these batch files in the chapters that follow is error-checking to avoid problems.

While A.BAT runs fine without a replaceable parameter and RONNYMD.BAT has a problem with one line, this final batch file—TOA.BAT—has significant problems when used with the wrong number of replaceable parameters. TOA.BAT, in Fig. 10-3 is designed to be run followed by exactly nine replaceable parameters. Each replaceable parameter designates a document to be copied to the A drive and must be entered without the .DOC extension. The batch file performs three steps for each replaceable parameter:

```
@ECHO OFF
REM NAME:     TOA.BAT
REM PURPOSE: Copy .CMP And .DOC Files To A Drive
REM          While Deleting .BAK Files
REM VERSION: 1.00
REM DATE:     May 12, 1992

DEL %1.BAK
COPY %1.DOC A:
COPY %1.CMP A:

DEL %2.BAK
COPY %2.DOC A:
COPY %2.CMP A:

DEL %3.BAK
COPY %3.DOC A:
COPY %3.CMP A:

DEL %4.BAK
COPY %4.DOC A:
COPY %4.CMP A:

DEL %5.BAK
COPY %5.DOC A:
COPY %5.CMP A:

DEL %6.BAK
COPY %6.DOC A:
COPY %6.CMP A:

DEL %7.BAK
COPY %7.DOC A:
COPY %7.CMP A:

DEL %8.BAK
COPY %8.DOC A:
COPY %8.CMP A:

DEL %9.BAK
COPY %9.DOC A:
COPY %9.CMP A:
```

10-3 TOA.BAT tries to copy nine sets of .DOC and .CMP files to the A drive and deletes nine sets of .BAK files, even if the user did not enter nine replaceable parameters.

1. Deletes the .BAK backup file.
2. Copies the .DOC document file to the A drive.
3. Copies the .CMP user dictionary for that file to the A drive.

As written, this batch file has several significant problems. In fact, I've included it because it has many of the problems associated with using replaceable parameters in batch files. The problems with this batch file are as follows:

- TOA.BAT doesn't check to make sure that nine replaceable parameters were entered. If only six were entered, then %7, %8, and %9 don't exist. For each of these, the DEL .BAK, COPY .DOC A:, and COPY .CMP A: commands generate a DR DOS "Invalid directory specified" error message. The filename is missing because the replaceable parameter is empty, and DR DOS treats the period before the extension as part of a path.
- TOA.BAT ignores are replaceable parameters beyond %9.
- TOA.BAT doesn't check to see if the .BAK file exists before it tries to delete it.
- TOA.BAT doesn't check to see if the .DOC and .CMP files exist before it tries to copy them.

In the chapters to come, we will see how to avoid each of these problems.

Summary

A replaceable parameter is information you enter on the command line after the name of a batch file when you run that batch file.

Replaceable parameters must be separated by a space, comma, or semicolon on the command line.

Replaceable parameters are global variables that are available anywhere in the batch file.

In addition to being available anywhere in a batch file, replaceable parameters can be passed by one batch file to another batch file or by a batch file to a program.

When a batch file name on the command line is followed by a slash and there is no space between the name of the batch file and the slash, DR DOS treats the command line as though there was a space between the batch file name, and the slash so the batch file name becomes %0, and the slash and the information that follows it becomes %1.

When a batch file name on the command line is followed by a slash and there is no space between the name of the batch file and the slash, MS DOS treats everything up to the first space as %0. This is different than DR DOS.

Replaceable parameters are used in a batch file using the terms %0-%9. The %0 is the name of the batch file, %1 is the first replaceable parameter, %2 is the second, and so on.

Everywhere DR DOS sees a %1, it replaces that %1 with the value of the first replaceable parameter as entered on the command line.

DR DOS places no limit on the number of replaceable parameters you can enter on the command line, other than the 127-character limit DR DOS places on the command line.

DR DOS is flexible enough to allow you to use replaceable parameters as commands inside your batch files.

A.BAT performs a directory of the A drive. If a file specification is entered on the command line, it uses that as part of the Dir command.

RONNYMD.BAT first creates a subdirectory branching off the current subdirectory and then changes to that subdirectory. RONNYMD.BAT expects the user to enter a valid subdirectory name and has problems if no name is entered.

TOA.BAT tries to copy nine .DOC and .CMP files matching the nine replaceable parameters it expects to the A drive as well as deleting the nine associated .BAK files. This batch file has significant problems.

11

Using more than nine replaceable parameters

As we mentioned in Chapter 10, DR DOS doesn't directly place a limit on the number of replaceable parameters you can specify on the command line. However, it does place an indirect limit. A command line is limited to 127 characters, and the name of the batch file and the first replaceable parameter as well as each set of replaceable parameters must be separated by a space, comma, or semi-colon. If you run a batch file with a single character name, like A.BAT, and you give it only single-character replaceable parameters, like

    A 1 2 3 4 5 6 7 8 9 0 A B C ...

Then you will have room for 63 replaceable parameters. However, only the replaceable parameters %0-%9 are valid in your batch file.

While dealing with %0-%9, a DR DOS batch file has access to at most ten replaceable parameters. While the particular set of ten replaceable parameters to which the batch file has access can be altered, a batch file is always limited to accessing only ten replaceable parameters.

☑ *Remember*   A batch file can only access ten replaceable parameters at a time.

The SHIFT command

Because a DR DOS batch file can only "see" at most ten replaceable parameters, DR DOS offers the SHIFT command. The SHIFT command discards the %0 parameter, moves the remaining parameters down one value, and brings in a new %9 value if one exists. So, after a SHIFT, the value in %1 moves into %0, the value in %2 moves into %1, and so on. This is illustrated in Fig. 11-1.

You can better understand the SHIFT command with an example. Figure 11-2 shows SHOWSHIF.BAT, the batch file I will use to illustrate the SHIFT command. But before that, let's talk briefly about the table I've used to present SHOWSHIFT.BAT.

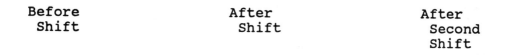

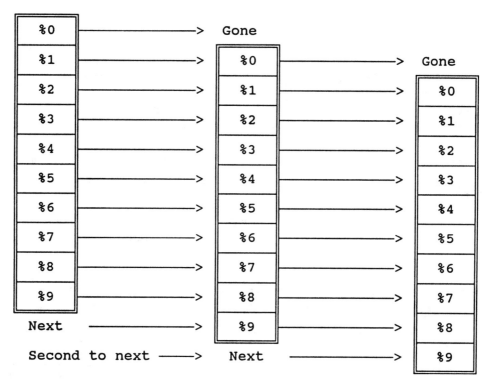

11-1 The SHIFT command discards the %0 replaceable parameter, moves the remaining replaceable parameters down one level, and then makes available one more replaceable parameter in the %9 slot.

Batch file tables

As you have seen in the first ten chapters, I've presented short batch files in the text. That is a neat way to show short batch files that need only a little explanation, and I will continue to use this approach where appropriate.

However, as we move through this book, many of our batch files will start to become longer and more complex. That is why I've developed the concept of this table. The batch file code is listed on the left side of the table. For each single line or group of very similar lines, the right side of the table has a detailed explanation of the function of that line or group of lines. That way, you can be assured that you can fully understand how each batch file works.

I've varied the width of the left side of the tables to avoid—to the extent possible—having to use word wrap on the batch file commands. When it proved to be necessary to use

Batch File Line	Explanation
@ECHO OFF	Turn command-echoing off.
REM NAME: SHOWSHIFT.BAT REM PURPOSE: Show The SHIFT Command REM VERSION: 1.00 REM DATE: May 12, 1992	Documentation remarks.
CLS	Clear the screen.
ECHO Before Shifting ECHO ----------------	Tell the user what will be displayed next.
ECHO %%0=%0 %%1=%1 %%2=%2 %%3=%3 %%4=%4 ECHO %%5=%5 %%6=%6 %%7=%7 %%8=%8 %%9=%9	Display the ten available replaceable parameters and their current assignment.
ECHO	Display a blank line by echoing an Alt-255.
SHIFT	Move all the replaceable parameters down one level and make available another replaceable parameter as %9.
ECHO After First Shift ECHO -----------------	Tell the user what will be displayed next.
ECHO %%0=%0 %%1=%1 %%2=%2 %%3=%3 %%4=%4 ECHO %%5=%5 %%6=%6 %%7=%7 %%8=%8 %%9=%9	Display the ten available replaceable parameters and their current assignment.
ECHO	Display a blank line by echoing an Alt-255.
SHIFT	Move all the replaceable parameters down one level and make available another replaceable parameter as %9.
ECHO After Second Shift ECHO ------------------	Tell the user what will be displayed next.
ECHO %%0=%0 %%1=%1 %%2=%2 %%3=%3 %%4=%4 ECHO %%5=%5 %%6=%6 %%7=%7 %%8=%8 %%9=%9	Display the ten available replaceable parameters and their current assignment.
ECHO	Display a blank line by echoing an Alt-255.
PAUSE	Pause the program until the user presses a key.
CLS	Clear the screen.

11-2   SHOWSHIF.BAT shows the SHIFT command in operation.

Batch File Line	Explanation
SHIFT	Move all the replaceable parameters down one level and make available another replaceable parameter as %9.
ECHO After Third Shift ECHO -----------------	Tell the user what will be displayed next.
ECHO %%0=%0 %%1=%1 %%2=%2 %%3=%3 %%4=%4 ECHO %%5=%5 %%6=%6 %%7=%7 %%8=%8 %%9=%9	Display the ten available replaceable parameters and their current assignment.
ECHO	Display a blank line by echoing an Alt-255.
SHIFT	Move all the replaceable parameters down one level and make available another replaceable parameter as %9.
ECHO After Fourth Shift ECHO -----------------	Tell the user what will be displayed next.
ECHO %%0=%0 %%1=%1 %%2=%2 %%3=%3 %%4=%4 ECHO %%5=%5 %%6=%6 %%7=%7 %%8=%8 %%9=%9	Display the ten available replaceable parameters and their current assignment.
ECHO	Display a blank line by echoing an Alt-255.
SHIFT	Move all the replaceable parameters down one level and make available another replaceable parameter as %9.
ECHO After Fifth Shift ECHO -----------------	Tell the user what will be displayed next.
ECHO %%0=%0 %%1=%1 %%2=%2 %%3=%3 %%4=%4 ECHO %%5=%5 %%6=%6 %%7=%7 %%8=%8 %%9=%9	Display the ten available replaceable parameters and their current assignment.
ECHO	Display a blank line by echoing an Alt-255.

11-2 Continued.

word wrap, I've indented every line except the first one. So, a batch file line in the table where word wrap was necessary might look like this:

ECHO This Is An Example Of A Batch Command Where Word Wrap Is Needed	Tell the user what is happening next.

I originated this method of displaying my batch files in the third edition of my MS DOS Batch File Programming book, and I've used it in all my "batch" books since then. While harder to set up, this method has provided my readers with unparalleled details on the operation of the more complex batch files in my books.

What SHIFT can do

Figure 11-3 shows the results of running SHOWSHIF.BAT in Fig. 11-2 with the command:

    showshif 1 2 3 4 5 6 7 8 9 10 11 12 13 14 15

```
Before Shifting
---------------
%0=showshift %1=1 %2=2 %3=3 %4=4
%5=5 %6=6 %7=7 %8=8 %9=9

After First Shift
-----------------
%0=1 %1=2 %2=3 %3=4 %4=5
%5=6 %6=7 %7=8 %8=9 %9=10

After Second Shift
------------------
%0=2 %1=3 %2=4 %3=5 %4=6
%5=7 %6=8 %7=9 %8=10 %9=11

After Third Shift
-----------------
%0=3 %1=4 %2=5 %3=6 %4=7
%5=8 %6=9 %7=10 %8=11 %9=12

After Fourth Shift
------------------
%0=4 %1=5 %2=6 %3=7 %4=8
%5=9 %6=10 %7=11 %8=12 %9=13

After Fifth Shift
-----------------
%0=5 %1=6 %2=7 %3=8 %4=9
%5=10 %6=11 %7=12 %8=13 %9=14
```

11-3 The results of running SHOWSHIF.BAT in Fig. 11-2, with the replaceable parameters "1 2 3 4 5 6 7 8 9 10 11 12 13 14 15".

As you can see, each time the batch file issues a SHIFT, the replaceable parameters move down one level with another replaceable parameter becoming available as %9.

The one thing you cannot see from Fig. 11-3 is what happens to the value contained in %0 after the SHIFT command. When SHOWSHIF.BAT is first run with the command line just shown, the value in %0 is "showshif." When the first SHIFT is issued, the "showshif" is removed to make room for moving the contents of %1 into %0. That value is unrecoverable. There is no "Unshift" command. Once you have shifted a value away, there is no way to access it, so use SHIFT with care.

💀 *Warning*   There is no "Unshift" command. The current contents of %0 is completely unavailable to the batch file after a SHIFT command.

Using the SHIFT command

The SHIFT command has two major purposes. First, by moving the parameters down into a lower replaceable parameter, a single replaceable parameter can be used for all coding by forcing the program to loop through the code. This makes it much easier to update the code when necessary. (I describe looping starting in Chapter 12.) Second, it allows the batch file to handle more than ten replaceable parameters. Just keep in mind that the total number of replaceable parameters is constrained by the 127-character command line limitation and the requirement to separate each replaceable parameter on the command line.

Of the three sample batch files introduced in Chapter 10, only TOA.BAT can benefit from the SHIFT command. First, take a quick look back at the original version of TOA.BAT in Chapter 10. Now, compare that to the modified version in Fig. 11-4. With this new version, the SHIFT command is used repeatedly so that TOA.BAT is always dealing with the same section of code:

```
DEL %1.BAK
COPY %1.DOC A:
COPY %1.CMP A:
SHIFT
```

which it uses nine times. If there was a way to reuse that code, TOA.BAT would be much shorter. As it turns out, there are two approaches to reusing this section of code: looping and subroutines. Looping is covered in the next Chapter 12, and subroutines are covered in Chapter 22. We will revisit TOA.BAT in both chapters.

```
@ECHO OFF
REM NAME:     TOA.BAT
REM PURPOSE:  Copy .CMP And .DOC Files To A-Drive
REM           While Deleting .BAK Files
REM VERSION:  2.00
REM DATE:     May 12, 1992

DEL %1.BAK
COPY %1.DOC A:
COPY %1.CMP A:
SHIFT
```

11-4   The modified version of TOA.BAT benefits from the SHIFT command. However, it still needs logic testing.

```
DEL %1.BAK
COPY %1.DOC A:
COPY %1.CMP A:
SHIFT

DEL %1.BAK
COPY %1.DOC A:
COPY %1.CMP A:
SHIFT

DEL %1.BAK
COPY %1.DOC A:
COPY %1.CMP A:
SHIFT

DEL %1.BAK
COPY %1.DOC A:
COPY %1.CMP A:
SHIFT

DEL %1.BAK
COPY %1.DOC A:
COPY %1.CMP A:
SHIFT

DEL %1.BAK
COPY %1.DOC A:
COPY %1.CMP A:
SHIFT

DEL %1.BAK
COPY %1.DOC A:
COPY %1.CMP A:
SHIFT

DEL %1.BAK
COPY %1.DOC A:
COPY %1.CMP A:
SHIFT
```

11-4 Continued

Summary

DR DOS places no limit on the number of replaceable parameters you can enter on the command line, other than the 127-character limit DR DOS places on the command line.

The SHIFT command discards %0, moves %1 to %0, %2 to %1, and so on. It also brings another replaceable parameter into the %9 slot.

The SHIFT command is not reversible.

When combined with looping or subroutines, SHIFT allows one section of a batch file to work with all the replaceable parameters.

12

Looping and program flow

So far, our simple batch files have done what I recommend my students do with term papers—start out at the beginning and end at the ending. While that results in some very useful batch files, it doesn't give the batch file any decision-making abilities. The batch file must start at the top and progress downwards even if the conditions that exist at the time of execution are different than when the batch file was designed.

The process of designing our batch files to react differently to different circumstances will span several different chapters. We begin in this chapter by examining several ways to alter the normal top-down progression of a batch file. By doing this, we create several alternative paths that the batch file can take depending on circumstances.

In Chapter 16, we will build on this concept by introducing decision-making tools to the batch file so it can choose from these different paths through the batch file depending on conditions. So, this chapter shows how to define multiple paths through your batch file, while the Chapter 16 shows how to have the batch file pick a path.

Pseudocode

If you program in a general-purpose computer language—like C or Pascal—you generally follow these steps:

1. The programs begin as an idea inside your mind.
2. You translate your idea into computer code. (Most computer tutorials recommend you draw a flowchart first, but no one ever does that!)
3. You run a "compiler" that converts the code that you wrote and understand into a program that the computer can understand.
4. Once your code is free of enough bugs for the compiler to successfully convert it into a program, you can begin running and testing it.

Pseudocode is really Step 1.5. Because no one ever does a flowchart anyway, pseudocode is a way of flowcharting without all the rigors.

Of course, with batch files or any language like GWBasic that acts as an interpreter, Step 3 disappears. Batch files don't need to be compiled because COMMAND.COM reads each line and interprets it as it executes rather than creating a program file of executable code.

☑ *Remember* Pseudocode is computer code written for a human to understand.

Pseudocode is computer code written in English for later conversion into a programming language. Consider the pseudocode example of a loop:

Mark the top of a loop
Do something
If some test is met, jump out of this loop
Go to top of loop

This program goes around in a continual loop until a certain condition forces it to jump out of the loop. However, the real point of this example is that you understand it without knowing any of the associated batch commands!

In addition, pseudocode is also language-independent. If I were to flesh out this example with a few actions and specify the condition for when to jump out of the loop, a Basic or C programmer could write a program to perform the same task in their respective languages.

Pseudocode is not new. I originally learned pseudocode while learning to program in dBASE II on an Apple II with a CP/M card over ten years ago. I will be using pseudocode occasionally in this book to explain the flow of longer batch files because it makes the logic very easy to follow.

Naming program lines

The first thing our loop pseudocode requires is that we "mark the top of a loop." In a batch file, there's no specific marking for the boundary of a loop. Instead, you can give any line a name so the batch file can then jump to that line. To name a line, start with a colon and then type in a name with the following characteristics:

- It must follow the colon with no spaces between the colon and name. While not required by DR DOS, it is a good idea to left-justify the colon and label. Some batch file compilers won't work with a batch file unless the label is left-justified.
- The name should have eight characters or less. Actually, the name can be longer than eight characters; DR DOS just ignores everything after the eighth character. That can cause problems if you have labels like GOTOTHIS1 and GOTOTHIS2, because they're identical through the first eight characters. As a result, both GOTO GOTOTHIS1 and GOTO GOTOTHIS2 will cause DR DOS to jump to the label that appears first in the batch file.
- There can be nothing after the name.
- Capitalization doesn't matter. The labels :END and :End work the same.
- There can be no spaces in the name.
- While you don't have to, it's a good idea to make the name mean something, like top or end.

These rules are quickly summarized in Table 12-1.

Table 12-1 Line-naming rules.

Begin the line to name with a colon in the left-most position.
Immediately follow the colon with a line name of eight or
  fewer characters.
Do not enter anything after the name.
Capitalization does not matter.
Do not use spaces in the name.
Try to have the label name mean something.

✍️ *Notice*   While not a requirement of DR DOS, some batch file compilers demand that the label be left-justified. So, unless you have a good reason to do otherwise, you should left-justify your labels.

The next two lines in the pseudocode above were "do something" and "if some test is met, jump out of this loop." The "do something" line represents your typical commands in a batch file. For example, a segment of the TOA.BAT batch file we have examined over the last two chapters might look like this:

```
:MAINPART
DEL %1.BAK
COPY %1.DOC A:
COPY %1.CMP A:
SHIFT
```

The first line is the label, and the next four lines are the "something" this section is doing.

The "if some test is met, jump out of this loop" line represents logic testing. This topic is covered in detail in the next chapter.

The GOTO command

The last line in the pseudocode above is "go to top of loop." In a batch file, you jump to another section of the batch file by jumping to a line with a name. Because the line containing the name doesn't perform any action, the batch file behaves as though it jumps to the line following the name.

The command used to jump to another line is the GOTO command. The GOTO must be followed by the name of the label to jump to *without* the colon that precedes the label in the batch file itself.

GOTO has two specific uses: repeating a series of commands more than once (in other words, looping) and transferring control to another section of the batch file. We will look at both uses.

Looping

One important use of GOTO is to loop through a section of code more than once. We can see this with a couple of simple examples. We'll call the first one ENDLESS.BAT:

```
@ECHO OFF
REM NAME:      ENDLESS.BAT
REM PURPOSE: Demonstrate GOTO Command
REM VERSION:  1.00
REM DATE:      May 13, 1992
:TOP
ECHO Before A GOTO Command
GOTO TOP
ECHO After A GOTO Command
```

There is a copy of ENDLESS.BAT on the disk that comes with this book. If you run ENDLESS.BAT, you will see a series of "Before A GOTO Command" messages scrolling up the screen.

Let's review the operation of this batch file and you'll see why. The steps in the batch file are as follows:

1. Process the @ECHO OFF command.
2. Skip over the REM commands.
3. Skip over the :TOP label. (Labels are completely ignored except when the batch file is looking at the batch file to figure out where to jump to after a GOTO command.)
4. The ECHO Before A GOTO Command line is executed, displaying the message on the top.
5. The GOTO TOP line is executed, causing the batch file to jump back up to Step 3.

Because it jumps back to the :TOP label each time it reaches the GOTO command, this batch file will continue looping until you force it to stop. This is called an endless loop because, if left alone, it would continue without ending.

By the way, you can stop ENDLESS.BAT by pressing Ctrl-Break or Ctrl-C and responding "yes" to the "Halt Batch Process (Y/N)?" message. In the next chapter, we will see how to add logic testing to batch files so that the batch file itself can figure out if it needs to jump out of a loop rather than depending on the user pressing Ctrl-Break. This "stopping logic" is almost always needed when using the GOTO command to construct a loop.

The steps between the :TOP label and the GOTO command in ENDLESS.BAT form a multi-line loop. It is standard programming practice to indent everything inside a loop—that is, everything except the top (the label) and the bottom (usually the GOTO command). This helps you visualize the loop as you look at the code and actually forms documentation of sorts. DR DOS doesn't require that the commands be indented; in fact, the indentation slows down the batch file a little. It does, however, make the batch file easier for someone to understand when they look at it.

Using this information, we can modify the TOA.BAT batch file we've looked at over the past two chapters. Look back at the version in Chapter 11. In that version, it performed the same few steps nine times. The new version uses a loop to consolidate those few steps inside a single loop. It looks like this:

```
@ECHO OFF
REM NAME:     TOA.BAT
REM PURPOSE: Copy .CMP And .DOC Files To A-Drive
REM          While Deleting .BAK Files
REM VERSION: 3.00
REM DATE:     May 12, 1992
:TOP
    DEL %1.BAK
    COPY %1.DOC A:
    COPY %1.CMP A:
    SHIFT
GOTO TOP
```

The first two versions of TOA.BAT had problems if fewer than nine replaceable parameters were entered because it was designed to handle exactly nine. This third version has a different problem. Because there is nothing in the batch file to cause it to stop, it wants to continue running forever. Of course, it soon runs out of replaceable parameters, and you must press Ctrl-Break to stop it. We will see how to avoid this in Chapter 16.

Transferring control

While it makes little sense, the following batch file is completely legal:

```
@ECHO OFF
GOTO END
ECHO This Message Never Seen
ECHO This Message Skipped Too
:END
```

When the batch file processes the second line, control is immediately transferred to the last line of the batch file and it terminates. It makes little sense because it has lines that are never executed.

While the unconditional jumping shown in this example makes little sense, it often makes good sense for a batch file to jump to different locations depending on conditions. Let's look at the pseudocode for the version of TOA.BAT we will be producing in Chapter 16.

```
Top Of Loop
    Test To See If There Is Another Replaceable Parameter Pending
        If No Then Jump To End Of Batch File
        If Yes Then Continue
    Erase The *.BAK File
    Copy The .DOC File To A-Drive
    Copy The .CMP File To A-Drive
    Shift Replaceable Parameters Down One Level
Go Through Loop Again
```

We haven't yet covered logic testing so we cannot yet produce this batch file as written, but you can see how the ability to jump out of that loop when the batch file "runs out of" replaceable parameters is useful.

In general, we will use this unconditional transfer of control to jump to different sections of the batch file, depending on the conditions the batch file finds when it begins operation. Of course, that means you must write different sections of the batch file to deal with these different conditions.

Quick exit

Many of the batch files in this book will have one or more GOTO END commands to exit the batch file quickly without processing the remainder of the batch file. When this command is executed to terminate a batch file and not a batch file functioning as a subroutine, there is actually a quicker way. In your batch file subdirectory, enter the command:

```
TYPE NOFILE>QUIT.BAT
```

NOFILE is the name of a non-existent file.

As an aside, make sure that you don't already have a QUIT.BAT because this command would erase it. This line creates a 0-length file called QUIT.BAT. Now, replace the GOTO END commands with the QUIT command. Running QUIT.BAT without CALL keeps control from returning to the original batch file; and because QUIT.BAT has no commands, the batch file immediately terminates. Note that you shouldn't use this to exit a subroutine when you want control to return to the batch file that called the subroutine.

💀 *Warning*   This new Quit command shouldn't be used in a batch file that's running as a subroutine.

Handy formatting option

When we mentioned looping earlier, I said that you should indent everything between the top and bottom of the loop as a visual aid in debugging and maintaining the batch file. If you do that, the loop from TOA.BAT looks like this:

```
:TOP
    DEL %1.BAK
    COPY %1.DOC A:
    COPY %1.CMP A:
    SHIFT
GOTO TOP
```

As we begin developing longer batch files, you will find these to be very compartmentalized. In many cases, the batch files will have many different sections for handling specific tasks. For example, a "full-blown" version of TOA.BAT might have sections to perform the following:

- Display help when the user starts the batch file with a /? switch.
- Display an error message when the user fails to enter a replaceable parameter.

- Display an error message when the user specifies a filename as a replaceable parameter and the .DOC version of that file doesn't exist. (Not all files have associated .CMP and .BAK files, so don't give an error message if one of those is missing.)
- Display an error message when the target disk is full or if other copying problems occur.
- Perform the actual copying.

Clearly, you need a method to keep these sections separate, both in execution and visually.

Code separation

Making sure the batch file executes only the right section of code is fairly easy. You jump into the appropriate section of code using the GOTO command as the result of a logic testing statement. At the end of the section, the batch file jumps to the next section of the batch file. You can see the TOA.BAT segment reproduced earlier. It doesn't need to jump into the loop because it reaches that sequentially, but it jumps at the end of the loop.

Visual separation

One way to visually separate the sections is to place one or more blank lines between the different sections. If the section is a loop, then you have the visual clue of the indenting used inside the loop. I tend to use the same form of indenting with sections that are not loops. For example, a section of TOA.BAT to display an error message when the user fails to enter a replaceable parameter might look like this:

```
:NOTHERE
        ECHO You Started TOA.BAT Without A Replaceable Parameter
        ECHO This Information Is Required For TOA.BAT To Run
        ECHO
        ECHO When You Start TOA.BAT, List The Names Of The Files
        ECHO To Copy On The Command Line After The TOA Command
GOTO END
```

Now, you have a visual clue that this section of code is a integral section of code.

The FOR command

Once we cover logic testing in the next chapter, we'll have everything that you'll need to know to write complex loops using the GOTO command. However, one limitation of looping via the GOTO command is that you must provide the parameters of the loop when you code the batch file. For example, you cannot go through the loop once for each .DOC file or for every file on the B drive. For that, you need the FOR command.

Looping with the FOR command

In its simplest form, the FOR command causes DR DOS to loop through a series of files and perform a single action on those files. There are two forms of the command. The first takes a list of files:

    FOR %%h IN (CHAPTER1.BAK CHAPTER2.BAK) DO ERASE %%h

The second form uses DR DOS wildcards to calculate all applicable files:

    FOR %%j IN (*.BAK) DO DEL %%j

In general, the command is

    FOR %% *variable* IN (set) DO *Command*

The FOR command must be on one line. Also, FOR commands cannot be nested, so only one FOR command can be on each line. The %%variable must be a single character: for example, %%A through %%Z. In addition, if you reference the %%variable after the DO command, you must use the same capitalization as you used in the beginning. For example,

    FOR %%J IN (*.*) DO ECHO %%J

and

    FOR %%j IN (*.*) DO ECHO %%j

are valid because both %%J's are the same case, but the command

    FOR %%J IN (*.*) DO ECHO %%j

is invalid because one J is uppercase and the other is lowercase.

Remember The FOR command must be all on one line and cannot be nested.

DR DOS will let you use %0 through %9 as variables in the For command, but it is a bad programming habit because DR DOS uses these as replaceable parameters. You can also use the FOR command from the command line prompt without a batch file. The only change is that you only use one percent sign rather than two, so the %%variable must be %variable.

Warning DR DOS allows you to use %0-%9 as the variable in a FOR command. Don't do it. This is poor programming because DR DOS uses %0-%9 as replaceable parameters.

Local variable

When we worked with replaceable parameters back in Chapter 10, we saw that the replaceable parameters were global variables. That is, you could use %1 anywhere in your batch file and the command would have access to the value stored in %1. However, the variables created by the For command are local variables. Their value is only usable while the batch file is running. That is, the following batch file segment:

```
@ECHO OFF
FOR %%J in (1 2 3) DO ECHO %%J
ECHO %%J
```

would not have a value for %%J to echo when it reached the third line so it would simply echo "%J". (Recall that you use no percent signs in an Echo command to echo a single percent sign.)

☑ *Remember*   FOR variables are local variables whose value is only usable within the FOR loop.

Running commands with a FOR loop

Every so often, the computer magazine hint columns will have a hint from someone who has just discovered that the things you put in the list of variables for a FOR command can be commands themselves. The authors of these hints are excited because the batch file runs faster this way; if you remember, DR DOS processes batch files one line at a time, and this strategy puts more commands on a single line.

Don't be fooled. While the batch files are truly a little faster, this method has a couple of drawbacks that greatly outweigh this slight dose of speed, with the biggest drawback being human readability. You and I could probably look at a batch file with the lines

```
DIR
CHKDSK
CD\
```

and tell exactly what it is supposed to do. However, the function of a batch file with the line

```
FOR %%j IN (DIR CHKDSK CD\) DO %%j
```

isn't nearly so clear. In the end, you will waste more time writing and debugging such complex code than you will save by stacking more commands on a single line.

This method has another drawback: you cannot use this trick with any command that requires more than one word. For example, you might want to run Chkdsk and then beep the bell by echoing a ^ G. With two lines, you would enter the commands

```
CHKDSK
ECHO ^ G
```

Using the For command, you would enter the command

```
FOR %%j IN (CHKDSK ECHO ^G) DO %%j
```

but because of the space, DR DOS would actually try to run

```
CHKDSK
ECHO
^ G
```

The final drawback is the most serious. Generally, you would run CHKDSK/F rather than CHKDSK. Other commands, like the DIR and FORMAT commands, use these command line switches. However, when used inside the (set) portion of a For command (like this)

FOR %J in (DIR/W CHKDSK/F FORMAT/S) DO %J

on either the command line or in a batch file, the FOR command immediately returns a "Batch file nested too deep" error message even when the command is executed from the command line! After this, additional FOR commands and some other DR DOS commands don't work properly until the computer is reset.

Warning   You should never use a FOR command to execute other commands under DR DOS, especially if those programs require command line parameters preceded with a slash!

This restriction won't create compatibility problems with MS DOS. When the slash command is used in the (set) portion of a FOR command under MS DOS, it is treated as a divider. So the command

FOR %J in (DIR/W CHKDSK/F FORMAT/S) DO %J

has six different elements (DIR, W, CHKDSK, F, FORMAT, and S) in its (set). Because MS DOS treats the slash as a divider, it strips it out when handing the elements off to the FOR command, just as both MS and DR DOS strip off the space between the elements in the (set).

For a quick reference chart for the FOR command, look at Table 12-2.

Table 12-2   FOR command summary.

The syntax of the command is FOR %%J IN (*Set*) DO *Command*
The *(Set)* can contain a list of files, wildcards, or simply a list of items to process.
The command to execute might or might not use the %%J variable.
FOR commands can also be issued from the command line: just replace the %%J variable with a %J variable having only a single percent sign.
If the %%J variable is referenced by the command, that reference must use the same capitalization as was used at the beginning of the FOR command.
The FOR command cannot be nested.
The variables %0 - %9 should not be used as FOR command variables although DR DOS allows it.
The %%J variable is a local variable that no longer contains a value once the FOR command terminates.
Command can be used in the *(Set)* list and executed by the command; however, that is poor programming.
Commands requiring a command line switch preceded by a slash cannot be included in the *(Set)* when executing commands using the FOR command.

Summary

Pseudocode is the process of outlining programs in English without worrying about which language will be used to create the program. Pseudocode is later turned into a program.

Lines are given a name in a batch file by preceding an eight-character or shorter name with a colon.

The GOTO command causes control to jump from the current line to the line named as part of GOTO.

The GOTO command can be used to loop or to permanently transfer control to another section of the batch file.

Loops created with GOTO need some logic added to tell the batch file when to stop looping.

Once the 0-length file QUIT.BAT has been created in a subdirectory in the path, the QUIT command can be used to quickly terminate a batch file without the need for a GOTO END command and the corresponding :END label.

When creating loops with the GOTO command, it is useful to indent everything between the label and the GOTO command to visually represent the loop.

The FOR command constructs a single-line loop that is automatically executed once for each item in the (set) of items specified with the command.

The FOR command must be all on one line and cannot be nested.

DR DOS has significant problems when commands are executed by listing the commands in the (set) and just executing the commands after the DO command—particularly when those commands require a command line parameter preceded with a slash. DR DOS users should avoid doing this.

13

The environment

DR DOS sets aside a portion of memory for storing system-wide variables. This area is called the *environment*, and the variables stored there are called *environmental variables*. In addition to storing the value of environmental variables, this area stores the prompt, path, and Comspec. Technically, these three values are nothing more than environmental variables, although they have such specific functions that they are usually treated differently. Because they are so important, let's take a moment to look at each one.

The prompt

The default prompt is C>, which tells you almost nothing (except that C is the default drive). You can use the PROMPT command to change the prompt to a wide range of prompts. The PROMPT command is normally just used in the AUTOEXEC.BAT file; when used by itself, it resets the prompt to C>.

Any printable character string can be included in the PROMPT command. In fact, one of the first tricks most computer users learn is to include their name or company name in the prompt. Special characters can be included in the prompt with the commands in Table 13-1. The most popular prompt is

    SET PROMPT=pg

This command adds the current subdirectory to the default disk display. It's important to remember that any prompt you develop is stored in the environmental space, along with the path and set variables. A long prompt combined with a long path, and a set variable might require you to expand your environmental space, as explained later in this chapter.

The path

DR DOS will accept four types of commands: internal commands, .EXE program names, .COM program names, and batch file names (.BAT). Every time DR DOS receives a command, it first checks to see if the command is an internal command, like ERASE. If so, it executes it. If the command isn't an internal command, DR DOS next checks the current

Table 13-1 Metacharacters to use in the PROMPT command.

Command	Action
$$	Display a dollar sign.
$_	Include a carriage return and line feed.
$b̄	Display a vertical bar.
$d	Display the date.
$e	Include an escape. This is useful for sending ANSI escape sequences via the prompt command.
$g	Display a greater-than sign.
$h	Display a backspace--thus deleting the prior character.
$l	Display a less-than sign.
$n	Display the current drive.
$p	Display the current subdirectory.
$q	Display an equal sign.
$t	Display the time.
$v	Display the DOS version.

subdirectory for an .EXE file by that name, then a .COM file, and finally a .BAT file. If DR DOS finds a program with the correct name, it executes that program. If DR DOS doesn't file in the current directory, it searches the path for a .COM, .EXE, or .BAT file. If DR DOS finds a program in the path with the correct name, it executes that program. Otherwise, DR DOS returns the "Command or filename not recognized" error message. The hierarchy of DR DOS commands is shown in Table 13-2.

Table 13-2 Hierarchy of DR DOS commands.

When The Path Is C:\FIRST;C:\SECOND;C:\THIRD

1. An internal command.
2. A .COM file in the current subdirectory.
3. A .EXE file in the current subdirectory.
4. A .BAT file in the current subdirectory.
5. A .COM file in the C:\FIRST subdirectory.
6. A .EXE file in the C:\FIRST subdirectory.
7. A .BAT file in the C:\FIRST subdirectory.
8. A .COM file in the C:\SECOND subdirectory.
9. A .EXE file in the C:\SECOND subdirectory.
10. A .BAT file in the C:\SECOND subdirectory.
11. A .COM file in the C:\THIRD subdirectory.
12. A .EXE file in the C:\THIRD subdirectory.
13. A .BAT file in the C:\THIRD subdirectory.

So the path is nothing more than a list of subdirectories for DR DOS to search when a program isn't in the current subdirectory. The syntax is

PATH=C:\;SUBDIRECTORY-11;SUBDIRECTORY-12;...;LAST-SUBDIRECTORY

So, if your path is

PATH=C:\;\DRDOS;\DATABASE;\WORDPROCESSOR

then DR DOS will search only those subdirectories on the default disk. This is normally what you want. However, if you're working on the A drive, then the path is really

PATH=C:\ ;A:\DRDOS;A:\DATABASE;A:\WORDPROCESSOR

because A is the default drive. So you're better off specifying the full path, like this:

PATH=C:\ ;C:\DRDOS;C:\DATABASE;C:\WORDPROCESSOR

A problem is that the Path command can contain only the same 127 characters as other DR DOS commands. The Subst command allows you to substitute a drive letter for a subdirectory. So

SUBST D: C:\DRDOS\LEVEL1\LEVEL2

allows you to use D: anywhere you would have used C:\DRDOS\LEVEL1\LEVEL2. Your PATH command can now be

PATH=C:\ ;D:\

instead of

PATH=C:\ ;C:\DRDOS\LEVEL1\LEVEL2

This makes the command shorter, as well as easier to read. Generally speaking, you won't have set the path before using the Subst command. Therefore, either SUBST.EXE must be in the root directory, you must change to the directory containing it before you issue the Subst command, or you must specify the full path to SUBST.EXE in the command. If you had the SUBST.EXE file in the C:\DRDOS directory, you would first change to that directory with the following command:

CD\DRDOS

and then give your Subst command, like

SUBST D: C:\DRDOS\LEVEL1\LEVEL2

or you could specify the full path to the command and not need to change subdirectories first:

C:\DRDOS\SUBST D: C:\DRDOS\LEVEL1\LEVEL2

If you enter PATH with nothing after it, DR DOS displays the current path. If you enter PATH followed by a semicolon, DR DOS resets the path to nothing; this causes DR DOS to search only the default directory for programs and batch files. If you specify a path incorrectly, DR DOS won't find the error until it needs to search the path. If you enter an invalid directory in the path, DR DOS ignores that entry—although DR DOS does display an error message when it tries to search that invalid subdirectory.

Comspec

Comspec is short for SET COMmand SPECification. It tells DR DOS where to find COMMAND.COM when it's overwritten by a program. DR DOS takes up a lot of memory.

When your computer is short of memory, either because it has less than 640K or because you have a lot of memory-resident software, things can get crowded. The lack of memory might prevent some programs from being run or even limit the size of others. DR DOS solves this problem by making part of itself provisionally resident (or transient) in memory. You need this part to enter DR DOS commands but not to run the application programs. If a program needs this space, it can overwrite the transient portion of DR DOS.

When you exit an application program that's overwritten the transient portion of DR DOS, part of DR DOS is missing. Thus, if you were to use this version, you wouldn't be able to enter most internal commands. DR DOS replenishes itself by rereading portions of COMMAND.COM into memory.

IIII▶ Note   This is why COMMAND.COM isn't a hidden file like the other two system files.

Usually, DR DOS reloads itself from the drive it booted from. Using

    SET COMSPEC=C: COMMAND.COM

you can force DR DOS to reload itself from some other place. You can also change COMSPEC using the SHELL command in the CONFIG.SYS file. Loading COMMAND .COM with the SHELL command rather than having the operating system load it automatically doesn't use any extra memory unless you expand the environment. And then, the only additional memory use is that of the extra environment. Many RAM-disk users copy COMMAND.COM to their RAM disk and then use the SET COMSPEC command to reload COMMAND.COM from the RAM disk. This is noticeably faster than reloading from disk.

Environmental variables

Think of the environment as a scratch pad, where the operating system leaves notes for itself. As we will see, batch files can also use this scratch pad.

Most programs distinguish between different types of variables. For example, you generally don't use the same type of variable for a string of characters as you do for numbers. The environment doesn't make this distinction. Every environmental variable is treated as a string of characters—even if it's all numbers.

Unlike filenames, environmental variable names aren't limited to a few characters. Therefore, it's a good idea to use descriptive names like SourceDrive and TargetDrive. Of course, these longer names take up more space in the environment; and, as we will see, environmental variable names are converted to uppercase.

▶ Remember   The environment is a scratch pad for the operating system.

Increasing the size of the environment

Most compilers use one or several environmental variables to point to their libraries. In fact, a couple of them use the same variables to point to different libraries! I once got a frantic call from a developer using two compilers from the same company—Basic and C. Both compilers used the same environmental variable to point to their (different) libraries. He didn't know how to deal with this problem. I told him to construct two batch files, one to start each compiler. He could then have each batch file custom-set the variables for that compiler.

He called me back, even more frantic, because it wouldn't work. I had him type in SET at the DR DOS prompt and read the contents back to me. It turned out that he hadn't expanded the environment; and, with his long path and prompt, there just wasn't enough room to store all the information he was trying to shove into the environment. I walked him through the procedure to expand the environment and then everything worked properly.

The default size of the environment for both DR DOS 5 and 6 is 256 bytes (which means that it can store 256 characters). This storage space must store the COMSPEC value, the PATH, the PROMPT, and any variables you want to enter. If this isn't enough room, you will get an "Environment Full" error message. To correct the problem, you need to expand the environment.

Under DR DOS, expanding the environment is easy. Adding the following line as the first line of your CONFIG.SYS file will expand the environment:

```
SHELL=C:\COMMAND.COM /E:yyyyy /P
```

If you're running off floppy disks, change the C:\ to an A:\. The yyyyy can be a number from 512 to 32,768 (which allows an environmental space up to 32K!). The /P is required to force COMMAND.COM to automatically run the AUTOEXEC.BAT file. Because the Shell command is in the CONFIG.SYS file and the CONFIG.SYS file is processed prior to the AUTOEXEC.BAT file, the AUTOEXEC.BAT file will be bypassed without the /P switch. It is also interesting to note that the default size for the environment is 256 bytes, but the minimum you can specify with the /E switch is 512 bytes.

The previous SHELL statement uses the /E and /P switches. These aren't SHELL switches but rather COMMAND.COM switches. The full set of switches is as follows:

/?	This switch displays help about COMMAND.COM.
/C	This tells COMMAND.COM to run the command listed after the /C switch.
/E	This switch changes the environment sizes.
/H	This switch displays help about COMMAND.COM.
/MH	This forces COMMAND.COM to load into high memory if enough memory is available.
/ML	This forces COMMAND.COM to load into conventional (low) memory.
/MU	This forces COMMAND.COM to load into upper memory if enough memory is available.
/P	This tells COMMAND.COM to load in permanent mode, which causes COMMAND.COM to set a couple of switches internally. One switch keeps it from unloading when you issue an Exit command, while another causes it to run the AUTOEXEC.BAT file after loading.

Note that you're required to put the .COM extension on the end of COMMAND .COM. And remember: these changes won't take effect until you reboot. Make sure you have a bootable system disk in case you make a mistake because some mistakes will hang the computer. If this happens, reboot from the floppy disk and switch over to the hard disk to edit the problem CONFIG.SYS. As a precaution, you should make a copy of your CONFIG.SYS file before trying this change.

Additionally, you should create a bootable floppy diskette if you don't already have one. Because the CONFIG.SYS is processed before COMMAND.COM is loaded, you cannot press Ctrl-Break to stop the CONFIG.SYS if you make a mistake that causes the computer to lock up. When that happens, you must boot from a floppy disk to correct the problem.

Environmental variables are transient

As mentioned earlier, all systems have a Comspec environmental variable, and most have a Path and Prompt environmental variable. Some hardware and software also creates environmental variables when you install them. Windows wants an environmental variable called Temp to point towards a place for its temporary files. My tape drive creates two, and my CD ROM creates three. You will find these added to your AUTOEXEC.BAT file. Usually, the installation program adds them automatically.

Variables in the environment are lost when you turn off or reboot the computer. Although these variables are transient, they can be very useful for communicating between different batch files or for storing information for use by more than one batch file.

📝 *Remember* Variables in the environment are lost when you turn off or reboot the computer.

Putting variables into the environment

You can place SET variables into the environment either with a batch file or interactively from the command line prompt. Either way, the syntax to place an environmental variable into the environment is

    SET variable=value

Note that the only space is between SET command and the variable name. Don't use spaces around the equal sign.

If you include spaces around the equal sign or elsewhere in the SET command, what ends up going into the environment depends on which version and brand of operating system you are using. With the command

    SET RONNY< >=< >Test

under all versions of MS DOS and under DR DOS 5, you end up with a variable named "RONNY< >" containing the value "< >Test". DR DOS 6 understands what you want and strips out the space so the variable is properly named "RONNY" and properly contains the value "Test". Regardless of the case you use, the environmental variable name is converted to uppercase.

In its attempt to be helpful, DR DOS 6 introduces some additional problems. On rare occasions, you might want to create an environmental variable containing internal spaces. For example, you might want to store a message like "Copyright (c) 1992 TAB Books" in the environment under the name Say and just have your batch files use the command ECHO %SAY% instead of including the message in all your batch files. The command

        SET SAY=Copyright (c) 1992 TAB Books

will store the environment properly under all MS and DR DOS. However, if you issue the command:

        SET SAY< >=< >Copyright (c) 1992 TAB Books

under DR DOS 6, it tries to be helpful and strip off the spaces around the equal sign—only it strips out all the spaces, and the text stored in the environment ends up being "Copyright(c)1992TABBooks"! The solution is to be extremely careful not to use spaces around the equal sign.

Warning When using the SET command, be sure not to use a space before or after the equal sign.

Once you store a variable in the environment, you cannot edit its value. However, you can replace the contents of an environmental variable using the same command—thus overwriting the contents of the environmental variable with a new value. You can also delete an environmental variable with the command

        SET variable=

where nothing follows the equal sign. Finally, you can view the contents of the environment by issuing the SET command by itself from the command line or in a batch file.

You can use a similar approach to transferring data between environmental variables. For example, if the environmental variable BEFORE contains a value you want to store in the environmental variable After, the command to do this is

        SET AFTER=%BEFORE%

Because of the percent signs, DR DOS replaces the %BEFORE% environmental variable with its contents; and because of the Set command, it then stores this value to AFTER. Two notes are important. First, the BEFORE environmental variable is surrounded by percent signs because we want to use its value, but the AFTER environmental variable isn't because we are using that name. Second, this command doesn't change the contents of the BEFORE environmental variable, so now we have the same information stored under two names. Of course, we could go ahead and work with either environmental variable to alter their contents.

Using the environment in batch files

Other than by placing them in memory and viewing them, you can't access environmental variables from the command line. However, environmental variables can be accessed by any batch file and used in commands—or even as a command—just like a replaceable parameter. The syntax is %variable%, so all you do to use the variable is surround the name with percent signs.

Remember Batch files can do more with environmental variables than you can from the command line.

What you can do with environmental variables

Programming languages generally let you perform mathematical operations on numbers but DR DOS doesn't have a command to do this on an environmental variable. However, the utility program Batcmd lets you add and subtract one from an environmental variable named Math. Batcmd is included on the disk that comes with this book, and this feature is reviewed in Chapter 25.

Environmental variables can be used for the following:

- *Display*. A batch file can display the contents of any environmental variable by surrounding its name with percent signs. For example, ECHO %PATH% will display the path. Also, when the expanded line is longer than 127 characters, as it might be with a long path and the command ECHO My Path Is: %PATH%, then the entire message will not display and the computer might lock up.
- *Combining Strings*. Two or more environmental variables can be displayed together. The technique is the same: just surround the respective names with percent signs. For example, if there are environment variables named DRIVE and FILE, the command ECHO %DRIVE%%FILE% will display them both side-by-side.
- *In Place Of Text*. Environmental variable can be used any place where text would be used. For example, the command PATH=%PATH%;C:\123 would append C:\123 onto the current path because the %PATH% is used just like the batch file entering the current path, and the command COPY C:\AUTOEXEC.BAT %DRIVE%%FILE% would copy your AUTOEXEC.BAT to the drive and filename stored under these environmental variables.
- *In Place Of Commands*. A batch file can run a command stored to an environmental variable by having that environmental variable, surrounded by percent signs, on a line by itself.

Note, while all these techniques work from within a batch file, none of them work from the command line.

Remember Batch files can use environmental variables much more extensively than they can be used from the command line.

Using the environment when shelling out of a program

While batch files work with the original—or master—copy of the environment, every time you start a program, DR DOS passes that program a full copy of the environment. The program is free to alter its copy of the environment, but when the program terminates, its copy of the environment is also terminated without passing the changes back to the master copy of the environment.

Remember our comparing the environment to a scratch pad. Well, when DR DOS runs a program, it provides that program with a "photocopy" of its scratch pad in case the program needs any of the information it contains. However, when the program is done, DR DOS ignores any notes the program has made on its photocopy.

Most programs make little or no use of the environment, so the first thing most programs do is free up any memory contained in their copy of the environment that isn't being used to store a value. They keep the values but little or no free environmental space. However, the environment must be created in 8-byte blocks, so this purging of free memory could result in 0–7 bytes of free environmental memory.

The action of the environment while a program is running leads to an interesting problem and a useful shortcut for experimenting with the environment. First, the problem, and then the shortcut.

Environment problem when shelling out of a program

Imagine you are setting up Windows to run a non-Windows program by running a batch file. For this example, we'll use WP.BAT from Chapter 10. This batch file will require one modification. Instead of running the menu as the last step, it will need to issue an Exit command to unload the copy of COMMAND.COM Windows used to run the batch file. The modified batch file looks like this:

```
@ECHO OFF
REM NAME:    WP.BAT
REM PURPOSE: Run Microsoft Word Under Windows
REM VERSION: 3.00
REM DATE:    May 12, 1992
C:
CD\WORD
WORD %1
CD\
EXIT
```

To avoid the problem of the user shelling out of Word and trying to run yet another program, you might want to add the modification examined in Chapter 3 of changing the prompt before starting Word and changing it back after Word terminates. That version of the batch file is shown below:

```
@ECHO OFF
REM NAME:    WP.BAT
REM PURPOSE: Run Microsoft Word Under Windows
REM VERSION: 3.01
REM DATE:    May 12, 1992
C:
CD\WORD
PROMPT Type EXIT To Return To Word $P$G
WORD %1
PROMPT $P$G
CD\
EXIT
```

However, this batch file won't run as expected under Windows! The problem is that Windows discards the free memory from its copy of the environment so there's no more than seven bytes of free environmental space. When Windows loads a second copy of COMMAND.COM, that COMMAND.COM gets a copy of this reduced-size environment.

Because the new "Type EXIT To Return To Word PG" prompt is much longer than the existing prompt, it will not fit and you'll get the "Environment full" error message.

This problem is not unique to Windows. If you shell out of Lotus or Word and try to run a batch file that adds information to the environment, you will find it also fails to run properly: Both Lotus and Word discard free environmental memory to have more conventional memory to run with and then pass along this reduced-size environment to COMMAND.COM when you shell out.

Increasing the size of the master copy of the environment won't help. This will just give the programs more free environment space to discard when they start.

The solution, then, is to find another approach to making environmental space available under programs that discard free environmental space. The steps are as follows:

1. In your AUTOEXEC.BAT file, create a long environmental variable containing enough information that, if deleted, would free up enough environmental space to make the environment usable under other programs. For this example, we'll call this variable Junk. So the AUTOEXEC.BAT file would have a statement like

   ```
   SET JUNK=AAAAAAAAAAAAAAAAAAAAAAAAAAAAAAAAAAAAAAAAAAAAAA
   ```

2. Before adding information to the environment in a batch file designed to run while shelled out of another program, delete the Junk environmental variable. The modified version of WP.BAT is shown next:

   ```
   @ECHO OFF
   REM NAME:      WP.BAT
   REM PURPOSE: Run Microsoft Word Under Windows
   REM VERSION: 3.02
   REM DATE:      May 12, 1992
   C:
   CD\WORD
   SET JUNK=
   PROMPT Type EXIT To Return To Word $P$G
   WORD %1
   PROMPT $P$G
   CD\
   EXIT
   ```

3. If you are modifying a batch file that will be used both from the command line and from within a program, then deleting the Junk environmental variable before adding information to the environment is OK. However, the current version of WP.BAT never recreates the Junk variable. As we said, when a program terminates, its copy of the environment is also terminated. Most programs shell out by running COMMAND.COM; this is always the case if you have to type Exit to return to the original program. When that copy of COMMAND.COM terminates, changes to its environment are lost.

However, when a dual-mode batch file is running from the command line, the environment isn't restored and the contents of the Junk environmental variable won't be available for other batch files to delete. To avoid that, add a command at the end of any dual-mode batch files to recreate the Junk environmental variable. That way, when they run by themselves, it is recreated properly. When run from inside a program, there might not be enough free memory to recreate the variable, but in that case it doesn't matter.

☑ **Remember** To create free environmental space while shelling out of another program, create a long environmental variable from the command line or in the AUTOEXEC.BAT file and then delete that variable to create free environmental space when shelling out of a program.

By following these three steps, you will always have free environmental memory no matter if your batch file is running from DR DOS directly or running while shelled out of Windows or some other program.

Environment benefits when shelling out of a program

As explained earlier, after you shell out of a program, the changes you make to the environment are lost when you enter the Exit command to return to the original program. However, as long as you follow the procedures just described to create a dummy environmental variable from your AUTOEXEC.BAT file that you can later delete, you will have free environmental space while shelled out of a program.

All that makes shelling out of a program the perfect place for testing batch files that modify the environment—especially if your system depends on a well crafted environment. No matter how many alterations you make to the environment, a simple Exit command restores the environment to its pristine form.

When I'm writing a batch file that works with the environment, I usually use Microsoft Word rather than Editor to write the batch file. That way, when I'm ready to test the batch file, I can shell out to test the batch file. If I find problems, an Exit command both restores the environment and returns me to Word where I can make the necessary changes.

Using the environment in a batch file

The environment is commonly used as an common exchange ground—for one batch file to place information into the environment for another batch file to use. Looking at this in more depth requires that we understand both the errorlevel and logic testing, so we'll postpone this topic until later in Chapter 18.

Batch files can use environmental variables just like replaceable parameters, including using them as filenames or even commands. This allows environmental variables to be used as a shortcut.

☑ **Remember** Batch files can use environmental variables just like replaceable parameters.

Imagine that you're writing a large database program using Quicksilver. You usually work on one program for most of the day, trying to get out all the bugs. You use batch files to start Microsoft Word in order to edit your program and to run Quicksilver in order to compile the program. If you store the name of the program in the environment as Compile, then the batch files can automate much of the work for you.

A batch file to compile the program for you, called COMPILE.BAT, would look like this:

```
@ECHO OFF
REM NAME:     COMPILE.BAT
REM PURPOSE: Compile A Quicksilver Program
REM VERSION:  1.00
REM DATE:     May 16, 1992
DB3C -A %COMPILE%
DB3L %COMPILE%
```

The DB3C -A command runs the Quicksilver compiler to produce the .OBJ file. It uses the Compile environmental variable so that the user doesn't have to enter the name of the program each time. The DB3L command runs the Quicksilver linker to produce the .EXE file and again uses the Compile environmental variable.

A similar batch file, called WORD2QS.BAT, could be written to similarly automate loading the program into Microsoft Word for editing. It would look like this:

```
@ECHO OFF
REM NAME:     WORD2QS.BAT
REM PURPOSE: Edit A Quicksilver Program
REM VERSION:  1.00
REM DATE:     May 16, 1992
WORD %COMPILE%
```

Because Word defaults to ASCII mode when editing an ASCII file, no special switches are required.

Summary

The environment is a portion of memory set aside for storing system-wide variables—much like a scratch pad for the operating system.

There are a number of special metacharacters for creating fancy prompts.

The path is a list of subdirectories for DR DOS to search for a program to run.

The Subst command lets you create a shorter path.

The Comspec environmental variable tells DR DOS where to find COMMAND.COM.

The prompt, path, and Comspec are stored in the environment.

The size of the environment is limited but can be expanded using DR DOS commands.

The values of environmental variables are lost when the computer is turned off or rebooted.

A copy of the environment is provided to each program, but any changes made to it are lost when the program terminates.

The Set command is used to store data in the environment. It also erases or changes existing data in the environment.

Be careful not to use spaces on either side of the equal sign in the Set command, as DR DOS is inconsistent in how it handles spaces.

Batch files—but not the command line—can access the contents of the environment by surrounding the environmental variable name with percent signs.

Batch files can display environmental variables, combine them together, transfer values between them, and even use them as commands.

Many programs give you very little free environmental space when you shell out to run other programs.

You can increase the environmental space available when you shell out of a program by creating a dummy environmental variable before you start the program and then deleting the dummy environmental variable when you shell out.

When you return to a program after shelling out to DR DOS, the environment is restored to its condition prior to your shelling out.

Batch files can use the environment to pass information between themselves.

Batch files can use the environment to store data that will be accessed by more than one batch file or that a single batch file needs to access each time it runs.

14
ERRORLEVEL

While a nice place for batch files, the environment is a very inhospitable place for programs to store information to communicate with each other. Each program is provided with a copy of the environment when it's first loaded. When it reads from or writes to the environment, it's dealing with its copy of the environment and *not* with the original. When the program terminates, its copy of the environment—along with all the changes the program made to it—are destroyed.

The ERRORLEVEL value was provided to overcome this problem. ERRORLEVEL isn't stored in the environment, so changes made to it aren't lost when a program terminates. Unlike the environment, there's only one copy of ERRORLEVEL, and every program changes the same one. ERRORLEVEL doesn't change unless a program changes it or you reboot, so you can perform multiple tests on it. However, ERRORLEVEL is automatically reset to 0 by DR DOS each time you start a new program, so each time a program runs the prior ERRORLEVEL value is lost.

The DR DOS manual is inconsistent in what it calls ERRORLEVEL, referring to it as both "ERRORLEVEL" and "error code." These terms refer to the same thing, and I'm consistently calling it ERRORLEVEL because I used it in logic testing, so it must be called "ERRORLEVEL."

✔ Reminder The DR DOS manual is inconsistent in how it refers to ERROR-LEVEL. Sometimes the manual calls it "ERRORLEVEL" and, other times, "error code." They mean the same thing, however.

Only three DR DOS commands support ERRORLEVEL command. Table 14-1 through 14-3 lists the ERRORLEVEL values returned by all the DR DOS commands supporting ERRORLEVEL, along with their associated meaning. Like DR DOS commands, only a few commercial programs use ERRORLEVEL. If a commercial program uses ERRORLEVEL, it will be listed in the program documentation.

Table 14-1   ERRORLEVEL values for the BACKUP command.

Value	Meaning
0	BACKUP ran normally.
1	BACKUP didn't find any files to back up matching the command line parameters.
2	A file-sharing problem caused some files not to be backed up.
3	The user terminated the backup with a Ctrl-Break or Ctrl-C.
4	BACKUP encountered some other form of error not listed above.

Table 14-2   ERRORLEVEL values for the RESTORE command.

Value	Meaning
0	RESTORE ran normally.
1	RESTORE didn't find any files to restore matching the command line parameters.
2	A file-sharing problem caused some files not to be restored.
3	The user terminated the restore with a Ctrl-Break or Ctrl-C.
4	RESTORE encountered some other form of error not listed above.

Table 14-3   ERRORLEVEL values for the XCOPY command.

Value	Meaning
0	XCOPY ran normally.
1	XCOPY didn't find any files to copy matching the command line parameters
2	The user terminated the copy with a Ctrl-Break or Ctrl-C.
3	Not used.
4	XCOPY ran out of memory; XCOPY ran out of disk space; the user specified an invalid drive or the user used invalid syntax.
5	XCOPY enountered an error while writing to the disk.

While DR DOS makes very little use of ERRORLEVEL, it is critical that you become familiar with ERRORLEVEL. Almost every batch utility uses ERRORLEVEL to communicate results back to the batch file. You will see this in action with the Batcmd utility included with this book. Batcmd is examined in detail in Chapter 19 and Chapter 25.

Remember   Almost every batch utility uses ERRORLEVEL to communicate results back to the batch file.

Summary

ERRORLEVEL is a single byte of information that is common to all programs and batch files.

15
DR DOS punctuation

DR DOS comes with some pretty cryptic commands. However, its punctuation is far more cryptic than the commands. If you have ever tried to direct input from one file into a filter and then direct the output to another file, then you know what cryptic means. Because punctuation is often used in batch files, I've devoted this chapter to helping you understand the topic.

Piping

Normally, you enter input from the keyboard and output goes to the screen, printer, or disk drive. This input and output is often called I/O. DR DOS has the ability, however, to redirect I/O to and from nonstandard locations. This is called *redirection*, or *piping*.

Remember Redirecting inputs and outputs is called piping.

All of the piping features of DR DOS are very similar to analogous Unix features. They aren't well understood, however, because there were no similar features in CP/M, an operating system for earlier computers and from which many of the features of DR DOS are derived. There are four piping symbols:

> This causes output from one location to flow to another location. Many times, it's treated as input by the receiving program. When the alternative location is a file, > piping causes the file to be overwritten if it exists. For this reason, you must be very careful when using a > in a batch file. You should always test first, using an If test, before piping to a file. If the file exists, you can issue an error message and stop, rename the existing file, or pipe to an alternative file—after checking to make sure that file doesn't exist.

>> This is used to route output to alternative locations. It's the same as the >, except that, when the alternative location is a file, >> piping causes the messages to be appended to the end of the existing file.

< This causes a program to get its input from the specified device or file.

| Instead of creating a permanent file like > or >>, this creates a temporary file

that's read and erased by the following program. A common use is in the command DIR | MORE. Another use of | is to pipe data that a program needs to run into that program. For example, ECHO Y | DEL *.* will erase all the files in the current directory without asking. That's because the DEL command requires you to confirm the deletion when deleting all the files, but that confirmation is piped into the DEL command using the ECHO Y command first. Basically, | means that you're using the output of what's on the left as input to what's on the right.

Devices

Generally, piping involves a DR DOS device. Those devices are the following:

CON   Depending on the usage, this is either the screen or the keyboard. When used as the target, it's the screen. When used as the source, CON is the keyboard.

LPT#   This is the printer port. LPT1 is the first port, and LPT2 is the second port. You can also use PRN to specify the default printer port.

COM#   This is the serial port. COM1 is the first port, and COM2 is the second. You can also use AUX as the default serial port.

NUL   This is an output device that causes any output sent to it to be discarded.

Filename   This can be used for either input or output. Any legal filename can be used.

Filters

DR DOS includes three "filters" you can use to manipulate the data coming out of or going into a pipe:

FIND   Searches each line of a file for specified text.

MORE   This displays one screen of information, pauses until you press any key, and then displays another screen of information. This continues until all the information has been displayed. MORE can't scroll backwards. The more common usages are DIR | MORE or TYPE FILE | MORE.

SORT   This sorts the file (or input) into ASCII order.

Problems

Piping can cause problems, with the major one being a "hung" computer. If you use piping to tell a program to get its input from a file, then that file must contain all the input the program requires. If it doesn't, you'll either have to reboot or else press Ctrl-Break; either of these acts aborts the program you were running. In addition, piping can get around the usual warning. For example, the command

ECHO Y | DEL *.*

will delete all your files without asking you if you want to because the Echo command supplies the necessary response. Those warnings are generally in place for a good reason, and it isn't a good idea to avoid them. Also, piping DR DOS error messages doesn't always work. Another problem crops up when you specify an invalid pipe, such as

```
DATE < NUL
PROGRAM < LPT1
```

In the first example, NUL is used as an input device, but NUL can never supply input. In the second case, the printer is used for input and, like NUL, can't supply input. DR DOS, unfortunately, won't spot either of these problems; the programs or commands will wait forever for a response (or until you press Ctrl-Break or reboot).

Finally, you can destroy data by using pipes improperly. For example, if you wanted to take the data in FILE.DAT and sort it using SORT.EXE, you might issue the command:

```
SORT < FILE.DAT > FILE.DAT
```

This tells DR DOS to run SORT.EXE and supply it with input from the file FILE.DAT. When SORT.EXE finishes, it's supposed to write the results back to the FILE.DAT file. However, because of the way DR DOS works, it erases FILE.DAT before sorting, so all the data is lost!

+ [Plus sign]

The plus sign is used to perform file *concatenation*, which is a fancy name for combining two or more files together. For example, the command

```
COPY File1+File2+File3 File4
```

will copy the first three files into one larger file, *File4*. This can cause problems if either of these first three files contains an end-of-file [eof] marker; most editors won't allow you to go beyond the point in a file where the first EOF marker is located.

You can also use file concatenation to append information to the bottom of a batch file without loading an editor. For example, the command

```
COPY CONFIG.SYS+CON
```

copies the current contents of the CONFIG.SYS file plus whatever you type after issuing this command (press F6 or ^Z to quit entering text) into a new version of the CONFIG.SYS file.

You should use this approach to appending text with care. If the file you are appending text to is large, the operation might not work properly. Plus, if the file doesn't end with a return, you must first press Return, or else the text you enter will be appended to the last line of the file.

: [Colon]

The colon is used to name lines in a batch file. This is explained in detail in Chapter 12.

. [Period]

MS DOS 3 and later would usually display a blank line in response to an ECHO. command, so you might see this in batch files you receive from others. This trick also works under DR DOS, so you don't need to modify these batch files to use them.

@ [Ampersand]

The ampersand is used to turn off command echoing for a single command in a batch file regardless of the global status of command echoing. This is covered in Chapter 5.

% [Percent sign]

The single percent sign is used to mark replaceable parameters in a batch file, as covered in Chapter 10. It is also used to name the variable in a For-loop when issued from the command line rather than in a batch file. This usage is covered in Chapter 12.

%% [Double percent signs]

Dual percent signs are used to name the variable in a For-loop when the For-loop is used as part of a batch file. See Chapter 12.

%Variable%

Percent signs surrounding a variable allow the value of that variable to be used in a batch file. This usage is covered in Chapter 13. This command does not work from the command line.

= [Equal sign]

The single equal sign is used to assign values to environmental variables and to erase those values. See Chapter 13.

== [Double equal signs]

Dual equal signs are used in If-tests to test to see if two strings are equal. See Chapter 16.

Summary

By using piping, DR DOS can get input from alternative sources as well as sending output to alternative locations.

The greater-than sign causes DR DOS to pipe output to an alternative location. When that location is a file, the file is overwritten.

Dual greater-than signs also cause DR DOS to pipe output to an alternative location. When that location is a file, the file is *not* overwritten.

The less-than sign cause a program to obtain its input from an alternative location.

The vertical bar causes the output of one program to be sent to another program without creating a permanent file.

Devices that can be used as alternative sources for pipes include the console (Con), the printer (LPT or PRN), the serial port (COM), nothing (NUL), and a file.

DR DOS includes three filters that can work with pipes: Find for locating specific text, More for displaying text one screen at a time, and Sort for placing data in order.

Improper use of piping can cause files to be overwritten.

The plus sign is used to perform file concatenation.

The colon is used to name lines in a batch file.

A period directly following an ECHO causes either DR or MS DOS to display a blank line in a batch file.

The ampersand is used to turn off command echoing for a single command in a batch file regardless of command echoing being turned on.

The single percent sign is used to mark replaceable parameters in batch files and for the variable name in a For-loop issued from the command line.

Dual percent signs are used for the variable name in a For-loop issued in a batch file.

Surrounding an environmental variable name with percent signs allows the contents of that variable to be used in a batch file.

The equal sign is used to assign values to environmental variables and to erase those values.

Dual equal signs are used in If-tests to test to see if two strings are equal.

16
Logic testing

Basically, logic testing in a batch file means that you should be able to specify a statement and then have the batch file react differently depending on whether the statement is true or false. The If-test allows a batch file to accomplish this. The basic syntax of the If-test is

IF *Statement Action*

If the statement being tested is false, then the batch file will skip to the next line and continue processing. If the statement is true, then the batch file will process the rest of this line.

The *Action* portion of the If-test can be a GOTO command. Using GOTO allows the batch file to take different paths through the batch file—and thus do different things—depending on the conditions the batch file finds while it is running.

Logic testing under DR DOS can take one of four forms:

- Are two strings of characters the same?
- What is the ERRORLEVEL?
- Does a file exist?
- Does a subdirectory exist?

When you comparing two strings of characters, you can acquire these strings from several different sources. They could be

- hardwired into the batch file.
- replaceable parameters.
- from the environment.

Are two values the same?

Batch files can only test to see if two character sets are the same; they cannot perform numeric calculations to see if two equations are equal. A set of characters is called a *string*, and comparing two strings is called a *string comparison*. The format of the If-test when used for string comparisons is

IF *String1==String2 Action*

where *String1* is the source of the first string, *String2* is the source of the second string, and *Action* is the command to be formed when the two strings are the same. Notice that two equal signs are used—not one. If you forget and use a single equal sign, DR DOS will give you a "syntax error" error message.

One of the strings in this comparison almost always come from either replaceable parameters or the environment—with replaceable parameters being the far most common source. The other string is generally hardwired into the batch file. I generally place the replaceable parameter on the left side of the two equal signs and the hardwired value on the right side.

One of the things we will use this for throughout the remainder of this book is to add help to our batch files. We will use /? to be consistent with DR DOS 6, but let's begin by looking at the problem associated with using the older form of /H, because it's a generic problem.

When the user starts the batch file with a /H, we want to briefly display a help message and then exit the batch file. You might think the command to do this is

```
IF %1==/H GOTO HELP
```

and this indeed might work. However, it suffers from two problems—one minor and one more serious.

The minor problem is that string comparisons in a batch file are case-sensitive. Recall that a batch file simply replaces the replaceable parameters with the values entered on the command line. When the user starts this batch file with /H, this test becomes

```
IF /H==/H GOTO HELP
```

which is true. However, when the user starts the batch file with /h, this test becomes

```
IF /h==/H GOTO HELP
```

which is not true. The solution to this problem is to test for both possible values, so the test becomes

```
IF %1==/H GOTO HELP
IF %1==/h GOTO HELP
```

In this case, if the user entered /H, the first test passes and the batch file jumps to the help section without ever reaching the second test. If the first test fails because the user entered /h, the batch file runs the second test and now finds the two strings equal, jumping to the help section. Of course, if the user enters some other replaceable parameter, both tests would fail and the batch file would continue without executing either GOTO command.

☑ *Remember* String comparisons in a batch file are case-sensitive.

While it's not difficult to check the different capitalizations for a single letter, it can become burdensome when multiple letters are involved. For example, if the first replaceable parameter was "daily," "weekly," or "monthly," then it would take nine If-tests to test for just the likely capitalization combinations of all-lowercase, all-uppercase, or first letter capitalized. The disk that comes with this book includes a utility to deal with this problem, which is explored deeper in Chapter 25.

Also, recall from Chapter 10 that when there is not a space between the batch file name and the slash one the command line, DR DOS splits the /H apart from the batch name but MS DOS does not. We will look at possible solutions to this problem when we examine adding help in Chapter 18.

When you compare strings where one or both of the values comes from replaceable parameters, you'll have more problems dealing with the way DR DOS treats replaceable parameters. Recall from Chapter 10 that everywhere you enter a %1 in the batch file, DR DOS replaces that %1 with the first replaceable parameter entered on the command line. Thus, if you have the test

        IF %1==/H GOTO HELP

and the user enters a replaceable parameter, then the test works properly—as shown earlier.

Unfortunately, MS DOS isn't very smart in making these comparisons. When the user does not enter a replaceable parameter, MS DOS substitutes nothing for %1 and the above comparison becomes

        IF ==/H GOTO HELP

When this happens, MS DOS thinks you left off part of the If-test and issues a "Syntax error" error message.

DR DOS is smarter than MS DOS with this test; it handles the test properly, and the test fails because "nothing" is not equal to /H. However, DR DOS also has problems with If-tests where both values are blank or when you are testing for a blank value. For example, if you wanted to test for whether or not the user failed to enter a replaceable parameter under DR DOS, you might try

        IF %1== GOTO NONE

thinking that DR DOS would compare the first replaceable parameter with the blank on the other side and make this a true statement. However, it does not; this test is treated as false when the first replaceable parameter is blank.

The solution to this minor dilemma is simple: surround the comparison with a set of symbols so that either DR DOS or MS DOS will compare something to something. I always use the ( ) symbols. The advantage to surrounding both items to compare with a set of parentheses is that you allow a single test to compare the two strings, while avoiding any problems when one—or even both—of the strings in the comparison are empty. It even allows testing for an empty string because ( )==( ) is a valid test. Thus, the command

        IF (%1)==( ) GOTO NONE

would successfully test for a blank first replaceable parameter under both MS DOS and DR DOS and would return the correct result.

Remember Both DR and MS DOS have problems performing string comparisons when one of the strings is a nul string. The solution is to surround both the strings with parentheses.

In addition to testing the replaceable parameters, we can use the same If-test to test environmental variables. The only difference is that the environmental variable must be surrounded by percent signs. So the If-test to see if the prompt is PG is this:

```
IF (%PROMPT%)==($P$G) ECHO Prompt Is $P$G
```

The percent signs around PROMPT tell DR DOS to replace it with the value of the PROMPT environmental variable so you do not need percent signs around the PG. Of course, like all other If-tests, this one is case-sensitive.

What is the ERRORLEVEL?

As we saw in Chapter 14, ERRORLEVEL has room for only one byte, so only an ASCII value of 0 to 255 can be stored in it. Using the statement

```
IF ERRORLEVEL #
```

a batch file can test the contents of ERRORLEVEL and make decisions based on that content. Unfortunately, the test isn't straightforward. The test If ERRORLEVEL 5 doesn't test to see if ERRORLEVEL is equal to 5, as you might expect from the section on string comparisons. Rather, it tests for an ERRORLEVEL of 5 or higher, so any number from 5 to 255 will result in a "true" response to this test.

Remember The If-ERRORLEVEL test is a greater-than-or-equal test and not an equality test.

Because the If-ERRORLEVEL test is a greater-than-or-equal test, you must always test from the highest possible ERRORLEVEL value to the lowest. In addition, you must branch away from the testing after the first match. Figure 16-1 shows CHECKERR.BAT, a batch file that will test for every possible ERRORLEVEL value and display that value on the screen.

Batch File Line	Explanation
@ECHO OFF	Turn command-echoing off.
REM NAME: CHECKERR.BAT REM PURPOSE: Show Errorlevel REM VERSION: 1.00 REM DATE: January 3, 1991	Documentation remarks.
IF (%1)==(/?) GOTO HELP	If the user starts the batch file with a request for help, jump to a section to display that help.
IF ERRORLEVEL 255 ECHO 255 ·	If the ERRORLEVEL is 255, echo that fact to the screen. Because the ERRORLEVEL test is a greater than or equal to test, you must start testing at the highest value of interest and work your way to the lowest.

16-1 CHECKERR.BAT checks the ERRORLEVEL from largest to smallest. When it finds a match, it displays the ERRORLEVEL value and then exits the batch file.

Batch File Line	Explanation
`IF ERRORLEVEL 255 GOTO END`	If the ERRORLEVEL is 255, skip to the end of the batch file. Once a match is found, you must exit the batch file because all the lower numbers will also match due to the greater than or equal to testing of the ERRORLEVEL test.
`IF ERRORLEVEL 254 ECHO 254` `IF ERRORLEVEL 254 GOTO END`	Test for an ERRORLEVEL of 254.
`IF ERRORLEVEL 253 ECHO 253` `IF ERRORLEVEL 253 GOTO END`	Test for an ERRORLEVEL of 253.
`Continues through all the possible ASCII values with two lines per number`	
`IF ERRORLEVEL   1 ECHO 1` `IF ERRORLEVEL   1 GOTO END`	Test for an ERRORLEVEL of 1.
`IF ERRORLEVEL   0 ECHO 0` `IF ERRORLEVEL   0 GOTO END`	Test for an ERRORLEVEL of 0. I used the same format for consistency. If the batch file reaches this point, then the ERRORLEVEL must equal 0.
`GOTO END`	Exit the batch file.

`:HELP`
`    ECHO Display The Current`
`    ECHO Errorlevel Value`
`GOTO END`
	Section that displays help when the user starts the batch file with a /? or a ? as the first replaceable parameter.

`:END`	Label marking the end of the batch file.

16-1 Continued.

Notice how CHECKERR.BAT operates. It first tests for a value of 255. Because the maximum value of ERRORLEVEL is 255, this first test is an equality test rather than the normal greater-than-or-equal test. If the value is 255, it displays that information and jumps to the end of the batch file. If the value is not 255, it next tests for 254. Because we know that the ERRORLEVEL is not 255 because the batch file has reached this point, the normal greater-than-or-equal test again functions as an equality test. Again, if the value is 254, it displays that value and jumps to the end of the batch file. If not, it tests for 253, 252, and so on down the line. By testing from the highest possible value to the lowest possible value, you can avoid the problems associated with the greater-than-or-equal ERRORLEVEL test.

While CHECKERR.BAT is very long, most batch files will be able to test every possible ERRORLEVEL value while remaining fairly short. Look back at Tables 14-1 through 14-3. None of the DR DOS commands has a possible ERRORLEVEL value higher than 5. DOXCOPY.BAT in Fig. 16-2 performs an XCOPY and report which errors it encountered. Notice that DOXCOPY.BAT tests for all possible ERRORLEVEL values from the XCOPY command but is still fairly short.

Batch File Line	Explanation
`@ECHO OFF`	Turn command-echoing off.

`REM NAME:     DOXCOPY.BAT`
`REM PURPOSE: Run XCOPY Program And`
`REM          Report Errors`
`REM VERSION: 1.00`
`REM DATE:    May 16, 1992`
	Documentation remarks.

`IF (%1)==(/?) GOTO HELP`	Jump to a help display section when the user requests help with /? as the first replaceable parameter.
`XCOPY %1 %2 %3 %4 %5 %6 %7 %8 %9`	Perform the XCOPY command. Any replaceable parameters not used by the user are ignored because they are treated as nul by the batch file.
`IF ERRORLEVEL 5 GOTO 5`	Test for the largest possible ERRORLEVEL value first and jump to an error-handling section if this is the ERRORLEVEL.
`IF ERRORLEVEL 4 GOTO 4`	If the ERRORLEVEL was not 5, then test for the next highest possible ERRORLEVEL value and jump to an error-handling section if this is the ERRORLEVEL.
`IF ERRORLEVEL 2 GOTO 2` `IF ERRORLEVEL 1 GOTO 1`	Test for the ERRORLEVEL values 1-2 in decreasing order and jump to an error-handling section if either is the ERRORLEVEL value. Recall that XCOPY does not use an ERRORLEVEL value of 3.
`GOTO 0`	If the batch file reaches this point, the ERRORLEVEL must be 0, so jump to the appropriate section. The batch file could just begin performing the tasks for an ERRORLEVEL value of 0 here, but that would be more confusing to someone trying to read and debug the batch file.

16-2 DOXCOPY.BAT runs XCOPY and then displays the appropriate error message.

Batch File Line	Explanation

`:0`
   `ECHO Normal Completion`
`GOTO END`
	Section for displaying the appropriate message when the ERRORLEVEL is 0. After displaying the message, it jumps to the end of the batch file.

`:1`
   `ECHO No Files Found To Copy`
`GOTO END`
	Section for displaying the appropriate message when the ERRORLEVEL is 1. After displaying the message, it jumps to the end of the batch file.

`:2`
   `ECHO User Pressed Ctrl-Break`
`GOTO END`
	Section for displaying the appropriate message when the ERRORLEVEL is 2. After displaying the message, it jumps to the end of the batch file.

`:4`
   `ECHO Not Enough Memory`
   `ECHO Or Not Enough Disk Space`
   `ECHO Or Invalid Drive Specified`
   `ECHO Or Syntax Error`
`GOTO END`
	Section for displaying the appropriate message when the ERRORLEVEL is 4. After displaying the message, it jumps to the end of the batch file.

`:5`
   `ECHO Disk Write Error`
`GOTO END`
	Section for displaying the appropriate message when the ERRORLEVEL is 5. After displaying the message, it jumps to the end of the batch file.

`:HELP`
   `ECHO Run XCOPY Command`
   `ECHO And Display Error Message`
`GOTO END`
	Section for displaying the appropriate message when the user requests help. After displaying the message, it jumps to the end of the batch file.

`:END`	Label marking the end of the batch file.

16-2 Continued.   •

Does a file exist?

The third possible type of If-test tests to see if a file exists. The format for the command is

    IF EXIST *Filename Action*

so the command

    IF EXIST C: AUTOEXEC.BAT ECHO AUTOEXEC.BAT File Exists

would check to see if your AUTOEXEC.BAT file existed in the root directory of the C drive and display a message if it did.

The If-test will not have any problem testing to see if a file exists, even if the replaceable parameter used in the test does not have a value. Thus, the test

    IF EXIST %1 *Action*

does not need anything special to protect it in case the user does not enter a replaceable parameter.

The If-test can use wildcards in the test, so the test

    IF EXIST C:\BAT*.BAT ECHO Batch Files Found

would be true if at least one .BAT file existed in the C:\BAT subdirectory.

If no path is specified in the If-Exist test, it only looks for the file in the current subdirectory on the current drive. If you like, you can specify the full path to the file, as is the case in the earlier tests.

Does a subdirectory exist?

The EXIST command is not designed to check to see if a subdirectory exists, but you have two different tricks that can dealing with that. First, the command

    IF EXIST C:\TESTSUB*.*

would check for any file in C:\TESTSUB, and this test would only pass if the subdirectory existed. However, it would not pass if the subdirectory existed but was empty. If you modify this test slightly to

    IF EXIST C:\TESTSUB\NUL

this command uses the DR DOS device NUL to test the subdirectory where the test passes even if the subdirectory is empty.

Earlier batch file revisited

Back in Chapter 10, we looked at three batch files: A.BAT, RONNYMD.BAT, and TOA.BAT. A.BAT worked fine, but the other two had problems. We've looked at TOA.BAT a couple of times since then, but it still has some problems. We have enough tools now that we can revisit these three files and put them into final form.

A.BAT

When last we examined A.BAT, it looked like this:

```
@ECHO OFF
REM NAME:     A.BAT
REM PURPOSE: Directory Of A-Drive
REM VERSION: 1.00
REM DATE:     May 12, 1992
DIR A:%1 /P
```

This batch file runs fine, but we can make it better. We'll add command line help to this batch file, and we'll also assume that if the user enters a %2, then the user wants to specify the switches, so we'll leave off the /P. In writing the command line help, we'll assume the batch file will not run under MS DOS; then we can ignore the problem mentioned in Chapter 10 of the /? being part of %0.

The resulting, and final, version of TOA.BAT is shown next:

```
@ECHO OFF
REM NAME:     A.BAT
REM PURPOSE: Directory Of A-Drive
REM VERSION: 2.00
REM DATE:     May 12, 1992

IF (%1)==(/?) GOTO HELP

IF (%2)==( ) DIR A:%1 /P
IF (%2)==( ) GOTO END

DIR A:%1 %2 %3 %4 %5

:HELP
    ECHO Performs A Directory Of The A Drive
    ECHO Allows You To Specify Files And Switches
    ECHO On The Command Line
GOTO END

:END
```

This new version has a line added at the top to jump to a help section if the user requests help plus four lines to display that help. It has an If-test added to the front of the old DIR line and only performs that line when the user entered a single replaceable parameter. The next line exits the batch file if the user entered a single replaceable parameter. Finally, it performs a directory using five replaceable parameters. It only reaches this point if the user entered two or more replaceable parameters; and if the user entered less than five, the extra ones in the batch file are ignored.

RONNYMD.BAT

When last we examined RONNYMD.BAT, it looked like this:

```
@ECHO OFF
REM NAME:     RONNYMD.BAT
REM PURPOSE: Make And Change To A Subdirectory
REM VERSION: 1.00
REM DATE:     May 12, 1992

MD %1
CD %1
```

The major problem with this batch file is it does not confirm that the user entered the name of a subdirectory to create. A minor problem—which we can not completely solve—is it also fails to check to see if the user specified a subdirectory that already exists.

Checking to see that the user entered a replaceable parameter is fairly easy. Checking to see if the subdirectory name the user specified already exists follows the technique shown earlier. The resulting, and final, version of RONNYMD.BAT is shown next:

```
@ECHO OFF
REM NAME:      RONNYMD.BAT
REM PURPOSE: Make And Change To A Subdirectory
REM VERSION: 2.00
REM DATE:      May 12, 1992

IF (%1)==(/?)   ECHO Makes And Changes To A Subdirectory
IF (%1)==(/?)   GOTO END
IF (%1)==()     ECHO No Subdirectory Specified
IF (%1)==()     GOTO END
IF EXIST %1\NUL ECHO %1 Subdirectory Exists
IF EXIST %1\NUL GOTO END

MD %1
CD %1

:END
```

The most interesting aspect of this modified version is the way it handles help and errors. Rather than jumping to a special section, it uses two If-tests: the first displays a brief message and the second jumps to the end of the batch file. This approach works when your messages are short. When you need more than one or maybe two lines of messages, you are better off jumping to a special section to handle it.

TOA.BAT

When last we saw TOA.BAT back in Chapter 12, it looked like this:

```
@ECHO OFF
REM NAME:      TOA.BAT
REM PURPOSE: Copy .CMP And .DOC Files To The A Drive
REM             While Deleting .BAK Files
REM VERSION: 3.00
REM DATE:      May 12, 1992
:TOP
    DEL %1.BAK
    COPY %1.DOC A:
    COPY %1.CMP A:
    SHIFT
GOTO TOP
```

It performs its assigned tasks of deleting the .BAK file and then copying the .DOC and .CMP files to the A drive for the first replaceable parameter. The SHIFT command then brings the next replaceable parameter into the %1 slot and the process is repeated. The one problem is, the batch file does not know when to stop. Even after using all the replaceable parameters, it continues trying to use non-existent replaceable parameters to copy non-existent files until the user presses Ctrl-Break.

Fixing TOA.BAT is as easy as adding two lines. First, it needs a label at the end of the batch file to jump to, and it needs an If-test to jump to the end-label when the batch files runs out of replaceable parameters. The corrected, and final, version of TOA.BAT is shown next:

```
@ECHO OFF
REM NAME:     TOA.BAT
REM PURPOSE: Copy .CMP And .DOC Files To The A Drive
REM              While Deleting .BAK Files
REM VERSION: 4.00
REM DATE:     May 12, 1992

:TOP
    IF (%1)==( ) GOTO END
    DEL %1.BAK
    COPY %1.DOC A:
    COPY %1.CMP A:
    SHIFT
GOTO TOP

:END
```

The only thing missing is command line help with the /? switch, and the disk version even has that. Notice that the batch file tests for a blank replaceable parameter at the top of the loop before any processing. That's important, just in case the user starts the batch file without any replaceable parameters. If the logic testing were at the end and the user started the program without a replaceable parameter, the first journey through the loop would generate error messages.

Preview of Chapter 18

Logic testing is so important to successful batch files that, after the review in Chapter 17, Chapter 18 is also devoted to logic testing. The techniques in Chapter 18 are more advanced than this chapter, but often these techniques make a complex problem easier to solve, so they are important techniques to understand.

Summary

The If-test is used to perform logic testing in a batch file.

The If-test can test to see if two strings are the same, what the ERRORLEVEL is, or if a file exists.

Batch file string comparisons are case-sensitive.

In a string comparison, the variables on both sides of the dual equal signs should be surrounded by parentheses to avoid problems when one of the strings is empty.

An If-test can test the ERRORLEVEL value; however, the test is a greater-than-or-equal test and not an equality test.

Because the If-test on ERRORLEVEL is a greater-than-or-equal test, ERRORLEVEL tests must cascade from largest to smallest.

The If-test can test to see if a single file, a group of files specified with a wildcard, or a subdirectory exists.

Command line help can be added by either jumping to a special section to display the help or by having an If-test display the help and a second If-test exit the batch file.

17

Applications and problems

It's time to stop and catch our breath. While we have only covered seven chapters since my last questions, we have covered a tremendous amount of material. You now know how to squirt information into a batch file from the command line, how to use that information in a batch file (no matter how much of it was entered on the command line), how to loop, and how to perform logic testing.

It's important for us to take a few moments and make sure that you're up-to-speed before we continue. What follows are three quick problems. Take a few moments and try to work them out. If you get stuck, glance back through the last few chapters. You need to have the skills necessary to solve these problems before you continue through the book; otherwise, you'll run into difficulty.

Problem 4

A friend of yours has a new computer. He is going away for the weekend but he wants to run the computer continually while he is gone. He purchased a diagnostic program called Check-It-Out; the command to run the program is CHKITOUT. This program performs a complete diagnostic on the computer. It creates a file containing a full report and sets the ERRORLEVEL to 1 when it encounters a problem, but it does not display any information on the screen.

Your friend has ask you to write him a batch file that could run CHKITOUT continually. Each time CHKITOUT terminates with an ERRORLEVEL of 1, the batch file should display an error message on the screen.

Problem 5

Your boss is having problems with her computer. It has a C and a D drive, but sometimes she has to reboot the computer several times before the D drive is operational. She has found a utility program called BOOT.COM that reboots the computer, and she has ask you to write a batch file she can call from her AUTOEXEC.BAT file to reboot the computer if the D drive is not operational. That way, each time it boots, the computer will automatically reboot itself until the D drive is operational.

Problem 6

You did such a good job on the last problem that your boss has asked you for another favor. It seems that she spends a lot of time on bulletin board systems and acquires a lot of ASCII files to read. Normally, she reads them with the command

```
TYPE file | MORE
```

but she is finding that method to be difficult when she has a lot of files to read. She has asked you for a batch file that loops through and displays all the files that she specifies on the command line. She has also mentioned she is considering you for a raise.

Answers

You have a number of ways to tackle each of these problems. My solutions are included in Appendix C in the back of the book. You don't need to match my answers; if you developed a working solution to the problem, then your solution is just as good as mine and might even be better.

PART FOUR
Advanced batch file topics

Now that you've seen the intermediate batch file commands, it is time to take a look at the advanced commands. By the time you finish this section, you will have seen all the native batch subcommands that are available for you to use in batch files.

Chapter 18: Advanced logic testing. In Chapter 13, we covered simple logic testing. This chapter expands logic testing to include all the available logic testing commands DR DOS offers and some more that are supplied by a utility program.

Chapter 19: Advanced getting information from users. DR DOS makes it fairly difficult to get information from the user, giving you just replaceable parameters and Ctrl-Break to do the job. This chapter shows how to use a utility program that comes with this book to greatly expand the ability of a batch file to interact with the user.

Chapter 20: Advanced screen design 1. Most batch files use a series of ECHO commands to communicate with the user in a very boring fashion. This chapter covers two ways to improve your screens using ASCII files: typing them to the screen, and converting them to a program with a screen compiler.

Chapter 21: Advanced screen design 2. This chapter continues where Chapter 17 leaves off by showing you how to used advanced ANSI commands to construct colorful and highly formatted screens. It also briefly covers the many other uses for ANSI.

Chapter 22: Batch file subroutines. Subroutines are one of the most powerful approaches available to writing complex batch files. This chapter shows you how to use them.

Chapter 23: When batch files don't work. Even after reading a book as good as this one, you are going to occasionally have problems with the batch files you write. While nothing can eliminate the need for you to work through the logic of your batch file to resolve this problem, this chapter shows you some ways to expedite the process.

Chapter 24: Applications and problems. Before moving on to the advanced batch subcommands, you should understand the commands and concepts covered so far. This chapter is a quick test. Pass it, and you're ready to move on.

18

Advanced logic testing

In Chapter 16, we began our look at logic testing in batch files. We saw that batch files could test for three conditions in a batch file:

- Whether or not two strings of characters are identical.
- What the ERRORLEVEL is.
- Whether or not a file exists.
- Whether or not a directory exists.

When you compare two strings of characters, you can acquire them from several different sources:

- Hardwired into the batch file.
- From replaceable parameters.
- From the environment.

In this chapter, we will examine logic testing in even more detail. Included in this text will be your first look at some of the utilities included on the disk that comes with this book. As you will see, these utilities will make your batch files extremely powerful.

NOT

The NOT modifier is used to reverse an If-test. If an If-Exist test is true, then the corresponding If-Not-Exist test is false. If an If-Exist test is false, then the If-Not-Exist test is true. For example, the batch file segment

```
IF EXIST C: AUTOEXEC.BAT ECHO AUTOEXEC.BAT Exists
IF NOT EXIST C: AUTOEXEC.BAT ECHO AUTOEXEC.BAT Missing!
```

will tell the user about her AUTOEXEC.BAT no matter if it exists or not.

Inter-batch communications

You can have batch files communicate with each other by placing values into the environment. ACCOUNT1.BAT performs monthly closing. The program CLOSE.EXE sets the ERRORLEVEL to show whether or not it ran without errors. ACCOUNT1.BAT needs to communicate that information to ACCOUNT2.BAT. It could depend on the ERRORLEVEL, but that could be reset if you ran another program in between the two batch files. To avoid that problem, ACCOUNT1.BAT places a value into the environment. The portion of ACCOUNT1.BAT that handles running the closing program and creating the environmental variable is shown here:

```
CLOSE
IF ERRORLEVEL 1 SET ACCOUNT=NO
IF ERRORLEVEL 1 GOTO END
IF ERRORLEVEL 0 SET ACCOUNT=YES
```

ACCOUNT2.BAT then checks for that value and won't run without a correct setting. The portion of ACCOUNT2.BAT that handles this is shown next:

```
IF (%ACCOUNT%)==( ) GOTO ERROR
IF (%ACCOUNT%)==(NO) GOTO NO
CLOSE2
GOTO END

:ERROR
    ECHO Run Account1 First
    PAUSE
    GOTO END

:NO
    ECHO Warning: Close Did Not Run Successfully
    ECHO Fix These Errors Before Running Account2
    PAUSE
    GOTO END

:END
    SET ACCOUNT=
```

Capitalization is not a problem here because ACCOUNT1.BAT always creates the variables in uppercase. Also note that ACCOUNT2.BAT resets the ACCOUNT environmental variable after running, which keeps ACCOUNT2.BAT from being run twice. This is something that you could not prevent with just ERRORLEVELs.

A logical question is "Why didn't CLOSE.EXE set the information into the environment itself?" Well, each program is passed a copy of the environment when it starts. When the program terminates, that copy of the environment is erased. So CLOSE.EXE couldn't set the environment directly because those changes would have been lost when CLOSE.EXE terminated. ERRORLEVEL isn't stored in the environment, so it isn't lost when CLOSE.EXE terminates.

Dealing with capitalization

Managing capitalization in batch files is a real pain. As we said in Chapter 16, just testing for the likely capitalization of three possible replaceable parameters—"Daily," "Monthly," and "Annual"—takes nine If-tests. That means the code just to handle the most likely capitalizations takes up nine lines, where three would work if capitalization were not a problem.

Even this elaborate scheme will not respond properly to replaceable parameters such as DAIly. There are a number of ways of dealing with the capitalization problem quickly without a lot of extra code. Each method has unique advantages, so we'll look at each in more detail.

GOTO %1

The first way to avoid the capitalization problem is to use the replaceable parameter as a label for the GOTO command because labels are case-insensitive. Keep in mind that DR DOS always replaces the replaceable parameters with their value. Take a look at this batch file segment:

```
GOTO %1
:DAILY
        DAILY
GOTO END
:MONTHLY
        MONTHLY
GOTO END
:ANNUAL
        ANNUAL
GOTO END
:END
```

If you run this batch file with the command line

```
BATCH daily
```

DR DOS replaces the GOTO %1 line with GOTO daily and the batch file runs properly.

This method is only a partial solution. If the user starts the batch file with an invalid parameter—"yearly," for example—the batch file will abort on the GOTO yearly line with a "Label not found" error message. Because the batch file "bombs" after a GOTO %1 command if the specified label does not exist, no commands are needed under the GOTO %1 other than the sections that are being jumped.

While there is no absolute protection against invalid labels when using this approach, there is partial protection. Each section can use multiple labels with all the labels the user is likely to use. For example, the Annual section might look like this:

```
:ANNUAL
:ANNUALLY
```

```
:YEAR
:YEARLY
:ENDOFYEAR
     ANNUAL
     GOTO END
```

This helps prevent the "Label not found" by putting as many possible labels in the batch file as the user is likely to use. Because label lines are not executed, having the batch file jump to the :ANNUAL or the :ENDOFYEAR line has the same effect on the execution of the batch file.

Environmental variables

A second method is to store the selected option in the environment as an environmental variable. The next batch file segment illustrates this:

```
SET DAILY=
SET MONTHLY=
SET ANNUAL=
SET %1=YES

IF %DAILY%==YES GOTO DAILY
IF %MONTHLY%==YES GOTO MONTHLY
IF %ANNUAL%==YES GOTO ANNUAL
GOTO ERROR

:DAILY
     DAILY
GOTO END

:MONTHLY
     MONTHLY
GOTO END

:ANNUAL
     ANNUAL
GOTO END

:ERROR
     ECHO You Entered An Invalid Parameter
GOTO END

:END
```

First, each possible environmental is deleted then the line SET %1=YES creates a single environmental variable with the name of the replaceable parameter and a value of YES.

This method works well for most replaceable parameters and avoids the missing label problem associated with the GOTO %1 method but has a minor problem of its own. If the replaceable parameter the user enters can be a number, the batch file will end up making unexpected tests. Suppose you wanted to run Lotus 1-2-3, so the user could be expected to use 123 as a replaceable parameter. The SET %1=YES line would work properly. In order to run Lotus, you would need a test line of IF %123%==YES. However, DR DOS would translate the %1 portion of this test as the first replaceable parameter.

The path

The path is the only environmental variable DR DOS converts to uppercase. You can use this to convert a replaceable parameter to uppercase by performing the following steps:

1. Store the current path under another variable name.
2. Set the path equal to the replaceable parameter. Note that you must use PATH= statement and not SET PATH= because DR DOS will not convert the path to uppercase using the SET PATH= method.
3. Store the replaceable parameter now stored under the path to another variable name.
4. Restore the proper path using the holding variable created in Step #1.
5. Clear out the holding variable created in step #1.

The batch file segment below illustrates this:

```
SET OLDPATH=%PATH%
PATH=%1
SET VARIABLE=%PATH%
PATH=%OLDPATH%
SET OLDPATH=
IF (%VARIABLE%)==(DAILY)     GOTO DAILY
IF (%VARIABLE%)==(MONTHLY) GOTO MONTHLY
IF (%VARIABLE%)==(ANNUAL)   GOTO ANNUAL
GOTO ERROR
```

This method handles all possible inputs without problem but requires the most environmental space; you must store the path under a different name before you store the replaceable parameter to the path variable, so at this point DR DOS must store two versions of the path in environmental memory at once.

Run a program

I became so frustrated trying to deal with capitalization that I wrote a program called CAPITAL.EXE to cure the problem once and for all. CAPITAL takes a single word as an input, converts it to all uppercase, and stores the results in the environment under the environmental variable name RONNY. Before we use this program, a couple of notes are in order.

Normally, a program like CAPITAL does not have access to the master copy of the environment. So, if CAPITAL were to just place the results in its copy of the environment, that information would be lost as soon as CAPITAL terminated. That is clearly not what we want. The only remaining "usual" way to pass the information back to the batch file is via the ERRORLEVEL, but that value is limited to one byte. CAPITAL avoids the problem by searching through all the computer memory to find the master copy of the environment. It then makes it changes there. This is the same approach taken by most batch utilities that work with the environment.

Second, because CAPITAL expects to store the results in the environment, it will not be able to run if there is not enough free environmental space. Third, CAPITAL only works on one word at a time. Send it more than one word, and it aborts and displays an error message. The next batch file segment illustrates using CAPITAL:

```
CAPITAL %1
IF (%RONNY%)==(DAILY)     GOTO DAILY
IF (%RONNY%)==(MONTHLY) GOTO MONTHLY
IF (%RONNY%)==(ANNUAL)   GOTO ANNUAL
GOTO ERROR
```

Of course, somewhere near the end of the batch file you would want a SET RONNY= command to reset this variable once you no longer needed it.

Capitalization conclusion

Each of these approaches has good points and bad points. The one you select really depends on your needs. However, I find that most of my batch files can be written using just the GOTO %1 and CAPITAL approach. I use the GOTO %1 approach when I have a lot of possible labels and the CAPITAL approach when there are fewer labels.

Multiple If-tests

Several If-tests can be combined to handle a complex decision or to help overcome the case problem associated with string comparisons. The format of a two-deep multiple If-test is

```
IF Statement IF Statement2 Action
```

When the first If-test fails, control flows to the next line in the batch file as it normally does. When the first If-statement is true, control passes to the remainder of the command as it normally does—only in this case, the remainder of the command is another If-test. Now, if the second If-test fails, control flows to the next line in the batch file; but if the second If-test is true, the *Action* command is executed. So each If-test acts as a gate, and the *Action* command is only executed when every If-test before it is true. If just one of the If-tests is false, the entire test fails and the *Action* command is not executed.

DR DOS does not place a direct limit on the number of If-tests you can combine in this fashion. You can use three or four or even five if you like. However, the command must be shorter than the 127-character limit DR DOS places on all batch file commands. In addition, the logic must clear enough that the batch file author and anyone who later needs to maintain the batch file can understand it.

A shorter way to show the ERRORLEVEL

Consider the following example:

```
IF ERRORLEVEL 3 IF NOT ERRORLEVEL 4 ECHO ERRORLEVEL Is 4
```

Three conditions are possible: the ERRORLEVEL is less than 3, the ERRORLEVEL is greater than 3, or the ERRORLEVEL equals 3.

When ERRORLEVEL is less than 3, the first If-test fails and the batch file would move on to the next line. When ERRORLEVEL is greater than 3, the first If-test would pass. When an If-test passes, the batch file executes the remainder of the line— which in this case contains another If-test. For this second If-test, the test IF ERRORLEVEL 4 is true, but the NOT modifier changes the results to false. Thus, the second If-test fails and the batch file continues on to the next line.

Now, when the ERRORLEVEL is equal to 3, the first If-test passes and again the batch file moves on to the remainder of the If-test. In this case, the test If ERRORLEVEL 4 is false because ERRORLEVEL is 3, so this test fails. However, the NOT modifier changes the results to true. Having passed both If-tests, the batch file moves on to the next portion of the line and displays the ERRORLEVEL value.

In general, the If-test

IF ERRORLEVEL *n* IF NOT ERRORLEVEL *n+1 Action*

is only true for an ERRORLEVEL value of exactly *n*. Figure 18-1 shows CHECKER1.BAT. This batch file takes advantage of these multiple If-tests to considerably reduce the number of lines needed to display all possible ERRORLEVEL values over CHECKERR.BAT in Chapter 16.

Batch File Line	Explanation
@ECHO OFF	Turn command-echoing off.
REM NAME: CHECKER1.BAT REM PURPOSE: Show Errorlevel REM VERSION: 1.00 REM DATE: January 3, 1991	Documentation remarks.
IF (%1)==(/?) GOTO HELP	If the user starts the batch file with a request for help, jump to a section to display that help.
IF ERRORLEVEL 255 ECHO 255	If ERRORLEVEL equals 255, it echoes that fact. Because 255 is the maximum possible value, only one test is required.
IF ERRORLEVEL 254 IF NOT ERRORLEVEL 255 ECHO 254	This multiple IF test overcomes the limitation of the greater than or equal ERRORLEVEL test. All values greater than or equal to 254 pass the first test. Without the NOT, all values 255 or greater pass the second test and the NOT reverses it, so only values less than 255 pass the test. The result is a test of only 254 passes.

18-1 Like CHECKERR.BAT in Fig. 13-1, CHECKER1.BAT shows the ERRORLEVEL. It uses multiple If-tests, so it is shorter but slower than CHECKERR.BAT.

Batch File Line	Explanation
`IF ERRORLEVEL 253 IF NOT` `   ERRORLEVEL 254 ECHO 253`	All values greater than or equal to 253 pass the first test. Without the NOT, all values 254 or greater pass the second test and the NOT reverses it , so only values less than 254 pass the test. The result is a test of only 253 passes.
`IF ERRORLEVEL 252 IF NOT` `   ERRORLEVEL 253 ECHO 252`	Test for an ERRORLEVEL value of 252.
`The batch file continues in a similar fashion for ERRORLEVEL` `values of 251 to 4`	
`IF ERRORLEVEL   3 IF NOT` `   ERRORLEVEL   4 ECHO   3`	Test for an ERRORLEVEL value of 3.
`IF ERRORLEVEL   2 IF NOT` `   ERRORLEVEL   3 ECHO   2`	Test for an ERRORLEVEL value of 2.
`IF ERRORLEVEL   1 IF NOT` `   ERRORLEVEL   2 ECHO   1`	Test for an ERRORLEVEL value of 1.
`IF ERRORLEVEL   0 IF NOT` `   ERRORLEVEL   1 ECHO   0`	Test for an ERRORLEVEL value of 0.
`GOTO END`	Exit the batch file.

`:HELP`
`   ECHO Display The Current`
`   ECHO Errorlevel Value`
`GOTO END`
	Section that displays help when the user starts the batch file with a /? or a ? as the first replaceable parameter.

`:END`	Label marking the end of the batch file.

18-1 Continued.

While CHECKER1.BAT is shorter, it will take much longer to run—especially when the ERRORLEVEL is a high number. When CHECKERR.BAT processes a high ERROR-LEVEL number—say 250—it only has to go through a few If-tests before it finds a match. For a value of 250, it would go through twelve If-tests before jumping out of the batch file. However, for each ERRORLEVEL value, CHECKER1.BAT processes all 255 of the first If-tests. In addition, it processes the second If-test for all ERRORLEVEL tests with lower test values than the ERRORLEVEL value. That is, for ERRORLEVEL test values of 0–250, CHECKER1.BAT must move on to the second If-test because the first is true. So for 250, CHECKER1.BAT ends up processing 305 If-tests rather than the 12 CHECKERR.BAT required and so it runs slower.

A very short way to show the ERRORLEVEL

Warning This explanation of a very short way to show the ERRORLEVEL is fairly complex and is not critical to your understanding the rest of the material. If you do not fully understand If-tests and For-loops, you should postpone reading this section until your skills improve.

While writing my *Dr. Batch File's Ultimate Batch File Utility* book, I developed an extremely short and fast batch file for displaying the ERRORLEVEL. I've found it so useful that I keep it in my utility subdirectory and find myself using it all the time. Because it's so useful, I want to share it with you now.

An easier way to find the ERRORLEVEL is to test each of the three digits individually. First, find out if the left digit is a 0, 1, or 2. This only takes one For-loop. The next batch file segment does this:

```
FOR %%J IN (0 1 2) DO IF ERRORLEVEL %%J00 SET ERROR=%%J
ECHO Left Digit Was %ERROR%
```

In addition to displaying the left digit, it also stores it in the environment under the environmental variable name ERROR. That is required for the remaining steps.

The next step is to find out if the middle digit is a 0-9. That takes only one FOR-loop as well. The following batch file segment does this:

```
FOR %%J IN (0 1 2 3 4 5 6 7 8 9) DO IF ERRORLEVEL %ERROR%%%J0 SET
    ERROR=%ERROR%%%J
ECHO Left Two Digits Are %ERROR%
```

Notice that the variable ERROR is being built as we go, from left to right. The right portion of the first line looks confusing but DR DOS interprets it properly. For your information, let's look at this line in more detail:

FOR %%J IN (0 1 2 3 4 5 6 7 8 9) DO   This is the typical beginning of a For-loop that causes it to loop through the numbers 0-9.

IF ERRORLEVEL   This specifies that for each For-loop, an If-test on the ERROR-LEVEL value will be performed.

%ERROR%   This is replaced by the environmental variable value. That will be the left digit of the ERRORLEVEL value—usually a 0.

%%J   This is replaced by the value of the loop counter variable on each loop.

0   Because we are testing for the middle variable, a place holder for the last variable is needed. Zero is the smallest value, so it is used.

SET ERROR=   When the test passes, the value of the test is stored in the environment.

%ERROR%%%J   When the value is stored to the environment because the If-test passed, %ERROR is replaced by the current value of the left digit stored in the environment and %%J is replaced by the loop counter value.

Testing for the right digit works the same way. The next batch file segment does this:

```
FOR %%J IN (0 1 2 3 4 5 6 7 8 9) DO IF ERRORLEVEL %ERROR%%%J SET
ERROR=%ERROR%%%J
ECHO ERRORLEVEL is %ERROR%
```

The For-loop in this batch file works much like the one above.

This method works properly for ERRORLEVEL values 0–199, but there is a problem for ERRORLEVEL values over 200. There are no restrictions in the batch file, so when the first digit is a 2, the remaining segments end up testing for values 256–299. The maximum

ERRORLEVEL value is 255, and DR DOS does not handle tests above 255 properly. As a result, we need some complex branching.

If the first digit is a 2, the batch file must branch to a separate test to make sure the test on the second digit does not exceed 5. If the second digit is a 5, it must branch again to make sure the test on the final digit does not exceed a 5. That way, the batch file never tests for an ERRORLEVEL greater than 255. In addition, there is no advantage in using separate batch files for each digit, so all three batch files can be combined into one. The resulting batch file is SAYERROR.BAT in Fig. 18-2.

Batch File Line	Explanation
`@ECHO OFF`	Turn command-echoing off.

`REM NAME:     SAYERROR.BAT`
`REM PURPOSE: Show ERRORLEVEL`
`REM VERSION: 1.00`
`REM DATE:     November 10, 1991`
	Documentation remarks.

`IF (%1)==(/?) GOTO HELP`	If the user starts the batch file with a request for help, jump to a section to display that help.
`SET ERROR=`	Reset the environmental variable to nul.
`FOR %%J IN (0 1 2) DO IF ERRORLEVEL %%J00` `    SET ERROR=%%J`	Find out if a) ERRORLEVEL > 200, b) ERRORLEVEL > 100 c) ERRORLEVEL > 0.
`IF %ERROR%==2 GOTO 2`	Jump to a special section if the ERRORLEVEL is 200 or larger. This is required because the maximum ERRORLEVEL is 255 and DOS does not handle ERRORLEVEL tests for numbers over 255 in a manner that will work with this batch file. When testing ERRORLEVEL 260 (for example) DOS subtracts increments of 256 until the number is less than 256, or 4 in this example.

18-2 SAYERROR.BAT quickly displays the ERRORLEVEL and stores its value in the environment for future reference.

Batch File Line	Explanation
`IF %ERROR%==0 SET ERROR=`	If the hundreds digit is a 0, remove it.

`FOR %%J IN (0 1 2 3 4 5 6 7 8 9) DO`
`    IF ERRORLEVEL %ERROR%%%J0 SET`
`    ERROR=%ERROR%%%J`
	As complex as this looks, DOS understands it. If the value of ERROR was 1 coming into this test and the FOR loop is on 6, the test line reads:
	IF ERRORLEVEL 160
	SET ERROR=16
	This test sets the value of the tens digit.

`IF %ERROR%==0 SET ERROR=`	If the tens digit is a 0 and there is no hundreds digit, remove the 0.

`FOR %%J IN (0 1 2 3 4 5 6 7 8 9) DO`
`    IF ERRORLEVEL %ERROR%%%J`
`    SET ERROR=%ERROR%%%J`
	This test sets the value of the ones digit.

`GOTO END`	Jump to the end of the batch file.
`:2`	This marks the beginning of the section that handles ERRORLEVEL greater than or equal to 200.
`FOR %%J IN (0 1 2 3 4 5) DO IF ERRORLEVEL` `    %ERROR%%%J0 SET ERROR=%ERROR%%%J`	Test for the tens digit. Because the maximum ERRORLEVEL value is 255, the test does not need to exceed 5.
`IF %ERROR%==25 GOTO 25`	If the ERRORLEVEL is 250 or larger, jump to a special section because the batch file needs to test only to five.

`FOR %%J IN (0 1 2 3 4 5 6 7 8 9) DO`
`    IF ERRORLEVEL %ERROR%%%J SET`
`    ERROR=%ERROR%%%J`
	Test for the ones digit.

`GOTO END`	Exit the batch file.
`:25`	Label marking the section of the batch file to testing ERRORLEVEL values greater than or equal to 250.

18-2 Continued.

Batch File Line	Explanation
FOR %%J IN (0 1 2 3 4 5) DO IF ERRORLEVEL %ERROR%%%J SET ERROR=%ERROR%%%J	Test for the ones digit.
GOTO END	Exit the batch file.

:HELP
    ECHO Displays The ERRORLEVEL
    ECHO And Stores It To The
    ECHO Environment
    ECHO All Values Reported
    ECHO Correctly
GOTO END
	Section that displays help when the user starts the batch file with a /? or a ? as the first replaceable parameter.

:END	Label marking the end of the batch file.

18-2 Continued.

SAYERROR.BAT quickly tests the ERRORLEVEL values. For every ERROR-LEVEL value, the test took under a second. In addition to displaying the ERRORLEVEL value, SAYERROR.BAT also stores the value in the environment under the name ERROR. That allows you to retain the ERRORLEVEL value while running another program. It also makes testing on the ERRORLEVEL value much easier. While the usual ERRORLEVEL test of IF ERRORLEVEL # is a greater than or equal test, the test IF %ERROR%==# is an equality test. This reduces the number of IF-statements required to test for any value in half.

▌▌▌▶ *Note*   While the operation of SAYERROR.BAT is difficult to follow, its operation is simple. Just enter SAYERROR at the command line and it stores the ERRORLEVEL value in the environment under the environmental variable ERROR and displays it on the screen. You can even use SAYERROR.BAT without understanding how it operates.

Setting the ERRORLEVEL

Testing the ERRORLEVEL value can be difficult. When I first started working with ERRORLEVEL If-tests, I did things like using XCOPY and leaving the drive open to force an ERRORLEVEL value into DR DOS. Then, I received my copy of Batcmd (short for Batch Commands). Batcmd is a program designed to be run from inside a batch file. The general format of the command is

BATCMD Keyword <Prompt>

where Keyword is a two-letter command abbreviation that tells Batcmd what to do and Prompt is an optional message to the user to tell him/her what information to enter. We'll talk about Batcmd in more detail later in this chapter, as well as in Chapter 19 and Chapter 25; but for now, I'll just say that one of Batcmd's nicer features is its ability to force any value into the ERRORLEVEL. The command to do that is

BATCMD EX #

where # is a number 0–255 to be forced into the ERRORLEVEL.

Being able to force any value 0–255 into ERRORLEVEL makes it easy to test batch files. It is also handy for resetting the ERRORLEVEL after an XCOPY or other command has failed and stored a value in the ERRORLEVEL. A copy of Batcmd is included on the disk that comes with this book.

Help

Back in Chapter 16, we hinted at batch file help while exploring the capitalization problem associated with If-test string comparisons. Now is the time to look at batch file help in more detail.

Beginning with version 6, DR DOS added the ability to get quick summary information about most programs by running the program with a /? switch. When you do this, the program displays summary information and then exits to the command line without doing anything other than displaying help. That way, you can read about a program without having to run it.

We can add this in DR DOS easily. The general format in pseudocode is

If the user requested help
    Display the help information
    Exit the batch file

The second and third line of the pseudocode is easy. You display help information using a series of Echo commands and you exit the batch file by having a line labeled :END at the end of the batch file and using a Goto End command.

If you are not concerned about being compatible with MS DOS, the first line is easy as well. The test

IF (%1)==(/?) GOTO HELP

works in all cases. DR DOS always splits the /? parameter from the batch file name so it's always %1, and the parentheses around the %1 and /? prevent a problem when the user does not enter a replaceable parameter. Of course, it has to jump to a special section because multi-line If- tests are not allowed under DR DOS as they are in some other languages.

Warning DR DOS and MS DOS handle replaceable parameters differently when the name of a batch file is followed immediately by a slash with information after the slash. DR DOS makes the slash and everything that follows %1, with the next replaceable parameter %2, and so on. Thus, if you enter BATCH/? under DR DOS, BATCH becomes %0 and /? becomes %1. However, MS DOS treats everything before the first space as %0, so if you enter BATCH/? under MS DOS, BATCH/? becomes %0. This makes it very difficult to write batch files that run under both MS and DR DOS and accept parameters with a slash.

If you are concerned about the batch file having to run under MS DOS as well as DR DOS, then this approach will not work. The problem is, MS DOS does not split the switch apart from the batch file name, so /? could be %1 or the last two characters of your batch file name. So, running BATCH.BAT under MS DOS and checking for a /? switch requires the following tests just to test for the most likely capitalizations:

IF (%1)==(/?)	GOTO HELP
IF (%0)==(BATCH/?)	GOTO HELP
IF (%0)==(batch/?)	GOTO HELP
IF (%0)==(Batch/?)	GOTO HELP

And even this will not catch unusual capitalizations. Also, note that I've used parentheses around %0. Because %0 always has a value, this is not necessary. However, it doesn't hurt either, so I've used the parentheses for the sake of consistency.

To avoid this problem, I wrote the program NEEDHELP.EXE; it's on the disk that comes with this book. To use NeedHelp, just pass it your %0 and %1 variables. It checks to see if the %1 variable or the last two characters of %0 is /?. If so, it sets the ERRORLEVEL to 1; otherwise, it sets it to 0.

If you do not pass NeedHelp a parameter, it sets ERRORLEVEL to 255. It does this because %0 always exists, so not receiving a parameter means you made an error. It does not object to only one parameter because %1 might not have a value.

To use NeedHelp, place these following lines near the top of your batch file:

NEEDHELP %0 %1
IF ERRORLEVEL 1 GOTO HELP

Now your batch files will work the same under MS DOS as they do under DR DOS, without you having to worry about how the specific operating system handles command line switches.

Windows

Occasionally, it would be nice for your batch files to know if they are running under Windows. For example, while the CHKDSK command is safe under Windows, the CHKDSK/f command can destroy your hard disk under Windows. Without knowing if Windows is running, your only choice is to not allow CHKDSK/f to run from your batch files just in case Windows is running.

Windows always creates an environmental variable called windir when it's running, and this variable points to the subdirectory where Windows is located. However, Windows is very tricky about this variable. DR DOS leaves the contents of your environmental variable alone, but it always converts environmental variable names to all uppercase. Additionally, DR DOS refuses to work with environmental variables where the name is lowercase. However, Windows bypasses DR DOS and creates the windir variable name in lowercase. This keeps you from being able to alter the windir environmental variable yourself. As a result, the normal batch If-tests to see if the windir environmental variable exists will not work.

To get around this problem, I've included a small program on the disk that comes with this book called ISITWIN.EXE. IsItWin sets ERRORLEVEL to 1 if it's running while you are shelled out from Windows, and it sets ERRORLEVEL to 0 if its run from the command line without Windows loaded in memory. That way, you can build Windows-checking into those batch files that need it.

Summary

The NOT modifier reverses the decision of any If-test.

By creating environmental variables, batch files can communicate with each other even when there is a time lapse between each of them running.

One way to deal with capitalization of replaceable parameters is with a GOTO %1 command.

When using GOTO %1 to deal with capitalization of replaceable parameters, the batch file bombs when the label does not exist. The chance of this can be reduced by using multiple labels.

Another way to deal with capitalization of replaceable parameters is by creating an environmental variable with the name of the replaceable parameter because environmental variable names are always converted to uppercase.

A third way to deal with capitalization of replaceable parameters is to temporarily store the replaceable parameter to the path because the path is converted to uppercase.

A final way to deal with capitalization of replaceable parameters is to run the CAPITAL program included on the disk that comes with this book.

Multiple If-tests can be combined on a single line.

When multiple If-tests are combined, the Action command is not executed unless all of the If-tests are true.

When multiple If-tests are combined, their length must not exceed 127 characters.

The SAYERROR.BAT batch file on the disk that comes with this book quickly displays the ERRORLEVEL as well as storing it to the environment under the name ERROR.

The Batcmd program on the disk that comes with this book allows you to set the ERRORLEVEL to any value 0–255.

Batch files that test to see if %1 is /? to display help might not work under MS DOS.

The NeedHelp program on the disk that comes with this book checks to see if the user requested help using the same commands under both MS and DR DOS.

When running, Windows creates a windir environmental variable that DR DOS can display but cannot modify or test on because the name is stored in lowercase.

The IsItWin program that comes on the disk that comes with this book sets ERRORLEVEL to 1 if Windows is running and to 0 if Windows is not running.

19

Advanced getting information from users

The DR DOS ERRORLEVEL (or error code) is one of the most useful items available to batch file authors, yet it is also one of the least used. Part of the reason that it's avoided is because of its idiotic name, which tells the user *nothing* about what ERRORLEVEL actually does and probably scares off a lot of potential users. The other reason ERROR-LEVEL is rarely used is that DR DOS does not give you any tools to take advantage of the ERRORLEVEL. At best, a very few DR DOS programs set the ERRORLEVEL when they exit.

So far, we have seen only two ways to get information from the user: replaceable parameters, and Ctrl-Break. With replaceable parameters, the user must remember the questions in advance—before running the batch file—in order to enter that information on the command line. That's asking for a lot! I have trouble remembering what batch file I need to run, much *less* what questions it is going to ask me. Many times, the questions change each time the batch file runs. "Do you really want to delete these files?" takes a lot of different meanings depending on which files the batch file shows me.

Pausing the batch file and asking the user to press any key to continue or Ctrl-Break to stop is one way of getting a yes/no response. It's inelegant but it works. However, because the batch file stops in response to a Ctrl-Break, it cannot perform any other tasks if the user wants to stop this operation.

▐▶ *Note*   The tools DR DOS gives you to query the user are a pretty sorry lot!

All-in-all, the tools DR DOS gives you to query the user are a pretty sorry lot! However, the single byte of ERRORLEVEL memory gives us a way to dramatically improve the situation.

Batcmd: Batch Commands

The idea is a simple one: use a utility program to ask the user a question and then code the user's response into ERRORLEVEL or into the environment. This book includes a program called Batch Commands—Batcmd for short—that makes it easy to get information from the user.

⏩ *Note* Batcmd makes asking the user questions via the ERRORLEVEL a snap.

Batcmd 1.0 was written by Doug Amaral of hyperkinetix—the maker of Builder and Builder Lite—especially for this book. I added a couple of commands and made some minor modifications to the help system to produce the v1.1 that is included in this book.

Batcmd is a program designed to be run from inside a batch file. The general format of the command is

BATCMD *Keyword Prompt*

where *Keyword* is a two-letter command abbreviation that tells Batcmd what to do and *Prompt* is an optional message to the user what information to enter. The prompt can contain multiple words and should *not* be enclosed in quotation marks because they would end up showing in the final prompt.

Querying the user is just one of the many functions of Batcmd. It also has the ability to query all parts of the computer and return information via the ERRORLEVEL. Using Batcmd, your computer can find out things like how much memory is installed and available, how may drives are available, how much space on a drive is free, if a mouse is installed, what the date is, and much more. Only the Batcmd tools for querying the user are described in this chapter. All of Batcmd is described in Chapter 25.

Single-character response questions

Most of the time, when you want to ask the user a question, you want to ask questions like "Do you really want to do this?" or "Which one of these menu items do you pick?" or even "Do you want to quit now?" Almost every time you ask the user a question, you will find that a single-character response is all you need. The ERRORLEVEL makes a perfect vehicle for communicating that information from the program to the batch file.

Batcmd offers several different methods of asking the user a question, depending on what type of information you need.

YN (Yes No) This commands accepts only a "n" or "y" keystroke in either upper- or lowercase. For an "n" in either case, Batcmd YN sets ERRORLEVEL to 0; for a "y" in either case, it sets them to 1.

☑ *Remember* The YN command in Batcmd is an excellent way to avoid the Halt Batch Process message and its associated problems.

This is probably the Batcmd option you will use the most. Many of the questions you will want to ask the user are things like "Do you really want to erase all these files? (Y/N)" or "This takes six hours, do you want to continue? (Y/N)" and using the YN option is so much nicer than using a Pause command and telling the user to press Ctrl-Break to stop the batch file. It also avoids bring up the Halt Batch Process (Y/N)? message and having to deal with the problem of DR DOS not processing a "no" response properly.

GN (Get Number) This command accepts any single-digit number from the user and exits with the ERRORLEVEL set to that number. If any other keystroke is entered, Batcmd beeps and continues waiting for a number. This command can display an optional prompt if it is included after the command.

When you need for the user to select between just a few options, this might be the best approach. If you need fewer than ten, just start your options at 0 and go back through the prompting loop if the user enters a number that is too high. You can do this with just one If-test. For example, if your last option is number 6, then loop back through the options anytime ERRORLEVEL is 7 or higher.

GL (Get Letter)   This command accepts any letter from the user and exits with the ERRORLEVEL set to 1 for an A, 2 for a B, and so on. If any other keystroke is entered, Batcmd beeps and continues waiting for a letter. This command can display an optional prompt if it is included after the command.

If you are designing a menu system where you want the user to be able to make a selection using any letter, this option is the best way to implement it. It's also the best approach when you have a lot of options you are willing to letter sequentially. Because the ERRORLEVELs run sequentially from A, if you options stop at N (ERRORLEVEL 14), then you can test for an invalid response with a single If-test that tests for an ERRORLEVEL of 15 or higher.

However, if you want the user to use only a few of the letters or you want to pick-and-choose certain letters to use, then using the GF (get from list) option is a better approach than using this option and jumping back through the loop for invalid options.

GU (Get Uppercase Letter)   This command accepts only uppercase letters from the user. If the user enters a lowercase letter or any non-letter keystroke, Batcmd beeps and continues waiting for an uppercase letter. ERRORLEVEL is set to the ASCII value of the uppercase letter, so A is reported as 65, B is reported as 66, and so on. This command can display an optional prompt if it is included after the command. This is a specialized version of the GL (get letter) option. For most applications, the GL option is a more useful option.

GF (Get From List)   This command accepts a keystroke from the user only when that keystroke is on the list of acceptable keystrokes. The format of the command is BATCMD GF *List Prompt*, where *List* is a listing of all valid keystrokes without spaces between them and *Prompt* is the user message to display. The list of keystrokes is case-sensitive, so in order to accept only A thru C from the user in either case, the command would have to be entered as BATCMD GF AaBbCc *Prompt*.

If the user enters an invalid keystroke, Batcmd beeps and continues waiting for a valid keystroke. Once the user enters a valid keystroke, Batcmd sets ERRORLEVEL to that keystroke's position in the list. So, for the above example, if the user entered B, the ERRORLEVEL would be set to 3 because the capital B is the third character in the list.

Batcmd checks the list from right to left. That is only an issue if you use duplicates in the list. If your list was Ronny, then *n* would be reported via an ERRORLEVEL of 4 and not 3 because the *n* in the fourth position was the first lowercase *n* encountered moving right to left.

This approach is designed for those occasions when you have a number of different selections for the user to pick from. If you have fewer selections, then having the user pick a number would be a better choice. At first glance, you might think that treating upper- and lowercase letters separately would double the number of If-tests in the batch file. That is not the case. Using the BATCMD GF AaBbCc *Prompt* shown earlier, we know ERROR-

LEVEL will be 1-6 and we want to treat upper- and lowercase the same. The following batch file segment does that:

```
BATCMD GF AaBbCc
IF ERRORLEVEL 5 GOTO C
IF ERRORLEVEL 3 GOTO B
IF ERRORLEVEL 1 GOTO A
```

We want to jump to the C section when ERRORLEVEL is 5-6; and because the IF ERRORLEVEL 5 statement is a greater-than-or-equal test and no values exceed 6, it handles both cases automatically. Once 5-6 have been eliminated, the IF ERRORLEVEL 3 statement tests for 3-4, which is B. The last statement could be replaced with just a GOTO A because everything else has been eliminated; I used an If-test just for consistency's sake.

Of course, you can test for each capitalization separately if you need to. The following example illustrates that:

```
BATCMD GF AaBbCc
IF ERRORLEVEL 6 GOTO LITTLEC
IF ERRORLEVEL 5 GOTO BIGC
IF ERRORLEVEL 4 GOTO LITTLEB
IF ERRORLEVEL 3 GOTO BIGB
IF ERRORLEVEL 2 GOTO LITTLEA
IF ERRORLEVEL 1 GOTO BIGA
```

GK (Get Key)   This command accepts any keystroke from the user and exits with the ERRORLEVEL set to the ASCII value of that keystroke. This command can display an optional prompt if it is included after the GK command.

Only very rarely will you need this tool. When you need to restrict entries, the GF option works better. The GF option also works better if you have less than 26 options because you can easily list all the letters. At 26 options, the GL is better because it handles getting just letters automatically. About the only time you will need this option is when you are doing something where you need to accept absolutely any keystroke from the user.

Multiple-character response questions

Occasionally, you want to ask the user a question that requires a multi-character response. Typically, this is used to ask the user for his name to customize the prompts or to ask for a specific filename. Multi-character responses can not be stored in ERRORLEVEL because that variable only has room for one byte of information.

Batcmd has a way around this. The GE option asks the user a question and stores the results in the master copy of the environment under the name Batcmd. This command will display a prompt if one is entered on the command line after the GE.

Normally, a program like Batcmd does not have access to the master copy of the environment; if Batcmd were to just place the results in its copy of the environment, that information would be lost as soon as Batcmd terminated. That is clearly not what we want. Batcmd avoids the problem by searching through all the computer memory to find the master copy of the environment. It then makes its changes there.

Before using Batcmd, you might want to check the environment to see how much space is free; Batcmd has a CE option that does this for you. It sets the ERRORLEVEL to the number of free bytes in the environment up to 255. If more than 255 bytes are free, it sets ERRORLEVEL to 255. Users can enter up to 65 bytes of information in response to the GE prompt, and you also need room for the environmental variable name and some internal markers DR DOS uses. Thus, to be absolutely certain of not running out of space, you would want to check for a value of around 73. However, most users enter far less than 65 characters, so I usually tailor my tests to the type of information I'm asking for.

Conclusion

Which of these many Batcmd options you use to query users really depends on the type of information you are asking for. To give you a better idea of how to use each option, SHOWGETS.BAT in Fig. 19-1 uses each of these options in a functioning batch file. Most of the examples perform logic testing on the user's response. SHOWGETS.BAT requires the Batcmd program and the SAYERROR.BAT batch file to either be in the current subdirectory or in the path when it runs.

Batch File Line	Explanation
@ECHO OFF	Turn command-echoing off.
REM NAME: SHOWGETS.BAT REM PURPOSE: Show Using Batcmd In Bat REM VERSION: 1.00 REM DATE: May 18, 1992	Documentation remarks.
CLS	Clear the screen.
ECHO This Demonstration Takes About ECHO Ten Minutes To Run	Explain what is happening to the user.
BATCMD SL	Use BATCMD to skip a line.
BATCMD YN Do You Want To Continue? (Y/N)	Use the yes/no option of BATCMD to ask the user a questions.
IF NOT ERRORLEVEL 1 GOTO END	If the user did not answer yes, jump to the end of the batch file.
ECHO I'm Glad You Decided To Stay	Acknowledge that the user answered yes.

19-1 SHOWGETS.BAT illustrates both using Batcmd to obtain information from the user and then acting on that information.

Batch File Line	Explanation
BATCMD CE	Use BATCMD to check and see how much environmental space is free.
IF NOT ERRORLEVEL 25 GOTO ERROR	If there are not 25 bytes of free environmental space, jump to an error-handling section.
BATCMD SL	Use BATCMD to skip a line.
BATCMD GE Please Enter Your Name:	Use BATCMD to ask the user's name. This is stored in the environment under the name BATCMD.
CLS	Clear the screen.
GOTO TOP1	Jump to the next section of the batch file.
:ERROR ECHO Your Environment Does Not Have Enough Free ECHO Space For The Entire Demonstration So I ECHO Am Skipping Asking Your Name ECHO In The Prompts, You Will See A Blank ECHO Where You Should See A Name PAUSE CLS GOTO TOP1	Section to explain the problem of inadequate free environmental space to the user.
:TOP1	Label marking the top of the first loop.
BATCMD SL	Use BATCMD to skip a line.
ECHO %BATCMD%:	Display the user's name if it was stored in the environment.
ECHO For The Next Question, Only A ECHO Number Will Be Acceptable, But ECHO You Might Want To Try Other ECHO Things First To See What Happens ECHO This Will Be Repeated Until ECHO You Answer With A 0	Tell the user what will happen next.

19-1 Continued.

Batch File Line	Explanation
`BATCMD GN Enter A Number 0-9`	Ask the user to enter a number 0-9 using BATCMD.

`IF ERRORLEVEL 9 ECHO 9 Entered`
`IF ERRORLEVEL 8 IF NOT ERRORLEVEL 9 ECHO 8 Entered`
`IF ERRORLEVEL 7 IF NOT ERRORLEVEL 8 ECHO 7 Entered`
`IF ERRORLEVEL 6 IF NOT ERRORLEVEL 7 ECHO 6 Entered`
`IF ERRORLEVEL 5 IF NOT ERRORLEVEL 6 ECHO 5 Entered`
`IF ERRORLEVEL 4 IF NOT ERRORLEVEL 5 ECHO 4 Entered`
`IF ERRORLEVEL 3 IF NOT ERRORLEVEL 4 ECHO 3 Entered`
`IF ERRORLEVEL 2 IF NOT ERRORLEVEL 3 ECHO 2 Entered`
`IF ERRORLEVEL 1 IF NOT ERRORLEVEL 2 ECHO 1 Entered`
`IF ERRORLEVEL 8 IF NOT ERRORLEVEL 1 ECHO 0 Entered`
	Test ERRORLEVELs in order to tell the user what number was selected.

`IF ERRORLEVEL 1 GOTO TOP1`	If the user entered anything other than 0, continue looping.
`CLS`	Clear the screen.
`:TOP2`	Label marking the top of the second loop.
`ECHO %BATCMD%:`	Display the user's name if it was stored in the environment.

`ECHO For The Next Demonstration Only`
`ECHO A Letter Will Be Accepted`
`ECHO You Might Want To Try Other Things First`
`ECHO The Demonstration Will Continue Until`
`ECHO You Enter An A`
	Tell the user what will happen next.

`BATCMD SL`	Use BATCMD to skip a line.
`BATCMD GL Enter Any Letter`	Use BATCMD to ask the user a question and accept any letter in response.

19-1 Continued.

Batch File Line	Explanation
IF ERRORLEVEL 1 IF NOT ERRORLEVEL 2 ECHO A Entered IF ERRORLEVEL 2 IF NOT ERRORLEVEL 3 ECHO B Entered IF ERRORLEVEL 3 IF NOT ERRORLEVEL 4 ECHO C Entered IF ERRORLEVEL 4 IF NOT ERRORLEVEL 5 ECHO D Entered IF ERRORLEVEL 5 IF NOT ERRORLEVEL 6 ECHO E Entered IF ERRORLEVEL 6 IF NOT ERRORLEVEL 7 ECHO F Entered IF ERRORLEVEL 7 IF NOT ERRORLEVEL 8 ECHO G Entered IF ERRORLEVEL 8 IF NOT ERRORLEVEL 9 ECHO H Entered IF ERRORLEVEL 9 IF NOT ERRORLEVEL 10 ECHO I Entered IF ERRORLEVEL 10 IF NOT ERRORLEVEL 11 ECHO J Entered IF ERRORLEVEL 11 IF NOT ERRORLEVEL 12 ECHO K Entered IF ERRORLEVEL 12 IF NOT ERRORLEVEL 13 ECHO L Entered IF ERRORLEVEL 13 IF NOT ERRORLEVEL 14 ECHO M Entered IF ERRORLEVEL 14 IF NOT ERRORLEVEL 15 ECHO N Entered IF ERRORLEVEL 15 IF NOT ERRORLEVEL 16 ECHO O Entered IF ERRORLEVEL 16 IF NOT ERRORLEVEL 17 ECHO P Entered IF ERRORLEVEL 17 IF NOT ERRORLEVEL 18 ECHO Q Entered IF ERRORLEVEL 18 IF NOT ERRORLEVEL 19 ECHO R Entered IF ERRORLEVEL 19 IF NOT ERRORLEVEL 20 ECHO S Entered IF ERRORLEVEL 20 IF NOT ERRORLEVEL 21 ECHO T Entered IF ERRORLEVEL 21 IF NOT ERRORLEVEL 22 ECHO U Entered IF ERRORLEVEL 22 IF NOT ERRORLEVEL 23 ECHO V Entered IF ERRORLEVEL 23 IF NOT ERRORLEVEL 24 ECHO W Entered IF ERRORLEVEL 24 IF NOT ERRORLEVEL 25 ECHO X Entered IF ERRORLEVEL 25 IF NOT ERRORLEVEL 26 ECHO Y Entered IF ERRORLEVEL 26 IF NOT ERRORLEVEL 27 ECHO Z Entered	Test ERRORLEVELs in order to tell the user what letter was selected.
IF ERRORLEVEL 2 GOTO TOP2	If the user entered anything other than the letter A, continue looping.
CLS	Clear the screen.
:TOP3	Label marking the top of the third loop.
ECHO %BATCMD%:	Display the user's name if it was stored in the environment.
ECHO For The Next Demonstration Only ECHO An Uppercase Letter Will Be Accepted ECHO You Might Want To Try Other Things First ECHO The Demonstration Will Continue Until ECHO You Enter An A	Tell the user what will happen next.
BATCMD SL	Use BATCMD to skip a line.

19-1 Continued.

Batch File Line	Explanation
`BATCMD GU Enter Any UPPERCASE Letter`	Use BATCMD to ask the user a question and accept any uppercase letter in response.

`IF ERRORLEVEL 65 IF NOT ERRORLEVEL 66 ECHO A Entered`
`IF ERRORLEVEL 66 IF NOT ERRORLEVEL 67 ECHO B Entered`
`IF ERRORLEVEL 67 IF NOT ERRORLEVEL 68 ECHO C Entered`
`IF ERRORLEVEL 68 IF NOT ERRORLEVEL 69 ECHO D Entered`
`IF ERRORLEVEL 69 IF NOT ERRORLEVEL 70 ECHO E Entered`
`IF ERRORLEVEL 70 IF NOT ERRORLEVEL 71 ECHO F Entered`
`IF ERRORLEVEL 71 IF NOT ERRORLEVEL 72 ECHO G Entered`
`IF ERRORLEVEL 72 IF NOT ERRORLEVEL 73 ECHO H Entered`
`IF ERRORLEVEL 73 IF NOT ERRORLEVEL 74 ECHO I Entered`
`IF ERRORLEVEL 74 IF NOT ERRORLEVEL 75 ECHO J Entered`
`IF ERRORLEVEL 75 IF NOT ERRORLEVEL 76 ECHO K Entered`
`IF ERRORLEVEL 76 IF NOT ERRORLEVEL 77 ECHO L Entered`
`IF ERRORLEVEL 77 IF NOT ERRORLEVEL 78 ECHO M Entered`
`IF ERRORLEVEL 78 IF NOT ERRORLEVEL 79 ECHO N Entered`
`IF ERRORLEVEL 79 IF NOT ERRORLEVEL 80 ECHO O Entered`
`IF ERRORLEVEL 80 IF NOT ERRORLEVEL 81 ECHO P Entered`
`IF ERRORLEVEL 81 IF NOT ERRORLEVEL 82 ECHO Q Entered`
`IF ERRORLEVEL 82 IF NOT ERRORLEVEL 83 ECHO R Entered`
`IF ERRORLEVEL 83 IF NOT ERRORLEVEL 84 ECHO S Entered`
`IF ERRORLEVEL 84 IF NOT ERRORLEVEL 85 ECHO T Entered`
`IF ERRORLEVEL 85 IF NOT ERRORLEVEL 86 ECHO U Entered`
`IF ERRORLEVEL 86 IF NOT ERRORLEVEL 87 ECHO V Entered`
`IF ERRORLEVEL 87 IF NOT ERRORLEVEL 88 ECHO W Entered`
`IF ERRORLEVEL 88 IF NOT ERRORLEVEL 89 ECHO X Entered`
`IF ERRORLEVEL 89 IF NOT ERRORLEVEL 90 ECHO Y Entered`
`IF ERRORLEVEL 90 IF NOT ERRORLEVEL 91 ECHO Z Entered`
	Test ERRORLEVELs in order to tell the user what letter was selected.

`IF ERRORLEVEL 66 GOTO TOP3`	If the user entered anything other than the letter A, continue looping.
`CLS`	Clear the screen.
`:TOP4`	Label marking the top of the fourth loop.
`ECHO %BATCMD%:`	Display the user's name if it was stored in the environment.

`ECHO For This Next Demonstration`
`ECHO Only The Letters "Ronny" Will Be Accepted`
`ECHO And The Capitalization Must Match Exactly`
`ECHO You Might Want To Try Other Entries First`
	Tell the user what will happen next.

19-1 Continued.

Batch File Line	Explanation
`BATCMD SL`	Use BATCMD to skip a line.
`BATCMD GF Ronny Select From The Letters "Ronny"`	Use BATCMD to ask the user a questtion and accept only letters in the list.

`IF ERRORLEVEL 1 IF NOT ERRORLEVEL 2 ECHO R Entered`
`IF ERRORLEVEL 2 IF NOT ERRORLEVEL 3 ECHO o Entered`
`IF ERRORLEVEL 4 IF NOT ERRORLEVEL 5 ECHO n Entered`
`IF ERRORLEVEL 5 IF NOT ERRORLEVEL 6 ECHO y Entered`
	Test the ERRORLEVELs in order to tell the user what letter was selected.

`IF ERRORLEVEL 2 GOTO TOP4`	If the user entered anything other than the letter R, continue looping.
`CLS`	Clear the screen.
`ECHO %BATCMD%:`	Display the user's name if it was stored in the environment.
`ECHO For This Next Demonstration Any Charater` `ECHO Will Be Accepted And Its Errorlevel Shown`	Tell the user what will happen next.
`BATCMD GK Enter Any Keystroke`	Use BATCMD to ask the user a question and accept any keystroke.
`CALL SAYERROR`	Run the SAYERROR.-BAT batch file to display the ERRORLEVEL.
`:END`	Label marking the end of the batch file.

19-1 Continued.

Summary

The YN option of Batcmd only accepts a y or n keystroke and reports the results via the ERRORLEVEL. This is perfect for yes/no questions.

The GN option of Batcmd only accepts numbers 0-9 and reports the results via the ERRORLEVEL. This option is perfect for menus or questions needing ten or fewer responses.

The GL option of Batcmd only accepts any letter without regard for case and reports the results via the ERRORLEVEL. The letter A is reported as 1, B as 2, and so on. This option is useful for menus or questions needed more than ten responses.

The GU option of Batcmd is a specialized version of the GL options that only accepts uppercase letters. The results are reported via ERRORLEVEL using the ASCII value of the letter.

The GF option of Batcmd only accepts keystrokes that are part of a list supplied to the GF command. The results are reported via ERRORLEVEL using the position of keystroke in the list of valid keystrokes. This option is useful for selecting from specialized lists.

The GK option of Batcmd accepts any keystroke and reports is ASCII code via the ERRORLEVEL.

The GE option of Batcmd accepts a multi-character response and stores that response in the environment under the name Batcmd.

The CE option of Batcmd reports on the amount of free environmental space and sets ERRORLEVEL to the number of bytes free up to 255. Over 255, the ERRORLEVEL is set to 255.

20

Advanced Screen Design 1

The main tool for displaying messages in a batch file is a series of ECHO commands, which works well for a few messages but soon gets old if your batch file has to display a lot of information. Fortunately, you have several alternatives. You can

- create a text file and using the TYPE command to send type that file to the screen.
- write a custom program.
- use a screen compiler.
- use ANSI.

The alternative you select depends on your specific needs.

Text files

Probably the easiest way to quickly display a screen full of information is to use the DR DOS Editor or your word processor to create each screen as a separate ASCII file. That way, you can use Editor to add blank lines where you want them, center text, and otherwise visually arrange the elements on the screen. Once you have the screens looking the way you want, just type them to the screen from your batch file. Of course, you'll need a PAUSE between each screen.

Using this method, a batch file might look like this:

```
@ECHO OFF
TYPE C:\TEXT\INTRO.TXT
PAUSE
TYPE C:\TEXT\SCREEN1.TXT
PAUSE
TYPE C:\TEXT\SCREEN2.TXT
PAUSE
```

Notice that this batch file segment specifies the full path to each text file. Because batch files are usually designed to run from anywhere on your hard disk, you cannot depend on the batch file and the associated text files being in the same subdirectory from which the batch file is executed.

This method is easier than a series of ECHO commands but it has several drawbacks. One drawback is simply remembering to send copies of all the associated text files when you send someone a copy of the batch file. A second drawback is that anyone wanting to run your batch file on their system must have a subdirectory of the same name you used to store your text files and must copy the text files to that subdirectory. That's a lot to expect users to do. Of course, you could write a batch file to install this batch file on their system. Finally, this method lacks the ability to control the screen color.

☑ *Remember*   Typing an ASCII file to the screen is an easy way for a batch file to display a screen full of information, but this method creates unique problems when batch files are to be distributed to other users. You must remember to give them all the files the batch file uses and they must store them in the right subdirectory.

Writing a program

You can also display menus by using a high-level programming language. Writing high-level programs is beyond the scope of this book, however, so I won't cover it in any detail. Most high-level programs compile to an executable .EXE file, so all you must do to display the menu is include the name of the .EXE file in a batch file. In addition, most high-level languages can control the screen color and execute very quickly.

This approach allows you to avoid the problem of needing a specific directory name to store the file in. As long as the resulting screen is anywhere in the path, it will execute whenever the batch file issues the command to run the program. However, while we've solved one problem, we've introduced another problem—namely the programing tools and abilities this approach requires—one thing many readers lack.

☑ *Remember*   Writing a program is a nice way to create custom screen, but also requires skills and tools that many readers do not have.

Using a screen compiler

What would nice would be having a method of creating screen display programs as nice as a programming language allows without the need to buy a programming language and learn to use it. Well, the disk that comes with this book has just that! It contains a screen compiler called BatScreen. BatScreen was written especially for this book by Doug Amaral of hyperkinetix, the maker of the Builder batch file compiler. The BatScreen screen compiler combines the ease of creating an ASCII file with the power of writing a program.

BatScreen takes an ASCII text file and converts it to a small .COM file. When you enter the name of the .COM file at the command line prompt or in a batch file, the file will flash up on the screen almost instantaneously.

To run BatScreen and compile a screen, first create the screen with any ASCII editor. Arrange the text in the file the way you want it to appear on the screen. Feel free to use high-ordered ASCII characters. Once the screen is ready, change to the subdirectory containing the ASCII file and enter BS at the command line prompt. BatScreen first presents a screen showing all the non-blinking color choices with a box around the currently selected color combination. Use the cursor to move the box to where it surrounds the color combination you want. If you want the text to blink, press PgDn and select from the blinking text in the same fashion.

Next, BatScreen prompts you for the name of an ASCII file. To completely fill the screen, the ASCII file should contain 80 columns and 24 rows. If the file is larger, BatScreen will ignore the extra. If you enter the name incorrectly, BatScreen won't spot it until it tries to create the .COM. Finally, BatScreen will ask you if you want to clear the screen when the program displays. Answer "Yes" and the .COM file will clear the entire screen, set it to the colors you selected, and display the contents of the ASCII file. Answer "No" and the .COM file will clear off only enough lines to display the message. Blinking text and not clearing the screen is perfect for error messages and other occasions where you want to grab the user's attention. Full screen solid colors are great for menus and general-purpose text.

The original ASCII file isn't modified and doesn't need to be present for the .COM file to operate, so you can modify and recompile it if you ever need to change the screen. Additionally, once you've created the .COM file, BatScreen is not needed to display the screen.

Remember The BatScreen screen compiler is probably the best way to create custom screens.

BatScreen makes excellent menus. It also has several other useful functions:

• Several of the programs I use don't properly reset the cursor when they terminate. I end up with a flashing box or some other strange shape for a cursor. I've compiled an ASCII file containing a single blank space; running the resulting .COM file will reset the screen colors and sometimes resets the cursor to its proper shape.

I like my display to have white letters and a blue background. This is initially set by the BatScreen menu that my AUTOEXEC.BAT file displays. However, these colors are easily reset to white on black by a CLS (clear screen) command or by a number of application programs that don't reset screen color when they terminate. I have a BatScreen file called COLOR.COM that was compiled from an ASCII file consisting of a single space. When I issue the Color command, the screen is cleared and my colors reset.

• Many times I need to display a message from within a batch file. By compiling them with BatScreen and using blinking colors, I can generate messages that flash up in unexpected colors. These messages get noticed!

After you try out BatScreen, I'm sure you'll agree that Doug has produced an excellent tool for batch file menus and screens. In fact, I use it almost exclusively for my screens.

ANSI

Because ANSI is such a large topic, I've devoted all of Chapter 21 to it. At the moment, I'll just say that ANSI allows you to control almost every aspect of the appearance of the screen but also requires loading the device driver ANSI.SYS— something most users do not do.

Summary

You can display a screen full of information with a series of ECHO commands.

Another way to display a screen full of information is by creating an ASCII file and typing it to the screen.

Using an ASCII file to display text when the batch file is shared with other users requires sharing the text files as well and requires the users to install the text files in the same subdirectory as was used on the original system.

Another way to display a screen full of information is by writing your own program. This requires programming tools and experience with a programming language.

If you use a program to display a screen full of information, the program must be shared with other users of the batch file; it can still be placed in any subdirectory along the path, though.

Another way to display a screen full of information is to create an ASCII file and compile it with the BatScreen screen compiler.

When a screen program is created with BatScreen and the batch file is shared with other users, the screen program must be shared as well and must be installed in a subdirectory along the path.

The final way to display a screen full of information is by using ANSI commands. ANSI is covered in Chapter 21.

21
Advanced Screen Design 2: ANSI.SYS

Your main tool for displaying messages in a batch file is a series of ECHO commands. That works well for a few messages but soon gets old if your batch file must display a lot of information. In the last chapter, we examined using text files and the TYPE command, writing custom programs, and using a screen compiler to design screens. A fourth method of screen design is ANSI. Because ANSI is such a complex program, I decided to cover it here in a separate chapter instead of including it with the other three methods.

Introduction

The device driver ANSI.SYS (ANSI for short) gives you an incredible amount of power over the appearance of the screen. By using that power, you can produce very attractive and eye-catching screens and messages in your batch files. However, writing batch files for others using ANSI is asking for problems because so few users load ANSI. Nothing looks worse than seeing ANSI escape sequences stream across a screen when ANSI is not running. The reason for ANSI's lack of popularity is that it's saddled with the worst user interface of any program on the market! ANSI makes Edlin look user-friendly!

☠ *Warning* ANSI is a great way to create colorful screens but only if everyone who runs the resulting batch file will be loading ANSI.

Getting started with ANSI

To use ANSI, you must first load it in your CONFIG.SYS file with a statement like

```
DEVICE=C: DRDOS ANSI.SYS
```

Of course, be sure to use the subdirectory where you have ANSI stored. This is generally your DR DOS subdirectory. ANSI will use around 4K of memory, which is actually very little memory to sacrifice for the power that ANSI gives you.

Before reading about ANSI, you might want to try a little experiment. Configure your computer to load ANSI and reboot. Once you have done that, run the ANSIDEMO.BAT batch file (shown in Fig. 21-1).

If you have a color display, ANSIDEMO.BAT gave you a blue background with bright white letters for the text. There was a flashing red title at the top of the menu and a bright yellow message at the bottom saying to make your selection. Now, to see the real power of ANSI, issue a CLS command.

With other utilities that set the color of the display, CLS returns the display to white characters on a black background. However, ANSI color assignments are permanent, at least until you reboot or issue a new ANSI command or reboot, so the CLS command retains the blue background with bright white lettering. Because ANSIDEMO.BAT used nothing but DR DOS and ANSI commands, this batch file will run on any computer that loads ANSI. As a result, you don't have to worry about the user owning a utility program to be able to change colors or position the cursor. You also do not have to worry about any supporting files.

Batch File Line	Explanation
@ECHO OFF	Turn command-echoing off.
REM NAME: ANSIDEMO.BAT REM PURPOSE: Show ANSI.SYS Power REM To Control The Screen REM VERSION: 2.00 REM DATE: July 22, 1991	Documentation remarks.
IF (%1)==(/?) GOTO HELP IF (%1)==(?) GOTO HELP	If the user starts the batch file with a request for help, jump to a section to display that help.
REM Change The Screen Colors REM Bright White On Blue	Documentation remarks.
ECHO ESC[37m	Send an ANSI sequence to set the foreground color to white. (Note: the batch file uses an ASCII-27 escape character, not ESC.)
ECHO ESC[44m	Send an ANSI sequence to set the background color to blue.
ECHO ESC[1m	Send an ANSI sequence to set the foreground color attribute to bright.
REM Clear the Screen REM Set Colors First So CLS REM Would Use New Colors	Documentation remarks.
ECHO ESC[2J	Send an ANSI sequence to clear the screen.
REM Change To Flashing Red REM Display Message And Reset	Documentation remarks.

21-1 ANSIDEMO.BAT demonstrates some of the formatting power of ANSI.SYS. Before running ANSIDEMO.BAT, you must load ANSI.SYS in your CONFIG.SYS file and reboot.

Batch File Line	Explanation

ECHO ESC[1;30HESC[31mESC[5mA Very
    Special MenuESC[0mESC[37mESC
    [44mESC[1m
	Send the following ANSI sequences:
	
	ESC[1;30H Position the cursor on row 1 and column 30.
	
	ESC[31m Set the foreground color to red. This affects only the text that is written to the screen after this, not the existing text.
	
	ESC[5A Set the foreground text to blinking.
	
	At this point, a message is written to the screen.
	
	ESC[0m Reset the screen display to white on black. Again, this affects only future text and is used here to stop the blinking.
	
	ESC[37mESC[44mESC[1m Set the display to bright white on blue.

REM Position Cursor & Display Options	Documentation remark.
ECHO ESC[6;20H1. Run Word Processing	Position the cursor on row 6 at column 20 and write text.
ECHO ESC[7;20H2. Run Spreadsheet ECHO ESC[8;20H3. Run Database ECHO ESC[9;20H4. Play Games ECHO ESC[10;20H5. Format A Disk ECHO ESC[11;20H6. Backup Hard Disk To Floppies	Write the remaining menu options to the screen.

ECHO ESC[15;20HESC[33mPress The
    Number of The Program You
    WantESC[37m
	Position the cursor on row 15 and column 20, change the foreground color to yellow, write text to the screen, and reset the foreground color.

ECHO PAUSE GOTO END	Pause until the user presses a key and then exit the batch file.

21-1 Continued.

Batch File Line	Explanation

`:HELP`
`ECHO This Batch File Is A`
`ECHO Demonstration Of ANSI`
`ECHO It Requires That You Load`
`ECHO ANSI.SYS In Your CONFIG.SYS File`
`GOTO END`
	Section that displays help when the user starts the batch file with a /? or a ? as the first replaceable parameter.

`:END`	Label marking the end of the batch file.

21-1 Continued.

If you like what you saw, read on: what follows is a tutorial on ANSI. ANSI has fifteen separate functions which fall into four broad categories:

- Screen Control. You have already seen this in the example. ANSI controls screen colors nicely and allows you to display different text on the screen in different colors. It also allows you to change your prompt to prompts far fancier than the pitiful (by comparison) prompts that DR DOS allows without ANSI.
- Cursor Control. ANSI allows you to position the cursor anywhere on the screen. ANSIDEMO.BAT used this to center text and otherwise control its position on the screen without the need to pad with spaces or issue a specific number of Echo commands to move the cursor down the screen.
- Video Control. ANSI allows you to easily change the display mode ant attributes.
- Keyboard Control. ANSI allows you to remap your keyboard and write keyboard macros.

First a warning: ANSI is very difficult to learn to use, due to the poor explanation in the manual plus its unusual user interface. Plan on spending a lot of time studying this tutorial and your DR DOS manual—along with doing a lot of experimenting—before you can consider yourself an ANSI master.

☠ Warning While very powerful, ANSI has a very poor interface that is difficult to learn and hard to use.

Entering ANSI commands

Every ANSI command starts with an escape followed by a left square bracket. The ANSI command to clear the screen, for example, is ESC[2J. (For all the commands and batch file listings that follow, I have used ESC to stand for the escape character so you can read it, both in the text and the batch file listings. However, the batch file or command must have the escape character, which has an ASCII value of 27 and a hexadecimal value of 1B.) Because the first character in an ANSI command is always an escape, the commands are often called escape sequences.

☞ Remember ANSI commands are called *escape sequences*.

From this description so far, you should immediately see the first problem with ANSI: you cannot enter any ANSI commands from the keyboard because when you press the Esc key, DR DOS thinks you want to abort the current command. Typing Alt-27 on the number pad does not bypass this problem; it's just another way of entering an escape. So that you can experiment, I have included a batch file called SENDANSI.BAT on the disk that comes with this book. It has command line help and remarks, so it's fairly long, but the only command it uses is ECHO ESC[%1. To use it, you enter the ANSI command you want to run without the escape and left bracket that begins the command. SENDANSI.BAT adds those two characters and issues the command. SENDANSI.BAT will not work with ANSI keyboard reassignment commands or any other ANSI commands that include a semicolon or requires more than one "word" of commands.

Word processors, editors, and the problem of "escaping"

Many word processors and editors make it difficult to create batch files with ANSI commands because they refuse to let you enter an escape character into the file. There is a trick to get around that. When you enter the CLS command, DR DOS responds with an ESC[2J command, even if ANSI is not loaded. You can pipe that to a file with the command CLS < file. Now, you can edit this file with your word processor. While many word processors do not allow you to enter an escape, most will edit a file containing an escape without any problem. You just copy the escape character to your scrap and paste it anywhere you need it.

☑ *Remember*   Pipe a CLS command to a file to easily get an escape into a file.

With the DR DOS 5 editor, you need this trick. However, the DR DOS 6 editor lets you enter the escape directly. Press ^QN, and when it asks you for the code, enter the number 27. You will see a ^[on the screen. That is just the escape character; you must still enter the left bracket that ANSI expects. So, if you entered the command to clear the screen in Editor you would see ^[[2J where the ^[is escape and the second square bracket is the bracket Ansi needs.

☑ *Remember*   With the DR DOS 6 Editor, enter ^ QN, followed by 27 to enter an escape into a file. You will see ^ [on the screen. Because this is how Editor represents the escape, you must enter a second left bracket for ANSI commands.

Sending ANSI commands by typing a file

While ANSI is loaded, all the text that is written to the screen through DR DOS is processed through ANSI. ANSI watches for the ESC[sequence. Anything beginning with ESC[is treated as an ANSI command and anything else is sent to the screen. That gives us a number of ways to send ANSI sequences to the screen. To see that, issue the following two commands:

```
CLS > TEMP.BAT
TYPE TEMP.BAT
```

If you look at the file TEMP.BAT with an editor, you will see it contains the text sequence "ESC[2J". However, when you try to display it with the TYPE command, ANSI sees the sequence beginning with ESC[as a command and execute it. So, in addition to echoing ANSI commands to the screen, you can put them in an ASCII file and type them to the screen. You can also copy these ASCII files to the screen with the command:

```
COPY TEMP.BAT CON
```

☑ *Remember* You can give ANSI commands by placing the escape sequences in an ASCII file and typing or copying that file to the screen.

Sending ANSI commands using the environment

Now, to continue with the experiment, load TEMP.BAT into an editor. Add the command SET TEMP= in front of the ANSI sequence so the line looks like SET TEMP=ESC[2J. Now, exit and run the batch file. Because you did not turn command echoing off, DR DOS tries to echo the command to the screen, and again ANSI intercepts it and executes it. However, the environmental variable was successfully created.

Now, enter the SET command. DR DOS displays the other environmental variables properly. However, when it reaches the TEMP variable and tries to display its contents, ANSI again intercepts and executes the escape sequence. In addition to ECHO, TYPE, and COPY, this gives us a fourth way to issue ANSI commands. It also turns out that this is the easiest way.

☑ *Remember* You can give ANSI commands by placing the escape sequences in an environmental variable and using the SET command to display the environmental variables.

Sending ANSI commands via the prompt

Most environmental variables are rarely displayed. There is, however, one exception. The prompt is an environmental variable that is displayed after every DR DOS command. It is also displayed for each batch file command if command echoing is on. The prompt is particularly useful for ANSI commands. The metacharacter $e issues an escape, so you avoid the problem of having to get an escape into the sequence. In addition, the prompt command has other metacharacters to spice up a prompt. Table 21-1 lists them.

☑ *Remember* You can give ANSI commands by placing the escape sequences in the prompt. This is especially easy because the prompt offers the $e metacharacter that represents the escape character.

You can see an example of the fancy prompts ANSI is capable of generating by issuing the following command from the command line prompt with ANSI loaded:

```
PROMPT=$e[s$e[1;1H$e[K$d..$t..$p$e[u$p$g$e[44m$e[37m$e[1m
```

Table 21-1 The metacharacters you can include in a prompt statement. For ANSI, $e is very useful because it issues an escape symbol.

Command	Action
$$	Display a dollar sign.
$_	Include a carriage return and line feed.
$b	Display a vertical bar.
$d	Display the date.
$e	Include an escape. This is useful for sending ANSI escape sequences via the prompt command.
$g	Display a greater-than sign.
$h	Display a backspace--thus deleting the prior character.
$l	Display a less-than sign.
$n	Display the current drive.
$p	Display the current subdirectory.
$q	Display an equal sign.
$t	Display the time.
$v	Display the DOS version.

Replace the dots with an equal number of spaces. This prompt shows the day of the week, the date, the time, and the current drive and subdirectory on the top line of the screen. It also sets the screen colors to bright white on blue and uses the standard PG prompt on the current line of the screen!

This prompt uses a couple of ANSI sequences I have not yet mentioned, but you see how elements of the prompt metacharacters and ANSI can be combined to produce an exceptional prompt. In case you do not want to take the time to enter and debug this complex prompt, the batch file NICEPROM.BAT on the disk that comes with this book will issue it for you.

You should be aware of two problems with using the prompt to send ANSI escape sequences in a batch file. Normally, the first command of a batch file is @ECHO OFF, to turn command-echoing off. However, this also causes DR DOS to stop displaying the prompt, which prevents ANSI escape sequences stored in the prompt from being sent to the screen so they can be processed. The solution is to issue an ECHO ON command when you want to sent ANSI escape sequences with the prompt. After a command has been processed that causes the prompt to be displayed, you can turn echo back off so that your batch file will execute cleanly. ANSIHIDE.BAT in Fig. 21-2 illustrates this.

Batch File Line	Explanation
`@ECHO OFF`	Turn command-echoing off.

`REM NAME:      ANSIHIDE.BAT`
`REM PURPOSE:  Use ANSI.SYS To Hide`
`                      Messages`
`REM VERSION:  1.00`
`REM DATE:      December 19, 1991`
	Documentation remarks.

21-2 ANSIHIDE.BAT uses the prompt to send ANSI escape sequences. It turns command echoing on and off as needed. This batch file also shows how to hide DR DOS messages that are being sent to the screen.

Batch File Line	Explanation
IF (%1)==(/?) GOTO HELP IF (%1)==(?) GOTO HELP	If the user starts the batch file with a request for help, jump to a section to display that help.
ECHO ON	Turn command-echoing back on. Because the ANSI escape sequences are being sent via the prompt, the prompt must be displayed for DOS to receive the escape sequences. For the prompt to be displayed, echo must be on.
PROMPT=$e[0;40;37m	Send the ANSI escape sequences to change the screen color to white-on-black.
ECHO	Display a blank line by echoing Alt-255. The real purpose is to display the prompt so DOS will receive the ANSI escape sequence.
@ECHO OFF	Turn command-echoing back off.
CLS	Clear the screen.
ECHO Message 1 (Visible) ECHO Message 2 (Visible)	Display two messages using DOS, the same method that the programs that come with DOS display their messages.
ECHO ON	Turn command echoing on in order to send another ANSI escape sequence to DOS.
PROMPT $e[0;30;40m	Send the ANSI escape sequence to change the screen color to black-on-black.
ECHO	Echo Alt-255 to force DOS to display the prompt so it can receive the ANSI escape sequences.
@ECHO OFF	Turn command-echoing back off.
ECHO Message 3 (Invisible) ECHO Message 4 (Invisible)	Send two more messages using DOS. Because these are displayed as black text on a black background, they are invisible.
ECHO ON PROMPT=$e[0;40;37m ECHO @ECHO OFF	Reset the screen colors to white-on-black.
ECHO Message 5 (Visible) ECHO Message 6 (Visible)	Display two more messages.

21-2 Continued.

160 *Advanced batch file topics*

Batch File Line	Explanation
`PROMPT $p$g`	Reset the prompt.
`GOTO END`	Exit the batch file.

`:HELP`
   `ECHO This Is A Demonstration`
   `ECHO Batch File That Uses ANSI`
   `ECHO To Hide Messages`
`GOTO END`
	Section that displays help when the user starts the batch file with a /? or a ? as the first replaceable parameter.

`:END`	Label marking the end of the batch file.

21-2 Continued.

☠ **Warning**   When using the PROMPT command in a batch file to send ANSI escape sequences, command echoing must be turned on. Otherwise, the prompt is never displayed.

Second, prompts used to send ANSI escape sequences tend to be much longer than "standard" prompts. Because your prompt is stored in the environment, you must make sure you have enough free environmental space for these longer prompts.

I created a batch file called SENDANS2.BAT (see Fig. 21-3) so that you could experiment with all the combinations of ANSI commands you like. To run it, you enter the command

    SENDANS2 *command1 command2 ...*

Batch File Line	Explanation
`@ECHO OFF`	Turn command-echoing off.

`REM NAME:     SENDANS2.BAT`
`REM PURPOSE: Send Multiple ANSI Commands`
`REM VERSION: 1.11`
`REM DATE:    July 23, 1991`
	Documentation remarks.

`IF (%1)==(/?) GOTO HELP` `IF (%1)==(?)  GOTO HELP`	If the user starts the batch file with a request for help, jump to a section to display that help.
`IF (%1)==() GOTO END`	If the user did not enter any ANSI sequences, exit the program.
`SET ANSI=`	Reset the environmental variable the batch file uses to construct the command.
`:TOP`	Label marking the top of a loop.

21-3 SENDANS2.BAT lets you send over fifty ANSI commands on a single line.

Batch File Line	Explanation
SET ANSI=%ANSI%ESC[%1	Add the next replaceable parameter to the series of ANSI sequences. (Note: the batch file uses an ASCII-27 escape character, not ESC.)
SHIFT	Decrease all the replaceable parameters by one.
IF (%1)==() GOTO SEND	If there are no more replaceable parameters, exit the loop.
GOTO TOP	There are more replaceable parameters, so continue looping.
:SEND	Label marking the section where the ANSI command is issued.
ECHO %ANSI%	Issue the ANSI command.
GOTO END	Jump to the end of the batch file.
:END	Label marking the end of the batch file.

21-3 Continued.

at the command line. SENDANS2.BAT adds the ESC[to the beginning of each command, so you should leave it off of all commands. It builds a large environmental variable containing the entire command string and then issues it all at once, so there are no linefeeds between commands. However, that means your environment must be large enough to store all of the commands you plan on issuing, plus the ESC[that SENDANS2.BAT adds to the beginning of each command. Finally, because SENDANS2 strips off one character from each parameter (the leading space) and adds two (ESC[), the environmental variable will be longer than the command you issue. If that causes it to exceed the 127 character limit DR DOS places on commands, the computer could lock, reboot, or misbehave in some other unpredictable manner. If you keep your commands to 80 characters or less, this will not affect you.

Like SENDANSI.BAT, SENDANS2.BAT cannot be used to send ANSI commands containing a semicolon because DR DOS treats the semicolon as a divider and strips it off before passing the replaceable parameter to the batch file. As a result, there is no way to get the colon on the command line into the batch file.

Screen control

The most common ANSI command is the command to change colors. The command is ESC[#m, where # is the number of the foreground or background color to use. The color numbers are all two digits; all foreground colors start with a 3 and all background colors start with a 4. The colors are as follows:

0   Black
1   Red
2   Green
3   Yellow
4   Blue
5   Magenta
6   Cyan
7   White

So the command ESC[44mESC[37m sets the screen to white letters on a blue background—my personal favorite. Table 21-2 shows all of the associated ANSI escape sequences.

Table 21-2   The ANSI escape sequences used to control the screen colors.

ANSI command sequence	Function
ESC[30m	Set foreground color to black
ESC[31m	Set foreground color to red
ESC[32m	Set foreground color to green
ESC[33m	Set foreground color to yellow
ESC[34m	Set foreground color to blue
ESC[35m	Set foreground color to magenta
ESC[36m	Set foreground color to cyan
ESC[37m	Set foreground color to white
ESC[40m	Set background color to black
ESC[41m	Set background color to red
ESC[42m	Set background color to green
ESC[43m	Set background color to yellow
ESC[44m	Set background color to blue
ESC[45m	Set background color to magenta
ESC[46m	Set background color to cyan
ESC[47m	Set background color to white

Three notes are in order here:

• These color numbers are not the same as the numbers you are use to using if you program in Basic.
• The clear screen command ended with an uppercase J, while the color command ended with a lowercase m. Most ANSI commands are case-sensitive, so pay attention to case while writing ANSI commands.
• An m ends every ANSI attribute setting command, but you only need one per line. Thus, the previous command could be shortened to ESC[44;37m. The m terminates

the command. You do not have to reissue the ESC[after the "44" because the ANSI command is not terminated due to the fact that there is no m.

Being able to control the colors leads to two somewhat useful utilities. BLANK.BAT uses ANSI sequences to blank the screen at the command line prompt by converting the screen to black text on a black background. BLANK.BAT is shown below:

```
@ECHO OFF
ECHO ESC[0m
ECl IO ESC[30m
ECHO ESC[40m
CLS
```

This keeps amateur snoops from looking at your files. I should note that the blank screen is really only blank at the command line and the few programs that use ANSI color settings. Most programs, however, display fine while ANSI is set for a blank screen. Of course, the user must be able to load the program without seeing the prompt of the commands being entered. Typing UNBLANK runs UNBLANK.BAT, shown here:

```
@ECHO OFF
ECHO ESC[37m
ECHO ESC[44m
ECHO ESC[1m
CLS
```

UNBLANK.BAT uses ANSI commands to restore the screen to bright white letters on a blue background. (You must, of course, be able to run UNBLANK.BAT without being able to see the screen.)

Note that the batch files on your disk have more documentation and command line help. However, that does not aid in the explanation here, so it is not reproduced here.

ANSI also provides for several types of screen erasing:

ESC[0J   Erases the screen from the cursor position to the end of the screen. (Note: Not all versions of ANSI support this command.)

ESC[0K   Erases the line the cursor is on, but only from the cursor position to the right.

ESC[1J   Erases the screen from the cursor position to the top of the screen. (Note: Not all versions of ANSI support this command.)

ESC[1K   Erases the line the cursor is on, from the beginning of the line to the current cursor position. (Note: Not all versions of ANSI support this command.)

ESC[2J   Clears the entire screen identically to a CLS command. In fact, the CLS command causes DR DOS to issue an ESC[2J command.

ESC[2K   Erases the entire line that the cursor is currently on. (Note: Not all versions of ANSI support this command.)

Cursor control

Ansi gives you the ability to position the cursor anywhere on the screen and to move the cursor around the screen as you see fit. In their simplest form, the commands to move around the screen are

ESC[A   Move the cursor up one row.
ESC[B   Move the cursor down one row.
ESC[C   Move the cursor to the right one column.
ESC[D   Move the cursor to the left one column.

If you precede the A through D with a number, the cursor is moved that many times, so ESC[5A moves the cursor up five rows. The command ESC[$r;c$H moves the cursor to row r and column c, so the command ESC[1;1H moves the cursor to the top left corner of the screen and ESC[24,80H moves it to the bottom right corner. One note: the lowercase f works identically to the uppercase H, so ESC[10;10H and ESC[10;10f do the same thing.

ANSI also has the ability to save the current cursor position with the command ESC[s. This command can only save one cursor position, so each time you use it, you overwrite the prior position it has saved. The ESC[u command returns to the position saved with the ESC[s command. You can also have ANSI report the cursor position with an ESC[6n command. This is generally used by programs and is of little value in a batch file.

Video control

The Mode command allows you to control the video mode, but ANSI does an even better job. For example, the ESC[=1h command configures the screen for 40×25 color mode so that text appears very large. The ESC[=3h returns the screen to 80×25 mode. The format of the command is slightly unusual because it has an equal sign in the middle. Assuming your display supports them, the ANSI commands to change the display mode are as follows:

ESC[=0h 40×25 monochrome text.
ESC[=1h 40×25 color text.
ESC[=2h 80×25 monochrome text.
ESC[=3h 80×25 color text.
ESC[=4h 320×200 4-color graphics.
ESC[=5h 320×200 monochrome graphics.
ESC[=6h 640×200 2-color graphics.
ESC[=13h 320×200 16-color graphics. (EGA and VGA only.)
ESC[=14h 640×200 16-color graphics. (EGA and VGA only.)
ESC[=15h 640×350 monochrome graphics. (EGA and VGA only.)
ESC[=16h 640×350 16-color graphics. (EGA and VGA only.)
ESC[=17h 640×480 2-color graphics. (VGA only.)
ESC[=18h 640×480 16-color graphics. (VGA only.)
ESC[=19h 320×200 256-color graphics. (VGA only.)

ANSI also has several commands to control other aspects of how the screen appears:

ESC[=7h   Causes lines longer than 80 characters to wrap around to the next line. This is the default mode.
ESC[=7l   Causes lines longer than 80 characters to be truncated so they do not wrap. Note that the last character is a lowercase L and not a 1.
ESC[0m   Turns off all screen attributes, returning the screen to white on black.

ESC[1m	Turns on high-intensity foreground colors.
ESC[2m	Returns the foreground colors to normal intensity.
ESC[4m	Turns on underlining on a monochrome display.
ESC[5m	Causes the foreground text to blink.
ESC[7m	Converts the display to inverse video.
ESC[8m	Blanks the screen by setting the foreground color to the background color.

As you can see, ANSI offers a lot of control over video attributes.

Remember   ANSI offers a lot of control over video attributes.

Keyboard control

ANSI is also able to reconfigure your keyboard. This topic is unrelated to batch files, so I will cover it only very briefly. The general format of the command is:

```
ESC[_;_p
```

The first blank is the ASCII value of the key to reassign. The second blank is the ASCII value the key is to take on. If you like, you can enclose the actual value in double quotes. For example, most of the time in DR DOS, you use the parentheses more than the brackets (although the left bracket gets a workout under ANSI). You can switch them in DR DOS using the command:

```
ECHO ESC[91;40p
ECHO ESC[93;41p
ECHO ESC[40;91p
ECHO ESC[41;93p
```

The reassignment works under DR DOS but not in programs like Microsoft Word that bypass DR DOS for keystrokes. To reset the keyboard reassignments, issue the command:

```
ECHO ESC[91;91p
ECHO ESC[93;93p
ECHO ESC[40;40p
ECHO ESC[41;41p
```

You could have started to remap these using the actual keystrokes. So the first command would have been

```
ECHO ESC["[";"("p
```

However, after remapping the square brackets to parentheses, you would not have been able to type them into the second two commands to map the parentheses to square brackets because they have been turned into something else. Using ASCII values avoids this problem.

The disk that comes with this book has two batch files that will help you experiment with ANSI keyboard reassignments. The first is ANSIKEY1.BAT. It takes pairs of numbers associated with the various keystrokes: the first number is the keystroke to modify, and the second keystroke is its new value. It issues the ANSI command necessary to make the first assignment, issues two SHIFT commands, and checks to see if another pair of numbers is waiting. It's shown next without internal documentation and command line help:

```
:TOP
    IF (%2)==( ) GOTO END
    ECHO %1;%2p
    SHIFT
    SHIFT
    GOTO TOP
```

To remap the square brackets and parentheses mentioned earlier, you would enter the command

```
ANSIKEY1 91 40 93 41 40 91 41 93
```

and to restore the keys to their original value, you would enter

```
ANSIKEY1 40 40 41 41 91 91 93 93
```

The second batch file is ANSIKEY2.BAT. It is similar to ANSIKEY1.BAT, only it accepts the actual keystrokes rather than the numbers. It is shown next without internal documentation and command line help:

```
:TOP
    IF (%2)==( ) GOTO END
    ECHO "%1";"%2"p
    SHIFT
    SHIFT
    GOTO TOP
```

To remap the square brackets and parentheses mentioned earlier, you would enter this command:

```
ANSIKEY1 ( [ ) ] [ ( ] )
```

Because none of the keys are remapped until this command is issued, you have no trouble issuing all the commands on the command line. To restore the keys to their original value, you would enter

```
ANSIKEY1 ( ( ) ) [ [ ] ]
```

Both batch files will accept over twenty-five reassignments on a single line, making it easy to reassign a lot of keys at once. If you find yourself using the same reassignment command more than once or twice, you might want to either write a custom batch file to issue the ANSI commands or just to store the commands you use to call one of these batch files.

In addition to remapping standard keys, you can also remap extended keystrokes like Ctrl-F1. These keystrokes have a two digit code that starts with "0;"—the number "zero", not the letter "O".) They are entered like any other keystroke; thus, to remap Ctrl-F1 to issue a DIR command, you would issue the command:

ECHO ESC[0;94;"DIR";13p

Because this type of assignment involves one number and one character string, you cannot issue this command with either ANSIKEY1.BAT or ANSIKEY2.BAT, although either could easily be modified to handle this. Table 21-3 shows many of the ASCII and extended keystrokes you can use.

Table 21-3   There are a number of extended keystrokes you can use with ANSI to remap the keyboard.

Keystroke	ANSI Key Code	Keystroke	ANSI Key Code	Keystroke	ANSI Key Code
Alt-;	0;131	Alt-L	0;38	Del	0;83
Alt-0	0;129	Alt-M	0;50	Down Arrow	0;80
Alt-1	0;120	Alt-N	0;49	End	0;79
Alt-2	0;121	Alt-O	0;24	F1	0;59
Alt-3	0;122	Alt-P	0;25	F10	0;68
Alt-4	0;123	Alt-Q	0;16	F2	0;60
Alt-5	0;124	Alt-R	0;19	F3	0;61
Alt-6	0;125	Alt-S	0;31	F4	0;62
Alt-7	0;126	Alt-T	0;20	F5	0;63
Alt-8	0;127	Alt-U	0;22	F6	0;64
Alt-9	0;128	Alt-V	0;47	F7	0;65
Alt-A	0;30	Alt-W	0;17	F8	0;66
Alt-B	0;48	Alt-X	0;45	F9	0;67
Alt-C	0;46	Alt-Y	0;21	Home	0;71
Alt-D	0;32	Alt-Z	0;44	Ins	0;82
Alt-dash	0;130	Ctrl-F1	0;94	Left Arrow	0;75
Alt-E	0;18	Ctrl-Left Arrow	0;115	NUL	0;3
Alt-F	0;33	Ctrl-Right Arrow	0;116	PgDn	0;81
Alt-F1	0;104	Ctrl-End	0;117	PgUp	0;73
Alt-F10	0;113	Ctrl-F10	0;103	Right Arrow	0;77
Alt-F2	0;105	Ctrl-F2	0;95	Shift-F1	0;84
Alt-F3	0;106	Ctrl-F3	0;96	Shift-F10	0;93
Alt-F4	0;107	Ctrl-F4	0;97	Shift-F2	0;85
Alt-F5	0;108	Ctrl-F5	0;98	Shift-F3	0;86
Alt-F6	0;109	Ctrl-F6	0;99	Shift-F4	0;87
Alt-F7	0;110	Ctrl-F7	0;100	Shift-F5	0;88
Alt-F8	0;111	Ctrl-F8	0;101	Shift-F6	0;89
Alt-F9	0;112	Ctrl-F9	0;102	Shift-F7	0;90
Alt-G	0;34	Ctrl-Home	0;119	Shift-F8	0;91
Alt-H	0;35	Ctrl-PgDn	0;118	Shift-F9	0;92
Alt-I	0;23	Ctrl-PgUp	0;132	Shift-Tab	0;15
Alt-J	0;36	Ctrl-Print Screen	0;114	Up Arrow	0;72
Alt-K	0;37				

As you can see, ANSI gives you a great deal of control over the screen. It is also difficult to learn; once you learn ANSI, though, it is fairly easy to use. Table 21-4 summarizes many frequently used ANSI commands.

Table 21-4   You can issue a number of different commands using ANSI.SYS. Here are the more common ones.

ANSI command sequence	Function
ESC[#;#p	Reassign the key defined by the first pound sign to the value of the second pound sign.
ESC[#A	Move the cursor up the number of rows specified by the number that replaces the pound sign.
ESC[#B	Move the cursor down the number of rows specified by the number that replaces the pound sign.
ESC[#C	Move the cursor left the number of rows specified by the number that replaces the pound sign.
ESC[#D	Move the cursor right the number of rows specified by the number that replaces the pound sign.
ESC[=0h	Set the display mode to 40x25 monochrome text.
ESC[=13h	Set the display mode to 320x200 16-color graphics.
ESC[=14h	Set the display mode to 640x200 16-color graphics.
ESC[=15h	Set the display mode to 640x350 monochrome graphics.
ESC[=16h	Set the display mode to 640x350 16-color graphics.
ESC[=17h	Set the display mode to 640x480 2-color graphics.
ESC[=18h	Set the display mode to 640x480 16-color graphics.
ESC[=19h	Set the display mode to 320x200 256-color graphics.
ESC[=1h	Set the display mode to 40x25 color text.
ESC[=2h	Set the display mode to 80x25 monochrome text.
ESC[=3h	Set the display mode to 80x25 color text.
ESC[=4h	Set the display mode to 300x200 4-color graphics.
ESC[=5h	Set the display mode to 320x200 monochrome graphics.
ESC[=6h	Set the display mode to 640x200 2-color graphics.
ESC[=7h	Turn line wrap on.
ESC[=7l	Turn line wrap off.
ESC[?7h	Turn line wrap on. This is needed only if line wrap has been turned off.
ESC[?7l	Turn line wrap off. When line wrap is off, once the cursor reaches the end of the line, each succeeding character is printed on top of the last one at the end of the line.
ESC[0h	Set the display mode to 40x25 monochrome.
ESC[0J	Erase the screen from the cursor position to the end of the screen. (Not all versions of ANSI support this command.)
ESC[0K	Erase the current line from the cursor position right.
ESC[0l	Set the display mode to 40x25 monochrome.
ESC[0m	Reset the screen display to white on black.
ESC[1h	Set the display mode to 40x25 color.
ESC[1J	Erase the screen from the cursor position to the top of the screen. (Not all versions of ANSI support this command.)

Table 21-4. Continued

ESC[1K	Erase the line the cursor is on, from the beginning of the line to the cursor position. (Not all versions of ANSI support this.)
ESC[1l	Set the display mode to 40x25 color.
ESC[1m	Set the foreground text to bold.
ESC[2h	Set the display mode to 80x25 monochrome.
ESC[2J	Clear the screen.
ESC[2K	Erase the entire line that the cursor is on. (Not all versions of ANSI support this.)
ESC[2l	Set the display mode to 80x25 monochrome.
ESC[2m	Return the foreground colors to normal intensity.
ESC[30m	Set foreground color to black.
ESC[31m	Set foreground color to red.
ESC[32m	Set foreground color to green.
ESC[33m	Set foreground color to yellow.
ESC[34m	Set foreground color to blue.
ESC[35m	Set foreground color to magenta.
ESC[36m	Set foreground color to cyan.
ESC[37m	Set foreground color to white.
ESC[3h	Set the display mode to 80x25 color.
ESC[3l	Set the display mode to 80x25 color.
ESC[40m	Set background color to black.
ESC[41m	Set background color to red.
ESC[42m	Set background color to green.
ESC[43m	Set background color to yellow.
ESC[44m	Set background color to blue.
ESC[45m	Set background color to magenta.
ESC[46m	Set background color to cyan.
ESC[47m	Set background color to white.
ESC[4h	Set the display mode to 320x200 color graphics.
ESC[4l	Set the display mode to 320x200 color graphics.
ESC[4m	Set the foreground text to underlined on a monochrome display. On a color display, this sets the foreground to blue.
ESC[5A	Set the foreground text to blinking.
ESC[5h	Set the display mode to 320x200 monochrome graphics.
ESC[5l	Set the display mode to 320x200 monochrome graphics.
ESC[5m	Set the foreground color to blinking.
ESC[6h	Set the display mode to 640x200 monochrome graphics.
ESC[6l	Set the display mode to 640x200 monochrome graphics.
ESC[6n	Report the cursor position.
ESC[7m	Set the display to reverse video, black text on a white background.
ESC[K	Erase the current line from the cursor position right.
ESC[r;cf	Position the cursor on row number r and column number c.
ESC[r;cH	Position the cursor on row number r and column number c.
ESC[s	Store the current cursor position.
ESC[u	Return to the cursor position stored by the ESC[s command.
ESC8m	Blank the screen by setting the foreground color equal to the background color.

Summary

You can display a screen full of information by using ANSI commands.

ANSI is used to control the screen, cursor, video, and keyboard.

ANSI escape sequences can be used to change the foreground and background colors of the screen.

When ANSI is used to change the color of the screen, a CLS command does not reset the colors to white-on-black.

ANSI commands are called escape sequences.

ANSI commands cannot be entered from the keyboard because they usually start with the escape character.

If your word processor cannot enter an escape character in a file, pipe the CLS command to a file and incorporate the escape from that file in your document.

ANSI processes any line that is sent to the screen that begins with an escape character followed by an open bracket, no matter how the characters are displayed.

ANSI escape sequences can be displayed using the ECHO command.

ANSI escape sequences can be displayed by storing them in an ASCII file and typing that file to the screen.

ANSI escape sequences can be displayed by storing them in environmental variables and then using the SET command or ECHO %variable% command to display one or more environmental variables.

ANSI escape sequences can be displayed using the PROMPT command, which has a built-in escape character.

When ANSI escape sequences are displayed in a batch file via the PROMPT command, command echoing must be turned on while the prompt is being used to send the ANSI commands.

ANSI provides several different ways to erase different portions of the screen.

ANSI provides the ability to move the cursor in any direction as well as to save and recall the cursor position.

ANSI can be used to set the video mode.

ANSI also allows you to remap the keyboard, although the remapping will not work with many programs that avoid DR DOS to get their keystrokes.

22

Batch file subroutines

In programming, a *subroutine* is a special type of program. When a program calls a subroutine, control is passed to the subroutine. When the subroutine is finished, control is passed back to the program that called the subroutine. The calling program continues from the point where it passed control to the subroutine. Figure 22-1 illustrates this graphically.

Subroutines are a way of writing a section of code once, storing it in a special way, and reusing it as many times as it is needed. In a batch file, this often makes the logic much easier to follow and the batch file easier to write and debug. For example, if you want to perform multiple commands based on the ERRORLEVEL value, you must have a series of If-tests for each possible ERRORLEVEL value. Each If-test must jump to a different section of the batch file to perform the multiple commands, and then the sections must reconverge. With subroutines, the batch file would have a single command for each If-test where that command ran a subroutine. Look at this example:

```
IF ERRORLEVEL 3 SUB-3
IF ERRORLEVEL 2 SUB-2
IF ERRORLEVEL 1 SUB-1
IF ERRORLEVEL 0 SUB-0
```

Of course, as we learn to write subroutines, we will replace the commands after the ERRORLEVEL-tests with the actual commands to run subroutines.

Remember Subroutines allow you to reuse your debugged batch file code.

What is a subroutine, and how do I write one?

A subroutine is nothing more than one or more lines of batch file commands—exactly like any other batch file commands. The question is not "What is it?" but rather "How do you use it?". Depending on the brand and version of operating system you have, your options are as follows:

  • You can store the subroutine as a separate batch file. Both DR and MS DOS support

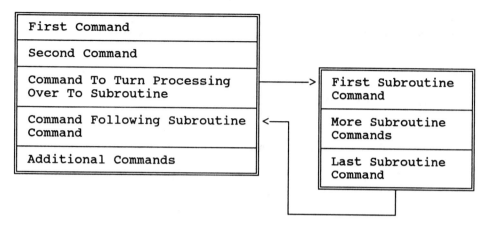

22-1 When one program or part of a program calls another program, the part being called is called a subroutine.

this, as do all versions of both operating systems—although the methods of running these separate batch files differ slightly depending on the version.

- You can store the subroutine inside the original batch files and use If-tests to jump to this section of code. Again, all versions of DR and MS DOS support this, and (again) the methods vary slightly.
- You can use the subroutine-specific batch subcommands built into DR DOS 6. Using this method, your batch files will not run under MS DOS or earlier versions of DR DOS.

As a separate batch file

The easiest way to write a subroutine is to write that subroutine as a stand-alone batch file. The method's biggest advantage is that it allows multiple batch files to call on a common subroutine; its worst disadvantage is that it uses more hard disk space because each batch file is allocated a full cluster of space no how small it is. Of course, this is not an issue if you use SuperStor for disk compression.

Remember The easiest way to write a subroutine is to write that subroutine as a stand-alone batch file.

Prior to DR DOS 5 and MS DOS 3.3

Early versions of MS and DR DOS did not support a batch file running other batch files as subroutines. With those older versions of the operating system, once a batch file passed control to another batch file, control never passed back to the original batch file.

This is not how a batch file behaves when it passes control to a program. When that program finishes, control is passed back to the calling batch file. This fact can be used to "trick" earlier versions of DR DOS into allowing one batch file to call another and gain back control when the subroutine batch file finishes.

While it is possible to "trick" older versions of DR DOS into treating other batch files as subroutines—and I'll show you how to do that in a moment—my suggestion is to simply upgrade to DR DOS 6. This new version has enough new and improved features that the upgrade will be well worth your time and money.

☑ *Remember*   COMMAND.COM is a program you can run just like any other program.

Normally, you do not think of COMMAND.COM as a program; yet, it is. Running COMMAND.COM by entering COMMAND at the command line prompt runs COM-MAND.COM. This loads a second copy of the command processor into memory. The command to exit this second command processor is EXIT; this command terminates the second command processor and returns control back to the first (and calling) command processor.

Try it yourself. Run MEM or CHKDSK to find out how much free memory your computer has. Now, run COMMAND and then rerun MEM or CHKDSK. You will see that you have less memory because a second copy of COMMAND.COM loaded into memory. Now, enter EXIT to unload that second copy of COMMAND.COM and rerun MEM or CHKDSK. You'll see that your memory level has returned to its original level.

The "trick" involves invoking a second command process, having that second command processor run the subroutine batch file, and then dropping out of the second command processor to return control to the calling batch file. The syntax to run the second batch file is

COMMAND /C Batch

The /C tells COMMAND.COM to run the following command, which in this case is a batch file. The last command of the subroutine batch file should be an EXIT. This returns control to the original batch file.

DR DOS 5, MS DOS 3.3, and later

DR DOS 5 added the CALL batch subcommand. Thus, a batch file can call another batch file with

CALL Batch

Once the subroutine batch file terminates, control automatically returns to the batch file that called the subroutine batch file. The subroutine batch file does not have to end with an EXIT command.

☑ *Remember*   The CALL command makes it easy for one batch file to run another batch file and regain control when it terminates.

An example

To illustrate this, we will look back to TOA.BAT. TOA.BAT was a batch file we began looking at in Chapter 10 as a way to copy .DOC and .CMP files to the A drive and delete the associated .BAK file when the user entered just the filename. This batch file evolved over the next several chapters, reaching its ultimate form in Chapter 16. That version of TOA.BAT is shown here:

```
@ECHO OFF
:TOP
    IF (%1)==( ) GOTO END
    DEL %1.BAK
    COPY %1.DOC A:
    COPY %1.CMP A:
    SHIFT
GOTO TOP

:END
```

The same batch file but with internal documentation and command line help is included on the disk that comes with this book.

The purpose of this batch file is to copy the modified versions of files to a floppy disk to be transported to another location. As it exists, it does not enforce this. If a .DOC file has been modified, then—on my system using Microsoft Word—a .BAK file always exists. Suppose we wanted to add the logic necessary to skip copying the file if a .BAK file does not exist. Our new version of TOA.BAT might look like this:

```
@ECHO OFF
:TOP
    IF (%1)==( ) GOTO END
    IF NOT EXIST %1.BAK ECHO %1 Not Modified So Not Copied
    IF NOT EXIST %1.BAK GOTO SKIP
    DEL %1.BAK
    COPY %1.DOC A:
    COPY %1.CMP A:
:SKIP
    SHIFT
GOTO TOP

:END
```

Now, suppose we wanted to add logic to the copy portion of the batch file to detect minor copying errors—like a full diskette—and warn the user. Plus, we wanted to make sure the user entered the name correctly warning him or her if the .DOC file does not exist. As you can imagine, the original three lines of the batch file that handled the repetitive tasks of copying and deleting files—

```
DEL %1.BAK
COPY %1.DOC A:
COPY %1.CMP A:
```

—are going to become very complex.

Predictably, because this chapter covers subroutines, the solution is to place these three commands in a separate batch file and treat them as a subroutine. The original version of TOA.BAT (called TOA-2.BAT on the disk) has these three lines stripped out and a single command added to call the subroutine. Within TOA-2.BAT, the files to be copied are known as %1. However, this replaceable parameter is only global while inside TOA-2.BAT and is not available to the subroutine—called TOA- 2SUB.BAT. In order to make the name of the file available to TOA-2SUB.BAT, we must pass it to that batch file as a replaceable parameter. The resulting TOA-2.BAT looks like this:

```
@ECHO OFF
:TOP
    IF (%1)==() GOTO END
    CALL TOA-2SUB %1
    SHIFT
GOTO TOP

:END
```

A version of TOA-2.BAT with internal documentation and command line help is included on the disk that comes with this book.

As we begin looking at TOA-2SUB.BAT, it looks like this:

```
@ECHO OFF
DEL %1.BAK
COPY %1.DOC A:
COPY %1.CMP A:
```

Two notes about this subroutine are important. First, it does not need to test to see if %1 exists because TOA-2.BAT takes care of that prior to calling the subroutine. Second, the @ECHO OFF command is not really necessary beause command echoing is always off when a batch file with command echoing turned off calls another batch file as a subroutine. You will see why I've added it later.

Because this subroutine is shorter and not already convoluted by the looping performed in TOA.BAT, we can add the additional checks we desired without the batch file becoming as complicated as TOA.BAT would have become. First, let's add the logic to test and make sure the file has been modified by testing to see if the .BAK file exists. The pseudocode for this is

If .BAK does not exist, tell user and exit subroutine
If .BAK exists, continue normally

The resulting subroutine looks like this:

```
@ECHO OFF

IF NOT EXIST %1.BAK ECHO File Not Modified—Not Copied
IF NOT EXIST %1.BAK GOTO END

DEL %1.BAK
COPY %1.DOC A:
COPY %1.CMP A:

:END
```

Next, we want to make sure the file actually exists before we try to copy it. If the file was created by Lotus or dBASE, a .BAK file might still exist but a .DOC file might not. If the .DOC file does not exist, we want to exit without copying anything; but if the .CMP file does not exist, we simply want to skip that COPY command because not all documents have .CMP files. The pseudocode for this is

If .DOC file does not exist, warn user and exit subroutine
If the .CMP file exists, copy it to the diskette

and the resulting subroutine looks like this:

```
@ECHO OFF

IF NOT EXIST %1.BAK ECHO File Not Modified—Not Copied
IF NOT EXIST %1.BAK GOTO END

IF NOT EXIST %1.DOC ECHO %1.DOC File Not Found
IF NOT EXIST %1.DOC GOTO END

DEL %1.BAK
COPY %1.DOC A:
IF EXIST %1.CMP COPY %1.CMP A:

:END
```

Because the second set of If-tests makes sure the .DOC file exists, no If-test is used in front of that COPY command. However, when it is time to copy the .CMP file, the batch file has not verified that it exists, so this COPY command is preceded by an If-test.

As our last modification to the logic, we want to make sure that the file was successfully copied to the A drive. Because COPY does not set the ERRORLEVEL, we must perform this test manually. The pseudocode for this is

If file is on current drive but not A drive warn user

The resulting subroutine looks like this:

```
@ECHO OFF

IF NOT EXIST %1.BAK ECHO File Not Modified—Not Copied
IF NOT EXIST %1.BAK GOTO END

IF NOT EXIST %1.DOC ECHO %1.DOC File Not Found
IF NOT EXIST %1.DOC GOTO END

DEL %1.BAK
COPY %1.DOC A:
IF EXIST %1.CMP COPY %1.CMP A:

IF NOT EXIST A:%1.DOC ECHO %1.DOC Not Copied Successfully
:END
```

This test will spot occasions when the file was too big to fit on the A drive but will not handle situations were there was a version of the file already on the A drive and some other problem prevented the successful copying, all because the batch file will find that A:%1.DOC exists. While COPY does not set an ERRORLEVEL value, XCOPY does. A 0 represents a successful copy, while a higher value represents some sort of problem. We can use that information to modify this subroutine to spot any copy problem by using XCOPY and ERRORLEVEL tests. The resulting subroutine looks like this:

```
@ECHO OFF

IF NOT EXIST %1.BAK ECHO File Not Modified—Not Copied
IF NOT EXIST %1.BAK GOTO END

IF NOT EXIST %1.DOC ECHO %1.DOC File Not Found
IF NOT EXIST %1.DOC GOTO END

DEL %1.BAK
IF EXIST %1.CMP XCOPY %1.CMP A:
XCOPY %1.DOC A:

IF ERRORLEVEL 1 ECHO %1.DOC Not Copied Successfully
:END
```

In addition to converting the COPY commands to XCOPY and converting the final If-Exist test to If-ERRORLEVEL, I also reversed the copying order of the .CMP and .DOC files. The ERRORLEVEL used in the If-ERRORLEVEL test is the final ERRORLEVEL value, and the .DOC document file is far more important than the .CMP dictionary file. So, by copying the .DOC file last, its ERRORLEVEL is the one tested. Interested readers might want to add tests on both values if the first XCOPY has a problem.

These are all the modifications the subroutine needs if it is to function solely as a stand-alone subroutine. However, because it exists as a stand-alone batch file, users are likely to try and run it to see what it does. We can help avoid problems with this by adding command line help when the user uses the now familiar /? switch, but this time also display the help if the batch file is started without a replaceable parameter. This final test works because TOA-2.BAT always calls it with a replaceable parameter; the batch file knows it is being run improperly if it does not receive a replaceable parameter. The final version of the batch file is shown next:

```
@ECHO OFF

IF (%1)==( )  GOTO HELP
IF (%1)==(/?) GOTO HELP

IF NOT EXIST %1.BAK ECHO File Has Not Been Modified—Not Copied
IF NOT EXIST %1.BAK GOTO END

IF NOT EXIST %1.DOC ECHO %1.DOC File Not Found
IF NOT EXIST %1.DOC GOTO END

DEL %1.BAK
IF EXIST %1.CMP XCOPY %1.CMP A:
XCOPY %1.DOC A:

IF ERRORLEVEL 1 ECHO %1.DOC Not Copied Successfully
GOTO END

:HELP
```

```
ECHO This Batch File Is A Subroutine Used By TOA-2.BAT
ECHO It Is Not Designed To Be Run By The User
GOTO END

:END
```

This version of TOA-2SUB.BAT is included on the disk that comes with the book. The only difference is that the disk version includes some additional internal documentation.

By now, you should also see why I included the @ECHO OFF command in the subroutine, although it's not needed when the batch file is running as a subroutine. If a user runs the batch file from the command line to find out what it does, the help section will take care of that, but everything would look very unattractive without the @ECHO OFF command.

Inside the calling batch file

Each batch file you write takes up a minimum of one cluster of disk space. Depending on several factors, that can be up to 8K and will most likely be at least 2K—unless you have created a SuperStor drive that you keep your batch files on. If you are running very short of hard disk space, that can seem like a large price to pay for a relatively small subroutine. You can avoid this by bundling all the subroutines within the main batch file.

When you include the subroutine(s) inside the batch file, it ends up running itself. A program or batch file that runs itself is said to be recursive. Recursive batch files have two advantages over batch files that call separate batch files as subroutines. First, as mentioned earlier, the resulting batch file is generally smaller than the separate batch file and subroutines. This is generally true in spite of the requirement in the recursive batch file for additional If-tests to direct it to the appropriate spot in the batch file to continue processing.

Remember   A program or batch file that runs itself is said to be recursive.

The second advantage of a recursive batch file is how easy it is to transfer it to different systems. If you need to copy a recursive batch file to another system, then that batch file is all you need to take to the new machine. If you want to transfer a batch file with external subroutines, then you have to remember to copy all the files—something I have trouble remembering to do.

There is, however, one very significant drawback to recursive batch files. The resulting batch file is longer and more complex and without the proper approach can be much more difficult to write. This additional complexity is an important consideration—one you should not overlook.

Warning   Building the subroutine inside the main batch file saves space but makes the resulting batch file more complex.

You have two approaches to storing the subroutine within the main batch file: the MS DOS compatible approach, and the DR DOS specific approach. We will look at both methods.

The MS DOS -compatible approach 1:
Skip the subroutine commands

The first MS DOS -compatible approach is fairly simple. A replaceable parameter functions as a signal to tell the batch file if it is being called by itself as a subroutine. When that signal is missing, the batch file knows it is being called from the command line. A series of If-tests at the beginning of the batch file direct it to the appropriate section of the batch file depending on the flag it receives as a replaceable parameter. That way, the batch file can contain more that one subroutine internally.

We'll start with TOA-2.BAT as written above and we'll include TOA-2SUB.BAT as an internal subroutine. We'll call the resulting batch file TOA-3.BAT. TOA-3.BAT needs to run exactly like TOA-2.BAT when it first starts. However, when TOA-2.BAT would be calling TOA-2SUB.BAT as a subroutine, TOA-3.BAT needs to call itself. We will use %2 as a flag to TOA-3.BAT that it is running as a subroutine—specifically, when TOA-3.BAT calls itself as a subroutine, it will pass XYZ123ABC as %2.

That means we have to have several If-tests at the top of TOA-3.BAT. One will direct the batch file to help if /? is entered and another will direct the batch file to the subroutine section if %2 is XYZ123ABC. Because TOA-3.BAT will be providing this replaceable parameter, capitalization will not be a problem. The end of the subroutine section will be a GOTO END command, so the subroutine copy of the batch file will exit and return control to the calling copy of TOA-3.BAT. Otherwise, the subroutine section is identical. The resulting batch file is shown next:

```
@ECHO OFF
:TOP
    IF (%1)==( ) GOTO END
    IF (%1)==(/?) GOTO HELP
    IF (%2)==(XYZ123ABC) GOTO SUB
    CALL TOA-3 %1 XYZ123ABC
    SHIFT
GOTO TOP

:HELP
    ECHO This Batch File Requires You To Enter File Names
    ECHO Without The Extension. For Each Name, It Erases
    ECHO The Associated .BAT File Then It Copies The
    ECHO Associated .DOC And .CMP Files To The A Drive
GOTO END

:SUB
    IF NOT EXIST %1.BAK ECHO File Not Modified—Not Copied
    IF NOT EXIST %1.BAK GOTO END

    IF NOT EXIST %1.DOC ECHO %1.DOC File Not Found
    IF NOT EXIST %1.DOC GOTO END

    DEL %1.BAK
    IF EXIST %1.CMP XCOPY %1.CMP A:
    XCOPY %1.DOC A:
```

```
IF ERRORLEVEL 1 ECHO %1.DOC Not Copied Successfully
GOTO END

:END
```

TOA-3.BAT calls itself as a subroutine without using the DR DOS batch subcommands for subroutines so that it can run under both MS and DR DOS. It also illustrates the best approach to writing recursive batch files. Because the individual-files approach is easier to write, that's what I used here. Only after TOA-2.BAT and TOA-2SUB.BAT were finished did I begin working on the single recursive batch file that incorporated both files.

This example also illustrates the reason for a habit you might be wondering about, one that I've developed when writing batch files. I have always closed out the last section of the batch file—generally the help section—with a GOTO END command, even when the next line was the :END label. By doing that, I avoid introducing problems when I rearrange the logic of the batch file—as I did when I created TOA-3.BAT by modifying TOA-2.BAT to include the subroutine.

It is also possible to reorder the If-tests in TOA-3.BAT to make it run more quickly. Because TOA-3.BAT calls itself as a subroutine for each file, it is likely to run as a subroutine more often than as a stand-alone batch file. As written, when running as a subroutine, it has to first pass through the two If-tests relating to command line help. By putting the subroutine If-test first, these two If-tests will be avoided when TOA-3.BAT runs as a subroutine. In general, when using branching If-tests in a batch file, they should be ordered from the most likely to be true to the least likely.

Remember   When using multiple If-tests to branch in a batch file, arrange them so the ones most likely to be true are the first in the series.

DR DOS 6-specific subroutines   DR DOS 6 introduced four batch subroutine commands that make building the subroutines into the main batch file a snap. However, these commands are not supported by MS DOS, so only use them if you are certain your batch file will not need to run under MS DOS. In addition, because most batch file compilers—like Builder and Builder Lite—only support the MS DOS format for commands, DR DOS 6 subroutine batch subcommands will not compile properly. Additionally, these batch files will not run under DR DOS 5.

Warning   DR DOS 6 batch files written with the subroutine batch subcommands will not run under MS DOS and will not compile with most batch file compilers.

The four subroutine batch subcommands are as follows:

EXIt	Causes a batch file to immediately terminate. This is useful in any DR DOS 6 batch file where it can replace the GOTO END commands.
GOSUB	Turns control over to a subroutine with the name that follows the GOSUB command. The subroutine must be included inside the batch file and marked with a label giving the name of the subroutine. Subroutine labels are assigned identically to the labels used with the GOTO command.
RETURN	Marks the end of a subroutine and causes control to return to the line in the batch file immediately following the GOSUB command.

SWITCH Allows the user to select the subroutine to jump to from the command line.

Only GOSUB and RETURN are needed to bundle a subroutine within a batch file. The EXIT command lets you skip a lot of extra GOTO END commands, so it's useful. The SWITCH command is useful for developing menus and is covered in Chapter 29.

The modified version of TOA-3.BAT—now called TOA-4.BAT—is shown here:

```
@ECHO OFF
:TOP
    IF (%1)==() EXIT
    IF (%1)==(/?) GOTO HELP
    GOSUB SUB
    SHIFT
GOTO TOP

:HELP
    ECHO This Batch File Requires You To Enter Filenames
    ECHO Without The Extension. For Each Name, It Erases
    ECHO The Associated .BAT File And Then Copies The
    ECHO Associated .DOC And .CMP Files To The A Drive
EXIT

:SUB
    IF NOT EXIST %1.BAK ECHO File Not Modified—Not Copied
    IF NOT EXIST %1.BAK EXIT

IF NOT EXIST %1.DOC ECHO %1.DOC File Not Found
    IF NOT EXIST %1.DOC EXIT

    DEL %1.BAK
    IF EXIST %1.CMP XCOPY %1.CMP A:
    XCOPY %1.DOC A:

    IF ERRORLEVEL 1 ECHO %1.DOC Not Copied Successfully
    IF ERRORLEVEL 1 EXIT
RETURN
```

In order to help you understand the subroutine commands used in TOA-4.BAT, Fig. 22-2 shows a line-by-line explanation of TOA-4.BAT.

One of the commands used in TOA-4.BAT is EXIT. Under DR DOS 6, this causes the batch file to immediately terminate. This command can be easily simulated under DR DOS 5 and all versions of MS DOS. Simply create a 0-length file called EXIT.BAT in your batch subdirectory. When the batch file issues EXIT, it will run EXIT.BAT. Because EXIT.BAT is run without CALL, control does not return to the original batch file. EXIT.BAT— because it has no commands—will run quickly.

The MS DOS-compatible approach 2:
Simulate the subroutine commands

The DR DOS GOSUB and RETURN commands are an excellent way to develop subroutines—but only if there is no chance of your needing to run the resulting batch file on

Batch File Line	Explanation
`@ECHO OFF`	Turn command-echoing off.

`REM NAME:      TOA-4.BAT`
`REM PURPOSE: Copy .CMP And .DOC Files To A Drive`
`REM           While Deleting .BAK Files`
`REM           This Version Uses A Subroutine Within`
`REM           Itself`
`REM VERSION: 1.00`
`REM DATE:     May 12, 1992`
	Documentation remarks.

`:TOP`	Label marking the top of a loop that is used to loop through all the replaceable parameters.
`    IF (%1)==() EXIT`	Once there are no more replaceable parameters, use the DR DOS 6 EXIT command to terminate the batch file.
`    IF (%1)==(/?) GOTO HELP`	Jump to a help display section when the user requests help with /? as the first replaceable parameter.
`    GOSUB SUB`	At this point, %1 exists and is not a /?, so jump to a subroutine to process the files.
`    SHIFT`	Move all the replaceable parameters down one level.
`GOTO TOP`	Continue looping.

22-2 TOA-4.BAT uses subroutine batch subcommands specific to DR DOS 6 to easily include the subroutine within the original batch file.

Batch File Line	Explanation
`:HELP`	Label marking the top of a section to display help when the user requests if from the command line.

`ECHO This Batch File Requires You To Enter`
`ECHO Names Without The Extension. For Each Name,`
`ECHO It Erases The Associated .BAT File And Then`
`ECHO Copies The Associated .DOC And .CMP Files`
`ECHO To The A Drive`
	Display the help information.

`EXIT`	Use the DR DOS 6 EXIT command to terminate the batch file.
`:SUB`	Label used to mark the beginning of a subroutine named SUB.

`IF NOT EXIST %1.BAK ECHO File Not Modified--`
`    Not Copied`
`IF NOT EXIST %1.BAK EXIT`
	If the file specified by the user has not been modified, display an error message and exit the batch file.

`IF NOT EXIST %1.DOC ECHO %1.DOC File Not Found` `IF NOT EXIST %1.DOC EXIT`	If the file specified by the user does not exist, display an error message and exit the batch file.
`DEL %1.BAK`	Delete the .BAK file. The batch file tested above to be sure this exists so an If-test is not needed here.
`IF EXIST %1.CMP XCOPY %1.CMP A:`	If the .CMP file exists, copy it to the A rive. Not all .DOC files will have .CMP files, so if it's missing, no error condition is generated.

22-2 Continued.

184 *Advanced batch file topics*

Batch File Line	Explanation
`XCOPY %1.DOC A:`	Copy the .DOC file to the A drive using XCOPY to allow for ERRORLEVEL testing.

`IF ERRORLEVEL 1 ECHO %1.DOC Not Copied`
`        Successfully`
`IF ERRORLEVEL 1 EXIT`
	If there was a problem copying the file, display an error message and exit the batch file.

`RETURN`	Exit the subroutine and return control to the batch file.

22-2 Continued.

an MS DOS machine. However, it is possible to "simulate" these commands under MS DOS or DR DOS 5 using environmental variables. The trick is remembering that MS or DR DOS can run environmental variables as commands.

To begin with, if we create an environmental variable named GOSUB containing "GOTO", then the command %GOSUB% SUB1 under MS DOS is the same as the command GOSUB SUB1 under DR DOS 6. If we then add a :BACK1 label on the line following our new GOSUB command and create an environmental variable named RETURN containing "GOTO BACK1" then the command %RETURN% under MS DOS is the same as the command RETURN under DR DOS 6.

Figure 22-3 shows MSDRSUB.BAT, a batch file that uses this approach to run three subroutines. Notice how similar it looks to a DR DOS 6 batch file that performs the same task. Most batch file compilers do not support environmental variables as commands, so the resulting batch files cannot be compiled.

Batch File Line	Explanation
`@ECHO OFF`	Turn command-echoing off.

`REM NAME:     MSDRSUB.BAT`
`REM PURPOSE: Show DR DOS-Line Subroutines`
`REM VERSION: 1.00`
`REM DATE:    May 28, 1992`
	Documentation remarks.

`NEEDHELP %0 %1`	Use the NeedHelp utility program to check and see if the user started the batch file with a /? switch.

22-3 MSDRSUB.BAT simulates DR DOS 6 subroutine batch subcommands using environmental variables under MS DOS.

Batch File Line	Explanation
IF ERRORLEVEL 1 GOTO HELP	If the user requested help, jump to a special section to display that information.
SET GOSUB=GOTO SET RETURN=GOTO BACK1	Create two environmental variables. The first is used as a command to jump to a subroutine and the second is used to tell the subroutine where to return to.
%GOSUB% SUB1	Jump to the subroutine by using the environmental variable as a command.
:BACK1	Label marking the return point for the subroutine.
ECHO Back In Main Program	Tell the user what is happening.
SET GOSUB=GOTO SUB2 SET RETURN=GOTO BACK2	Create two more subroutine environmental variables.
%GOSUB% SUB2	Jump to the subroutine by using the environmental variable as a command.
:BACK2	Label marking the return point for the subroutine.
ECHO Back In Main Program	Tell the user what is happening.
SET GOSUB=GOTO SUB3 SET RETURN=GOTO BACK3	Create two more subroutine environmental variables.
%GOSUB% SUB3	Jump to the subroutine by using the environmental variable as a command.
:BACK3	Label marking the return point for the subroutine.
ECHO Back In Main Program	Tell the user what is happening.
GOTO END	Exit the batch file.
:SUB1	Label marking the top of the first subroutine.
ECHO In Subroutine 1	Tell the user what is happening.

22-3 Continued.

Batch File Line	Explanation
%RETURN%	Exit the subroutine and return to the appropriate portion of the main batch file by using the environmental variable as a command.
:SUB2	Label marking the top of the second subroutine.
ECHO In Subroutine 2	Tell the user what is happening.
%RETURN%	Exit the subroutine.
:SUB3	Label marking the top of the third subroutine.
ECHO In Subroutine 3	Tell the user what is happening.
%RETURN%	Exit the batch file.

:HELP
   ECHO Shows MS DOS Compatible Subroutines
   ECHO That Look Like DR DOS Subroutines
GOTO END
	Display a help screen and exit the batch file when the user requests help.

:END	Label marking the end of the batch file.
SET GOSUB= SET RETURN=	Delete these environmental variables before exiting.

22-3 Continued.

Conclusion

If you are writing a subroutine that can possibly be called by more than one batch file, then it makes a lot of sense to create that subroutine as a stand-alone batch file. That way, all the batch files can access that single subroutine. If the subroutine will only be used by one batch file, then it makes more sense to create that subroutine as part of the original batch file. Unless you are certain the batch file will never need to be compiled or run on an MS DOS machine, you should probably avoid the DR DOS 6 subroutine batch subcommands and use the approach outlined here that will work for both MS and DR DOS.

Summary

A subroutine is reusable code that one or more batch files can access when needed to perform some specific function.

Subroutines can be stored as separate batch files and run with the CALL command.

Storing subroutines as stand-alone batch files is the easiest way to write and debug subroutines; but it takes up more disk space and you must remember to provide all the subroutines when you give a batch file to another user.

When using the CALL command to access another batch file, that called batch file does not have access to the replaceable parameters of the original batch file, so it must be passed any information it needs.

It's important that stand-alone batch file subroutines protect themselves from being run by users from the command line. The safest form of protection is to test for a specific replaceable parameter provided by the batch file that is supposed to call the subroutine batch file.

Storing the subroutine inside the original batch file saves space and makes it easier to transport the batch file, but it also makes the resulting batch file more complex.

Subroutines can be stored inside the original batch file in two ways while remaining compatible with MS DOS and batch file compilers: by using a series of If-tests to direct the batch file to the appropriate location each time it starts, and by using a replaceable parameter as a flag when calling the batch file as a subroutine.

The DR DOS 6 GOSUB and RETURN commands make it easy to include subroutines inside the original batch file but results in batch files that are not compatible with MS DOS or most batch file compilers.

The EXIT command causes a DR DOS 6 batch file to immediately terminate execution but results in batch files that are not compatible with MS DOS or most batch file compilers.

DR DOS 6 subroutine batch subcommands can be simulated under MS DOS using environmental variables.

23

When batch files don't work

By now, you should have a good understanding of the basics of writing and using batch files. You should be able to create a batch file that uses standard DR DOS commands as well as batch-specific commands and even some Batcmd commands. You should also know how to use replaceable parameters and If-tests to control the flow of the batch file. As you begin to use this knowledge in your computing, however, you're going to occasionally have a batch file that doesn't work properly—so you need to know what to do.

If your batch file is in a loop or doesn't appear to be doing anything, hit ^C or ^Break. This should stop the batch file and give you a "Halt batch process (Y/N)?" prompt. Answer Y for yes and press Enter. This is the only way to stop a batch file. If it doesn't work, you'll have to reboot. Once you get it stopped, you need to locate the problem. You can list the file on screen with the command:

TYPE FILE.BAT

However, you'll need to use Editor to make changes, so you might as well load it into Editor to begin with.

While it is not possible to give you a checklist of everything you should do when your batch file fails, what follows is a list of what I've found to be the most common troubleshooting approaches I've found useful.

Possible error messages

If you are lucky, the operating system will tell you why your batch file is not working properly. However, the message is likely to be cryptic and difficult to understand. Listed next are some of the error messages you are likely to see, along with their causes and possible solutions. The wording sometimes changes slightly between different versions and brands of DOS, so be sure to check to messages similar to the ones you are getting and not just for an exact match.

Syntax Error

This is the nastiest error to deal with because it gives you so little information. Generally, a command like an If-test is using the wrong syntax. The solution is to turn command echoing on so you can see which line is the problem line and then review the syntax for that command to see where the problem is. Far and away, the two most common problems here are using a single equal sign for the If-test and testing a replaceable parameter with a test like

    IF %1==A

without first making sure the replaceable parameter has a value. You can avoid this error by always surrounding the replaceable parameter you are testing and the test value with parentheses, so there is never a nul value on either side of the test. Thus, this test should be rewritten as

    F (%1)==(A)

Bad Command Or Filename
Command Or Filename Not Recognized

The batch file is trying to run a program that is not in the current subdirectory or path. Usually, this is caused by misspelling the name of a program or batch subcommand or by forgetting to change subdirectories or drives before running a program from a subdirectory not in your path. The solution is to verify the spelling of the program or batch subcommand or make sure the batch file changes to the proper drive and subdirectory. You should always have a batch file change to the proper drive before changing to a subdirectory because you never know for sure if the user has changed drives before running the batch file.

Label ... Not Found

The batch file issued a GOTO command, but the label listed after GOTO does not exist. The solution is to rewrite the batch file to include the specified label.

Abort, Retry, Ignore, Fail?
Abort, Ignore, Retry
Abort, Retry, Fail
Data Error
Drive Not Ready
Physical Media Error
Sector Not Found

The batch file or a program being run by the batch file is unable to read from or write to the drive it is trying to use. The most common cause is trying to read from or write to a floppy disk drive without a diskette in it, without the drive door shut, or with an unformatted diskette in the drive. The second most common cause is a defective disk or diskette.

If you forgot to insert a diskette, go ahead and insert it and press Retry. However, you should never change disks while one is being read from or written to. For any other problem, press Fail and troubleshoot from the operating system. If you have a defective diskette, replace it. If you have a defective hard disk, you can generally correct the problem with a utility program like the Norton Utilities or PC Tools.

Access Denied
Access Denied For File
Access Denied On Source Directory
Access To File ... Denied

The file is either a read-only file or a password-protected file. If the file is read-only and you want to modify it, you must change the read-only flag with the ATTRIB command. If the file is password-protected, you must access the file by entering its name followed by a semicolon and the password.

Batch File Missing
Batch file ... missing retry [Y/N]?

This is usually an MS DOS error message. MS DOS only reads batch files one line at a time. After executing that line, it goes back to the batch file to read the next line. When MS DOS cannot find the batch file to read the next line, you get this error message.

The most common cause of this error message is a batch file that deletes itself. For example, BATCH.BAT

```
@ECHO OFF
DEL BATCH.BAT
DIR
```

will generate this error message because when MS DOS reads the DEL BATCH.BAT line, it knows there is another line; but after deleting the batch file, it goes back to read the next line and the batch file is not there. Other less common reasons for this error message are batch files that rename themselves, substituting or unsubstituting drives containing the batch file, or swapping a floppy disk that contains the batch file for a different disk.

The solution is simple. Review the logic of the batch file and make sure that nothing in the batch file causes the operating system to "lose" the batch file. It's usually easy to find the problem line. Just turn command echoing on and look to see which is the last line the batch file executes; that's generally the problem line.

If you want a batch file to delete itself, you can have it do so without generating this error message; however, because the resulting batch file only runs once, it's usually easier to just ignore the error message. In order for the operating system to delete the batch file without complaining about it being missing, absolutely nothing must follow the DEL BATCH.BAT command—not even a return. The easiest way to make sure this is the case is to enter the batch file from the command line via the COPY CON BATCH.BAT command

and press F6 or ^ Z immediately after entering DEL BATCH.BAT *without* pressing Return first.

You will not see this error message as often under DR DOS 5 or 6, and BATCH.BAT will run properly. Unlike MS DOS, DR DOS reads ahead for a few lines in the batch file and stores that information, so the DIR command in BATCH.BAT would be preread and executed properly. If several commands follow the command to delete the batch file, DR DOS reads and executes as many of them as it can and generally ignores the rest. Occasionally, that results in a "Command or Filename Not Recognized" error message because DR DOS did not read in an entire command so instead of CHKDSK, it tried to execute CHKD.

Batch Files Nested Too Deep

One batch file can call another with CALL. When that happens, the second batch file is said to be nested inside the first. That second batch file can then call a third, and so on. If these batch files become nested too deeply, they abort with the "Batch Files Nested Too Deep" error message. The solution is to reduce the number of nested batch files you have.

Not Enough Memory
Not Enough Memory For …
Not Enough Memory To …

The batch file is trying to load a program but there is not enough memory to run that program. The solution is to increase available memory by removing unnecessary device drivers or memory resident software.

Not Ready Error

The device the batch file is trying to access (e.g. LPT1, CON or COM1) is not ready, the disk drive is not ready to use, the hard disk has failed. For non-drive devices, try rebooting. If the problem continues, verify that the requested device is actually installed. If it is, the computer needs to be repaired. For a disk drive, try inserting a new and formatted disk and making sure the drive door is shut. For a hard disk, try using a utility program like PC Tools or the Norton Utilities to repair the drive. If you do not have experience in this area, get help.

Warning Repairing a defective disk can be difficult. If you are not sure what you are doing, get experienced help.

Cannot Start Command, Exiting
No Free File Handles/Cannot Start Command, Exiting
Too Many Files Open
Too Many Open Files

The operating system is trying to open more files than is allowed. This generally happens when running a second batch file with the command rather than using CALL. The solution is to either rewrite the batch file or increase the values for the FILE switch in the CONFIG.SYS file and reboot.

Environment Full

The batch file is trying to create an environmental variable but doesn't have enough room. The solution is to either delete unwanted environmental variables or expand the size of the environment.

Environment Error

DR DOS cannot find the current environment. The only solution is to reboot.

Filename Too Long

DR DOS only supports filenames of eight characters or less and extensions of three characters or less. The solution is to shorten the filename to an acceptable length.

Disk Full

The batch file is trying to COPY or otherwise write to a disk that either has no more room or (when writing/copying to the root directory) has no more room in the file allocation table [FAT] for directory entries. The solution is to erase unwanted files.

Write Protect Error

The diskette the batch file or application is trying to write to is write-protected. The solution is to remove the write-protection.

File Sharing Conflict

This error only occurs on a network. The action the batch file or application running from within the batch file conflicts with actions of another network user. For example, trying to delete a file that is in use by another user. The solution is to rewrite the batch file to avoid conflicting with other users.

On Or Off Parameter Required

The batch file issued a BREAK followed by something other than an On/Off switch. These two switches, or using BREAK by itself, are the only three valid ways of issuing a BREAK command. The solution is to rewrite the batch file to use BREAK properly.

Invalid Path Or Path Not Found
Invalid Path Specified: Check Path

The batch file has issued a command that required DR DOS to search the path. While searching the path, DR DOS found an invalid entry in the path. The solution is to make sure your path contains only valid subdirectories.

Other

Many other error messages are possible because any application your batch file runs can itself trigger an error message from the operating system. In addition, the applications the batch file is running might themselves display an error message. When you see an error message you do not recognize while your batch file is running, check the back of your DR DOS manual to see if it is listed there along with possible solutions. If not, check the manual for the software your batch file is currently running to see if it lists that error message and possible solutions.

Check the spelling

The next thing to check is the spelling. It's very easy to make a spelling error, especially when you're copying the file from the console. Sometimes it is visually difficult to spot a word that is slightly misspelled, like Eche for Echo. I use Microsoft Word, a processor that lets you specify your own dictionaries, so I've developed a dictionary of just batch commands and the common DR DOS commands and messages I use in batch files. When I think a typo or spelling error might exist, I run the batch file through the spelling checker in Word using this dictionary. If your dictionary allows custom dictionaries, you might try the same thing.

If your word processor does not allow custom dictionaries or you do not want to go through the trouble of creating one, you might try an old proofreading trick. When reading anything forwards, you tend to get interested in the content and anticipate the words or spelling that should be there. That makes it harder to catch errors. The solution is to read backwards, or in the case of batch files, where lines usually cannot be split up, from the last line to the first. While you will not be able to follow the logic (that's the idea), you will be much more likely to spot syntax errors.

Look closer

Sometimes, it's hard to follow the execution of a batch file. With command echoing turned off and a fast computer, it can be very hard to follow your batch files as they run. When I have this problem, I remove the @ECHO OFF line and slow my computer down to its slowest speed before running the batch file. If the commands still go by too fast, I load Windows and run the batch file from inside Windows. Usually, that slows down the batch file enough so I can watch it.

Isolate the problem

As you begin taking a closer look at your batch file, you will most likely find that most of it runs fine but breaks down at some particular point. Once I've isolated the problem to a particular section of the batch file, I turn off command echoing for the rest of the batch file and just turn it on for that section by using an ECHO ON command at the beginning of the section and an @ECHO OFF at the end. I also insert several PAUSE commands in the problem section so that I can take my time examining the information on the screen while the problem section runs.

Split out the problem section

Occasionally, a particular section just seems so wrong that nothing I do seems to make it work right. When that happens, I remove the problem section and make it a separate batch file. That way, I can run it by itself—supplying the inputs it needs—without the rest of the batch file getting in the way. I can add ECHO commands to see the values of variables and any number of PAUSE commands to review the screen. When I finally get this batch file working, I merge it back into the original batch file.

Diagram the logic

When you have a problem involving logic testing, the best solution to resolving the problem is to draw a "map" of the logic of the batch file. That way, you can make sure all the paths end up where they should and none of them end up "dangling" without reaching a proper conclusion. It's been my experience that these dangling paths are one of the major sources of logic errors. Figures 23-1 and 23-2 show a map of the logic of COPYTHE2.BAT, the solution to Problem 9 in Chapter 24.

Put it aside for a while

Sometimes, when nothing seems to work, the best thing you can do is put the batch file aside for a while and come back to it. A number of times, I've put aside a batch file with what seemed to be an impossible task only to come back to it later and see an obvious problem. This approach works for many problems, not just batch files.

Start over

If all else fails, the final solution is to erase the problem batch file or batch file segment and start over. Often, this second attempt will turn out better than the first because you have experience with the problem already.

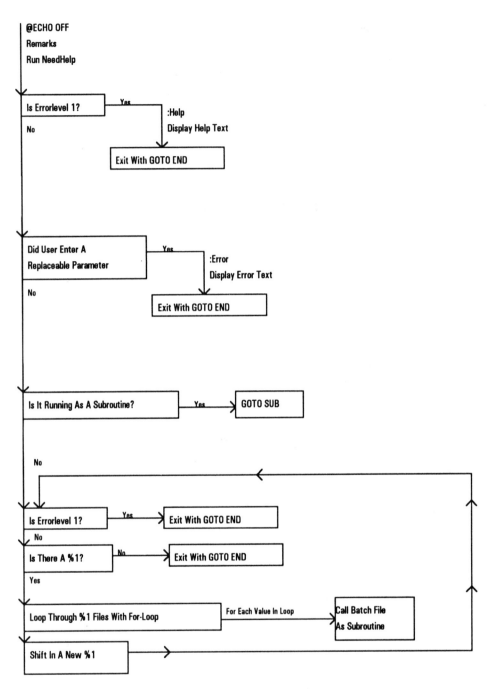

@ECHO OFF
Remarks
Run NeedHelp

Is Errorlevel 1? — Yes →
No

:Help
Display Help Text

Exit With GOTO END

Did User Enter A Replaceable Parameter — Yes →
No

:Error
Display Error Text

Exit With GOTO END

Is It Running As A Subroutine? — Yes → GOTO SUB
No

Is Errorlevel 1? — Yes → Exit With GOTO END
No

Is There A %1? — No → Exit With GOTO END
Yes

Loop Through %1 Files With For-Loop — For Each Value In Loop → Call Batch File As Subroutine

Shift In A New %1

23-1 A diagram of the logic of the main portion of COPYTHE2.BAT.

196 *Advanced batch file topics*

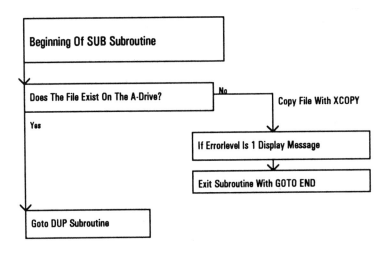

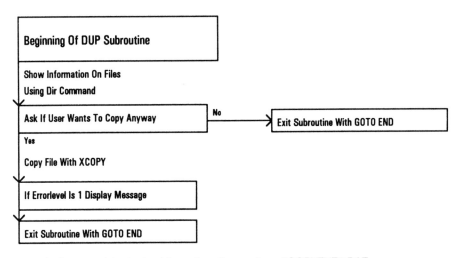

23-2 A diagram of the logic of the subroutine portion of COPYTHE2.BAT.

Summary

If your batch file generates an error message, that message can help you find the problem with your batch file.

If your batch file appears to lock up, you can often regain control by pressing Ctrl-Break.

After looking for error messages, the next thing to check when a batch file does not work is to check the spelling of the commands.

When checking the spelling does not resolve the problem, try turning command echoing on and adding PAUSE commands to watch command execution closer.

When a closer review does not resolve the problem, try isolating the problem portion of the batch file into a separate batch file.

When the problem with a batch file involves logic testing, try drawing a map of the logic.

As a last resort, try putting the problem batch file aside for a while or even starting over.

_____24_____
Applications and problems

We've covered a tremendous amount of advanced material, so we should take a few moments and make sure you're up to speed before we continue. What follows are three quick problems. Take a few moments and try to figure them out. It's important that you have the skills necessary to solve these problems before you go on; otherwise, you will find the new material difficult.

Problem 7

A friend of yours is always copying files between two different machines. Several times, she has made the mistake of copying a file to a floppy disk when another version of that very file was already on the floppy disk. She has asked you to write a batch file to copy all the files she specifies on the command line to the A drive—but only if the file does not already exist on the A drive.

    The complete file name with extension will be provided on the command line, so no assumptions about the name should be made. When wildcards are used, the batch file should copy all the files to the A drive that do not exist there while skipping the ones already on the A drive. Also, keep the user informed of the process. Finally, one of the two machines she uses is an MS DOS machine, so do not use any DR DOS-specific commands.

Problem 8

You are working with a program that you do not normally use, and you find yourself entering the same long command over and over. You will only be using this program for a few weeks, so you first elected not to construct a batch file to issue this one command. However, you've run into this circumstance before, so you change your mind and decide to write a batch file to handle it.

    When you run this new batch file with a command after its name, the batch file will store that command in the environment and then run it. When you run the batch file alone, it will issue the command stored in the environment. Some of your commands are very long, so you want to avoid limiting the commands to nine pieces, corresponding to %1–%9. You do have a lot of free environmental space so you are not worried about running out.

Problem 9

Your friend from Problem 7 likes your batch file but asks you for a modification. Sometimes, she wants to overwrite the file on the disk with the one on the hard disk. Rather than just skipping all the files that exist on the floppy disk, she wants the batch file to show her information on both versions and ask her what to do.

Answers

You can tackle each of these problems in a number of ways. My solutions are shown in Appendix C in the back of the book. It is not important that you match my answers; if you developed a working solution to the problem, your solution is just as good as mine and maybe even better.

PART FIVE
Improving batch files with software

As useful as batch files are, software can make them even more useful. We have already looked at several handy utilities. This section looks at three major software packages that can make your batch files even more useful.

Chapter 25: Batcmd: New batch file commands. In order to write really powerful batch files, you need a batch file utility to provide a few commands that DR DOS does not offer. This book includes a very powerful batch utility called Batch Commands, or Batcmd for short. You have already seen some of its power from Chapter 19. This chapter documents the full power of Batcmd.

Chapter 26: Builder and Builder Lite. When you decide that batch files are not powerful enough for your needs, the next step up is a batch file compiler. One of the most powerful and easy-to-use batch file compilers available is Builder from hyperkinetix. If you want to try a less powerful version, hyperkinetix, TAB Books and myself have combined to bring you Builder Lite.

Chapter 27: Dual Boot Utility. If you have not decided for sure to convert to DR DOS or if you have to maintain batch files that will run under both MS and DR DOS, then you will appreciate this nice utility from Keith Ledbetter. It lets you keep DR DOS 6 and MS DOS 5 on one hard disk and boot from either one easily without using floppy disks! Not only that, it is easy to install.

25

Batcmd: New batch file commands

When I started writing about batch files, I was very frustrated by their inability to perform some of the simplest tasks, like asking the user a question. However, many utilities are now available to get around the limitations of batch files—so many, in fact, that I was able to write a whole book describing many of them.

That still left me with the problem of writing about batch files that needed one or more of these utilities. I could not very well dictate which ones for the reader to buy; and without knowing what utilities the reader already had, writing a batch file any reader could use was impossible. So I sat down and designed a batch file utility that would perform those functions I needed in my batch books.

Once I had designed the program, I turned that design over to Doug Amaral of hyperkinetix. (hyperkinetix is the company that wrote Builder and Builder Lite, two batch file compilers.) Doug kindly wrote Batcmd (short for "Batch Commands") especially for my batch file books. Thanks, Doug!

Batcmd is free with the book, so I expect that most of you will end up using it. However, keep in mind that, with all of these batch files, you can substitute any other batch utility that performs the same function. You do not have to use Batcmd.

Using Batcmd

The general format of the command is

BATCMD *Keyword Prompt*

where *Keyword* is a two-letter command abbreviation that tells Batcmd what to do and *Prompt* is an optional message to the user what information to enter. The *Prompt* can contain multiple words and should *not* be enclosed in quotation marks. A few of the commands require additional information and are explained later under the specific command discussion.

Most of the Batcmd keywords cause Batcmd to either get information from the user or from the computer. In most cases, that information is passed back to the batch file through the ERRORLEVEL.

Next comes a description of each of the Batcmd commands.

AD (Add 1 To MATH Environmental Variable)

This command adds one to the contents of the MATH environmental variable. If the MATH environmental variable does not exist, Batcmd displays an error message and does nothing. If MATH exists but contains something other than a number, its contents are treated as though they were a 0. As a result, its value is replaced with a 1 (0 + 1).

 The AD command was not included in Batcmd to give batch files mathematical power. In fact, it would be difficult to perform anything other than the simplest math via the AD command. Rather, the AD command was added to allow your batch files to go through loops a specific number of times. For example, you might ask the user for a password with the GE and use the AD command to make sure the user only gets three attempts at the password.

BE (Beep The Speaker)

This command beeps the speaker. If the command is entered as BATCMD BE, then it beeps the speaker once. If it is entered as BATCMD BE *n*, then it will beep the speaker *n* times. Once started, this beeping cannot be aborted without rebooting so Batcmd limits *n* to 99 or less. If you have a specific need to beep the speaker more than 99 times, you can repeatedly run BATCMD BE *n* or include it in a For-loop.

BS (Blank The Screen)

This command clears the screen, identically to the DR DOS CLS command. However, if you enter colors after the command, it clears the screen to those colors. The command format is BATCMD BS *Foreground Background*. Table 25-1 shows the color numbers that can be used with the BS command. All sixteen numbers can be used for the foreground color, but only the first eight can be used for the background color.

Table 25-1 The colors that can be used with the BATCMD BS **command.**

Number	Color	Number	Color
0	Black	8	Gray
1	Blue	9	Bright Blue
2	Green	10	Bright Green
3	Cyan	11	Bright Cyan
4	Red	12	Bright Red
5	Magenta	13	Bright Magenta
6	Brown	14	Yellow
7	White	15	Bright White

CC (Check Conventional Memory)

This command checks to see how much conventional memory is available and returns through ERRORLEVEL the number of 32K blocks; an ERRORLEVEL value of 10 would indicate that 320K is free. You would use this command to make sure enough memory was available if a program being run by a batch file was particularly sensitive to available memory. Keep in mind that the available memory is reduced by the memory used by Batcmd before this measurement is made.

CE (Check Environmental Memory)

This command checks to see how much environmental space is free and returns through ERRORLEVEL the number of free bytes. Because ERRORLEVEL is limited to an integer from 0 to 255, this command returns 255 for any environment where the free environmental space exceeds 255 bytes. This is a good way for batch files that depend on the environment to check before running to make sure space is available. In particular, you might want to use the CE command before the GE command if the information GE is storing in the environment is critical.

CH (Check Number of Hard Drives)

This command checks to see how many hard drives are installed. It returns a 0 if there are no hard drives; otherwise, it sets ERRORLEVEL equal to the number of hard drives. This command checks the number of *physical* hard drives, not the number of partitions. Thus, a 100M drive that is partitioned into three 32M partitions and a fourth 4M partition will still count as one physical drive to Batcmd. It does not include any CD ROM drives or other nonstandard drives in the calculation.

CL (Check LIM Memory)

This command checks to see how much LIM memory is free and returns with an ERRORLEVEL equal to the number of 32K blocks of expanded memory. This is useful as a check prior to running a program that requires a minimum amount of LIM memory.

CM (Check Mouse)

This command sets ERRORLEVEL to 1 if it finds a mouse and to a 0 otherwise. Some older programs need a special command line switch in order to use a mouse; this command lets the batch file check for the presence of a mouse when it runs rather than forcing the batch file to behave in a certain fashion.

CS (Check Space)

This command checks to see how much free space is available on a drive and returns the number of 32K blocks of free space in ERRORLEVEL. When free space exceeds 255*32K or 8160K, it returns 255. If the command is entered as BATCMD CS, it uses the default drive. If the command is entered as BATCMD CS drive, then it checks the amount of free space on the specified drive. This command is especially useful before running a database program where you will be working with large files because many database programs create a lot of working files on the disk.

EX (Exit)

This command is entered as BATCMD EX n, where n is a number from 0 to 255. Batcmd sets the ERRORLEVEL to the number specified and exits. If no number is specified, Batcmd sets ERRORLEVEL to 0. If a fractional number is specified, Batcmd uses only the integer portion of the number, so BATCMD EX 33.3 would result in an ERRORLEVEL value of 33. If a number over 255 is specified, 256 is repeatedly subtracted from the specified number until the resulting number falls between 0 and 255, the only valid values for ERROR-LEVEL. If a negative number is specified, 256 is repeatedly added to the specified number until the resulting number is between 0 and 255.

One use for this command is to give your batch files the ability to report their results via the ERRORLEVEL, just as programs do. Another use is to reset the ERRORLEVEL to 0. Sometimes when working with subroutines, it is useful to put ERRORLEVEL- testing at the top of a loop—as COPYTHIS.BAT (the solution to Problem 7 in Chapter 24) does. However, this can cause problems if a program run before this batch file has set ERRORLEVEL because the first time through the loop, COPYTHIS.BAT has not yet run XCOPY, so ERRORLEVEL still contains the value from the last program. Adding a BATCMD EX 0 to the top of any batch file using ERRORLEVEL testing avoids this problem.

GE (Get To Environment)

This command accepts a multi-character response from the user and stores it in the master copy of the environment under the variable BATCMD. This command will display a prompt if one is entered on the command line after the GE.

This command limits user inputs to 65 characters and will stop accepting keystrokes when that limit is reached. If there is inadequate free environmental space to store the response in the environment, the response is lost and nothing is stored in the environment.

Normally, a program like Batcmd does not have access to the master copy of the environment, so if Batcmd were to just place the results in its copy of the environment, that information would be lost as soon as Batcmd terminated. That is clearly not what we want. Batcmd avoids the problem by searching through all the computer memory to find the master copy of the environment. It then makes it changes there.

GF (Get From List)

This command accepts a keystroke from the user only when that keystroke is on the list of acceptable keystrokes. The format of the command is BATCMD GF *List Prompt*, where *List* is a listing of all valid keystrokes without spaces between them and *Prompt* is the user message to display. The list of keystrokes is case-sensitive, so in order to accept only A to C from the user in either case, the command would have to be entered as BATCMD GF AaBbCc *Prompt*.

If the user enters an invalid keystroke, Batcmd beeps and continues waiting for a valid keystroke. Once the user enters a valid keystroke, Batcmd sets ERRORLEVEL to that keystroke's position in the list. So, for the previous example, if the user entered B, the ERRORLEVEL would be set to 3 because the capital B is the third character in the list.

Batcmd checks the list from right to left. That is only an issue if you use duplicates in the list. If your list was Ronny, then n would be reported via an ERRORLEVEL of 4 and *not* 3 because the n in the fourth position was the first lowercase n encountered moving right to left.

This approach is designed for those occasions when you have a number of different selections for the user to pick from. If you have fewer selections, then having the user pick a number would be a better choice. At first glance, you might think that treating upper- and lowercase letters separately would double the number of If-tests in the batch file if you want to make the batch file case-insensitive. That is not the case. Using the BATCMD GF AaBbCc *Prompt* shown earlier, we know ERRORLEVEL will be 1–6 and we want to treat upper- and lowercase the same. The following batch file segment does that:

```
BATCMD GF AaBbCc
IF ERRORLEVEL 5 GOTO C
IF ERRORLEVEL 3 GOTO B
IF ERRORLEVEL 1 GOTO A
```

We want to jump to the section C when ERRORLEVEL is 5–6, and because the IF ERRORLEVEL 5 statement is a greater-than-or-equal test and no values exceed 6, it handles both cases automatically. Once 5–6 have been eliminated, the IF ERRORLEVEL 3 statement tests for 3–4, which is B. The last statement could be replaced with just a GOTO A because everything else has been eliminated; I simply used an If-test for consistency's sake.

Of course, you can test for each capitalization separately if you need to. The following example illustrates that:

```
BATCMD GF AaBbCc
IF ERRORLEVEL 6 GOTO LITTLEC
IF ERRORLEVEL 5 GOTO BIGC
IF ERRORLEVEL 4 GOTO LITTLEB
IF ERRORLEVEL 3 GOTO BIGB
IF ERRORLEVEL 2 GOTO LITTLEA
IF ERRORLEVEL 1 GOTO BIGA
```

GK (Get Key)

This command accepts any keystroke from the user and exits with the ERRORLEVEL set to the ASCII value of that keystroke. This command can display an optional prompt if it is included after the GK command.

Only very rarely will you need this tool. When you need to restrict entries, the GF option works better. The GF option also works better if you have less than 26 options because you can easily list all the letters. At 26 options, the GL is a better option because it handles getting just letters automatically. About the only time you will need this option is when you are doing something where you need to accept absolutely any keystroke from the user.

GL (Get Letter)

This command accepts any letter from the user and exits with the ERRORLEVEL set to 1 for an A, 2 for a B, and so on. If any other keystroke is entered, Batcmd beeps and continues waiting for a letter. This command can display an optional prompt if it is included after the command.

If you are designing a menu system where you want the user to be able to make a selection using any letter, this option is the best way to implement it. It's also the best approach when you have a lot of options you are willing to letter sequentially. Because the

ERRORLEVELs run sequentially from A, if your options stop at N (ERRORLEVEL 14), then you can test for an invalid response with a single If-test that tests for an ERRORLEVEL of 15 or higher.

However, if you want the user to use only a few of the letters or you want to pick-and-choose certain letters to use, then using the GF (get from list) option is a better approach than using this option and jumping back through the loop for invalid options.

GN (Get Number)

This command accepts any single-digit number from the user and exits with the ERROR-LEVEL set to that number. If any other keystroke is entered, Batcmd beeps and continues waiting for a number. This command can display an optional prompt if it is included after the command.

When you need for the user to select between just a few options, this might be the best approach. If you need fewer than 10, just start your options at 0 and go back through the prompting loop if the user enters a number that is too high. You can do this with just one If-test. For example, if your last option is number 6, then loop back through the options anytime ERRORLEVEL is 7 or higher.

GU (Get Uppercase Letter)

This command accepts only uppercase letters from the user. If the user enters a lowercase letter or any non-letter keystroke, Batcmd beeps and continues waiting for an uppercase letter. ERRORLEVEL is set to the ASCII value of the uppercase letter, so A is reported as 65, B is reported as 66, and so on. This command can display an optional prompt if it is included after the command. This is a specialized version of the GL (get letter) option. For most applications, the GL option is a more useful option.

PC (Position Cursor)

This command positions the cursor at the specified coordinates on the screen. The format of the command is BATCMD PC *row column*, where *row* is the row number to move the cursor to (1-24) and *column* is the column number to move the cursor to (1-80). If a non-integer row or column number is used, the fractional portion of the number is ignored. If a 0, negative number, or number outside the acceptable boundaries is used, Batcmd aborts with an error message and sets the ERRORLEVEL to 1.

This command replicates the ability of ANSI to position the cursor without needing ANSI. Being able to position the cursor can make it easier to draw complex screens and can help keep the screen uncluttered.

RB (Reboot The Computer)

This command performs a warm reboot of the computer, which can be useful if you are writing a batch file to change the configuration of the computer or as a way of aborting a password batch file after a specific number of attempts.

SD (Store Day)

This command stores the day of the month in ERRORLEVEL. If the date were March 21, BATCMD SD would set ERRORLEVEL to 21. This command—and the date and time commands that follow—are useful for performing specific tasks on a specific day. For example, you might perform an incremental backup every Friday from the AUTOEXEC .BAT and a full backup the first of every month.

SH (Store Hour)

This command stores the hour of the day, in twenty-four-hour format, in ERRORLEVEL. If the time is 6:30PM, BATCMD SH sets ERRORLEVEL to 18.

SL (Skip Line)

This command causes a batch file to skip a single line on the screen, just like echoing an Alt-255. While not needed too much in DR DOS—where echoing two spaces results in a blank line on the screen—it is very useful in MS DOS where echoing a blank line is more difficult or where a batch file must run under both DR and MS DOS.

SM (Store Minute)

This command stores the minute of the hour in ERRORLEVEL. If the time is 6:30PM, BATCMD SM sets ERRORLEVEL to 30.

SO (Store Month)

This command stores the month of the year in ERRORLEVEL. If the date is March 21, BATCMD SO would set ERRORLEVEL to 3.

SS (Store Second)

This command stores the second in ERRORLEVEL. Of course, this information changes rapidly, but ERRORLEVEL is only updated each time the command is run. If the time is 6:30:15, BATCMD SS sets ERRORLEVEL to 15.

SU (Subtract 1 from MATH Environmental Variable)

This command subtracts one from the contents of the Math environmental variable. If the Math environmental variable does not exist, Batcmd displays an error message and does nothing. If Math exists but contains something other than a number, its contents are treated as though they were a zero. Like the AD command discussed above, SU is designed for looping and not really for adding mathematical power to batch files.

SY (Store Year)

This command stores the last two digits of the year in ERRORLEVEL, so 1992 is stored as 92 and 2000 is stored as 0.

YN (Yes No)

This command accepts only a n- or y-keystroke in either upper- or lowercase. For an n, BATCMD YN sets ERRORLEVEL to 0; for a y, it sets ERRORLEVEL to 1.

This is probably the Batcmd option you will use the most. Many of the questions you will want to ask the user are things like "Do you really want to erase all these files? (Y/N)" or "This takes six hours, do you want to continue? (Y/N)," and using the YN option is so much nicer than using a PAUSE command and telling the user to press Ctrl-Break to stop the batch file. It also avoids bring up the "Halt Batch Process (Y/N)?" message and having to deal with the problem of DR DOS not processing a no response properly.

Summary

Table 25-2 shows a brief summary of the Batcmd keywords and their function.

Table 25-2   The Batcmd keywords.

Short command	Command name	Function
AD	ADd	Add 1 to the number stored in the MATH environmental variable.
BE	BEep	Beep the speaker.
BS	BlankScreen	Clear the screen, optionally using the colors specified after the BS command.
CC	CheckConventional	Return in 32K blocks the amount of free conventional memory.
CE	CheckEnvironmental	Return with an ERRORLEVEL equal to the amount of free environmental space up to 255 bytes, setting it to 255 for that amount and over.
CH	CheckHard	Return with an ERRORLEVEL 0 if no hard disk is installed; otherwise, set the ERRORLEVEL equal to the number of logical hard disk drives installed.
CL	CheckLim	Return with an ERRORLEVEL equal to the number of 32K blocks of expanded memory.
CM	CheckMouse	Return with an ERRORLEVEL equal of 1 if there is a mouse and a 0 otherwise.
CS	CheckSpace	Return with an ERRORLEVEL equal to the number of 32K blocks free on the specified drive. If no drive is specified, use the default.
EX	EXit	Set the ERRORLEVEL to the number specified after the EX and exit.
GE	GetEnvironment	Display an optional prmopt, accept a multi-character input from the user, and store it in the environment under the name BATCMD.
GF	GetFromlist	Display an optional prompt and accept an input only if it is contained in the list following the prompt; exit with an ERRORLEVEL equal to 1 for the first item in the list, 2 for the second item, and so on.
GK	GetKey	Display an optional prompt, accept any keystroke, and exit with the ASCII value of that keystroke.

Table 25-2. Continued

GL	GetLetter	Display an optional prompt, accept a letter, and exit with an ERRORLEVEL equal to the ASCII value of the letter. If the user presses any other keystroke, beep and continue waiting for a letter.
GN	GetNumber	Display an optional prompt, accept a single-digit number, and exit with an ERRORLEVEL equal to that number. If the user presses any other keystroke, beep and continue waiting for a number.
GU	GetUpper	Display an optional prompt, accept an uppercase letter, and exit with an ERRORLEVEL equal to the ASCII value of the letter. If the user presses a lowercase letter or any non-letter keystroke, beep and continue waiting for an uppercase letter.
PC	PositionCursor	Position the cursor on the row and column specified after the PC.
RB	ReBoot	Reboot the computer.
SD	StoreDay	Return with an ERRORLEVEL equal to the day of the month.
SH	ShowHour	Return with an ERRORLEVEL equal to the hour of the day, in 24-hour format.
SL	SkipLine	Skip one blank line on the screen.
SM	StoreMinute	Return with an ERRORLEVEL equal to the minute of the hour.
SO	StoremOnth	Return with an ERRORLEVEL equal to the month.
SS	StoreSecond	Return with an ERRORLEVEL equal to the second.
SU	SUbtract	Subtract 1 from the number stored in the MATH environmental variable.
SY	StoreYear	Return with an ERRORLEVEL equal to the last two digits of the year. If possible, have it work properly for 2000 and beyond.

SHOWGETS.BAT (look back at Fig. 19-1) illustrates using Batcmd to obtain information from the user and then acting on that information.

DOBATCMD.BAT (see Fig. 25-1) shows using most of the remaining commands in a batch file to obtain information from the computer.

Batch File Line	Explanation
`@ECHO OFF`	Turn command-echoing off.

`REM NAME:     DOBATCMD.BAT`
`REM PURPOSE: Illustrate Non-Input`
`REM          Batcmd Commands`
`REM VERSION: 1.00`
`REM DATE:    May 27, 1992`
	Documentation remarks.

`SET SPACE=`	The environmental variable Space contains ten spaces and is used several times to erase text from a particular line.
`BATCMD BS 15 1`	Run Batcmd and use the BS (Blank Screen) option to clear the screen to bright white on blue.
`ECHO Creating Math Environmental Variable`	Tell the user what is happening.
`SET MATH=0`	Create the MATH environmental variable.
`ECHO Will Now Count To Fifty`	Tell the user what is happening.
`PAUSE`	Pause the program until the user presses a key.
`BATCMD BS 13 1`	Use the BATCMD BS option to clear the screen to bright magenta on blue.
`:TOPAD`	Label marking the top of a loop.
`  BATCMD PC 12 40`	Use the BATCMD PC (Position Cursor) command to position the cursor on the screen.

25-1 DOBATCMD.BAT shows using most of the Batcmd commands not involved in obtaining information from the user.

Batch File Line	Explanation
ECHO %MATH%	Display the current value of the MATH environmental variable. Because the BATCMD PC option is used before this command each time, it always appears in the same location on the screen.
BATCMD AD	Use the BATCMD AD (Add) command to increment the MATH environmental variable by 1.
IF NOT %MATH%==51 GOTO TOPAD	Until MATH reaches 51, continue looping.
BATCMD PC 22 01	Position the cursor.
ECHO Now Will Count Down To Zero	Tell the user what is happening.
SET MATH=50	Reset MATH to 50 because the previous loop went past 50 to 51.
PAUSE	Pause the program until the user presses a key.
BATCMD BS 12 1	Clear the screen to bright red on blue.
:TOPSU	Label marking the top of a loop.
BATCMD PC 12 40	Position the cursor.
IF %MATH%==9 ECHO IF %MATH%==9 BATCMD PC 12 40	When counting down, this batch file has a problem going from 10 to 9 because the 9 is written over the 1 but the 0 remains on the screen, resulting in a 90 on the screen. These two lines correct the problem by echoing two blank spaces (Alt-255) when 9 is reached. This moves the cursor so it is also repositioned.

25-1 Continued.

Batch File Line	Explanation
`ECHO %MATH%`	Display the current value of the MATH variable.
`BATCMD SU`	Decrease the MATH variable by one using the BATCMD SU (Subtract) command.
`IF NOT %MATH%==0 GOTO TOPSU`	If the value of MATH has not yet reached 0, continue looping.
`PAUSE`	Pause the program until the user presses a key.
`SET MATH=`	Reset this environmental variable because it is no longer needed.
`BATCMD BS 15 1`	Clear the screen to bright white on blue.
`BATCMD PC 05 01`	Position the cursor.
`ECHO Beeping Speeker Five Times`	Tell the user what is happening.
`BATCMD BE 5`	Beep the speaker five times using the BATCMD BE (Beep) command.
`BATCMD PC 07 01`	Position the cursor.
`BATCMD CC`	Check available memory using the BATCMD CC (Check Conventional) command.
`CALL SAYERROR`	Run SAYERROR.BAT to store the ERRORLEVEL value in the environment under the name ERROR. Note that SAYERROR.BAT must be in the path for DOBATCMD.BAT to run properly.

25-1 Continued.

Batcmd: New batch file commands **213**

Batch File Line	Explanation
BATCMD PC 07 01	SAYERROR.BAT displays a single line of information on the line the cursor was positioned on with the BATCMD PC command. By repositioning the cursor on the same line, the ECHO command that follows overwrites the message from SAYERROR.BAT.
ECHO %ERROR% 32K Blocks of Conventional Memory	Display the results of the BATCMD CC command.
BATCMD PC 09 01	Position the cursor.
BATCMD CE	Check the amount of environmental memory using the BATCMD CE (Check Environmental) command.
CALL SAYERROR	Run SAYERROR.BAT to store the ERRORLEVEL in the environment.
BATCMD PC 09 01	Position the cursor.
ECHO %ERROR% Bytes Of Environmental Memory	Display the results of the BATCMD CE command.
BATCMD PC 11 01	Position the cursor.
BATCMD CH	Check the number of hard disks using the BATCMD CH (Check number of Hard disk) commands.
CALL SAYERROR	Run SAYERROR.BAT to store the ERRORLEVEL in the environment.
BATCMD PC 11 01	Position the cursor.
ECHO %ERROR% Hard Disk(s)%SPACE%	Display the results of the BATCMD CH command.
BATCMD PC 13 01	Position the cursor.
BATCMD CL	Check the amount of LIM memory using the BATCMD CL (Check LIM memory) command.

25-1 Continued.

Batch File Line	Explanation
`CALL SAYERROR`	Run SAYERROR.BAT to store the ERRORLEVEL in the environment.
`BATCMD PC 13 01`	Position the cursor.
`ECHO %ERROR% 32K Blocks of LIM Memory`	Display the results of the BATCMD CL command.
`BATCMD PC 15 01`	Position the cursor.
`BATCMD CM`	Check to see if a mouse is installed using the BATCMD CM (Check Mouse) command.
`IF ERRORLEVEL 1 ECHO Mouse Found` `IF NOT ERRORLEVEL 1 ECHO No Mouse Found`	Display the results of the BATCMD CM command.
`BATCMD PC 17 01`	Position the cursor.
`BATCMD CS`	Check the amount of free space on the current drive using the BATCMD CS (Check Space) command.
`CALL SAYERROR`	Run SAYERROR.BAT to store the ERRORLEVEL in the environment.
`BATCMD PC 17 01`	Position the cursor.
`ECHO %ERROR% 32K Blocks of Free Space` `      On Default Drive`	Display the results of the BATCMD CS command.
`BATCMD PC 19 01`	Position the cursor.
`PAUSE`	Pause the program until the user presses a key.
`BATCMD BS 15 1`	Clear the screen to bright white on blue.
`BATCMD PC 03 01`	Position the cursor.
`BATCMD SD`	Find the day of the month using the BATCMD SD (Store Day) command.
`CALL SAYERROR`	Run SAYERROR.BAT to store the ERRORLEVEL in the environment.
`BATCMD PC 03 01`	Position the cursor.
`ECHO Day Of Month Is %ERROR%`	Display the results of the BATCMD SD command.

25-1 Continued.

Batch File Line	Explanation
SET DAY=%ERROR%	Store this information to another environmental variable to keep the value.
BATCMD PC 05 01	Position the cursor.
BATCMD SO	Store the month to the ERRORLEVEL using the BATCMD SO (Store mOnth) command.
CALL SAYERROR	Run SAYERROR.BAT to store the ERRORLEVEL in the environment.
BATCMD PC 05 01	Position the cursor.
SET MONTH=%ERROR%	Store this information to another environmental variable to keep the value.
IF %MONTH%==1 ECHO Month Is January IF %MONTH%==2 ECHO Month Is February IF %MONTH%==3 ECHO Month Is March IF %MONTH%==4 ECHO Month Is April IF %MONTH%==5 ECHO Month Is May IF %MONTH%==6 ECHO Month Is June IF %MONTH%==7 ECHO Month Is July IF %MONTH%==8 ECHO Month Is August IF %MONTH%==9 ECHO Month Is September IF %MONTH%==10 ECHO Month Is October IF %MONTH%==11 ECHO Month Is November IF %MONTH%==12 ECHO Month Is December	Display the results of the BATCMD SO command.
BATCMD PC 07 01	Position the cursor.
BATCMD SY	Store the year to the ERRORLEVEL with the BATCMD SY (Store Year) command.
CALL SAYERROR	Run SAYERROR.BAT to store the ERRORLEVEL in the environment.
BATCMD PC 07 01	Position the cursor.
SET YEAR=19%ERROR%	Store this information to another environmental variable to keep the value.

25-1 Continued.

Batch File Line	Explanation
`ECHO Year Is %YEAR%%SPACE%`	Display the results of the BATCMD SY command. Because this message is shorter than the message from SAYERROR.BAT, the message displays the SPACE variable (10 spaces) at the end to erase the rest of the SAYERROR.BAT message.
`BATCMD PC 09 01`	Position the cursor.
`ECHO Date Is %MONTH%/%DAY%/%YEAR%`	Display the entire date using the environmental variables used to store this information.

`SET MONTH=`
`SET DAY=`
`SET YEAR=`
	Delete these variables that are no longer needed.

`BATCMD PC 11 01`	Position the cursor.
`BATCMD SH`	Store the hour to ERRORLEVEL using the BATCMD SH (Store Hour) command.
`CALL SAYERROR`	Run SAYERROR.BAT to store the ERRORLEVEL in the environment.
`BATCMD PC 11 01`	Position the cursor.
`ECHO Hour Is %ERROR%%SPACE%`	Display the results of the BATCMD SH command.
`SET HOUR=%ERROR%`	Store this information to another environmental variable to keep the value.
`BATCMD PC 13 01`	Position the cursor.
`BATCMD SM`	Store the minute to ERRORLEVEL using the BATCMD SM (Store Minute) command.
`CALL SAYERROR`	Run SAYERROR.BAT to store the ERRORLEVEL in the environment.
`BATCMD PC 13 01`	Position the cursor.

25-1 Continued.

Batch File Line	Explanation
`ECHO Minute Is %ERROR%%SPACE%`	Display the results of the BATCMD SM command.
`SET MINUTE=%ERROR%`	Store this information to another environmental variable to keep the value.
`BATCMD PC 15 01`	Position the cursor.
`BATCMD SS`	Store the second to the ERRORLEVEL using the BATCMD SS (Store Second) command.
`CALL SAYERROR`	Run SAYERROR.BAT to store the ERRORLEVEL in the environment.
`BATCMD PC 15 01`	Position the cursor.
`ECHO Second Is %ERROR%%SPACE%`	Display the results of the BATCMD SS command.
`SET SECOND=%ERROR%`	Store this information to another environmental variable to keep the value.
`BATCMD PC 17 01`	Position the cursor.
`ECHO Time Is %HOUR%:%MINUTE%:` `    %SECOND%%SPACE%`	Display the entire time using the environmental variables used to store this information.

`SET HOUR=`
`SET MINUTE=`
`SET SECOND=`
`SET ERROR=`
	Delete these variables that are no longer needed.

`BATCMD SL` `BATCMD SL`	Skip two lines using the BATCMD SL (Skip Line) command.
`ECHO Leaving With Errorlevel Set To 240` `ECHO Run SAYERROR.BAT To Check`	Tell the user what is happening.
`BATCMD EX 240`	Set the ERRORLEVEL to 240 using the BATCMD EX (EXit) command.

25-1 Continued.

26

Builder and Builder Lite

As powerful and useful as batch files are, when I work with them, I always have this nagging feeling that I could make them really powerful if they could just do a *little* bit more. With a batch file, even simple activities—like asking the user a question and getting a response—require a utility program.

☞ *Remember*   With a batch file, even what should be simple activities like asking the user a question require a utility program.

There are literally hundreds of utilities designed to enhance batch files. Most of these programs, however, introduce a new headache if you're writing a batch file for use on another system: How do you ensure that the other system has the batch file utility you plan to use? If the utility is in the public domain, you can include a copy. If it's shareware, you can still include a copy, along with a note suggesting the user register the copy. However, if you need a commercial utility you're just plain stuck.

Even if you're able to send the user a copy of the utility, you still have the problem of managing the files so the user gets all the necessary files and puts the utility program(s) in a subdirectory in the path so that the batch file can use it.

If you are using DR DOS, you have yet another problem. DR DOS offers batch subcommands not supported by any version of MS DOS. As a result, when you share your batch files with other users who might have MS DOS, you must be very careful about which batch subcommands you use. You also must be careful about sharing with DR DOS users because v.5 does not support the GOSUB and RETURN commands.

So when you're writing batch files for other people, you must worry about which brand and version of operating system they have, *plus* you must worry about which batch utilities they have and what the syntax is. As a result, batch files intended for multiple users tend to end up being a real pain.

▎▶ *Notice*   Writing batch files intended for multiple users on different platforms can end up being a real pain.

Multipurpose batch languages

Several do-it-all batch languages, like Enhanced Batch Language and Batchman, can add an incredible amount of power to your batch files. But you still come back to the problem of trying to share those powerful batch files with other users. Unless those other users have the same utility, your fancy batch file will not run on their system.

Builder

What you need is a way of legally bundling the utilities you use together with the resulting batch file so you can distribute everything and not worry about what batch utilities the user has. Builder does just that. But Builder does much more: it gives you the power and flexibility of a programming language, the speed of a compiled language, and full compatibility with the MS DOS batch subcommands, as well as the ease of learning with this batch language.

Remember With Builder, you can legally bundle the utilities you use together with the resulting batch file and distribute everything together as one program.

Bundling

Builder converts a batch file into a stand-alone program through a process called *compiling*. Compiling a batch file means that all the commands are converted to instructions that the computer can understand—including commands that use all of the extensions Builder builds into the batch language. And because the resulting program does not need the Builder language to run—it's nothing but instructions that the computer already understands—you can distribute this program royalty-free, and everyone running your program can use all the language extensions you used when you wrote the program.

Because you're sending them everything they need as part of the program, you don't need to worry about what utilities they have. Because all the code is in one .EXE program, file management is easy. Plus, because you are distributing a program, you have the security of knowing that the user cannot change it.

Remember Builder programs are powerful, easy to distribute and royalty free!

Power and flexibility of a programming language

The main reason for using Builder is its many enhancements. To give you an idea of the power of Builder, the Batcmd utility that comes with this book was written using only a small subset of the features of Builder, and Batcmd is a very powerful extension to the batch language!

The NEEDHELP.EXE, ASCII.EXE, and CAPITAL.EXE programs that come with this book were also written in Builder. I wrote these three programs and neither one took longer that thirty minutes to write, debug, and test! Anything you might want a batch file to do can be easily programmed into Builder. Additionally, Builder is so powerful that it generally has a command or function to do exactly what you want to do.

One of the most common uses of batch files is to write menus. Imagine if you were not limited to the simple menus batch files offer but could write fancy menus like the one used in the README.EXE program that comes on the disk included with this book. Take a moment to run this program. Notice that the menu gives you three ways to select an item from the menu:

- Move the cursor to that item and press Return.
- Press the highlighted letter for the item you want to run.
- Click with the mouse on the item you want to run.

Now notice that the menu has a shadow background, and notice the colors. The menu is in one color, the menu items are in another, and the screen background is still another color. This entire program was written and debugged in under an hour, using Builder Lite—a subset of the Builder program!

Builder gives you far too many extensions to the batch language for me to list them all here, but these are some of the ones I like best:

- Menus. The menus in README.EXE are just the beginning. Builder can produce moving lightbar, popup, and dropdown menus, as well as a special menu that allows you to place individual menu items anywhere on the screen. You could use this to write a menu where option one is in the top left corner, option two is in the bottom right corner, and option three is in the middle.
- User Input. All of the user input features of Batcmd (see Chapter 19) were written in Builder. Builder has a number of different ways to get input from the user, including single characters and long strings. You can ask the user a yes/no question, accept only numbers, letters or function keys, and much more.
- Math. While batch files have no mathematical abilities, Builder can perform a full set of mathematical and logical operations on integers between plus and minus two billion.
- String Operations. Builder includes a full set of string manipulation and string logic testing functions. You can easily find the length of a string, convert it to all lower- or uppercase, or pick out three characters in the middle of a string.
- No More Spaghetti Code. Builder supports structured programming methods like Case, While, Repeat and If-Then-Else.
- Subroutines. While it does not support the DR DOS 6 GOSUB and RETURN statements directly, Builder offers far more subroutine support than does DR DOS 6. Subroutines can be built into a program just like they can under DR DOS 6, or they can be written as stand-alone programs and attached to the main program while compiling.

This is only a very partial list. Builder offers so much that it can do anything that you'd ever want from a batch file!

Speed of a compiled language

Batch files generally run slow because DR DOS reads them a little at a time and then has to pause and figure out what to do, all because batch files are written in instructions that a human (and not a computer) can understand. However, when the computer reads a program like the ones produced by Builder, it reads the entire program into memory so that it does not have to access the disk again for that program. Additionally, the compiler converts your program into instructions that the computer can understand, thus not forcing the computer to perform any translations when running the program. This results in a much faster program.

Full compatibility with the MS DOS batch subcommands

Builder will read in any existing MS or DR DOS batch file and convert it automatically to a Builder program. Builder does not convert DR DOS-specific batch subcommands like GOSUB and RETURN. It does offers similar commands, though, so manual conversion is easy. Because of all the enhancements Builder offers, you will be able to do away with almost all of your other batch file utilities.

Ease of learning of the batch language

I could write pages and pages about how easy it is to learn to program in Builder, but you probably would not believe me. Rather than doing that, I'm going to show you the source code to a Builder program; I'm willing to bet that you'll understand most of the program, without having any prior knowledge of the Builder language.

The program shown next is CAPITAL.EXE; it takes a single input from the user, converts it to all uppercase, and stores the results in the environment under the environmental variable name RONNY. Additionally, it has built-in documentation, offers command line help if you start it with a /? or just a question mark, and performs extensive error-checking to make sure that it was passed exactly one word to convert to uppercase. Knowing just that, does this code still make sense to you?

```
'CAPITAL.BLD
'Convert A Single Input To Uppercase
'Store In The Environment Under The Name Ronny
'1.00
'May 16, 1992

STRING Input1

IF (("%1"=="/?") OR ("%1"=="?"))
        SAY "Converts A Single Word Input To Uppercase"
        SAY "And Stores The Results In The Environment";
        SAY "Under The Name Ronny"
        SAY "Sets Errorlevel To 1 If There Is A Problem"
        EXIT 0
END

IF "%1"==""
        SAY "Nothing To Convert"
        BEEP
        EXIT 1
END
```

```
IF NOT ("%2"=="")
    SAY "Only One Word Can Be Converted But Both ";
    SAY "<YELLOW>%1 And %2<NORMAL> Were Entered"
    BEEP
    EXIT 1
END
    Input1 := "%1"
Input1 := UPPERCASE Input1
SET "Ronny" = Input1
EXIT 0
```

Most of this code is devoted to documentation, help and error-checking. The Builder code to just convert a string to uppercase and store the results in the environment—without everything else is:

```
STRING Input1
Input1 := "%1"
Input1 := UPPERCASE Input1
SET "Ronny" = Input1
```

The first line declares a string variable that the program needs for this example. The second line stores the first replaceable parameter into this variable. The third line converts this variable to uppercase and stores the results back to the same variable name and the last line stores the results in the environment.

✍ *Notice*   So easy, and it even looks like a batch file. Builder does it all!

Builder Lite

If Builder sounds like an excellent idea to you, you will find a coupon in the back of this book for a discount on the program. If you are looking for something to improve your batch files but Builder sounds like more than what you need, TAB Books has a special deal: we have worked with hyperkinetix to take the Builder features most beginners want and have combined them into a less powerful program called Builder Lite.

Builder Lite is a book/software combination available from TAB. In the book, I explain how to use all the features of Builder Lite with lots of examples. This is a good way to get started. Once you have mastered Builder Lite, if you feel like you need even more power, you can upgrade to Builder.

Summary

Distributing batch files to other users is complicated because they might have a different brand or version of operating system than you do. Also, they probably will have different batch file utilities than you do.

Builder programs have all of the Builder batch language enhancements compiled into the program, so anyone who receives a copy of your Builder program has access to all the enhancements you used.

Builder offers a wealth of enhancements to the batch language such as menus, user input, math, string operation, structured code, subroutines, and much more.

Builder programs run much faster than batch files.

Builder is fully compatible with all MS DOS batch commands, and DR DOS specific batch commands are easy to convert.

If you already know batch programming, then the Builder language is easy to learn.

Builder Lite offers the most popular features of Builder at a lower price.

Dual Boot Utility

If you have been reading this book, are currently using MS DOS 5, and think that you might want to try DR DOS 6 but aren't sure, boy, have I got a deal for you! I've got the same deal if you're a DR DOS 6 user who occasionally needs to run MS DOS 5 or who wants to double-check your batch files to make sure they run under MS DOS 5.

Keith Ledbetter has create a very nice utility called Dual Boot Utility (DBU). DBU allows you to have a copy of both DR DOS 6 and MS DOS 5 on your hard disk and boot from either one. Not only that, Keith allowed me to include a copy in this book. Because DBU depends on batch files for its operation, it's especially fitting to have a copy of it in a book on batch files.

✍ **Notice** Dual Boot Utility allows you to boot off your hard disk and easily select between MS DOS 5 or DR DOS 6.

The steps we will follow to install this neat utility are as follows:

1. Create a boot disk. This is critical because a mistake can cause your hard disk to become unbootable—the data will still be on the hard disk, but you won't be able to boot from it.
2. Make a backup of the hard disk. This is just a precaution because the worst thing that can happen is temporarily making the disk unbootable.
3. Install DBU. Don't worry, this part is really easy.
4. Modify the batch files that drive DBU. Its batch files need to be modified slightly to fit your installation. Don't worry: full instructions are included.

Creating a boot disk

The procedures in this chapter can potentially make your hard disk unbootable if you make a mistake. This is a minor problem if you have a boot disk handy but a major problem if you don't, so take the time to create a boot disk.

☠ *Warning*   If you make a mistake while installing Dual Boot Utility, you might be unable to boot from your hard disk. Making a boot disk first will allow you to correct the problem.

The steps for creating a boot disk are as follows:

1. Format a floppy disk using the /S option. If your computer uses two different disk sizes, the boot disk must be the correct one for the A drive. The /S option adds the DR DOS files necessary for the disk to be bootable.
2. Examine your CONFIG.SYS file to see if any of the device drivers are required to operate your system. For example, some add-on hard disks—like the Plus Development Hardcard—require a device driver. You can ignore drivers like the mouse driver that are nice to have but not necessary to the operation of your system.
3. Copy the necessary device drivers you found in Step 2 to the boot floppy disk.
4. Create a CONFIG.SYS file on the boot floppy that loads all these necessary device drivers. It should load them from the floppy disk and *not* from the hard disk. It should also set files and buffers to values you normally use.
5. Create an AUTOEXEC.BAT file on the boot floppy that specifies the path you normally use. It's best not to load any memory resident software here. If you use this disk to troubleshoot, these will just get in the way.
6. Boot from your boot disk just to be sure it works. Don't just make sure you can get a directory of the C drive; actually go in and run your normal applications to make sure they all work properly. If you have problems, work through all these steps again until you resolve all your problems.
7. Place a copy of SYS.COM on this boot disk. This will be critical to restoring your hard disk if it becomes unbootable, so don't skip this step.
8. Depending on how much room is left on this boot disk, copy some of your more useful recovery tools onto the disk. Some suggestions of what to include are your backup program (so you can restore from a backup), an editor (so you can fix problems with the hard disk version of the CONFIG.SYS and AUTOEXEC.BAT file), and an unerasing program.

Once you create this boot disk, you make one or two copies of it using the DISKCOPY program so that the copies are also bootable. You must also keep the DR DOS version current. Any time you upgrade the DR DOS on your computer, you must update the DR DOS versions on all your boot disks.

A few computers include a nasty "Got you" in their setup program by allowing you to specify the drives to boot from. Generally, these computers can be configured to only boot from the C drive, although that is not the default. With the computer configured in this fashion, it will be unusable if the hard disk fails or if you make an error when altering a configuration file that prevents the computer from booting from the hard disk (unless you can reconfigure it without booting from a floppy disk). If you own a machine with this type of setup program, use this setting with a great deal of care!

Back up your hard disk

While nothing that we plan to do will endanger your data, there's a small chance that the hard disk could become temporarily unbootable. Rather than take this chance, make a backup of your hard disk.

☑ *Remember*   Play it safe and make a backup first.

Installing Dual Boot Utility

I'm glad you stuck with me. This procedure involves keeping two copies of the operating system files and writing over the boot sector of your hard disk. The installation is straightforward and as safe as is possible but under no circumstances is TAB Books, myself, or Keith Ledbetter responsible for damages to your system, so make sure that you have both a boot disk with SYS.COM *and* a recent backup.

The steps for installing DBU are as follows:

1. Copy the DBU files from the disk that comes with this book to a subdirectory on your hard disk that is always in your path.
2. Install DR DOS 6 on your hard disk. DBU installation needs to begin with DR DOS 6 installed first. The author believes DBU will work with DR DOS 5 but has not tested it. I tried it on my machine and it worked fine. He is sure that it will not work with earlier versions of DR DOS.
3. Create a subdirectory called C:\BOOTS to store the files DBU creates. It does not need to be in your path. Off the C:\BOOTS subdirectory, create two subdirectories: MS and DR.
4. Issue the command BOOTSECT READ C:\BOOTS\BOOTSECT.DR. This reads your boot sector (which tells the computer what hidden system file to process when booting) and stores it as a file called BOOTSECT.DR in the C:\BOOTS subdirectory.
5. Copy the CONFIG.SYS and AUTOEXEC.BAT files to C:\BOOTS\DR. Copy COMMAND.COM to C:\DRDOS. If you used another name for the subdirectory to store your DR DOS files, you will have to modify the batch file that comes with DBU.
6. Install MS DOS 5 on your hard disk, placing the system files in C:\DOS50. Again, you can use a different name for the subdirectory, but you'll have to modify the DBU batch files. Because MS DOS 5 and DR DOS 6 use different names for their hidden system files, both versions are stored on the hard disk. It's the boot sector that tells the computer which one to use. That is why all we need to save for each version is the boot sector and the files with a common name, COMMAND.COM, AUTOEXEC.BAT and CONFIG.SYS. Installing MS DOS 5 overwrites the DR DOS 6 boot sector with the MS DOS boot sector.
7. Issue the command BOOTSECT READ C:\BOOTS BOOTSECT.MS. This reads your new MS DOS boot sector and stores it as a file called BOOTSECT.MS in the C:\BOOTS subdirectory.
8. Copy the CONFIG.SYS and AUTOEXEC.BAT files for MS DOS to

C:\BOOTS\MS. Copy COMMAND.COM to C:\DOS50. If you used another name for the subdirectory to store these files, you will have to modify the batch file that comes with DBU.

9. Modify the DRDOS.BAT and MSDOS.BAT files that come with the DBU package. If you have used the same subdirectory names (\DRDOS and \DOS50) suggested in these instructions, only one minor change is needed. One of the lines in each batch file is D:\CACHES\HYPER\HYPERKDK D > NUL, which the author uses to flush his disk cache because it uses staged writes, where something you save to disk is not immediately written to the disk. Flushing the cache causes everything that is pending to be written to disk. If you don't use a cache or your cache does not stage writes, just delete this line. Otherwise, you must check your cache manual and substitute the command your cache uses for this function.

That's all there is to it. Now, the command DRDOS configures the computer for DR DOS 6 and reboots, while the command MSDOS configures it for MS DOS 5 and reboots.

Troubleshooting

If you make a mistake, you might not be able to boot from your hard disk. If that happens, the recovery steps are as follows:

1. Boot from your bootable floppy disk.
2. Issue the command SYS C: to make the hard disk bootable. Now copy the DR DOS 6 configuration files (AUTOEXEC.BAT and CONFIG.SYS) and COMMAND .COM to the root directory.
3. Reboot from the hard disk and check all the steps and filenames to see where you made a mistake.

When I first tried to install DBU, I mistyped the name of a file and ended up with BOOTSECT.DB rather than .DR as the extension. I was still able to correct the problem and get everything working properly in under thirty minutes.

Summary

Using Dual Boot Utility, you can boot off of MS DOS 5 or DR DOS 6 without resorting to floppy disks.

Before installing Dual Boot Utility, you should create a boot disk and make a backup.

Installing Dual Boot Utility involves saving the boot sector and files with the same name for both DR DOS 6 and MS DOS 5 in separate locations.

Batch files copy the proper files back into place and reboot.

PART SIX
Batch file applications

We've learned so much about batch files, and now it's time to put that into practice. So far, you've seen a number of batch files that solve very specific problems. For the next few chapters, we will look at how batch files can be a part of the solution for larger problems.

Chapter 28: An automated batch file help system. One problem with having a lot of batch files is remembering which batch file does what. As it turns out, batch files can solve this problem and, in the process, give you a set of very powerful tools for locating the right batch file for your needs.

Chapter 29: Simple batch file menus. The most common thing you do with your computer is run different programs. Often, this involves entering several different commands. Well, batch files can automate the process and make it simple for you to start your different applications.

Chapter 30: Anti-viral batch files. It's hard to imagine why anyone would want to write a program to harm someone else's data. Nevertheless, a few sick individuals have done just that. Your best defense is safe computing, and any number of other books will explain this in detail for you. Another form of defense is an anti-viral software program; a number of good ones are available. If you do not want to spend the money for an anti-viral software package, then at least protect yourself with the approaches outlined in this chapter. In addition to some DR DOS-based approaches, it outlines a batch file that will tell you if COMMAND.COM becomes infected. Because COMMAND.COM is the most commonly infected program, you should be able to determine whether or not it's OK.

Chapter 31: A document archival system. Never lose an important file again! That is a strong claim, but this chapter will show you how.

Chapter 32: Simulating Doskey using batch files. The one thing I missed most when I switched over to DR DOS 6 was the Doskey program from MS DOS 5. Doskey gives you command line recall, keyboard macros, and the ability to enter multiple commands on a single command line. As it turns out, all these features can be added to DR DOS using nothing more than batch files and this chapter shows how. It even turns out that there are significant advantages to using batch files over Doskey.

Chapter 33: Smaller batch file applications. This chapter presents a number of batch file applications that were too small to put in a separate chapter.

Chapter 34: Applications and problems. Think of this as a final exam. You get to try out everything you have learned in this book so far.

28

An automated batch file
help system

One problem with having a lot of batch files is that it is difficult to remember which batch file does what. One way around this is with a menu. Menus are nothing more than a list of available options along with some method of selecting one of those options. Menus are discussed in detail in Chapter 29. However, if you write a menu system with an entry for every one of your batch files, you are going to have to work through a lot of menus to find a specific batch file.

☑ **Remember** One approach to providing batch file help is a menu.

Help files

Another approach is to write your own help file, like HELP.BAT shown below without documentation and command line help (the disk version has both):

```
@ECHO OFF
CLS
ECHO DISCARD.BAT
ECHO -----------
ECHO Will Move All Unwanted Files
ECHO To A Directory For Holding
ECHO SYNTAX: DISCARD FILE1 FILE2
BATCMD SL

ECHO MAINTAIN.BAT
ECHO ------------
ECHO Will Erase Temporary Files,
ECHO Sort Files, And Run Your
ECHO File Defragmentation Program
ECHO SYNTAX: MAINTAIN
ECHO WARNING: Takes Two Hours To Run
BATCMD SL
```

ECHO PRINT.BAT
ECHO ---------
ECHO Will Print ASCII Files Automatically
ECHO SYNTAX: PRINT FILE1 FILE2 FILE3
ECHO WARNING: Make Sure Printer Is On
ECHO Or Computer Will Lock Up

This batch file displays a friendly reminder of the purpose of each batch file.

Remember A second approach to providing batch file help is a batch file that displays topical information.

As written, HELP.BAT simply displays a brief explanation of each batch file. Once you have accumulated a lot of batch files, it can be time-consuming to read through all those messages looking for a specific batch file. As HELP1.BAT in Fig. 28-1 shows, If-tests can be used to make this help batch file somewhat context-sensitive. However, this help is limited to the few categories preprogrammed into the batch file.

Batch File Line	Explanation
@ECHO OFF	Turn command-echoing off.
REM NAME: HELP1.BAT REM PURPOSE: Display Batch Help REM VERSION: 1.00 REM DATE: January 3, 1991	Documentation remarks.
NEEDHELP %0 %1	Use the NeedHelp utility program to check and see if the user started the batch file with a /? switch.
IF ERRORLEVEL 1 GOTO HELP	If the user requested help, jump to a special section to display that information.
IF (%1)==() GOTO NOTHING	If the user did not enter a replaceable parameter to be used to decide which topic to display help on, jump to an error-handling section.
CAPITAL %1	Use the Capital utility to convert this value to uppercase and store it in the environment under the variable name Ronny.

28-1 HELP1.BAT adds limited context sensitivity to a batch-based help facility.

Batch File Line	Explanation
| ```
IF NOT (%RONNY%)==(UTILITY) GOTO NOUTIL
    ECHO DISCARD.BAT
    ECHO -----------
    ECHO Will Move All Unwanted Files
    ECHO To A Directory For Holding
    ECHO SYNTAX: DISCARD FILE1 FILE2...
    BATCMD SL

    ECHO MAINTAIN.BAT
    ECHO ------------
    ECHO Will Erase Temporary Files, Sort
    ECHO Files, And Run Your
    ECHO File Defragmentation Program
    ECHO SYNTAX: MAINTAIN
    ECHO WARNING: Takes Two Hours To Run
GOTO END
``` | If the user requested information about utility programs, display that information and exit the batch file. |
| ```
:NOUTIL
IF NOT (%RONNY%)==(PRINTING) GOTO NOPRINT
    ECHO PRINT.BAT
    ECHO ---------
    ECHO Will Print ASCII
    ECHO Files Automatically
    ECHO SYNTAX: PRINT FILE1 FILE2 FILE3
    ECHO WARNING: Make Sure Printer Is On
    ECHO Or Computer Will Lock Up
GOTO END
``` | If the user did not request information on utilities, check to see if they requested information on printing. If they did, display that information and exit the batch file. |
| ```
:NOPRINT
IF NOT (%RONNY%)==(BACKUP) GOTO NOBACK
    ECHO BACKUP.BAT
    ECHO ----------
    ECHO Will Backup All (Or Some)
    ECHO Subdirectories On Your Hard Disk
    ECHO SYNTAX: BACKUP
    ECHO To Backup Entire Hard Disk
    ECHO SYNTAX: BACKUP Directory
    ECHO To Backup One Subdirectory
GOTO END
``` | If the user did not request information on printing, check to see if they requested information on backups. If they did, display that information and exit the batch file. |

28-1 Continued.
```

Batch File Line	Explanation
| ```
:NOBACK
IF NOT (%RONNY%)==(MISC) GOTO WRONG
    ECHO GAME.BAT
    ECHO --------
    ECHO Will Bring Up The Game Menu
    ECHO SYNTAX: GAME
GOTO END
``` | If the user did not request information on backups, check to see if they requested miscellaneous information. If they did, display that information and exit the batch file. If not, jump to an error-handling section because all topics have been covered. |
| ```
:WRONG
    ECHO INVALID SYNTAX
GOTO NOTHING
``` | The batch file only reaches this point when the user enters an invalid replaceable parameter. This section displays an error-message and jumps to another section to display additional information. |
| ```
:NOTHING
    ECHO SYNTAX IS HELP1 CATEGORY
    ECHO Valid categories are:
    ECHO Utilities, Backup, Printing, Misc
GOTO END
``` | When the user does not enter a replaceable parameter or when another error-handing section jumps here, this section displays instructions. |
| ```
:HELP
    ECHO HELP1.BAT Displays Help On
    ECHO Specific Batch Files
GOTO NOTHING
``` | Display a help screen and exit the batch file when the user requests help. |
| ```
:END
``` | Label marking the end of the batch file. |

28-1 Continued.

Customized help

While writing menus or custom help batch files works, it is a difficult system to maintain. Each time you write a batch file or discard an existing batch file, you must update everything to reflect that change. Otherwise, your help system gets out of "sync" with your batch files and gives outdated information.

☠ *Warning* While writing menus or topical batch files does work, it is difficult to keep these systems in sync with all your batch files.

One approach allows you to add and delete batch files at will and never gets out of sync; however, it requires some special considerations when you create your batch file. First, it helps if you store all your batch files in a common subdirectory. I use the C:\BAT subdirectory for this, although the name does not matter; if you use a different subdirectory name, you will need to modify these batch files to work with your subdirectory name.
```

While you don't need to keep all your batch files in one subdirectory, it makes the help system work much better. If you have your batch file arsenal scattered across multiple subdirectories, the help system can only give you information on one subdirectory at a time. Also, for these batch files to work across different subdirectories, you will need to modify them to either take the subdirectory as an input or always use the current subdirectory.

Second, your batch files must be created with the proper internal documentation and must use consistent capitalization. This requirement affects only the first five lines of the batch file, and every batch file should begin with these same first five lines:

```
@ECHO OFF
REM NAME:
REM PURPOSE:
REM VERSION:
REM DATE:
```

Chapter 4 examines this in more detail. If you have not read Chapter 4 yet, you should do that before you continue with this chapter.

Remember   The easiest way to display batch file help is using a system that keys off of the information built into the batch file itself.

HELPBAT.BAT in Fig. 28-2 uses this documentation to display custom help about each batch file. It begins with a For-loop that loops through each batch file in the C:\BAT subdirectory. For each batch file, it calls itself with a special flag that causes HELPBAT .BAT to jump to a special routine the second time through.

Batch File Line	Explanation
`@ECHO OFF`	Turn command-echoing off.

`REM NAME:     HELPBAT.BAT`
`REM PURPOSE: Display .BAT Purpose`
`REM VERSION: 1.00`
`REM DATE:     November 6, 1991`
	Documentation remarks.

`IF (%2)==(DISPLAY) GOTO DISPLAY`	This line checks to see if the second replaceable parameter is a DISPLAY, indicating the batch file is calling itself as a subroutine. If so, it jumps to the subroutine section.
`NEEDHELP %0 %1`	Use the NeedHelp utility program to check and see if the user started the batch file with a /? switch. This is placed after the test on %2 to avoid running this utility each time the batch file calls itself as a subroutine.

28-2   HELPBAT.BAT displays the name of each batch file and its purpose line.

Batch File Line	Explanation
`IF ERRORLEVEL 1 GOTO HELP`	If the user requested help, jump to a special section to display that information.
`FOR %%J IN (C:\BAT\*.BAT) DO` `CALL HELPBAT %%J DISPLAY`	When running as the main routine, loop through each batch file in the C:\BAT subdirectory and call this batch file as a subroutine and pass it the name of the batch file and a flag to indicate its subroutine status. If you keep your batch files in a different subroutine, change the C:\BAT to the name of that subdirectory. To cause this batch file to work with the batch files in the current subdirectory, change the first portion of the command to: FOR %%J IN (*.BAT)
`GOTO END`	After looping through all the batch files in the main routine, exit the batch file.
`:DISPLAY`	Label marking the beginning of the subroutine.
`ECHO %1`	Display the name of the batch file by echoing the %1 replaceable parameter, which contains the name because it was passed when the batch file called itself as a subroutine.
`ECHO --------------------`	Underline the name of the batch file to set it off from the purpose.
`TYPE %1	FIND "PURPOSE:"`	Type the batch file and use the FIND filter to search for the line containing the phrase "PURPOSE:". In most batch files, this line will be the purpose line; although, a few batch files--like this one--will have "PURPOSE:" as part of a command. When that happens, two lines will be displayed.
`BATCMD SL`	Use the BATCMD utility to display a blank line.

28-2 Continued.

Batch File Line	Explanation
`GOTO END`	The subroutine is finished, so exit the batch file. Control will return to the version of HELPBAT.BAT running as the main routine.

`:HELP`
    `ECHO Reads Batch Files & Displays`
    `ECHO The Name And Purpose Line`
`GOTO END`
	Display a help screen and exit the batch file when the user requests help.

`:END`	Label marking the end of the batch file.

28-2 Continued.

That special subroutine first displays the name of the batch file and underlines it. It has access to the name because the name is passed to it as a replaceable parameter. After displaying the name, it types the batch file using the TYPE command. It pipes this information to the FIND filter, which then displays only the line containing PURPOSE:. This is the reason for the recommendation in Chapter 4 to put your entire purpose statement all on one line; that way, this display completely explains the purpose of the batch file.

If you must use multiple lines for your purpose statement, you could start each one with a PURPOSE: to make sure these help batch files display the entire purpose. That does, however, tend to make the help screens look fairly cluttered. After that, control returns to the original version of HELPBAT.BAT that loops through to the next batch file, if any remain.

On a 16MHz IBM Model 80, this system runs slow enough that I can read all the lines as they scroll up the screen. However, on a Northgate 386/20, the lines scroll too fast to read. If that happens to you, you can replace the ECHO %1 line with a TYPE %1 ¦ FIND "NAME:" line. That will cut the speed of the display in half because the batch file now has to type the batch file twice and use the FIND filter twice to locate specific text. If it still runs too fast, you can add lines to display the version and last modified date. If you display all four pieces of information, that version of HELPBAT.BAT will run at one-fourth the speed of the original version.

When you delete a batch file, it ceases to exist, so the For-loop bypasses any reference to it and it is automatically removed from this system. When you add a new batch file, it contains all the information required by HELPBAT.BAT and the For-loop automatically includes it, so it is automatically included in this system. As a result, this system is automatically current with your batch files without any modification when you modify your batch files.

Context-sensitive help

While HELPBAT.BAT is a very effective method of displaying general batch file help, it can be overpowering when you have a lot of batch files. For example, I have over 700 batch files for all the books I have written. Finding a specific batch file using HELPBAT.BAT would take a long time and a lot of reading.

Fortunately, narrowing the search is fairly easy. You simply only need to add a filter to the line that types the batch files, as shown by HELPBAT2.BAT in Fig. 28-3. When you do not enter any text, you get all the purpose lines as you do with HELPBAT.BAT. However, when you enter a phrase, HELPBAT2.BAT displays the purpose line for only those batch files that contain that phrase.

Batch File Line	Explanation
`@ECHO OFF`	Turn command-echoing off.

`REM NAME:    HELPBAT2.BAT`
`REM PURPOSE: Display .BAT Purpose`
`REM          For Matching Text`
`REM VERSION: 1.00`
`REM DATE:    November 9, 1991`
	Documentation remarks.

`IF (%2)==(DISPLAY) GOTO DISPLAY`	This line checks to see if the second replaceable parameter is a DISPLAY, indicating the batch file is calling itself as a subroutine. If so, it jumps to the subroutine section.
`NEEDHELP %0 %1`	Use the NeedHelp utility program to check and see if the user started the batch file with a /? switch. This is placed after the test on %2 to avoid running this utility each time the batch file calls itself as a subroutine.
`IF ERRORLEVEL 1 GOTO HELP`	If the user requested help, jump to a special section to display that information.
`SET FIND=`	Reset the environmental variable to nothing.

28-3 HELPBAT2.BAT allows you to get help about your batch files for a specific topic; however, it still displays the names of all the batch files.

Batch File Line	Explanation
`IF (%1)==() GOTO RUN`	If the user did not enter a replaceable parameter, jump to the run section and start running the batch file.
`:TOP`	Label marking the top of a loop used to build the environmental variable FIND that contains the text to search for.
`IF NOT (%FIND%)==() SET FIND=%FIND% %1` `IF (%FIND%)==() SET FIND=%1`	Add the contents of the first replaceable parameter onto the FIND environmental variable. Treating FIND different when it contains a value allows for a space to be inserted between the contents of FIND and the next word to add.
`SHIFT`	Move all the replaceable parameters down one level and make available another replaceable parameter as %9.
`IF (%1)==() GOTO RUN`	If there are no more replaceable parameters, jump to the section for performing the actual search.
`GOTO TOP`	Continue looping. It jumps out of this loop above if there are no more replaceable parameters so it only reaches this point where replaceable parameters remain.
`:RUN`	Label marking the beginning of the section that loops through all the batch files.

28-3 Continued.

Batch File Line	Explanation
`FOR %%J IN (C:\BAT\*.BAT) DO` `    CALL HELPBAT2 %%J DISPLAY`	When running as the main routine, loop through each batch file in the C:\BAT subdirectory and call this batch file as a subroutine and pass it the name of the batch file and a flag to indicate its subroutine status. If you keep your batch files in a different subroutine, change the C:\BAT to the name of that subdirectory. To cause this batch file to work with the batch files in the current subdirectory, change the first portion of the command to: FOR %%J IN (*.BAT)
`SET FIND=`	Reset the variable that is no longer needed.
`GOTO END`	After looping through all the batch files in the main routine, exit the batch file.
`:DISPLAY`	Label marking the beginning of the subroutine.
`ECHO %1`	Display the name of the batch file by echoing the %1 replaceable parameter, which contains the name because it was passed when the batch file called itself as a subroutine.
`ECHO --------------------`	Underline the name of the batch file to set it off from the purpose.

28-3 Continued.

Batch File Line	Explanation
`TYPE %1	FIND "%FIND%"	FIND "PURPOSE:"`	Type the batch file and use the FIND filter to search for the line containing the words entered on the command line plus phrase "PURPOSE:". All of this must be on the same line to pass this test.
`BATCMD SL`	Use the BATCMD utility to display a blank line.
`GOTO END`	The subroutine is finished, so exit the batch file. Control will return to the version of HELPBAT.BAT running as the main routine.

`:HELP`
   `ECHO Reads Batch Files & Displays`
   `ECHO The Name And Purpose Line`
   `ECHO And Will Search The Purpose For`
   `ECHO Text Entered On The Command`
   `ECHO Line`
`GOTO END`
	Display a help screen and exit the batch file when the user requests help.

`:END`	Label marking the end of the batch file.

28-3 Continued.

The phrase you enter to search on must appear on the purpose line, and it must appear in exactly the same order specified without anything else in the middle. If the purpose line was

REM PURPOSE: Runs The Menu Program

then the phrases "Menu," "Menu Program," and "The Menu" would all display this line. However the phrases "Run The Menu" (with "Run" instead of "Runs"), "Runs Menu" (without the "The"), and "Menu Program Now" (extra word) would all fail to display this line.

Because you are using the DR DOS FIND filter, the search is not case-sensitive. MS DOS users using the same batch file would have to match the capitalization used in the batch files because the MS DOS FIND command *is* case-sensitive. That is the reason for recommending standardizing on one capitalization method in Chapter 4. MS DOS 5.0 users can add the /I switch to ignore case.

While HELPBAT2.BAT only displays the purpose line for those batch files that contain the text the user specifies on the command line, it displays the underlined file names of every batch file in the subdirectory. That too is avoidable, although avoiding it requires using DR DOS-specific commands that will cause the batch file to work improperly under all versions of MS DOS.

The heart of this modification is the fact that when the DR DOS FIND filter only displays a line from a file, it displays the name of the file as well. (MS DOS does not do this, so this batch file will not run properly under MS DOS.) Because the DR DOS FIND filter can also take a list of filenames as input, this new version does not need looping either. Figure 28-4 shows HELPBAT3.BAT, our final help batch file.

Batch File Line	Explanation
`@ECHO OFF`	Turn command-echoing off.

`REM NAME:      HELPBAT2.BAT`
`REM PURPOSE: Display .BAT Purpose`
`REM          For Matching Text`
`REM VERSION: 2.00`
`REM DATE:    June 1, 1992`
	Documentation remarks.

`IF (%1)==(/?) GOTO HELP` `IF (%1)==(?)  GOTO HELP`	Test to see if the user requested help. Because this batch file will not run properly under MS DOS, it does not use the Needhelp utility to be compatible with MS DOS.
`SET FIND=`	Reset the environmental variable that will be used to store the string to search for.
`IF (%1)==() GOTO RUNALONE`	If the user did not enter text to search file, jump to a special section to handle that.
`:TOP`	Label marking the top of a loop used to build the environmental variable FIND that contains the text to search for.

28-4 HELPBAT3.BAT allows you to get help about your batch files for a specific topic and only display the names of the batch files that match your search criteria. This batch file uses DR DOS-specific commands.

Batch File Line	Explanation
`IF NOT (%FIND%)==() SET FIND=%FIND% %1` `IF (%FIND%)==() SET FIND=%1`	Add the contents of the first replaceable parameter onto the FIND environmental variable. Treating FIND different when it contains a value allows for a space to be inserted between the contents of FIND and the next word to add.
`SHIFT`	Move all the replaceable parameters down one level and make available another replaceable parameter as %9.
`IF (%1)==() GOTO RUN`	If there are no more replaceable parameters, jump to the section for performing the actual search.
`GOTO TOP`	Continue looping. It jumps out of this loop above if there are no more replaceable parameters, so it only reaches this point where replaceable parameters remain.
`:RUN`	Label marking the beginning of the section that performs the actual search.
`FIND "PURPOSE:" C:\BAT*.BAT	FIND "%FIND%"`	Search through all the batch files in C:\BAT for "PURPOSE" first and then for the string the user entered. DR DOS takes care of displaying the name and looping through all the values.

28-4 Continued.

An automated batch file help system 243

Batch File Line	Explanation
`SET FIND=`	Reset the variable that is no longer needed.
`GOTO END`	Exit the batch file.

`:RUNALONE`
`    FIND "PURPOSE:" C:\BAT\*.BAT`
`GOTO END`
	Section that handles the user not entering a string to search for. It is the same as the first section, except a second FIND is not performed and the FIND environmental variable is not reset because it is never created.

`:HELP`
`    ECHO Reads Batch Files & Displays`
`    ECHO The Name And Purpose Line`
`    ECHO And Will Search The Purpose For`
`    ECHO Text Entered On The Command`
`    ECHO Line`
`GOTO END`
	Display a help screen and exit the batch file when the user requests help.

`:END`	Label marking the end of the batch file.

28-4 Continued.

When you start HELPBAT3.BAT without any replaceable parameters, it displays the name and purpose of each batch file on a single line. When you enter the test to search on, it again displays the name and purpose of the batch files on a single line, but this time it only displays those batch files that contain the specified test within the purpose line.

✔ Remember HELPBAT3.BAT uses the information built into the batch file itself to display help on only those batch files relating to the topic you specify.

Depending on how many batch files you have, you will find either HELPBAT.BAT or HELPBAT3.BAT a big help in figuring out which batch file does what. I know I use HELPBAT3.BAT constantly on my system.

Summary

One way to keep track of all your batch files is to access them through a menu system.

If you track your batch files with a menu system, you must update the menu system every time you add or delete a batch file.

Another way to track your batch files is to write yet another batch file to provide help on existing batch files. This batch file can be non-context-sensitive like HELP.BAT or context-sensitive like HELP1.BAT.

Before you can write a more advanced help system, you must store your batch files in a common subdirectory and construct them with the proper internal documentation.

HELPBAT.BAT automatically displays the purpose line for each batch file automatically. It does not require any modifications when you add or delete batch files.

HELPBAT2.BAT uses the FIND filter to only display the purpose line for batch files that contain a specified piece of text. However, HELPBAT2.BAT still displays the name of all the batch files.

HELPBAT3.BAT uses the FIND filter to only display the purpose line for batch files that contain a specified piece of text. By using DR DOS-specific syntax, HELPBAT3.BAT avoids displaying the names of batch files that do not match the search criteria.

29

Simple batch file menus

Back in 1983, the organization I worked for got its first few computers. These computers were shared by over twenty users, most of whom didn't know much about computers at that time. After answering the question "How do I start Lotus?" constantly for several weeks, I developed a menu system very much like the first menu system I will describe in this chapter. I placed this menu system on the most frequently used computer. The MIS manager saw it and laughed at it, saying that no one would ever use it. Several days later, I saw him copying it onto the other computers! He thought it wasn't necessary, but the users loved it.

▐▐▶ *Note*   Menus might not seem necessary, but users love them.

The purpose of a menu system is to handle much of the overhead involved in performing routine tasks with a hard disk like changing subdirectories and starting programs. For the most part, menus are more trouble than they're worth for a floppy-disk system. Before developing a menu system, however, you should have a well-structured hard disk; let's spend a few moments discussing hard disk structure.

✔ *Remember*   The purpose of a menu system is to handle much of the overhead involved in performing routine tasks.

Structuring your hard disk

A floppy disk is like a desk. You can just toss all your papers on a desk and usually find what you need. Similarly, you can copy files onto an available floppy disk and likely find the file later, especially if you label the disk.

A hard disk, on the other hand, is like a filing cabinet. If you just toss in all your papers, it's unlikely that you'll ever find anything. An average user will create or accumulate over one thousand files a year. Of course, if you install Windows and a few Windows-based applications, your total will be much higher. If they were all in a single directory, simply getting a listing would take a long time; finding one specific file would be next to impossible. Just as you categorize all the papers in a filing cabinet into files, you should categorize the files on a hard disk into directories and subdirectories.

An additional reason to create these divisions is that DR DOS places an arbitrary limit on the number of files that can be created in the root directory. My copy of DR DOS 5, for example, limits the root directory to 512 files. Because of the way DR DOS stores subdirectories, this limit doesn't apply to them.

The first division from the root directory is considered a directory, and further divisions from there are subdirectories. Keep in mind, however, that these two terms are often used interchangeably.

Remember A subdirectory is a logical subdivision of a disk.

Each subdirectory is stored as a file in the parent directory. Because the subdirectory is a file, it can expand to hold as many files as needed. A subdirectory is a logical subdivision of a disk, much as a folder is a logical division of a filing cabinet. DR DOS treats each subdirectory much like a separate floppy disk. Each subdirectory has a separate directory listing, and each one can have files with the same name. Subdirectories don't significantly slow down most DR DOS operations, and they don't take up much room, so there's no real disadvantage to creating as many as you need. Each subdirectory can also grow to fill all the available space on the hard disk, so using subdirectories doesn't make it more difficult to fit files on a hard disk.

While a subdirectory can have as many files as you want, there are technical reasons to limit the number of files in a single subdirectory to a manageable number. DR DOS tries to hold all the filenames of a subdirectory in memory, which speeds directories and searches. However, when the number of files is too large to fit into memory, DR DOS slows down dramatically. You'll notice this problem because DR DOS will have to read the disk more than once when you perform a DIR. At this point, you should either reduce the number of files in the offending subdirectory or increase the number of buffers specified in the CONFIG.SYS file.

The DR DOS commands for managing subdirectories are CD (ChDir), FDISK, MD (MkDir), and RD (RmDir). These commands perform the following functions:

CD *path* Changes the currently active directory to the one named in the path.
FDISK Used to prepare a new hard disk. If the disk has any information already on it, FDISK will destroy the information. Unlike MS DOS, the FDISK command in DR DOS both prepares and formats the hard disk.
MD *name* Makes a subdirectory with the name you specify that branches off the currently active directory.
RD *name* Removes the subdirectory name if it branches off the current directory and if it doesn't contain any files.

Remember The DR DOS commands for managing subdirectories are CD, FDISK, MD, RD, MOVE /T, and RENDIR.

Think of the subdirectories of a disk as a tree. Each disk has only one root (or base) directory, which is created automatically when you format the disk. The root directory can contain as many subdirectories as you need, although the technical limit is the number of files DR DOS allows in the root directory. Each of these subdirectories can have subdirectories, and so on. The limit is that the path statement (C: subdirectory1\subdirectory2\etc.) must be less than 63 characters long.

When a directory is created, it will be a *child* (or *branch*) of the current directory (called the *parent*). So if you create a subdirectory while in the root directory, that subdirectory would be a branch off the root directory. If it were created when you're in a subdirectory, it would be a branch of that subdirectory. A drawing of all the subdirectories in a hard disk, therefore, looks a lot like an inverted tree. Figure 29-1 shows a diagram of the subdirectory structure of a typical hard disk.

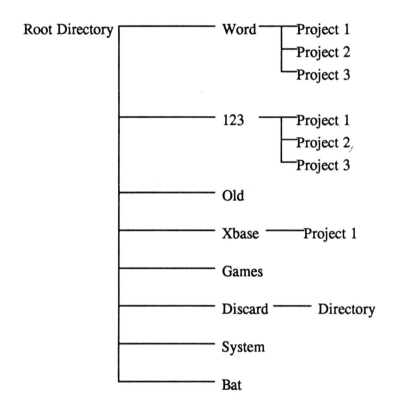

29-1 A typical hard disk configuration.

Each subdirectory (except the root directory) will automatically contain two files when you create it; these show up as a dot and double dot file when you perform a DIR. These two files have special meanings to DR DOS and allow for two handy shortcuts. The double dot file stands for the parent subdirectory, so you can move one subdirectory closer to the root directory with the CD.. command. You can continue issuing this command until you reach the root directory. The single dot file represents all the files in the subdirectory, and can be used in place of *.* when copying or erasing files.

248 *Batch file applications*

To remove a directory, that directory must not have any files except the required dot and double dot files. If you find you can't remove a subdirectory, first check to see if it has any files in it. If so, you must erase them. When DIR doesn't show any files, you most likely have hidden files. The hidden status of the file can be changed with the ATTRIB program, but be sure you know what you are doing because some files—like some of the operating system files—must be hidden files to run.

When you're changing directories, you can move only along a continuous path. For example, in the hard disk diagrammed in Fig. 29-1, you can't move directly from C:\WORD\PROJECT1 to C:\123\PROJECT2. You must first move back to the root directory. However, you can move back to the root directory and on to the desired subdirectory with the single command CD\123\PROJECT2. The CD is the change directory command, and specifying the entire path, from just to the right of the C:, moves you back to the root directory and on to the desired subdirectory. CD\ by itself always returns you to the root directory.

Typically, the first level of subdirectories (or directories) are functional. There is one for system files, one for word processing, one for spreadsheets, and so on. Each of these directories can then have subdirectories. So the word processing directory could have subdirectories for personal letters, course outlines, tests, consulting, and so on. If you teach several courses, the test subdirectory could even be subdivided by course. At some point, however, further division is more trouble than it's worth.

The root directory should have only a few files in it. The operating system requires it to have COMMAND.COM unless you use a SHELL command in your CONFIG.SYS file and two hidden system files. DR DOS also requires two hidden files that you will not see in a directory listing. If you plan to use an AUTOEXEC.BAT file or a CONFIG.SYS file, they must also be in the root directory.

Introduction to menus

A menu is nothing more than a list of options on the screen. The menu will give numbers for each option. A sample menu is shown in Fig. 29-2. This example menu, along with the hard disk layout in Fig. 29-1, will form the basis for the remaining examples in this chapter.

Press	For
1	Run Word Processor
2	Run Spreadsheet
3	Run Database
4	Play Chess
5	Format A Floppy Disk
6	Backup Hard Disk To Floppies

29-2 A sample menu.

Menu options can do more than just automatically run a program; they can also control how dangerous programs are used. For example, if you try to format a floppy disk without the drive specification (FORMAT A:), you could erase your entire hard disk with some versions of MS DOS. This can be avoided if you format disks from the menu. The menu option to format a disk runs a batch file, thus preventing the user from entering the format command incorrectly.

Displaying the menu

The menu itself is nothing more than text on the screen, and text can be displayed using any of the methods explored in Chapters 20 and 21. For all of the examples in this chapter, I will be using .COM files produced by the BatScreen screen compiler included with this book. Refer to Chapter 20 for documentation on this program.

Types of menus

Menus fall into four very broad categories:

- Non-resident non-nested menus
- Resident non-nested menus
- Non-resident nested menus
- Resident nested menus

The first menu type is called a *non-resident menu* because, after displaying the menu screen, the menu gets out of memory—leaving you with nothing but DR DOS. Entering a selection, say 1, at the DR DOS prompt to run a word processing program with a non-resident menu does nothing by itself; you must also create a batch file called 1.BAT to perform the action under the first option in the menu. Entering 1 runs 1.BAT. In addition to running the word processor, 1.BAT would typically contain a final command to redisplay the menu.

The first menu type was also called *non-nested* because none of the menu items call other menus. When one of the menu items calls another menu, the menu being called is said to be *nested* inside the first menu. Menus can be nested as deeply as you like.

The second menu type is called a *resident* menu because the menu remains in memory, watching over your selection and then executing that selection. The advantage of this approach is the menu can watch over users and make sure that they do not enter an invalid selection. The disadvantage of this approach is that the batch file driving a resident menu is much more complex.

The third and fourth menu types are duplicates of the first two, only with additional menus nested inside them. These types of menus are much more complex. A single menu screen can comfortably display forty or more options in two or even three columns, so it's rarely necessary to write nested menus. If you need menus this complex, you are usually better off using one of the commercial or shareware menu development packages rather than depending on batch files. For these reasons, this chapter only has a very general description of nested menus and not a full-blown description of their programming.

Non-resident non-nested menus

We will be developing a complete non-resident non-nested menu system as an example in this chapter. All of the files for this demonstration system are stored in the \MENU1 subdirectory on the disk that comes with this book. In order to allow you to experiment with the non-resident non-nested menu system, I've included on the disk slightly altered copies of the batch files shown in the book. These modifications are as follows:

- The batch files always return to the \MENU1 subdirectory rather than the root directory. Because this action only takes place in the MENU.BAT subdirectory, you only need to make this change in one location.
- The batch files do not automatically return to the C drive; instead, they remain on whatever drive you ran them from. Each batch file changes to the drive containing the application it's running, while MENU.BAT takes care of returning to C:\, so each batch file would need to be modified to make the system operational.
- Because there are no applications to run on the floppy disk, the batch files that run the applications merely simulate running them by displaying a screen and pausing until you press a key. Of course, on your own system, you would want to modify each batch file to run your specific applications.

As mentioned above, a non-resident non-nested menu is nothing more than a method of displaying the menu screen and a batch file to run each option. The batch file to display the menu screen is called MENU.BAT and is shown next without command line help and without most of its internal documentation:

```
@ECHO OFF

REM C:
REM Change The Line Below To CD\ On Your System
CD\MENU1
SCREEN1
```

As you can see, the only thing it does is change to the appropriate drive and subdirectory and then display the menu via SCREEN1. This runs SCREEN1.COM, a compiled copy of the screen.

Remember A non-resident non-nested menu is nothing more than a method of displaying the menu screen and a batch file to run each option.

The location of the batch files and screen compiler .COM files that drive this system is important. They must be in a subdirectory that is always in your path. I keep all my files in my batch subdirectory along with all my other batch files.

Now, let's create the first batch file, 1.BAT, to run the word processor program. The entire batch file is shown here because we need to look at it fairly closely:

```
@ECHO OFF
REM NAME:      1.BAT
REM PURPOSE:   Run Word Processor
REM VERSION:   1.00
REM DATE:      June 2, 1992

NEEDHELP %0 %1
```

```
IF ERRORLEVEL 1 GOTO HELP

REM C:
REM CD\WORD
PROMPT EXIT To Return To Word
REM WORD
REM Delete The Next Two Lines
WORD
PAUSE
PROMPT $P$G
MENU

:HELP
    ECHO Runs Word Processor
GOTO END

:END
```

After the internal documentation and checks to see if the user requested help, the batch file changes to the drive and subdirectory containing the word processing program, changes the prompt (as mentioned earlier, in order to remind users shelling out of the word processor that it's loaded into memory), and then runs the program. In this batch file, the command WORD runs WORD.COM on the disk—another screen created with BatScreen to simulate a word processor. Users planning on converting this batch file for use on their system should remove this line and the PAUSE command.

After running the applications, the batch file resets the prompt and then runs MENU.BAT to redisplay the menu. However, it runs MENU.BAT without using CALL, so control never returns to 1.BAT. At this point, MENU.BAT picks up, returning to the appropriate subdirectory and redisplaying the menu. The other batch files—2.BAT through 6.BAT—run in a similar fashion. The batch files for formatting a floppy disk and making a backup can easily run from any location on the hard disk, so they skip changing location. Also, because these programs do not allow you to shell out, they also skip changing the prompt.

The real advantage of this sort of system is its flexibility of use. If you want to run the spreadsheet and remember that 2.BAT can do that, you can issue the 2 command anywhere and load the spreadsheet. You don't have to load the menu program first, and you don't have to change to a specific location on the hard disk first. Because 2.BAT is in your path, it works automatically when you issue the 2 command.

Remember The real advantage of a non-resident non-nested menu is the commands work anytime and anywhere, even if the menu itself is not shown on the screen.

This is the very system I installed back in 1983, only back then I displayed the menu options with ECHO commands in the batch file. That system has been upgraded once to replace the ECHO commands with output from an earlier version of the screen compiler, and it's still in use today. As you can imagine, for an organization to continue using this type of application for almost nine years through three generations of computers means they find it both powerful and easy to use. While I will explain resident non-nested menus in detail and briefly cover nested menus, I'm absolutely convinced that this approach just mentioned creates the best menus you are going to find. It is, in fact, the menu system I use on my personal machines.

🔊 *Notice*   For an organization to continue using this type of application for almost nine years means they find it both powerful and easy to use.

Resident non-nested menus

With a non-resident menu, the batch file displays the menu and then quits running. With a resident menu, the batch file hangs around and waits for the user to press a key. The advantage of this approach is the batch file can watch over users and make sure that they do not push the wrong key. The disadvantage is that writing such a batch file is more difficult, plus the system can be more complex to use. Because you're trading off extra "hand-holding" against more complex development and use, I only recommend this approach when you are developing a system that will be used by very inexperienced users.

📝 *Remember*   A resident menu remains in memory to validate the user's selection.

You have two approaches when writing resident menus: the hybrid batch file and the stand-alone batch file. With a hybrid batch file, the menu system stays in memory to validate your selection but then calls on stand-alone batch files to run the menu selection. With a stand-alone batch file, a single batch file both validates the user's selection, executes that selection, and then redisplays the menu.

Both of these approaches require something that the non-resident menu does not: an EXIT or QUIT. Occasionally, someone will want to issue a command or run a program that's not on the menu. Because the non-resident menu simply leaves you at the DR DOS prompt after displaying the menu, that's simple. Because the resident menu keeps you within the cocoon of a batch file, you need a specific command to exit the menu to get to the DR DOS prompt.

Hybrid batch file   In this chapter, we will be developing a sample complete hybrid resident non-nested menu system. All of the files for this demonstration system are stored in the \MENU2 subdirectory on the disk that comes with this book. In order to allow you to experiment with the hybrid resident non-nested menu system, the batch files shown in the book have been slightly modified for the disk. These modifications are the same modifications that were mentioned earlier for the non-resident non-nested menu system.

As explained before, the hybrid system uses the same batch files to run the menu select as does the non-resident system. For that reason, none of the batch files to run the software is printed in this chapter, although all of them are included on the disk.

The difference comes in with MENU.BAT, now called MENU2.BAT. After displaying the menu, it stays in memory waiting for the user to enter a keystroke. When the user makes a selection, MENU2.BAT first verifies that the user made a valid selection. If her solution was valid, it simply runs the proper batch file. Because that batch file will reload

MENU2.BAT, it runs the batch file without the CALL command. If the user makes an invalid selection, MENU2.BAT displays an error message and waits for the user to make another selection. MENU2.BAT is shown in detail in Fig. 29-3.

☑ *Remember* A hybrid menu system offers the advantages of a non-resident system plus user selection validation.

As you can see from Fig. 29-3, MENU2.BAT is only somewhat more complex than MENU.BAT shown above. Additionally, 1.BAT through 6.BAT will still function as stand-alone batch files. So you have the additional error-checking that the resident menus offer, plus the advantage of the batch files working from anywhere without having to run the menu that the non-resident menus offer. Thus, at the expense of a slightly more complex menu batch file, a hybrid menu system offers all of the advantages of both the non-resident and resident systems without the complexities of the full resident menu system. That makes the hybrid system well suited for those applications—like new users—where you want the control of a resident system without the added complexity.

Batch File Line	Explanation
@ECHO OFF	Turn command-echoing off.
REM NAME: MENU2.BAT REM PURPOSE: Display Menu And Position DOS REM In Proper Location & Validate REM User Selections REM VERSION: 1.00 REM DATE: June 2, 1992	Documentation remarks.
NEEDHELP %0 %1	Use the NeedHelp utility program to check and see if the user started the batch file with a /? switch.
IF ERRORLEVEL 1 GOTO HELP	If the user requested help, jump to a special section to display that information.
REM C: REM Change Line Below To CD\ On Your System CD\MENU2	Change to the appropriate drive and subdirectory on your system.
SCREEN2	Display the screen.
:RETRY	Label used to loop when the user makes an invalid selection.

29-3 MENU2.BAT drives a hybrid non-nested menu system.

Batch File Line	Explanation
BATCMD GN	Use the BATCMD command to obtain a number from the user.
IF ERRORLEVEL 7 GOTO WRONG	If the user entered 7-9, that is an invalid selection, so jump to an error-handling section. Because ERRORLEVEL tests are greater-than or equal, the possible values from BATCMD (0-9) must be tested from largest to smallest.
IF ERRORLEVEL 6 6 IF ERRORLEVEL 5 5 IF ERRORLEVEL 4 4 IF ERRORLEVEL 3 3 IF ERRORLEVEL 2 2 IF ERRORLEVEL 1 1	If the user entered 1-6, then they made a valid selection corresponding to a batch file, so run that batch file. Because the batch file is run without the CALL command, control does not return directly to MENU2.BAT; however, each batch file calls MENU2.BAT as its last command.
IF ERRORLEVEL 0 GOTO END	If the user selected 0, they want to exit the menu system to leave the batch file.
:WRONG	Label marking the beginning of the error-handling section. The batch file only reaches this section and beyond via a GOTO command.
BATCMD PC 19 1	Position the cursor using the BATCMD program.
ECHO Invalid Selection	Display an error-message.
BATCMD BE	Beep the speaker using the BATCMD program.
GOTO RETRY	Go back through the user selection loop again.

29-3 Continued.

Simple batch file menus **255**

Batch File Line	Explanation
:HELP ECHO Displays The Menu GOTO END	Display a help screen and exit the batch file when the user requests help.
:END	Label marking the end of the batch file.

29-3 Continued.

Stand-alone batch file   In this chapter, we will be developing a sample complete stand-alone resident non-nested menu system. All of the files for this demonstration system are stored in the \MENU3 subdirectory on the disk that comes with this book. In order to allow you to experiment with the stand-alone resident non-nested menu system, the batch files shown in the book have been slightly modified for the disk. These modifications are the same modifications explained for the non-resident non-nested menu system earlier.

☑ *Remember*   A stand-alone resident menu is one where a single batch file displays the menu, validates selections and runs menu options.

A stand-alone resident non-nested menu is one where a single batch file displays the menu, handles user selection validation, and handles running all of the applications. These tend to be massive batch files that are difficult to write and harder to maintain. The stand-alone approach is most useful under three circumstances:

- Compilers. You plan on compiling the batch file using a batch file compiler, like Builder or Builder Lite. However, most batch file compilers offer their own menuing options that are usually much more powerful than those in batch files, so here you are better off using the native language to develop the menu than you are the batch language. A few compilers (like Bat2Exec) offer no native menu support, so you must write them in the batch language.
- Space. If your hard disk is very pushed for space, you can often save a little space by using one massive batch file over several smaller ones. However, this approach requires the presence of a utility like Batcmd to get information from the user. If you have that on your hard disk anyway, it's not a consideration. If you do not have Batcmd on your hard disk, then the combination of Batcmd and the large batch file can exceed the space required for the individual batch files.
- Security. If you want to control who runs the applications or how they are run, then building that security into a central batch file is much easier than building it into each individual batch file. Additionally, not being able to run individual batch files adds additional security. In fact, security is the very best justification for a stand-alone approach to resident menus.

While the batch file that drives a stand-alone resident menu is long and complex, it possesses one secret that makes it easy to write and fairly easy to debug. This batch file is nothing more than the batch file used for the hybrid menu, only instead of running another batch file for valid selections, it runs one of its own internal routines using the GOTO command.

▶ **Remember** Stand-alone resident menus are easier to create and debug if you start by developing a hybrid resident or a non-resident system and merging all the batch files together once it is operational.

MENU3.BAT is the driving menu for my sample stand-alone resident menu. It is shown in Fig. 29-4. To create MENU3.BAT, I took MENU2.BAT (Fig. 29-3) and modified the ERRORLEVEL tests to GOTO a separate section of the batch file rather than running a separate batch file. For each of these six sections, I imported 1.BAT through 6.BAT, stripped off the documentation and command line help, and added a GOTO command to the bottom. Once I finished those two steps, MENU3.BAT was finished and ready to use.

Batch File Line	Explanation
@ECHO OFF	Turn command-echoing off.
REM NAME: MENU3.BAT REM PURPOSE: Stand-Alone Resident REM Non-Nested Menu REM VERSION: 1.00 REM DATE: June 2, 1992	Documentation remarks.
NEEDHELP %0 %1	Use the NeedHelp utility program to check and see if the user started the batch file with a /? switch.
IF ERRORLEVEL 1 GOTO HELP	If the user requested help, jump to a special section to display that information.
:TOP	Label marking the top of the menu portion of the batch file. As each menu option terminates, it will jump to this label to redisplay the menu.
REM C: REM Change Line Below To CD\ On Your System CD\MENU3	Change to the appropriate drive and subdirectory on your system.
SCREEN2	Display the screen.

29-4 MENU3.BAT drives a stand-alone non-nested menu system.

Batch File Line	Explanation
`:RETRY`	Label used to loop when the user makes an invalid selection.
`BATCMD GN`	Use the BATCMD command to obtain a number from the user.
`IF ERRORLEVEL 7 GOTO WRONG`	If the user entered 7-9, that is an invalid selection, so jump to an error-handling section. Because ERRORLEVEL tests are greater-than or equal, the possible values from BATCMD (0-9) must be tested from largest to smallest.

`IF ERRORLEVEL 6 GOTO 6`
`IF ERRORLEVEL 5 GOTO 5`
`IF ERRORLEVEL 4 GOTO 4`
`IF ERRORLEVEL 3 GOTO 3`
`IF ERRORLEVEL 2 GOTO 2`
`IF ERRORLEVEL 1 GOTO 1`
	For each of these valid selections, jump to a separate section of the batch file to handle the selection.

`IF ERRORLEVEL 0 GOTO END`	If the user selected 0, they want to exit the menu system to leave the batch file.
`:WRONG`	Label marking the beginning of the error-handling section. The batch file only reaches this section and beyond via a GOTO command.
`BATCMD PC 19 1`	Position the cursor using the BATCMD program.
`ECHO Invalid Selection`	Display an error-message.
`BATCMD BE`	Beep the speaker using the Batcmd program.
`GOTO RETRY`	Go back through the user selection loop again.

29-4 Continued.

Batch File Line	Explanation

`:1`
    `REM C:`
    `REM CD\WORD`
    `PROMPT EXIT To Return To Word`
    `REM WORD`
    `REM Delete The Next Two Lines`
    `WORD`
    `PAUSE`
    `PROMPT $P$G`
`GOTO TOP`
	Section to handle the first menu option. Notice how these commands exactly mirror the commands in 1.BAT. That makes it fairly easy to convert a hybrid system to a stand-alone system.

`:2`
    `REM C:`
    `REM CD\123`
    `PROMPT EXIT To Return To 1-2-3`
    `REM 123`
    `REM Delete The Next Two Lines`
    `123`
    `PAUSE`
    `PROMPT $P$G`
`GOTO TOP`
	Section to handle the second menu option.

`:3`
    `REM C:`
    `REM CD\XBASE`
    `PROMPT EXIT To Return To XBASE`
    `REM XBASE`
    `REM Delete The Next Two Lines`
    `XBASE`
    `PAUSE`
    `PROMPT $P$G`
`GOTO TOP`
	Section to handle the third menu option.

`:4`
    `REM C:`
    `REM CD\GAMES`
    `PROMPT EXIT To Return To Chess`
    `REM Chess`
    `REM Delete The Next Two Lines`
    `Chess`
    `PAUSE`
    `PROMPT $P$G`
`GOTO TOP`
	Section to handle the fourth menu option.

29-4 Continued.

Batch File Line	Explanation

`:5`
   `FORMAT-1 A:`
   `PAUSE`
`GOTO TOP`
	Section to handle the fifth menu option.

`:6`
   `BACKUP-1 C:\ A: /S`
   `PAUSE`
`GOTO TOP`
	Section to handle the sixth menu option.

`:HELP`
   `ECHO Displays The Menu`
`GOTO END`
	Display a help screen and exit the batch file when the user requests help.

`:END`	Label marking the end of the batch file.

29-4 Continued.

Nested menus

A nested menu is nothing more than one menu that has one or more of its menu items as additional menus rather than a program. Nested menus are more difficult to set up using stand-alone or hybrid batch files than they are with stand-alone batch files. The reason is numbering. Suppose the menu we have been working on had option four "Play Chess" replaced by "Play Games," and that menu selection brought up a selection of the different games you have installed on your system. The first menu used options 1–6 corresponding to 1.BAT to 6.BAT, so this second menu cannot easily reuse these numbers. This second menu might use A–G corresponding to A.BAT to G.BAT. Now, if you add a third and fourth menu, what are you going to use to select the items with?

You might try A–G for the first menu, H–M for the second, and N–S for the third. But what do you do when you need to add a menu item to the first menu? If you make it H, all the menus have to be renumbered and the commands the users have learned no longer work the same. If you use T, because it's the next available letter, then the menu items are not numbered sequentially. There is no good solution to this problem with a stand-alone system.

You have the same problem with a hybrid system if you want the menu options used within the hybrid system to correspond with the batch files—that is, if selecting option 1 runs 1.BAT. If you are willing to give that up and have option 1 run a batch file like WP.BAT, then nesting menus with a hybrid system is no more difficult than it is with a stand-alone system. However, this gives up the advantage of a hybrid system because knowing the menu option used inside the hybrid system does not allow you to run that program from anywhere on the hard disk without working through the menu first.

![skull icon] **Warning** Finding unique, single-digit names for each menu option in a nested menu is difficult with non-resident and hybrid systems.

Because everything is built into a stand-alone system, the numbering scheme used for one menu cannot interfere with the number scheme used for another menu, so you are free to reuse numbers or letters at will. That makes developing nested menus much easier in a stand-alone system.

I must warn you that programming nested menus with batch files is difficult; and the more complex the menu structure, the more difficult it is. Your best approach if you have a lot of programs to run is to try and fit all the options on one, or at most two, menus. By using short descriptions and a multi-column format, you can easily list sixty or more menu options on a single screen. By using the twenty-six letters and ten single-digit numbers, the most programs you can run with a single- digit command is thirty-six, and that will easily fit on a two-column screen with room left for instructions and formatting.

If you need more menu items than this, you are probably better off using a dedicated menu system rather than batch files. One of the better dedicated menu systems is Automenu from Magee Enterprises. This is a shareware program, so you'll find it on many bulletin board systems.

DR DOS 6 specific menus

If you are designing a menu system that will run only on DR DOS 6 machines, then DR DOS 6 has all the tools that you need to build that menu, so you won't need a batch utility program like Batcmd. The secret here is the SWITCH command. The format of SWITCH is

SWITCH *Label1, Label2, Label3, ... , Label9*

where the SWITCH is followed by up to nine labels separated by commas. When DR DOS 6 encounters a SWITCH command, it pauses and waits for the user to press a key, ignoring any keys other than 1–9. When the user presses a valid key, DR DOS 6 jumps to the associated label using the equivalent of a GOSUB command. If the user presses a 3, the batch file acts as though a GOSUB LABEL3 command was issued.

SWITCH-M.BAT in Fig. 29-5 illustrates the SWITCH command with a working batch file. Before SWITCH-M.BAT would be operational, it would need to be modified to issue the commands needed to run these applications rather than simply displaying messages. One interesting note about SWITCH-M.BAT is it is completely self-contained; it needs no utility to key a keystroke from the user, it needs no other batch files to run, and it handles all text display itself. As a result, you could easily share SWITCH-M.BAT with other users.

Batch File Line	Explanation
@ECHO OFF	Turn command-echoing off.
REM NAME: SWITCH-M.BAT REM PURPOSE: Show SELECT Command REM VERSION: 1.00 REM DATE: June 11, 1992	Documentation remarks.

29-5 The SWITCH command allows you to build a stand-alone resident menu system using all DR DOS 6 commands.

Batch File Line	Explanation
NEEDHELP %0 %1	Use the NeedHelp utility program to check and see if the user started the batch file with a /? switch.
IF ERRORLEVEL 1 GOTO HELP	If the user requested help, jump to a special section to display that information.
:TOP	Label marking the top of the menu loop.
CLS	Clear the screen.
ECHO 1 = Run Word Processor ECHO 2 = Run Spreadsheet ECHO 3 = Run Database ECHO 4 = Play Chess Echo 5 = Format A Floppy Disk ECHO 6 = Backup Hard Disk To Floppy ECHO 9 = Exit	Display the menu.

SWITCH WP, LOTUS, DATABASE, CHESS,
    FORMAT, BACKUP, INVALID,
    INVALID, END
	Use the DR DOS 6 Switch command to select a section to function as a subroutine. Pressing 1 selects WP, pressing 2 selects LOTUS, and so on. Notice that the INVALID section is used twice. This is a quick way to handle invalid selections. Notice also how the EXIT option selects the END section and exits the batch file.

GOTO TOP	After returning from the subroutine, loop through the menu again.

:HELP
    ECHO Show Using The SELECT Command
    ECHO To Build A Menu
GOTO END
	Display a help screen and exit the batch file when the user requests help.

:CHESS
    ECHO Playing Chess
    PAUSE
RETURN
	Section to handle the chess game option on the menu. Notice the section ends with a RETURN command and the sections do not have to appear in the batch file in the same order they appear after the SELECT command.

29-5 Continued.

Batch File Line	Explanation

``
:FORMAT
    ECHO Formatting A Floppy Disk
    PAUSE
RETURN
``
	Section to handle formatting a disk. In all of these sections, you would want to replace the existing commands with the commands needed to run the software on your system.

``
:BACKUP
    ECHO Backing Up Hard Disk
    PAUSE
RETURN
``
	Section to handle performing a backup.

``
:INVALID
    ECHO Invalid Option Selected
    ECHO Press Any Key To Try Again
    PAUSE > NUL
RETURN
``
	Section to handle an invalid selection. Notice it displays an error-message, pauses so the reader can read the error-message and then uses a RETURN command to go back to the menu.

``
:WP
    ECHO Running Word Processor
    PAUSE
RETURN
``
	Section to handle running the word processor.

``
:LOTUS
    ECHO Running Spreadsheet
    PAUSE
RETURN
``
	Section to handle running the spreadsheet.

``
:DATABASE
    ECHO Running Database
    PAUSE
RETURN
``
	Section to handle running the database.

``` :END ```	Label marking the end of the batch file. Notice that this label is referenced in the SWITCH command for the option to exit the menu.

29-5 Continued.

If less than nine labels are listed on the line, the DR DOS 6 ignores numbers higher than the number of labels on the line. For example, with the command

SWITCH WP SPREAD DATABASE

DR DOS 6 would ignore any number higher than 3 because there are no labels beyond the third label.

Several other structural considerations are important:

• The SWITCH command has no built-in facilities for displaying the pending options.

As a result, you have to handle that in the batch file prior to issuing the SWITCH command. You can, of course, use ECHO commands for this.

- Like all resident menus, the menu being displayed by the SWITCH command needs an EXIT. You see this in SWITCH-M.BAT in Fig. 29-5 as the :END label being used as the last label in the SWITCH command. I almost always have EXIT as option 9 in these menus.

- It can be confusing for the user to press a number and have nothing happen. I usually avoid this by having a single section to handle invalid selections. Because I always have the exit option as number 9, I use this invalid selection section to pad all the selections between the last acceptable selection and the number 9 exit selection.

- Because you normally want to stay in a resident menu until the user selects the exit option, the SELECT command needs to be followed by a GOTO command to cause the batch file to loop through the menu again.

In addition, it is important to remember that the SWITCH command is a DR DOS 6-specific command. It will not work under DR DOS 5 or any version of MS DOS. It also will not work when using a batch file compiler.

☠ *Warning*   While the SWITCH command makes it easy to write menus under DR DOS 6, the resulting batch files will not run under DR DOS 5 or MS DOS and cannot be compiled with a batch file compiler.

While SWITCH-M.BAT is a stand-alone menu and this section has focused on the stand-alone menu, you can also develop a hybrid menu using the SWITCH command. To do that, each section in the batch file would need to call a stand-alone batch file to perform the work. For example, the WP section of SWITCH-M.BAT could be replaced with

```
:WP
     CALL 1.BAT
RETURN
```

By modifying all the sections in a similar fashion, SWITCH-M.BAT would run as a hybrid resident menu system.

Because the SWITCH command always uses the numbers 1 through 9, it isn't possible to develop a hybrid nested menu system because the batch file would need to call on batch files named other than 1.BAT through 9.BAT in order to handle all the menu options. While it still uses external batch files, that difference in names would prevent the user from using the same keystroke inside and outside the menu system.

Summary

The purpose of a menu system is to handle much of the overhead involved in running programs and other routine tasks.

A hard disk is like a filing cabinet; it needs a consistent filing system.

A subdirectory is a logical subdivision of a hard disk.

The CD or CHDIR command is used to change subdirectories.

The FDISK command is used to prepare a hard disk for use. Using it erases anything stored on the hard disk.

The MD or MKDIR command is used to create a subdirectory.

The RM or RMDIR command is used to remove an existing subdirectory once the files have been erased.

A map of the subdirectories on a hard disk looks like an inverted tree.

First-level subdirectories are typically functional with subdirectories below that for data.

The four broad types of menus are non-resident non-nested, resident non-nested, non-resident nested, and resident nested.

A non-resident menu displays the menu option and then leaves the user at the DR DOS prompt to make your selection.

A resident menu displays the menu option and then remains in memory to validate the user's selection.

A non-nested menu is one where none of the menu items is an additional menu.

A nested menu is one where one or more of the menu items brings up additional menus.

A non-resident menu displays a test on the screen and then depends on batch files to run the menu options.

A non-resident non-nested menu allows you run the menu options anytime and anywhere on the hard disk, even if the menu is not being displayed.

Resident menus are more complex than non-resident menus.

A hybrid resident menu turns over the execution of menu options to other batch files after it has validated the selection.

A stand-alone resident menu handles menu display, selection validation, and option execution.

Nested menus are more difficult in non-resident and hybrid systems because of the difficulty of arranging for different batch file names for each menu option.

Nested menus are easier in stand-alone systems, but if you need to nest more than one or two menus, you are probably better off with a dedicated menu system.

The DR DOS 6 SWITCH command can be used to develop stand-alone and hybrid menus.

30

An anti-viral batch file

I'm not going to get into the controversy about whether viruses are actually a serious problem. Some people believe they represent a significant danger to our data, while others claim they're mostly marketing hype from the people selling anti-viral software. In either case, it makes sense to protect yourself, and it makes especially good sense to take those protection measures that don't require you to purchase additional software. I'll leave it to others to explain "safe" computing, but I'll show you how you can use the operating system and a batch file to protect yourself.

If basic safe computing practices aren't enough to make you feel safe but you don't want to spend the money to purchase an anti-viral software package, then try the following three steps. While they don't offer nearly as much protection as anti- viral software, they use nothing but DR DOS and a tiny utility that comes with this book, so they're free. Plus, they're all fairly unobtrusive (in other words, they rarely get in the way). That's important. If the anti-viral procedures you use generate too many false alarms, you'll end up deactivating them.

Warning   If the anti-viral procedures you use generate too many false alarms, you'll get frustrated and deactivate them.

The three DR DOS-based anti-viral procedures are as follows:

1. Write-protect your program files.
2. Moving COMMAND.COM out of the root directory.
3. Test your critical program files to make sure they have not been altered.

Each step is examined here in more detail.

Remember   The three approaches DR DOS offers to virus protection are write-protecting critical files, moving COMMAND.COM, and comparing your critical files against an unaltered copy.

Write-protect program files

DR DOS comes with a program called ATTRIB that will let you mark files as read-only. While a smart virus can bypass this, it will stop some viruses. Not only that, but it will protect you against accidentally erasing the program files yourself, on most systems, this being a bigger threat. The command to mark files as read-only is

ATTRIB *Filename* +r

ATTRIB accepts wildcards, so you can mark more than one file at a time. You can also use the /s switch to mark all the files along the current path. You should be able to mark all your program files (*.EXE and *.COM) as read-only without any problems. If you later need to erase a file, you can turn off the read-only setting with the following command:

ATTRIB *Filename* −r

Move COMMAND.COM out of the root directory

More viruses hit COMMAND.COM than any other file, primarily because almost every computer has COMMAND.COM and it runs every time the computer runs. Because COMMAND.COM runs every time the computer boots, infecting it gives a virus the largest opportunity to be running when other disks are available for infection.

Most computers have COMMAND.COM in the root directory, so some viruses won't take the time to look elsewhere. However, you can put COMMAND.COM into any subdirectory you like. On my system, I have it in the \SYSLIB (system library) subdirectory.

To move COMMAND.COM to another subdirectory, follow these easy steps:

1. Copy COMMAND.COM to the subdirectory on your hard disk where you store your DR DOS files.
2. Leave a copy in the root directory as a sacrificial lamb. DR DOS won't be using that copy, so it doesn't matter as much if it becomes infected.
3. Add the following line to your CONFIG.SYS file:

   'SHELL=C:\SYSLIB\COMMAND.COM /P

4. Add the following line to your AUTOEXEC.BAT file:

   SET COMSPEC=C:\SYSLIB\COMMAND.COM

Replace C:\SYSLIB in this command with the subdirectory you use to store your copy of COMMAND.COM. In Step 3, you must specify the .COM after COMMAND and you must specify /P, or DR DOS won't run your AUTOEXEC.BAT file. You can expand the environment at the same time. Chapter 13 has the details.

This is by no means a foolproof method. First, your COMSPEC variable always points to your real COMMAND.COM, so any virus can check its contents and infect COM-MAND.COM no matter where it's located or what it's named. There's also a second, though less obvious, problem. You must make sure that your path statement doesn't point to the root directory, or you could end up running the "fake" COMMAND.COM.

For example, Microsoft Word lets you shell to the DR DOS prompt by "running" COMMAND.COM. What it does is run a second copy of the command processor. If your root directory is in your PATH and comes before the directory containing the proper version of COMMAND.COM, Word will run the fake version. No matter how your path is set, Word will run the fake version if it's logged into the root directory when you issue this command. If the fake version is infected and you run it, then you risk infecting other files.

Test your critical files

You can test COMMAND.COM against a good copy with a batch file. This requires that you have a good copy stored under a different name available for testing.

The approach to this problem requires some trickery as well. Both DR DOS 5 and 6 come with the COMP program for comparing two files, and DR DOS 6 adds the FC program (file compare) to also compare files. However, none of these programs sets ERRORLEVEL, so there's no direct way of informing the batch file how the test went. Doing that will take three tricks.

The first trick is fairly easy. Both the DR DOS 5 and 6 versions of COMP display the message "*n* Mismatches" when files do not match, where *n* is a number representing the number of mismatches. Because we don't care how many mismatches occurred, only that at least one occurred, we can use the FIND filter to search for the text "Mismatches" and pipe the results to a file. If the resulting file is a 0-length file, then no mismatches were found and the files were the same. If one or more mismatches were found, then this file contains text and one of these two versions of COMMAND.COM has been modified.

Neither DR or MS DOS has a direct way of checking to see if a file is a 0-length file, but MS DOS offers an indirect way. MS DOS will not copy 0-length files, so you can test a file in MS DOS by trying to copy it. If the copy is successful and the new file exists, the file is not a 0-length file; if it fails, the file *is* a 0-length file. However, this test fails under DR DOS because both the COPY and XCOPY commands successfully copy 0-length files.

So, our second trick involves testing to see if a file is a 0-length file. To do this, the disk includes a copy of a program called IsItZero. The command to use IsItZero is

ISITZERO *File*

where the *File* does not contain wildcards. IsItZero returns one of five different ERROR-LEVELs:

0   The user requested command line help, so IsItZero performs no testing.
1   The file you requested IsItZero to test does not exist.
2   No file to test was specified on the command line.
3   The file size is greater than 0.
4   The file is a 0-length file. Because this is the highest ERRORLEVEL IsItZero returns, testing for a 0-length file can involve the single IF ERRORLEVEL 4 rather than a nested If-test or even several tests.

A third trick overcomes a bug in both the DR DOS 5 and 6 versions of COMP. When you use COMP to compare two files of different lengths from the command line, COMP displays the message "Files are not the same size. Compare them anyway (Y/N)?" and you must answer yes to continue the test. However, when asked to compare two files of different lengths from a batch file, COMP does not display this message; although, it still expects a yes response. To overcome this, the batch file pipes a "Y" to COMP when it runs it. If COMMAND.COM is unmodified, and therefore the same length, this "Y" is ignored. However, if COMMAND.COM has been modified in such a way that the lengths are different, this "Y" allows the batch file to continue without user intervention.

TESTCOMM.BAT in Fig. 30-1 pulls all this together and tests the integrity of COMMAND.COM with a batch file.

Batch File Line	Explanation
`@ECHO OFF`	Turn command-echoing off.

`REM NAME:      TESTCOMM.BAT`
`REM PURPOSE: Verify COMMAND.COM Good`
`REM VERSION: 2.00`
`REM DATE:     June 3, 1992`
	Documentation remarks.

`NEEDHELP %0 %1`	Use the NeedHelp utility program to check and see if the user started the batch file with a /? switch.
`IF ERRORLEVEL 1 GOTO HELP`	If the user requested help, jump to a special section to display that information.

`REM Simple Anti-Viral Program`
`REM to Test COMMAND.COM`
`REM I Have COMMAND.COM Stored in`
`REM My \SYSLIB Subdirectory Rather`
`REM Than in my Root Directory`
`REM There is an Identical`
`REM Copy in my \MISC Subdirectory`
`REM Under the Name TEST.TXT`
	Documentation remarks.

`ECHO Y	COMP C:\SYSLIB\COMMAND.COM` ` C:\MISC\TEST.TXT	FIND "Mismatches"` ` > JUNK`	Run the COMP program to compare these two files, piping it a "Y" in case they have a different length. Then, searching for the word "Mismatches" and piping the results of that search to another file.

30-1 TESTCOMM.BAT tests for modifications to COMMAND.COM.

Batch File Line	Explanation
`ISITZERO JUNK`	Running the IsItZero utility program that comes with this book to see if this is a 0-length file.
`IF ERRORLEVEL 4 ECHO COMMAND.COM OK` `IF ERRORLEVEL 4 GOTO END`	If JUNK is a 0-length file, no mismatches were found, so display a quick message and exit.
`IF ERRORLEVEL 3 GOTO VIRUS`	If JUNK contains text, then COMP found differences, indicating that COMMAND.COM has been modified, so jump to an error-handling routine.
`GOTO OTHER`	
	IsItZero encountered some other kind of error so jump to an error-handling routine.

`:OTHER`
   `ECHO Non-Virus Problem Encountered`
   `ECHO Check Batch File For Modification`
   `ECHO And Review Instructions In`
   `ECHO DR DOS Batch File Programming Book`
`GOTO END`
	Tell the user what happened and exit the batch file.

`:VIRUS`
   `ECHO COMMAND.COM MODIFIED!`
   `ECHO Find Problem Before Continuing`
   `PAUSE`
`GOTO END`
	Tell the user COMMAND.COM has been modified. Pause the batch file to give the reader long enough to read the message and then exit the batch file.

`:HELP`
   `ECHO TESTCOMM.BAT Compares The`
   `ECHO Existing COMMAND.COM With A`
   `ECHO Version Known To Be Good And`
   `ECHO Reports The Results`
`GOTO END`
	Display a help screen and exit the batch file when the user requests help.

`:END`	Label marking the end of the batch file.
`DEL JUNK`	Delete this working file before leaving the batch file.

30-1 Continued.

This test is not a perfect test because of the way COMP tests files of different lengths. When one file is 1000-bytes long and the other is 1200-bytes long but both are identical for the first 1000 bytes, then Comp reports that they are the same rather than reporting a mismatch. Thus, if anything is appended onto the end of COMMAND.COM without affecting the portion up to the original end of the file, this test will not spot the change.

This test isn't restricted to COMMAND.COM, or even program files. You could have the batch file test any or all critical files on your hard disk. That would require a lot of room, however, because you need a second copy of any files you're testing. The test takes about ten seconds on my 386/20, so doing more than one or two tests in the AUTOEXEC.BAT file could significantly slow down booting. For multiple tests, you might want to create a separate batch file that you run once a day or even once every few days.

✔ *Remember*   This virus test isn't restricted to COMMAND.COM; you can use it on any important file.

Conclusion

None of these methods are as good as running a good anti-viral software package, but users with only a low chance of infection might find these measures adequate.

Summary

Making COMMAND.COM and other program files read-only might stop a simple virus.

Hiding COMMAND.COM in a subdirectory and even changing its name might stop some viruses.

You can compare COMMAND.COM and other mission-critical programs against known good copies to see if they've been modified.

31

A document archival system

What I'm going to describe in this chapter is a complete system for making sure that you never lose an important file. Because it consists of several major sections, you can adopt only those sections that are critical to your own applications. The major sections to my overall document archival system are listed next.

Ⅲ➡ *Note* This is a complete system to make sure you never again lose an important data file!

- Periodic backups. Absolutely nothing is more important than periodically backing up your hard disk or important floppy disks. This is the only part of this plan that I recommend to everyone. In fact, without periodic backups, the rest of this system is fairly useless. If you don't care enough about your data to protect it without a backup, then why waste time protecting it in any other fashion?
- Systematically copy critical data files. Many important data files undergo routine revisions. Prior to making a major revision, I copy the file to be revised to a special holding subdirectory.
- Never delete old files. I never erase an old file. Instead, I copy it to a special holding subdirectory. When that subdirectory is full of files, I copy the files to a disk and erase them from the subdirectory. I then store the disk in a safe place. I currently have 125 such disks.
- Index document files. I use a commercial indexing package to index my word processing documents so I can find them faster.

Each part of my overall document archival system is explained in much more detail, as follows next.

Periodic backups

Back when everyone used floppies, the most damage you could do with one mistake was 320K. Like mistakes, bad disks or defective hardware rarely damaged more than 320K. Large hard disks, however, now give us the ability to damage 200M or more of data with one mistake, or as the result of an errant command or defective hardware. 200M is over 135 high capacity floppy disks!

☠ *Warning*   If you don't care enough about your data to back it up, then why waste time protecting it in any other fashion?

I insure my computer with a company called Safeware. Recently, they sent out a newsletter listing some of the more unusual claims they had paid. This list included the following:

- A California man carried some work home with him. He kept the disks in a box that looked like his cat's litter box. As you might expect, the cat used the disk box to relieve himself and destroyed all the data on the disks.
- A California boy was hiding behind the family computer during a friendly game of hide-and-seek. When a friend found him, the boy made a heroic dash to avoid being tagged. While dashing, he tripped over the power cord. That sent a shock through the computer that caused the hard disk to crash.
- A Los Angeles motorist collided with a fire hydrant, sending a column of water into the air. That water entered a nearby office building, damaging several computers.
- A California man knocked his fish tank over, spilling all the water into his computer.
- A Florida man had his laptop out near the pool. The family dog bumped the table and sent the computer to the bottom of the pool.

As you can see, computers can be damaged by a number of unexpected events. While an insurance policy like the one from Safeware can protect your hardware and even your programs, it's up to you to protect your data.

I just saw a graphic reminder of the importance of backups on CNN. As I am writing this chapter, the presidential primaries are over and the political news has quieted down until the conventions. However, CNN reported on a break-in at the campaign headquarters of Ross Perot. The only damage reported was the erasure of a file containing the names of 17,000 supporters. As you can imagine, this has the potential of doing millions of dollars of damage to a campaign if these 17,000 supporters are the more generous supporters. In a close race, it could even determine the outcome! However, at the close of the report, the CNN reporter noted that the Perot campaign had a backup disk.

Many small businesses maintain all their records—all the payroll records, tax information, bid information, and more—on a single microcomputer. Imagine the impact to that business if those records were lost. I know of one company that had their three computers stolen. To make matters worse, they didn't have backups. They were so desperate for the data that they ran ads saying that the thieves could keep the computers and they wouldn't press charges if they could just get their data back. They never did, and they ended up going out of business.

I know of a large utility company that maintains a lot of their rate case information on microcomputers. One of the analysts tried to format a floppy with (you guessed it) the FORMAT command at the C prompt. He was lucky: a recent backup had been made and he lost only a few hours of work. The manager told me that losing the files on his hard disk would have delayed a multi-million-dollar rate case. He now requires daily backups.

IIII► *Note* Losing the files on a hard disk could cost a great deal of money and permanently damage a business.

I have about twenty articles in progress, the final version of my dissertation, a copy of this book, the related batch files, and several other books on my hard disk. Until recently, I make a daily incremental backup and two full weekly backups. One backup is stored at home and the other is stored at my office.

Is this carrying things too far? I don't think so. An incremental backup takes about two minutes, and the two full backups take less than half an hour. So I spend about an hour a week on backups, this hour being insurance. It would take an experienced typist over twenty hours to rekey just my dissertation, and it would take me thousands of hours to redo the research if I lost the hard disk copy and couldn't locate a printed copy. Even my notes are on the hard disk. Now add in the time to redo all the other files, and you begin to see why I make backups.

As I said, that was my approach until recently. I now have a very fast tape drive that can perform a full backup on both my hard disks in about twenty minutes, which is so fast that I've forgone incremental backups. I now make two full backups daily (one during supper and one after I quit for the night), and I keep the three latest versions of these two backup sets. One set is stored at home and the other is stored at the office.

Which file to back up?

You should have copies of most of your software on the original distribution disks, so you don't need to back up these files very often. Just keep the originals in a safe place so they can't be damaged. Even in the worst case of fire or theft, you can always replace your software by buying a new copy, so you will not lose your software.

☑ *Remember* Software comes with its own backup in the form of the distribution disks, making backing up your software less important.

Except during installation, programs don't often change. The software is "tied together" with system files that include batch files, AUTOEXEC.BAT, CONFIG.SYS, and subdirectories. You can safely go a long time between backups of these files. They generally change only when you install new software or remove existing software.

If damaged, these system files can be replaced from an old backup or the original distribution disks. However, things aren't that simple with your data files. You create them and then usually modify them quite often. It's important, therefore, to back up these files frequently.

☑ *Remember* You create your data, so it's important to back up these files frequently.

Types of backup

Your first hard-drive backup should be a full backup. This gives you a good copy of installed software and system files, as well as a copy of your data files. When you change a data file, DR DOS automatically changes a flag it maintains to indicate that a current backup no longer exists. At the end of the day (or week, if you want to live dangerously), you can make an incremental backup. The backup software looks through your hard disk for files with the archive flag. The software backs up that file and resets the flag, and then looks for the next file.

This process is fairly painless because incremental backups are very quick. As you continue making incremental backups, the disks will begin to pile up. If you're constantly updating a 300K database, then you'll create a new copy of this file on disk every day. Most backup software won't remove earlier versions of this file from the backup disks during an incremental backup. Another problem is that files you've erased from the hard disk still exist on the backup disks. Files that have been renamed will exist on the backup disks under both names. If you have to restore from backup disks, you can end up with a lot of extra files.

You can reduce these minor problems by using LISTFILE.BAT. LISTFILE.BAT is shown here without command line help or internal documentation but the version on the disk has both.

```
@ECHO OFF
C:
CD
ATRIB *.* /S > C:  CHANGED.TXT
```

All LISTFILE.BAT does is create a file containing a list of all the files on the hard disk. On my 386/20 with a bulging 105M hard disk, it takes less than two minutes to run.

By running it before backing up, this file will also be backed up—even by an incremental backup because you just changed it. If you must restore, you can compare the files that exist after the restore to LISTING.TXT. Any files that exist on the hard disk but not in LISTING.TXT were either erased or renamed, so they can be deleted.

While incremental backups are quick, restoring from them can be cumbersome if they have been going on too long. At some point you'll have so many disks from incremental backups that it will be time to erase them and make another full backup.

These types of backups will protect you from hardware problems and mistakes but not from theft, fire, or other types of damage. For that, you need a second backup set, stored off-site. In order to create a second incremental backup, your backup program must give you the option of not resetting the archive flag, and not all of them do.

Warning Frequent backups alone will not protect your data against fire or theft. For that, you need an off-site backup.

Many organizations with very critical files maintain their three or so newest incremental backups. These are often called the grandfather, father, and son. The purpose of these multiple backups is that you can recreate changes to important files.

Multiple backups also give you a way to recover if your primary backup fails. I once needed to restore from a backup made when I was using PC Tools for backups. PC Tools had not displayed any error messages when making the backup but when I went to restore, not a single file on the backup was recoverable. I sent the diskettes to Central Point Software and they could not recover any data either. Luckily, I had a full backup from the day before, and it restored properly, so all I lost was one day's work. However, without that second backup, all of my data would have been lost.

Systematically copy critical data files

If you need multiple backups for only a few files, there's a better way than running your backup program several times a day. I have a subdirectory called C: OLD just for old copies of files. Every time I make a major change to a file, I copy it to this subdirectory with a number extension. So the first version of this chapter is CHAP-31.001, the second is CHAP-31.002, and so on. This way, I can always go back to an earlier version if I decide I don't like the changes I've made.

Figure 31-1 shows the layout of the example hard disk for this chapter. Figure 31-2 shows COPYBACK.BAT, a batch file to automate the copying of important files to the backup subdirectory. Note that it checks to make sure that the target filename doesn't exist before copying.

As these files continue to accumulate, you have a choice. You can erase older versions of the now modified (several times over) files, or you can copy them to floppy disks.

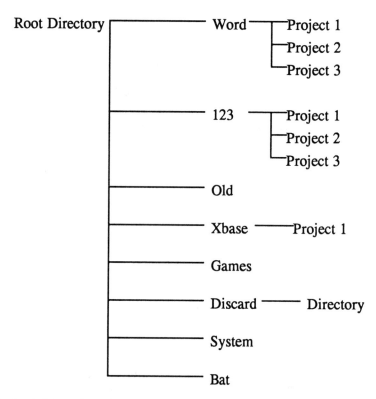

31-1   The hard disk configuration used by the batch files in this chapter.

Batch File Line	Explanation
`@ECHO OFF`	Turn command-echoing off.

`REM NAME:     BACKUP-3.BAT`
`REM PURPOSE: Copy Files To Backup Directory`
`REM VERSION: 1.00`
`REM DATE:    June 3, 1992`
	Documentation remarks.

`NEEDHELP %0 %1`	Use the NeedHelp utility program to check and see if the user started the batch file with a /? switch.
`IF ERRORLEVEL 1 GOTO HELP`	If the user requested help, jump to a special section to display that information.
`IF (%1)==() GOTO ERROR` `IF (%2)==() GOTO ERROR`	If the user did not enter the source or target filenames, jump to an error-handling section.
`IF EXIST C:\OLD\%2 GOTO EXISTS`	If the target filename already exists, jump to an error-handling section.
`COPY %1 C:\OLD\%2/V` `GOTO END`	Perform the actual copy if the batch file reaches this point then exit the batch file.

`:ERROR`
`    ECHO Source Or Target Name Not Entered`
`    ECHO At The Command Prompt Enter:`
`    ECHO BACKUP-S SOURCE TARGET`
`GOTO END`
	This is an error section that display an error-message and exits when the user does not enter the source and target filenames.

`:EXISTS`
`    ECHO %2 Already Exists!`
`    ECHO Select Another Name And Try Again`
`GOTO END`
	This is an error section that displays an error-message and exits when the target name entered by the user already exists.

`:END`	Label marking the end of the batch file.

31-2 COPYBACK.BAT makes a copy of important files in a backup subdirectory.

Never delete old files!

One of the things I learned a long time ago is that, just as soon as you erase a file, you end up needing it. As a result, I never completely erase a file unless I can easily recreate it. There are a lot of files on your hard disk that you can easily recreate, such as these:

- .OBJ files. When you run most compilers, they first turn your source code into .OBJ files, and then they turn the .OBJ files into .EXE files. If you have the source code, you can easily recreate the .OBJ files by running the compiler again.
- .BAK files. With most word processors, every time you save a file, the prior version is saved under the same name with a .BAK extension. Because I save all critical versions to a special subdirectory (as I explained previously), I routinely erase these files.
- .PRN files. These are ASCII files created by printing a spreadsheet file to a document. These can easily be recreated by reprinting the spreadsheet.
- .$$$ and .TMP files. These are working files created by some commercial packages. They're usually erased by the package when you exit, but a reboot or disk problem can leave them on your hard disk.
- Commercial program files. These are the files that come on your software disks. If you need to recreate these, you can copy them from the original disks.

These are about all the files I erase. For the rest of my files, when I'm finished using them, I copy them to a holding subdirectory called C:\DISCARD, and then I erase the original. Figure 31-3 shows DISCARD.BAT, the batch file I use for this. It copies all the files I list on the command line. Prior to copying, it checks to make sure that a file doesn't already exist in the \DISCARD subdirectory with the same name. After successfully copying the file, it erases the original.

Batch File Line	Explanation
`@ECHO OFF`	Turn command-echoing off.

`REM NAME:    DISCARD.BAT`
`REM PURPOSE: Moves Files To \DISCARD`
`REM VERSION: 1.00`
`REM DATE:    June 3, 1992`
	Documentation remarks.

`NEEDHELP %0 %1`	Use the NeedHelp utility program to check and see if the user started the batch file with a /? switch.
`IF ERRORLEVEL 1 GOTO HELP`	If the user requested help, jump to a special section to display that information.
`:TOP`	Label marking the top of the main loop.

31-3 DISCARD.BAT is a batch file to copy files to a discard subdirectory.

Batch File Line	Explanation
`IF (%1)==() GOTO END`	Once there are no more replaceable parameters, exit the batch file.
`IF EXIST C:\DISCARD\%1 GOTO ERROR`	If the file to be discarded already exists in the C:\DISCARD subdirectory, jump to an error-handling routine.
`COPY %1 C:\DISCARD\%1 /V`	If the batch file reaches this point, the file does not exist in the discard subdirectory, so copy it there.
`IF EXIST C:\DISCARD\%1 DEL %1`	If the copy was successful, erase the original file.
`SHIFT`	Move all the replaceable parameters down one level and make available another replaceable parameter as %9.
`GOTO TOP`	Continue looping.

`:ERROR`
`  ECHO %1 Already Exists In C:\DISCARD`
`  ECHO You Must Decide Which File To Keep`
`GOTO END`
	Display an error-message and exist when the file already exists in C:\DISCARD.

`:HELP`
`  ECHO Moves Files To \DISCARD`
`  ECHO List Files To Move After Name`
`GOTO END`
	Display a help screen and exit the batch file when the user requests help.

`:END`	Label marking the end of the batch file.

31-3 Continued.

Once I get a lot of files in the C:\DISCARD subdirectory, I copy them to a floppy disk and then delete them from the hard disk. Each of my floppy disks is numbered, from one to my latest one. After copying the files to a floppy disk, I perform three steps. First I erase the copied files from the hard disk. Next, I create a list of the files on the floppy disk. This list stays on the hard disk for easy retrieval when I want to search for a file. Finally, I index the document files on the hard disk.

Deleting all the files on the hard disk that were copied to the discard floppy disk would be easy if all the files were copied—all it would take is a DEL *.* command. However, I sometimes have more files than will fit on a single floppy, but not enough to justify using two. The problem is then to delete only those files that were actually copied to the discard floppy disk. DELOLD.BAT does just that. While it contains a number of lines to handle command line help and internal documentation, the operational commands are

```
A:
FOR %%j IN (*.*) DO DEL C:\DISCARD\%%j
C:
```

The batch file changes to the A drive first because it would be more difficult to write this batch file to run from the C drive.

To create a file on the hard disk containing a listing of all the files on the floppy disk, I change over to the C:\DIRECTORY subdirectory and issue the command

```
DIR A: > 99.DIR
```

replacing the 99 with the number of the current floppy disk. By maintaining a directory of all my discard floppy disks on my hard disk, I can rapidly search them for a file.

This might sound like overkill, especially if you rarely go back to a file after you're finished with it. The advantage to this system is that it's dirt cheap. In my area, 1.44M floppy disks currently cost about $10 per box of ten. So I have less than $125 invested in storing every one of my old files. The way I figure it, using just one of those files again saves me much more than $125. I've been using this system for several years now, and I'm very pleased with the results. In fact, I find these disks so useful, I recently started using DISKCOPY to make a duplicate to keep off-site for safety.

⏩ *Note*   I've been using this system for several years now and I'm very pleased with the results.

Index document files

Currently, a number of good word processing indexing programs are available. These programs take a word processing file or an ASCII file and create an index of it. These aren't indexes like you find in the back of a book; rather, they're indexes that allow you to search for every document that contains a specific phrase.

ZyIndex is such a package. It will index most word processing documents, using the format they're stored in. All you have to do is tell ZyIndex the format. I use ZyIndex to index all the text files on my discard floppy disks so I can rapidly locate information on them. A big drawback to ZyIndex, and all other indexing programs, is that it will index only text information; it won't index dBASE database files or Lotus spreadsheet files. To get around that problem, I create a small text file with the same name but a different extension that explains what the attached file does. For example, I create .WKT files to explain worksheet (spreadsheet) files. So HP.WKT explains in ASCII text what the file HP.WK1 does. I use .DBT files to explain the function of .DBF dBASE database files.

ZyIndex lets you assign names up to 30 characters to the floppy disks. These names can't include spaces, so I use an underscore to simulate a space. Because all the floppy disks are numbered, I give them the same name combined with their unique number. Disk number 43 would be named DISCARD_DISK_43.

INDEX.BAT runs the indexing program. It is shown below without the command line help or internal documentation of the version on the disk:

```
@ECHO OFF
IF (%1)==() GOTO NONE
```

```
CD\ZYINDEX
IF EXIST A:*.DOC ZYINDEX D:\ZYINDEX \ A:*.DOC/03 DISCARD_DISK_%1
IF EXIST A:*.WKT ZYINDEX D:\ZYINDEX \ A:*.WKT/01 DISCARD_DISK_%1
IF EXIST A:*.DBT ZYINDEX D:\ZYINDEX \ A:*.DBT/01 DISCARD_DISK_%1
GOTO END

:NONE
    ECHO You Did Not Enter A Number
    ECHO For The Floppy Disk
GOTO END

:END
```

It knows that the name should include the DISCARD_DISK_ specification, so I don't have to enter that. It also knows a number should be entered, so it checks to make sure that one was.

Conclusion

By following all four steps outlined in this chapter, you can be sure that you will never lose an important data file. Additionally, you will have the tools and techniques to quickly locate any single data file in your set of floppy disks that you use to store the old data files. I would be interested in hearing from any users who have success with this system or who find ways to improve this system.

Summary

By planning ahead and implementing a system of file control using a combination of commercial programs and batch files, you can make sure that you never again lose an important data file.

The major steps to this plan are periodic backups, duplicating critical data files before modification, copying old files to floppy disks rather than erasing them, and indexing data files with a commercial indexing program.

Periodic backups are critical to the health of your data.

Regular full backups and daily incremental backups will ensure the safety of your data.

For further protection, you must keep rolling backups where you keep the last two or backups.

For full protection, you need to keep both on-site and off-site copies of all your backups.

Program files and the batch files that support the operation of your system need backing up far less frequently than your data files.

LISTFILE.BAT makes sure every incremental backup includes a list of all the files currently on the hard disk.

If you make a backup copy of critical data files before modifying them by copying the file to a new name in a backup subdirectory, you can always revert to the prior version if you decide you do not like the changes you made.

COPYBACK.BAT automates the copying of important files to the backup subdirectory so you can keep multiple copies of those important files as you make modifications to them. This allows you to revert to earlier versions as needed.

For additional protection, as this subdirectory of prior versions of critical files grows, it can be copied to floppies rather than simply deleting files.

Program files can be safely deleted because you can restore them from the distribution diskettes as required.

Data files that are easily recreated, such as .PRN and .OBJ, can safely be deleted as required.

All other data files should be moved to a holding subdirectory rather than being deleted.

As this holding subdirectory fills up or when you need additional space on the hard disk, the files can be copied to floppy disks and then deleted from the hard disk.

A list of files for each floppy disk can be maintained on the hard disk to make locating a specific file quicker.

A commercial program can index the data files on the floppy disk to speed file location even more.

32

Simulating Doskey using batch files

MS DOS 5 comes with a wonderful keyboard enhancement program called Doskey. This memory resident program gives you three major command line enhancements:

- Command line macros
- Recall of prior command lines
- The ability to enter multiple commands on a single command line

When I've talked to MS DOS 5 users who have switched to DR DOS 6, far-and-away the most common complaint I hear is about having to give up Doskey. Well, I have a solution for you. In this chapter, you will see how to write batch files that give you much of the functionality of Doskey without any memory-resident component. In some cases, the batch files will even outperform Doskey!

Command line macros

With a command line macro, you enter a macro name and a command or series of commands on the command line. Unlike a command line recorder, a macro is not run immediately after it is created—it's merely stored in memory for later use. After that, every time you enter the macro name at the start of a command line, MS DOS 5 replaces it with the command assigned to it.

With Doskey, these assignments are stored in memory. That means they are lost when you turn the computer off or reboot. While you can save them to a file, you must edit that file before you have a way of recalling the definitions by using the file.

In order to recreate command line macros with a batch file, the batch file will have to be able to do the following things:

- Store a new macro. It can do this by piping the commands entered on the command line to a batch file.
- Run a macro stored in a file. It can do this by running the batch file containing the macro.
- Display the available macros. It can do this by simply typing the contents of each macro to the screen.

MACRO.BAT in Fig. 32-1 does all this. It restricts you to the macro names of 0–9, but clever users can modify this easily. It also limits your commands to nine "words" because %1, which contains the name of the macro, is shifted down to %0. However, clever users can easily modify this as well. Note that the lines that appear to only contain an echo command display a blank line by echoing an Alt-255 to the screen.

Batch File Line	Explanation
`@ECHO OFF`	Turn command-echoing off.

`REM NAME:     MACRO.BAT`
`REM PURPOSE: Run Macros From File`
`REM VERSION: 1.00`
`REM DATE:    November 6, 1991`
	Documentation remarks.

`NEEDHELP %0 %1`	Use the NeedHelp utility program to check and see if the user started the batch file with a /? switch.
`IF ERRORLEVEL 1 GOTO HELP`	If the user requested help, jump to a special section to display that information.
`IF NOT EXIST C:\MACRO\NUL MD C:\MACRO`	If the subdirectory used by this batch file to store macros does not exist, create it.
`IF (%1)==()  GOTO MISSING`	If the user failed to tell the batch file what to do, jump to an error-handling section.
`IF (%1)==(D) GOTO DISPLAY` `IF (%1)==(d) GOTO DISPLAY`	If the user requested a listing of the available macros, jump to a section to handle that.
`IF (%1)==(ABC123XYZ) GOTO SHOWTHEM`	If the first replaceable parameter is a special flag indicating the batch file is being called as a subroutine, jump to the subroutine section.
`IF (%2)==()  GOTO RUN`	If the second replaceable parameter is blank, then the user wants to run a macro so jump to the section to handle that.

32-1 MACRO.BAT allows you to define, view, and run keyboard macros.

Batch File Line	Explanation
`FOR %%J IN (0 1 2 3 4 5 6 7 8 9) DO` `    IF (%1)==(%%J) GOTO DEFINE`	If the batch file reaches this point, the user wants to define a macro. Loop through the acceptable names and jump to the definition routine if the user entered a valid name.
`GOTO ERROR1`	If the batch file reaches this point, the user entered an invalid macro name so jump to an error-handling routine.

`:ERROR1`
`    ECHO You Entered An Invalid Code On`
`    ECHO The Command Line`
`    ECHO`
`GOTO MISSING`
	When the user enters an invalid macro name, display an error-message and then jump to another error-handling section to display more information.

`:ERROR2`
`    ECHO The Command You Entered Was Too`
`    ECHO Long And Everything After The`
`    ECHO %9 Is Missing From The Macro`
`    ECHO`
`    ECHO Try To Shorten Your Command`
`GOTO END`
	When the user tries to create a macro containing more than nine words, display a warning that it was not created properly and then exit the batch file.

`:ERROR3`
`    ECHO The Macro You Selected (%1) Does`
`    ECHO Not Exist`
`    ECHO`
`GOTO MISSING`
	When the user tries to run a macro that does not exist, warn the user and then exit the batch file.

`:RUN`	Label marking the section that runs the macro.
`    IF NOT EXIST C:\MACRO\%1.BAT GOTO ERROR3`	Make sure the requested macro exists. If not, jump to an error-handling routine.
`    C:\MACRO\%1.BAT`	Run the macro. Because the CALL command is not used, control does not return to this batch file.

32-1 Continued.

Simulating Doskey using batch files **285**

Batch File Line	Explanation
`GOTO END`	Control does not return to this batch file, so this is used only for formatting to close the loop.

`:MISSING`
   `ECHO To Define A Macro, Enter The Number`
   `ECHO Followed By The Macro Defination`
   `ECHO`
   `ECHO Numbers 0-9 Are Allowed`
   `ECHO`
   `ECHO To Run An Existing Macro, Enter`
   `ECHO The Number Of That Macro`
   `ECHO`
   `ECHO The Available Macros Are:`
`GOTO DISPLAY`
	When a required value is missing, display an error-message and exit the batch file.

`:DISPLAY`	Label marking the top of the section to handle display each macro.
`FOR %%J IN (0 1 2 3 4 5 6 7 8 9) DO` `CALL MACRO ABC123XYZ %%J`	Loop through the ten possible macro names and for each one, call MACRO.BAT as a subroutine and pass it the name of the batch file.
`GOTO END`	Exit the batch file.
`:SHOWTHEM`	Label marking the top of the section that functions as a subroutine to display the existing macros.
`IF NOT EXIST C:\MACRO\%2.BAT GOTO END`	If this particular macro does not exist, exit the subroutine.
`ECHO --%2--`	The subroutine only reaches this point if the macro exists. Here, it displays the macro name because it was passed to the subroutine as the second replaceable parameter with the macro flag being the first.

32-1 Continued.

Batch File Line	Explanation
`TYPE C:\MACRO\%2.BAT|FIND /V "@ECHO OFF"`	Type the batch file and use the find filter to display the line without the @ECHO OFF command.
`ECHO`	Display a blank line.
`GOTO END`	Exit the subroutine.
`:DEFINE`	Label marking the beginning of the section to create a new macro.
`SHIFT`	Move all the replaceable parameters down one level and make available another replaceable parameter as %9. This makes the macro name %0.
`ECHO @ECHO OFF > C:\MACRO\%0.BAT`	Pipe an @ECHO OFF command into the macro.
`ECHO %1 %2 %3 %4 %5 %6 %7 %8` `%9 >> C:\MACRO\%0.BAT`	Pipe the commands entered on the command line into the macro.
`SHIFT`	Move all the replaceable parameters down one level and make available another replaceable parameter as %9.
`IF NOT (%9)==() GOTO ERROR2`	If %9 still exists, then something was left out of the macro so jump to an error-handling section.
`GOTO END`	Exit the batch file.

`:HELP`
`   ECHO MACRO.BAT Allows You To Define`
`   ECHO Up To Ten Macros (0-9) That Are`
`   ECHO Stored On Disk So They Do Not`
`   ECHO Use Any Memory`
`GOTO END`
	Display a help screen and exit the batch file when the user requests help.

`:END`	Label marking the end of the batch file.

32-1 Continued.

If you enter MACRO D, it displays all the available macros. If you enter MACRO #, it runs the macro stored under the number you enter on the command line. And if you enter MACRO # *commands*, it stores those commands in a macro without executing them. Macros are stored in the C:\MACRO subdirectory. The subdirectory should *not* be in your path. They remain until you overwrite them or manually erase them so macros are retained between sessions.

Users interested in implementing this system but concerned about just being allowed to enter one line of commands should note that once MACRO.BAT has created a macro, nothing prevents you from going behind it and enhancing the macro batch files it creates because they are nothing but regular batch files. Additionally, there is nothing preventing you from creating one or more of the macro batch files yourself without using MACRO .BAT. You will still be able to use MACRO.BAT to display and run the resulting batch file.

Command line recorder

I really dislike the way Doskey and every other keyboard program I've seen stores old command lines. Every single command line gets stored. I tend to enter a lot of short commands, like DIR or D:, and I prefer not to have to search through all these looking for one or two long commands. That is the nice thing about a batch file approach: only those command lines you enter via the command line batch file are stored, so you control which ones are stored. Enter the command normally and it bypasses the macro program, which is just perfect for short commands. Enter the command after the batch file name and the command is executed, plus it's stored for later use, which is just perfect for longer commands.

Like the macro batch file, old command lines are kept in batch files so they are not affected by rebooting or turning the computer off. In addition, for especially complex command lines, you can edit the batch file directly.

In fact, the command line recorder is very similar to the macro recorder. It does have three differences:

- After storing a command line, that command line is immediately executed.
- You assign macro names but command lines are stored in the next available name.
- After all the names have been used, the oldest command line is discarded and the remaining ones moved down one name to make room for the new command line to be stored.

As it turns out, all three of the differences are easy to accomplish with a batch file. To run a command line after storing it only requires one additional line in the batch file—a line to run the just-created batch file. Assigning the name to the command line only requires searching for the first available name and if none is found, deleting 0.BAT, renaming the remaining batch files to a number one lower, and then using the name of 9.BAT to store the current command line. Beyond this, the batch file, called CL.BAT, is very similar to MACRO.BAT explained earlier. CL.BAT is reviewed in detail in Fig. 32-2.

Batch File Line	Explanation
`@ECHO OFF`	Turn command-echoing off.

`REM NAME:     CL.BAT`
`REM PURPOSE: Store Command Lines`
`REM          Using Files Not Memory`
`REM VERSION: 1.00`
`REM DATE:    November 6, 1991`
	Documentation remarks.

`IF (%1)==(ABC123XYZ) GOTO SHOWTHEM`	If CL.BAT is being called as a subroutine, jump to the subroutine portion of the batch file.
`SET USE=`	Reset the environmental variable used by the batch file.
`NEEDHELP %0 %1`	Use the NeedHelp utility program to check and see if the user started the batch file with a /? switch.
`IF ERRORLEVEL 1 GOTO HELP`	If the user requested help, jump to a special section to display that information.
`IF (%1)==(D)   GOTO DISPLAY` `IF (%1)==(d)   GOTO DISPLAY`	If the user requested the display of the available command lines, jump to a section to handle that.
`IF NOT EXIST C:\CL\*.* MD C:\CL`	If the command line storage subdirectory does not exist, create it.
`FOR %%J IN (0 1 2 3 4 5 6 7 8 9) DO` `   IF (%1)==(%%J) GOTO RUN`	Loop through the ten available macros to see if the user has requested running one. If so, jump to a section to run it.
`FOR %%J IN (9 8 7 6 5 4 3 2 1 0) DO` `   IF NOT EXIST C:\CL\%%J.BAT SET USE=%%J`	If the batch file reaches this point, then the user is entering a command line to store and run , so find the first available slot.
`IF NOT (%USE%)==() GOTO USE`	If a slot was found, jump to the section that processes the command.

32-2 CL.BAT stores, displays, and reruns command lines.

Batch File Line	Explanation
`GOTO ALLUSED`	If no slot was available, jump to a section to create one.

`:RUN`
  `C:\CL\%1.BAT`
`GOTO END`
	Section that runs the command line selected by the user. Because it is not run with the CALL command, the GOTO command is used just for formatting and is never executed.

`:USE`	Label marking the beginning of the section that stores a command line and then runs it.
`SHIFT`	Move all the replaceable parameters down one level and make available another replaceable parameter as %9 because %0 is not needed for anything.
`ECHO @ECHO OFF > C:\CL\%USE%.BAT`	Pipe an *@ECHO OFF* to the batch file that was selected to store the command line.
`ECHO %0 %1 %2 %3 %4 %5 %6 %6 %7 %8` `%9 >> C:\CL\%USE%.BAT`	Pipe the commands to the batch file that was selected to store the command line.
`C:\CL\%USE%.BAT`	After creating the batch file to store the command line, run it.
`GOTO END`	Because the batch file was run without the CALL command, control never returns to this batch file, so this command is only used for formatting.

32-2 Continued.

Batch File Line	Explanation

`:ALLUSED`
   `DEL C:\CL\0.BAT`
   `REN C:\CL\1.BAT 0.BAT`
   `REN C:\CL\2.BAT 1.BAT`
   `REN C:\CL\3.BAT 2.BAT`
   `REN C:\CL\4.BAT 3.BAT`
   `REN C:\CL\5.BAT 4.BAT`
   `REN C:\CL\6.BAT 5.BAT`
   `REN C:\CL\7.BAT 6.BAT`
   `REN C:\CL\8.BAT 7.BAT`
   `REN C:\CL\9.BAT 8.BAT`
   `SET USE=9`
`GOTO USE`
	When all the available slots have been used, erase the oldest command line file, move the remaining ones down one level, and use the last slot to store the current command line.

`:DISPLAY`
   `FOR %%J IN (0 1 2 3 4 5 6 7 8 9) DO`
      `CALL CL ABC123XYZ %%J`
`GOTO END`
	When the user requests display of the command lines, loop through them and call CL.BAT as a subroutine to display them.

`:SHOWTHEM`	Label marking the beginning of the subroutine for displaying the available command lines.
`IF NOT EXIST C:\CL\%2.BAT GOTO END`	If this particular command line does not exist, exit the batch file.
`ECHO --%2--`	Display the command line name.
`TYPE C:\CL\%2.BAT	FIND /V "@ECHO OFF"`	Display the contents of the batch file.
`ECHO`	Display a blank line by echoing an Alt-255.
`GOTO END`	Exit the batch file.

`:MISSING`
   `ECHO You Did Not Enter Anything`
   `ECHO After The Name So CL Does`
   `ECHO Not Know What To Do!`
   `ECHO`
`GOTO EXPLAIN`
	Display an error-message when the user does not tell the batch file what to do and jump to another section to show additional information.

32-2 Continued.

Batch File Line	Explanation
| ```
:EXPLAIN
    ECHO Enter CL D To Display The
    ECHO Existing Command Lines
    ECHO
    ECHO Enter CL # To Reuse One Of
    ECHO The Existing Command Lines
    ECHO Where # Is The Number Of
    ECHO The Command Line To Reuse
    ECHO
GOTO DISPLAY
``` | Explain what the batch file does and then jump to another section to display additional information. |
| ```
:HELP
    ECHO Enter CL D To Display The
    ECHO Existing Command Lines
    ECHO
    ECHO Enter CL # To Reuse One Of
    ECHO The Existing Command Lines
    ECHO Where # Is The Number Of
    ECHO The Command Line To Reuse
GOTO END
``` | Display a help screen and exit the batch file when the user requests help. |
| `:END` | Label marking the end of the batch file. |

32-2 Continued.

Running multiple commands

MULTI.BAT in Fig. 32-3 allows you to enter as many commands as you like on a command line, up to the limit of 127 characters on the command line. It constructs an environmental variable containing the command by looping through the replaceable parameter and adding each one to this environmental variable until it reaches a replaceable parameter that is a caret (^); the caret tells it that the command is complete. At that point, it executes that command and then resets the environmental variable and starts over. Because replaceable parameters must be separated by spaces, the caret must have a space on each side.

Batch File Line	Explanation
`@ECHO OFF`	Turn command-echoing off.
| ```
REM NAME:     MULTI.BAT
REM PURPOSE: Issue Multiple DR DOS
REM          Commands On a Single Line
REM VERSION: 1.10
REM DATE:     May 7, 1991
``` | Documentation remarks. |

32-3 MULTI.BAT lets you enter multiple commands on a single command line.
```

Batch File Line	Explanation
NEEDHELP %0 %1	Use the NeedHelp utility program to check and see if the user started the batch file with a /? switch.
IF ERRORLEVEL 1 GOTO HELP	If the user requested help, jump to a special section to display that information.
SET COMMAND=	Reset the environmental variable used by this batch file.
IF (%1)==() GOTO ERROR	If the user did not tell the batch file what to do, jump to an error-handling routine.
IF (%1)==(^) GOTO ERROR	If the first replaceable parameter is a caret, the user specified the command wrong so jump to an error-handling routine.
:TOP	Label marking the top of the main loop.
SET COMMAND=%COMMAND% %1	Add the current word on to the end of the environmental variable that contains the command to run.
SHIFT	Move all the replaceable parameters down one level and make available another replaceable parameter as %9.
IF (%1)==() GOTO RUNLAST	If there are no more replaceable parameter, then the batch file has reached the end of the last command, so jump to a section to run it.
IF (%1)==(^) GOTO RUN	If the next replaceable parameter is a caret, then the batch file has reached the end of a command with another one following, so jump to another section to run this command.
GOTO TOP	Continue looping.
:RUN	Beginning of the section that runs a command with other commands pending.
SHIFT	Shift to move the caret that separated the commands out of the %1 position.

32-3 Continued.

Batch File Line	Explanation
`   CALL %COMMAND%`	Run the command. When the command is a program, the CALL command is ignored; but when the command is a batch file, the CALL command allows this batch file to regain control.
`   SET COMMAND=`	Reset the environmental variable that contains the command now that the command has been executed.
`GOTO TOP`	Continue looping.
`:RUNLAST`	Label marking the beginning of the section that handles running the last command.
`   %COMMAND%`	Run the last command. Because the CALL command is not used, control does not return to this batch file if the command is a batch file; however, control does return if the command is a program.
`GOTO END`	Exit the batch file.

`:ERROR`
`ECHO Invalid Commands Specified`
`ECHO The Command Is Multi Followed`
`ECHO By Command Lines`
`ECHO Each Line Must Be Separated By ^`
`PAUSE`
`GOTO END`
	Display an error message and exit the batch file.

`:HELP`
`   ECHO MULTI.BAT Runs Multiple`
`   ECHO Commands Entered On The`
`   ECHO Command Line`
`   ECHO ----------------------`
`   ECHO To Run, Enter:`
`   ECHO MULTI Command ^ Command`
`   ECHO Where The Commands Are`
`   ECHO Separated By A ^ With`
`   ECHO Spaces Around It`
`GOTO END`
	Display a help screen and exit the batch file when the user requests help.

32-3 Continued.

Batch File Line	Explanation
:END	Label marking the end of the batch file.
SET COMMAND=	Reset the environmental variable used by the batch file before exiting.

32-3 Continued.

The caret was used because it is not likely to be used on the command line and because there is no lowercase version of it to complicate testing. Readers needing to use the caret in commands while surrounded by spaces can substitute another unused symbol.

MULTI.BAT uses one nifty trick and has one limitation you need to be aware of. It executes all of its commands using the command:

CALL %COMMAND%

MULTI.BAT must do this so it can regain control if the command you enter executes a batch file. Interestingly, the CALL has no impact if the command is not a batch file, so CALL DIR and DIR perform exactly the same function.

Its one limitation is piping. DR DOS processes pipes before handing processing over to MULTI.BAT, so the pipes will never even get to MULTI.BAT. As a result, none of the commands you execute using MULTI.BAT can use pipes. Otherwise, commands execute the same under MULTI.BAT as they do when run from the command line.

Summary

Between MACRO.BAT, CL.BAT and MULTI.BAT, you have most of the functions of MS DOS 5's DOSKEY program.

With MACRO.BAT and CL.BAT, you also have the advantage of storing information between sessions automatically without your having to do anything special.

33

Smaller batch file applications

This chapter presents a number of shorter batch file applications, some of them mundane and others unique. This diversity has two purposes. First, I want you to see how you can use fairly simple batch files to solve everyday problems. Second, by presenting you with batch files that are used for unusual purposes, I hope to make you think about how you can solve your own unique problems with a batch file.

Changing subdirectories

Many users have a very complex directory structure that's nested several levels deep. They often need to leave one subdirectory to check something in another subdirectory and then switch back, and are looking for a way to automate this.

You can actually attack this problem in a couple of different ways. The best way is probably using a quick directory changing program like the NCD program in the Norton Utilities or the shareware QC (Quick Change) program from Steven Flores. You can find QC on many bulletin board services, like CompuServe or PC-Link. You can also get it from many local users groups. If you want to order it directly, send $20 to

Steven Flores
11711 E. 27th St.
Tulsa, OK 74129

Be sure to tell Steven where you heard about his program.

If you need or want to tackle the problem with batch files, you have a couple of alternatives. If you're always switching between just a couple of subdirectories, you can write a custom batch file to change to each subdirectory. For example, you could write a batch file called 0-9.BAT with the single command

    CD\D\LOTUSFIG\0-9

to change to that subdirectory. I use this method to change back to my home directory on the network at the office, because entering CD\D\USERS\RICHARDS is a bit much.

Of course, this can become a complex solution if you have a lot of subdirectories to change between. You can write a batch file to partially solve this problem. This batch file marks the current directory as home and builds a second batch file to always return you to the home directory. The next time you run this batch file, it creates a new home directory and a new batch file to change you to there.

The batch file RETURN.BAT—

```
COPY C:\BAT\RETURN C:\BAT\RETURNTO.BAT
CD >> C:\BAT\RETURNTO.BAT
```

—copies a file called RETURN to the batch file named RETURNTO.BAT. RETURN contains the single line

```
CD ^z
```

where ^z is an end-of-file marker. Because there's no return in the file, when the next line of RETURN.BAT pipes in the subdirectory, it gets added to the same line as the CD. The result is a line similar to this:

```
CD C:\D\LOTUSFIG\0-9
```

Because the batch file must be in a subdirectory in the path in order for it to work, RETURN.BAT is configured to always use the C:\BAT subdirectory. For that reason, every time you run RETURN.BAT, it overwrites RETURNTO.BAT with a new version. You can expand RETURN.BAT to handle multiple subdirectories by using a replaceable parameter on the command line and creating RETURN1.BAT, RETURN2.BAT, and so on. I'll leave this up to you.

If you don't want to create a custom batch file, you can use the batch file RETURN2.BAT as follows:

```
@ECHO OFF
CD %HOME%
```

There's no way to pipe the current subdirectory into the environment, so this batch file requires you to manually issue the command

```
SET HOME=C:\D\LOTUSFIG\0-9
```

to tell RETURN2.BAT which subdirectory is home. The only real drawback to RETURN2.BAT is that you have to manually type the home subdirectory into the environment. You can avoid that, as shown in RETURN3.BAT in Fig. 33-1.

Batch File Line	Explanation
`@ECHO OFF`	Turn command-echoing off.

`REM NAME:      RETURN3.BAT`
`REM PURPOSE: Change & Return`
`REM          To A Subdirectory`
`REM VERSION: 1.00`
`REM DATE:      April 15, 1991`
	Documentation remarks.

33-1 RETURN3.BAT records your home directory into the environment when you originally change to it, allowing you to automatically change to it later.

Batch File Line	Explanation
`NEEDHELP %0 %1`	Use the NeedHelp utility program to check and see if the user started the batch file with a /? switch.
`IF ERRORLEVEL 1 GOTO HELP`	If the user requested help, jump to a special section to display that information.
`IF (%1)==() GOTO GOHOME`	Jump to one section if the user did not enter a subdirectory.
`CD\%1`	If the batch file reaches this point, the user entered a subdirectory to change to, so change to that subdirectory.
`SET HOME=%1`	Store the home subdirectory in the environment.
`GOTO END`	Exit the batch file.
`:GOHOME`	Label marking the top of the section to handle the user running the batch file without a replaceable parameter.
`CD %HOME%`	Change to the subdirectory stored in the environment.
`GOTO END`	Exit the batch file.

`:HELP`
`ECHO RETURN3 Subdirectory`
`ECHO Stores That Subdirectory`
`ECHO In The Environment And`
`ECHO Changes To It`
`BATCMD SL`
`ECHO Entering RETURN3 By Itself`
`ECHO Changes Back To The Last`
`ECHO Subdirectory Stored In`
`ECHO The Environment`
`GOTO END`
	Display a help screen and exit the batch file when the user requests help.

`:END`	Label marking the end of the batch file.

33-1 Continued.

Using RETURN3.BAT to change to a subdirectory originally (which you must do anyway) records that subdirectory into the environment automatically. When you use RETURN3.BAT without a subdirectory, it changes back to the last subdirectory you changed to, using RETURN3.BAT with a subdirectory name. Like RETURN1.BAT, you can modify RETURN3.BAT to record multiple home subdirectories in the environment.

If you routinely change between only a few subdirectories, it is possible to duplicate the power of the Norton Utilities NCD program with a batch file. RCD.BAT in Fig. 33-2 illustrates this. You run RCD.BAT by including the nickname of a subdirectory to change to after the batch file name. RCD.BAT uses a GOTO %1 to jump to that label where it issues a command to change to that subdirectory. Because you can have multiple labels together in a batch file, it's possible to assign multiple shortcut names to a single subdirectory as RCD.BAT illustrates. The problem with RCD.BAT is that you must manually append each new subdirectory. Additionally, if you specify a shortcut name that does not exist, the batch file aborts with a DR DOS "Label Not Found" error message.

Batch File Line	Explanation
`@ECHO OFF`	Turn command-echoing off.

`REM NAME:     RCD.BAT`
`REM PURPOSE: Ronny's Change Directory`
`REM VERSION: 1.00`
`REM DATE:    November 15, 1991`
	Documentation remarks.

`NEEDHELP %0 %1`	Use the NeedHelp utility program to check and see if the user started the batch file with a /? switch.
`IF ERRORLEVEL 1 GOTO HELP`	If the user requested help, jump to a special section to display that information.

`ECHO If You See The Error Message`
`ECHO Label Not Found`
`ECHO Then You Selected A Subdirectory`
`ECHO Not Stored In RCD.BAT`
	Because the batch file will abort if the user entered an invalid label, these messages warn the user about the problem.

`GOTO %1`	Jump to the label issued as the first replaceable parameter.

`:BAT`
`   C:`
`   CD\BAT`
`GOTO END`
	If the first replaceable parameter was BAT, change to C:\BAT subdirectory and exit the batch file.

`:SYSLIB`
`:DOS`
`   C:`
`   CD\SYSLIB`
`GOTO END`
	If the first replaceable parameter was SYSLIB or DOS, change to C:\SYSLIB subdirectory and exit the batch file.

`:BOOKBAT`
`   D:`
`   CD\BATFIG\BAT`
`GOTO END`
	If the first replaceable parameter was BOOKBAT, change to D:\BOOKBAT subdirectory and exit the batch file.

`The user should add their own shortcut names and subdirectories` `to this batch file in this area before using it.`	

33-2 RCD.BAT allows you to quickly change subdirectories.

Batch File Line	Explanation

:HELP
   ECHO RCD Nickname
   ECHO Changes To That Subdirectory
   BATCMD SL
   ECHO RCD.BAT Must Be Preconfigured
   ECHO To Use The Nickname
GOTO END
	Display a help screen and exit the batch file when the user requests help.

:END	Label marking the end of the batch file.

33-2 Continued.

Running inflexible programs

At an office I used to work at, we had one computer that we used for all our communications. One of the things we did was log onto a remote database that supplied us with custom communications software. Because of the unique features of this database, we had to use their software. One limitation of this software was that it stored the account number, password, and other information in a file called MENU.INF. We had two people who used this database, and they both had different account numbers, passwords, and so on. This communications software could not handle multiple users. The vendor suggested keeping two versions in two different subdirectories. We used batch files as a better solution.

The first user ran the configuration program to create MENU.INF with his information. We then copied MENU.INF to a file called RONNY.INF. The second user ran the configuration program, and we once again copied MENU.INF to a file—this time DAVID.INF.

This database software required just this one special file—MENU.INI—for each user. We created several versions of that special file under different names. STARTDAT.BAT the batch file in Fig. 33-3 copies the appropriate one to MENU.INF.

Batch File Line	Explanation
@ECHO OFF	Turn command-echoing off.
REM NAME: STARTDATA.BAT REM PURPOSE: Allow Two Users To REM Access Database REM VERSION: 1.00 REM DATE: April 15, 1991	Documentation remarks.
NEEDHELP %0 %1	Use the NeedHelp utility program to check and see if the user started the batch file with a /? switch.

33-3 STARTDAT.BAT activates different setups for a database program.

Batch File Line	Explanation
`IF ERRORLEVEL 1 GOTO HELP`	If the user requested help, jump to a special section to display that information.
`IF (%1)==() GOTO NOTHING`	If the user did not enter his name, jump to an error-handling routine.
`CAPITAL %1`	Use the CAPITAL utility to convert this value to uppercase and store it in the environment under the variable name RONNY.
`IF %RONNY%==DAVID GOTO OK` `IF %RONNY%==RONNY GOTO OK`	If the user entered a valid name, jump to a section to run the database program.
`GOTO ERROR`	If the batch file reached this point, jump to an error-handling routine.

`:NOTHING`
`    ECHO Enter Your Name After`
`    ECHO The STARTDAT Command`
`GOTO END`
	When the user does not enter a name, display an error-message and exit.

`:ERROR`
`    ECHO Invalid User Name`
`    ECHO Try Again Or See Manager`
`GOTO END`
	When the user enters an invalid name, display an error-message and exit.

`:OK`	Label marking the beginning of the section to run the database program when a valid name is entered.
`    COPY %1.INF MENU.INF`	Copy the appropriate configuration file to the file MENU.INI, the name used by the database.
`    MENU /1200/5551212`	Start the database, giving it the baud rate and phone number.
`GOTO END`	After running the database, exit the batch file.

33-3 Continued.

Batch File Line	Explanation

`:HELP`
    `ECHO This Batch File Allows Ronny`
    `ECHO Or David To Access Remote`
    `ECHO Database`
    `BATCMD SL`
    `ECHO Enter STARTDAT RONNY/DAVID`
    `ECHO To Start The Database`
`GOTO END`
	Display a help screen and exit the batch file when the user requests help.

`:END`	Label marking the end of the batch file.

33-3 Continued.

This same technique can be used with any program that stores the default values in a special file. For example, Microsoft Word stores the document you're working on, your place, and several optional settings in a file called MW.INI. Figure 33-4 shows a batch file that Ronny and David could both use to maintain their own versions of MW.INI. There's only one major difference between the batch files in Fig. 33-3 and Fig. 33-4. Because Microsoft Word allows you to change the defaults while running the program, each user's defaults are copied back to the holding file when that user exits Word. The /L is required to force Word to use some of the defaults from the MW.INI file.

Batch File Line	Explanation
`@ECHO OFF`	Turn command-echoing off.

`REM NAME:     STARTWORD.BAT`
`REM PURPOSE: Allow Two Users To Store`
`REM          Custom Word Configuration`
`REM VERSION: 1.00`
`REM DATE:    April 15, 1991`
	Documentation remarks.

`NEEDHELP %0 %1`	Use the NeedHelp utility program to check and see if the user started the batch file with a /? switch.
`IF ERRORLEVEL 1 GOTO HELP`	If the user requested help, jump to a special section to display that information.
`IF (%1)==() GOTO NOTHING`	If the user did not enter his name, jump to an error-handling routine.
`CAPITAL %1`	Use the CAPITAL utility to convert this value to uppercase and store it in the environment under the variable name RONNY.

33-4 STARTWOR.BAT is a word processing version of STARTDAT.BAT, the batch file in Fig. 33-3.

Batch File Line	Explanation
`IF %RONNY%==DAVID GOTO OK` `IF %RONNY%==RONNY GOTO OK`	If the user entered a valid name, jump to a section to run Word.
`GOTO ERROR`	If the batch file reached this point, jump to an error-handling routine.

`:NOTHING`
`    ECHO Enter Your Name After`
`    ECHO The STARTWOR Command`
`GOTO END`
	When the user does not enter a name, display an error-message and exit.

`:ERROR`
`  ECHO Invalid User Name.`
`  ECHO Try Again Or See System Manager`
`GOTO END`
	When the user enters an invalid name, display an error-message and exit.

`:OK`	Label marking the beginning of the section to run WORD when a valid name is entered.
`    CD\WORD`	Change to the WORD subdirectory.
`    COPY %1.INI MW.INI`	Copy the appropriate configuration file to the file MW.INI, the name used by Word.
`    WORD/L %2`	Run Word.
`    COPY MW.INI %1.INI`	Because Word changes the configuration file each time it runs, copy this version back to the filename used to store the configuration for this user.
`GOTO END`	Exit the batch file.

`:HELP`
`    ECHO This Batch File Allows Ronny`
`    ECHO Or David To Use Microsoft Word`
`    BATCMD SL`
`    ECHO Enter STARTWOR RONNY/DAVID`
`    ECHO To Start Program`
`GOTO END`
	Display a help screen and exit the batch file when the user requests help.

`:END`	Label marking the end of the batch file.

33-4 Continued.

Several readers of the MS DOS version of this book have told me that they use this same method with Ventura Publishing by using multiple copies of its VP.INI file. However, rather than using this trick for multiple users, they report using it to store multiple configurations of Ventura for a single user.

Controlling your printer

Changing your dot-matrix printer between compressed and regular print or between type styles can be a real problem. First you have to remember the proper syntax, and then you must start up Basic. Then you run a Basic program. All this can be done with batch files:

```
@ECHO OFF
ECHO ESC27 > LPT1
```

This batch file configures an Epson printer for compressed print. The >LPT1 pipes the setup string to the printer. Of course, the escape character is substituted in the batch file itself for the Esc in this listing. You can change this to another port if your printer is connected differently.

Finding files

While the batch file is not as flexible as some of the commercial programs, you can use it as a fast file-searching program. The DR DOS ATTRIB (short for Attribute) program was designed to change the attributes of files. It works across subdirectories using a /S switch. Because running ATTRIB without any switches to change the status of files causes it to list all the files it finds matching your file specification, ATTRIB can work as a file finding utility. Figure 33-5 shows FASTFIND.BAT, the resulting batch file, and explains how it operates.

Batch File Line	Explanation
`@ECHO OFF`	Turn command-echoing off.

`REM NAME:     FASTFIND.BAT`
`REM PURPOSE: Find A File`
`REM VERSION: 2.00`
`REM DATE:     April 15, 1991`
	Documentation remarks.

`NEEDHELP %0 %1`	Use the NeedHelp utility program to check and see if the user started the batch file with a /? switch.
`IF ERRORLEVEL 1 GOTO HELP`	If the user requested help, jump to a special section to display that information.

33-5 FASTFIND.BAT uses ATTRIB to create a fast file-searching program.

Batch File Line	Explanation
`IF (%1)==() GOTO NOFILE`	If the user did not enter the name of a file to search file, jump to an error-handling routine.
`GOTO FILE`	If the batch file reaches this point, the user entered a file to search for, so jump to a section to do that.

`:NOFILE`
`    ECHO No File Entered On Command Line`
`    ECHO Syntax is C>FASTFIND file`
`    ECHO Where file is the File You`
`    ECHO Wish to Find`
`GOTO END`
	The user did not enter the name of a file to search for, so display an error-message and exit the batch file.

`:FILE`
`    ATTRIB \%1 /S | MORE`
`GOTO END`
	When the user enters a file name, use the ATTRIB command to search for that file or files and use the MORE filter in case the number of files exceeds a screen full. After doing that, exit the batch file.

`:HELP`
`    ECHO Entering: FASTFIND File`
`    ECHO Will Search The Entire Hard`
`    ECHO Disk Looking For That File`
`    ECHO Wildcards Are Allowed`
`GOTO END`
	Display a help screen and exit the batch file when the user requests help.

`:END`	Label marking the end of the batch file.

33-5 Continued.

Printing return mailing labels

You can use a batch file to create your own return address labels. The standard $1 \times 3.5''$ labels have room for five lines of text. They also require a sixth blank line to skip over the blank area between labels. Create a text file called LABEL.TXT with six lines. The last line must be blank. The batch file that actually creates the labels looks like this:

```
@ECHO OFF
:TOP
    COPY LABEL.TXT LPT1:
GOTO TOP
```

It will run continually, so you need to press Ctrl-Break to stop it. If you knew how many labels you wanted to print, you could use the adding capabilities of Batcmd to print the number you want. The following batch file will print one hundred labels:

```
@ECHO OFF
SET MATH=0
:TOP
    COPY LABEL.TXT LPT1:
    BATCMD AD
    IF %MATH%==100 GOTO END
GOTO TOP

:END
```

Of course, this only works with a dot matrix printer. Printing multi-column labels on a laser printer would be much more complex and is probably best left to a word processor.

Running commands occasionally

If you use your computer to store important data, you should make daily incremental backups. If your data is less important, you may decide to forgo daily backups in favor of less frequent backups. The problem with those is remembering to do them. One approach is to occasionally back up the computer.

Normally, you think of batch files as being either the AUTOEXEC.BAT file, which is run every time you turn your computer on, or a stand-alone batch file that's run only when you enter its name. However, there are some things you want your computer to do only occasionally, like make a backup.

OCCASION.BAT in Fig. 33-6 illustrates this concept. To run this from your AUTOEXEC.BAT file, you'll need a CALL OCCASION.BAT statement. This batch file maintains a counter in the form of a file. When the batch file first starts, it creates COUNT.00. The next time it runs, it renames this file COUNT.01, the next time it renames it COUNT.02, and so on. When it encounters COUNT.09, it renames it COUNT.00 and performs the task it's suppose to perform occasionally—the backup, in this example. That gives this batch file a period of ten.

Batch File Line	Explanation
`@ECHO OFF`	Turn command-echoing off.

`REM NAME:      OCCASION.BAT`
`REM PURPOSE: Run Programs Occasionally`
`REM VERSION: 1.00`
`REM DATE:      April 15, 1991`
	Documentation remarks.

`NEEDHELP %0 %1`	Use the NeedHelp utility program to check and see if the user started the batch file with a /? switch.

33-6 OCCASION.BAT backs up the hard disk once every ten times the computer is rebooted.

Batch File Line	Explanation
`IF ERRORLEVEL 1 GOTO HELP`	If the user requested help, jump to a special section to display that information.
`FOR %%J IN (00 01 02 03 04 05 06 07 08` `    09) DO IF EXIST COUNT.%%J GOTO %%J`	Loop through ten values. If a file named COUNT exists with that extension, jump to a section corresponding to the extension.
`GOTO NOFILE`	If the batch file reaches this point, COUNT does not exist with the ten acceptable extensions, so jump to a section to create it.

`:00`
`    REM All Work Done Here`
`    BACKUP C:\ A:`
`    REN COUNT.00 COUNT.01`
`GOTO END`
	When the file COUNT.00 exists, perform the backup and rename the file to COUNT.01 to increment the counter.

`:01`
`    REN COUNT.01 COUNT.02`
`GOTO END`
	Increment the counter and exit the batch file.

`:02`
`    REN COUNT.02 COUNT.03`
`GOTO END`
	Increment the counter and exit the batch file.

`:03`
`    REN COUNT.03 COUNT.04`
`GOTO END`
	Increment the counter and exit the batch file.

`:04`
`    REN COUNT.04 COUNT.05`
`GOTO END`
	Increment the counter and exit the batch file.

`:05`
`    REN COUNT.05 COUNT.06`
`GOTO END`
	Increment the counter and exit the batch file.

`:06`
`    REN COUNT.06 COUNT.07`
`GOTO END`
	Increment the counter and exit the batch file.

`:07`
`    REN COUNT.07 COUNT.08`
`GOTO END`
	Increment the counter and exit the batch file.

`:08`
`    REN COUNT.08 COUNT.09`
`GOTO END`
	Increment the counter and exit the batch file.

33-6 Continued.

Batch File Line	Explanation
```:09 REN COUNT.09 COUNT.00 GOTO END```	Increment the counter and exit the batch file.
```:NOFILE REM Restore Counter File REM Then Restart Process TYPE NOFILE > COUNT.00 GOTO 00```	When the counter file does not exist, create it by typing a file that does not exist and piping the results to the counter file. After this, jump to the section that performs the backup.
```:HELP ECHO OCCASION.BAT Demonstrates How ECHO Commands Can Run Occasionally ECHO By Performing A Backup Every ECHO Tenth Time It Is Run GOTO END```	Display a help screen and exit the batch file when the user requests help.
```:END```	Label marking the end of the batch file.

33-6 Continued.

The batch file counts reboots, not days. If you're working with problem software that frequently locks up, therefore, it could end up running backups several times a day. If you leave your computer on for days at a time or use it infrequently, ten reboots could end up being several weeks.

OCCASION.BAT has two interesting tricks in it. The first trick is the counter test on line 2. The batch file needs to perform ten IF EXIST COUNT.00 GOTO 00 tests for the values 00-09. Because these tests will be exactly the same except for the digit used, all ten tests are combined into a single For-loop. The second trick is the 0-length file.

You can create a 0-length file by typing a file that does not exist and piping the results to a file. Because there's nothing to type, the resulting file is empty. Because the file has a length of zero, it does not take up any disk space, so you get to use the name as a counter holder without any disk space penalty.

You can also use occasional batch files for other kinds of applications. For example, my disk testing program has two levels of testing. The first is the quick mode that takes only a few minutes to run. The complete mode spots more errors but takes much longer to run. The batch file that runs the program normally runs it in quick mode; however, it occasionally runs it in complete mode. You can have as many different occasional batch files as you need. The only trick is to remember to use a different name for each counter.

The approach in OCCASION.BAT works if you only have a fairly short period. However, if you wanted to have a longer period, having a separate section for each possible value of the counter would make for a long and slow batch file. However, it is possible to avoid this, as OCCASIN2.BAT in Fig. 33-7 illustrates.

OCCASIN2.BAT first jumps to other sections if the value of the counter is 0 or if the file is missing. Then it uses two If-tests to handle the special case of the last counter value

Batch File Line	Explanation
`@ECHO OFF`	Turn command-echoing off.

`REM NAME:     OCCASIN2.BAT`
`REM PURPOSE: Run Programs Occasionally`
`REM VERSION: 1.00`
`REM DATE:    June 5, 1991`
	Documentation remarks.

`NEEDHELP %0 %1`	Use the NeedHelp utility program to check and see if the user started the batch file with a /? switch.
`IF ERRORLEVEL 1 GOTO HELP`	If the user requested help, jump to a special section to display that information.
`SET MATH=`	If the MATH environmental variable already exists, reset its value.
`FOR %%J IN (0 1 2 3 4 5 6 7 8 9) DO IF` `   EXIST COUNT.%%J SET MATH=%%J`	Loop through the acceptable counter values. If the file COUNT exists with that extension, store the value to the MATH environmental variable. To increase the period, just add more items to the loop.
`IF (%MATH%)==(0) GOTO 00`	If the MATH environmental variable equals "00", then jump to the section that performs the backup.
`IF (%MATH%)==() GOTO NOFILE`	If the MATH environmental variable does not exist, jump to a section to create the counter variable.
`IF (%MATH%)==(9) REN COUNT.9 COUNT.0` `IF (%MATH%)==(9) GOTO END`	If the MATH environmental variable equals the maximum value for the counter, reset the counter and exist the batch file. These lines must also be changed to increase the period.
`SET NOW=%MATH%`	Store the value of the MATH environmental variable to the NOW environmental variable.
`BATCMD AD`	Use BATCMD to increase the value of the MATH environmental variable by 1.

33-7 OCCASIN2.BAT also backs up the hard disk once every ten times the computer is rebooted only it is shorter than OCCASION.BAT in Fig. 33-6.

Batch File Line	Explanation
`REN COUNT.%NOW% COUNT.%MATH%`	Increase the counter by 1 by renaming the counter file.
`GOTO END`	Exit the batch file.

`:00`
`    REM All Work Done Here`
`    BACKUP C:\ A:`
`    REN COUNT.0 COUNT.1`
`GOTO END`
	When the counter reaches the proper value, perform the backup, reset the counter and exit.

`:NOFILE`
`    REM Restore Counter File`
`    REM Then Restart Process`
`    TYPE NOFILE > COUNT.0`
`GOTO 00`
	When the counter file does not exist, create it and jump to the section to perform the backup.

`:HELP`
`    ECHO OCCASION.BAT Demonstrates How`
`    ECHO Commands Can Run Occasionally`
`    ECHO By Performing A Backup Every`
`    ECHO Tenth Time It Is Run`
`GOTO END`
	Display a help screen and exit the batch file when the user requests help.

`:END`	Label marking the end of the batch file.

33-7 Continued.

where the counter has to be reset to zero. After that, all that is needed is to increment the counter value by 1. It's possible to compute this new counter value by using Batcmd to add one to the environmental variable and storing the counter that matched the extension. Because Batcmd strips off the leading 0 when it performs addition, OCCASIN2.BAT does not use the leading 0 in the counter the way OCCASION.BAT did. For periods longer than five to ten, this approach is much faster.

Using the volume in a batch file

When you format a floppy diskette or hard disk, DR DOS gives you the option of assigning an eleven-digit volume label to the disk. Occasionally, it can be useful to access this volume label in a batch file. For example, if you sent the user three disks of data to install and a batch file to handle the installation, checking the volume label is one way to make sure the user inserted the correct disk at each stage of the installation. (Checking for a unique filename on each disk is another approach.)

DR DOS does not give you any built-in functions to access the volume label from within a batch file. In fact, all it has is the VOL command to display the volume label on the screen. We can use this as the first of several steps to make the volume available to the batch file. Using the VOL command, we can pipe the information DR DOS displays into a file with the command

```
VOL > STOREVOL.BAT
```

in a batch file called GETVOL.BAT. The VOL command only displays information and does not need input like the DATE or TIME commands, so we do not need to use piping to send a Return to the command.

If you run VOL from the keyboard, you will see a message like "Volume in drive C is RICHARDSON". When you pipe this to a batch file, the batch file contains the same information.

The trick now is to run STOREVOL.BAT. We can automate this by including a STOREVOL command as the last command in GETVOL.BAT. STOREVOL.BAT immediately issues the command "Volume in drive C is RICHARDSON". This runs VOLUME-.BAT and passes it the following information:

```
%1    in
%2    drive
%3    C
%4    is
%5    RICHARDSON
```

So VOLUME.BAT can place the volume into the environment with this command:

```
SET VOLUME=%5
```

To summarize, the steps in the process are as follows:

1. Run GETVOL.BAT. This file first pipes the volume label into the file STORE VOL.BAT, and then runs STOREVOL.BAT. Because the CALL command isn't used, control never returns to GETVOL.BAT.
2. STOREVOL.BAT runs and enters the single command VOLUME to run VOLUME.BAT. The volume label is passed as %5. The CALL command isn't used, so control never returns to STOREVOL.BAT.
3. VOLUME.BAT runs and places the contents of the volume label into an environmental variable.

So far, the process has been fairly simple, but you must consider one major complication: Volume labels can have spaces in them. In fact, your volume label could be a b c d e f, which has five spaces in it. Using the process above, only the a part of the volume label would be placed into the environment. Although GETVOL.BAT and STOREVOL.BAT can remain the same, VOLUME.BAT must be modified to handle volume labels with spaces.

Figure 33-8 shows VOLUME.BAT with the necessary modifications. This version issues four SHIFT commands to move the first component of the volume label into the first replaceable parameter position. VOLUME.BAT then loops through all the remaining replaceable parameters, appending a space and the next component onto the VOLUME environmental variable.

When a disk does not have a volume label, DR DOS displays a "Volume in drive C does not have a label" message. Because nothing in VOLUME.BAT limits the volume label

Batch File Line	Explanation
@ECHO OFF	Turn command-echoing off.
REM NAME: VOLUME.BAT REM PURPOSE: Store Volume In Environment REM VERSION: 2.00 REM DATE: December 24, 1991	Documentation remarks.
NEEDHELP %0 %1	Use the NeedHelp utility program to check and see if the user started the batch file with a /? switch.
IF ERRORLEVEL 1 GOTO HELP	If the user requested help, jump to a special section to display that information.
SHIFT SHIFT SHIFT SHIFT	Shift the batch file four times to bring the first component of the volume label into the first replaceable parameter.
SET VOLUME=%1	Set the environmental variable VOLUME equal to the first word in the volume label.
:TOPLOOP	Label marking the top of the loop that processes the remainder of the volume label.
SHIFT	Move all the replaceable parameters down one level and make available another replaceable parameter as %9.
IF (%1)==() GOTO END	Once the replaceable parameters are processed, exit the batch file.
SET VOLUME=%VOLUME% %1	If the batch file reaches this point, another component of the volume label exists, so append it on to the environmental variable that is storing the volume label.
GOTO TOPLOOP	Continue looping.

33-8 This version of VOLUME.BAT will properly handle spaces in the volume label.

Batch File Line	Explanation

`:HELP`
    `ECHO VOLUME.BAT Stores Volume`
    `ECHO In Environment`
    `ECHO Must Be Called By Another`
    `ECHO Program.`
    `BATCMD SL`
    `ECHO Cannot Run From Command Line`
`GOTO END`
	Display a help screen and exit the batch file when the user requests help.

`:END`	Label marking the end of the batch file.

33-8 Continued.

to eleven characters, it ends up creating an environmental variable containing "does not have a label," which is what you might want when the drive does not have a volume.

Of course, once you get the volume label into the environment, you need something to do with it. Typically, it's tested to see if it matches some predefined value. You could do this with a standard If-test. It's important to remember that many aftermarket utilities allow volume labels with lowercase letters, so you can't make any assumptions about the capitalization. However, if you are testing disks you created, then you know what capitalization to expect.

Batch file floppy-disk catalog

Batch files can catalog disks and work fairly well if you have only a few disks. If you have more than a few, however, you're probably better off buying one of the many shareware disk cataloging programs that are available because the batch file method is fairly slow and lacks important error checking. Be careful when you use it and make frequent backups.

Figure 33-9 shows CATALOG.BAT, the batch file that creates the catalog. Notice that it lacks any error-checking at all—I've left this for the user to add. The batch file should determine that it's logged into the proper drive and subdirectory before running. As written, the batch file makes sure the user enters a name and then uses the For-loop to cycle through all the files on the A drive. Notice that this would be a good application for grabbing the volume label and including it in the ECHO command.

Batch File Line	Explanation
`@ECHO OFF`	Turn command-echoing off.

`REM NAME:     CATALOG.BAT`
`REM PURPOSE: Cataloging Floppy Disks`
`REM VERSION: 2.00`
`REM DATE:    November 15, 1991`
	Documentation remarks.

33-9 CATALOG.BAT creates a catalog of files on a floppy disk.

Batch File Line	Explanation
REM Assumes You Are Using The B drive REM For The Floppies And The C drive REM For The Catalog.	More documentation remarks.
NEEDHELP %0 %1	Use the NeedHelp utility program to check and see if the user started the batch file with a /? switch.
IF ERRORLEVEL 1 GOTO HELP	If the user requested help, jump to a special section to display that information.
IF (%1)==() GOTO NONAME	If the user did not enter a name for this catalog entry, jump to an error-handling routine.
C: CD\CATALOG	Change to the appropriate drive and subdirectory.
ECHO Insert Disk To Catalog In A Drive ECHO And Press Any Key When Ready	Tell the user what to do next.
PAUSE>NUL	Pause the program until the user presses a key.

FOR %%j in (B:*.*) DO ECHO %%j
    %1 %2 %3 %4 %5 %6 %7 %8 %9 >>
    C:CATALOG.TXT
	For each file on the B-drive, pipe the file name, some spaces and the first nine words of the catalog entry name into the catalog file.

GOTO END	Exit the batch file.

:NONAME
    ECHO You Must Enter Catalog Name
    ECHO Where Name Describes The Disk
GOTO END
	When the user does not enter a catalog name, display an error-message and exit the batch file.

:HELP
    ECHO Creates A Catalog In The
    ECHO C:\CATALOG Subdirectory That
    ECHO Lists All The Files In the
    ECHO B Drive Along With The Name
    ECHO You Enter On The Command Line
GOTO END
	Display a help screen and exit the batch file when the user requests help.

:END	Label marking the end of the batch file.

33-9 Continued.

Figure 33-10 shows REMOVE.BAT, a batch file for removing entries. It also lacks much error checking, but it's impossible to add enough error checking with batch commands. The basic problem is using the FIND command to select lines to delete. If you start the batch file with the replaceable parameter OFFICE, it will not only delete the lines with the added label OFFICE, it will also delete the file OFFICE.TAX and any other line containing the line OFFICE. For this reason, this cataloging method must be used with a great deal of care and frequent backups.

Batch File Line	Explanation
`@ECHO OFF`	Turn command-echoing off.

`REM NAME:     REMOVE.BAT`
`REM PURPOSE: Removes Entries From Catalog`
`REM VERSION: 2.00`
`REM DATE:    November 15, 1991`
	Documentation remarks.

`NEEDHELP %0 %1`	Use the NeedHelp utility program to check and see if the user started the batch file with a /? switch.
`IF ERRORLEVEL 1 GOTO HELP`	If the user requested help, jump to a special section to display that information.
`IF (%1)==() GOTO NoName`	If the user did not enter a name for this catalog entry, jump to an error-handling routine.
`SET FIND=%1`	Store the first word of the catalog title to search file in the environment.
`SHIFT`	Move all the replaceable parameters down one level and make available another replaceable parameter as %9.
`:TOPLOOP`	Label marking the top of the loop to process any remaining words in the catalog title.
`IF (%1)==() GOTO CONTINUE`	Once there are no more words in the catalog title to process, jump out of this processing loop.

33-10 REMOVE.BAT will remove entries from the catalog.

Batch File Line	Explanation
`SET FIND=%FIND% %1`	When the batch file reaches this point, more words exist for the catalog title, so append this word onto the existing environmental variable.
`SHIFT`	Move all the replaceable parameters down one level and make available another replaceable parameter as %9.
`GOTO TOPLOOP`	Continue looping.
`:CONTINUE`	Label used to jump out of the above loop.

`ECHO All Floppy Catalog Entries Containing`
`ECHO %FIND% Will Be Deleted`
`ECHO If This Is Not OK, Press Control-Break`
`ECHO Otherwise, Press Any Other Key`
`PAUSE`
	Tell the user what will happen next.

`C:` `CD\CATALOG`	Change to the appropriate drive and subdirectory.
`COPY CATALOG.TXT CATALOG.BAK`	Make a backup copy of the catalog before modifying it.
`TYPE CATALOG.TXT|FIND/V "%FIND%" > JUNK.TMP`	Type the catalog, use the FILE filter to search for all lines not containing the catalog text to delete and pipe the results to an output file.
`DEL CATALOG.TXT`	Delete the current catalog.
`REN JUNK.TMP CATALOG.TXT`	Rename the temporary file to make it the catalog file.
`GOTO END`	Exit the batch file.

33-10 Continued.

Batch File Line	Explanation
| ```
:HELP
    ECHO This Batch File Deletes The
    ECHO Entries From The Disk Catalog In
    ECHO The C:\CATALOG Subdirectory That
    ECHO Contain The Name You Enter On The
    ECHO Command Line
GOTO END
``` | Display a help screen and exit the batch file when the user requests help. |
| ```
:END
``` | Label marking the end of the batch file. |

33-10 Continued.

Adding to and deleting from your path

Most people simply include every subdirectory they need DR DOS to search through in the path and forget it. There are occasions, however, when you might want to have two separate paths (for example, if you're testing a new program and you don't want DR DOS to search anywhere other than the current subdirectory; if you have added a subdirectory for a special program and you want it in the path for only a short period of time; or if you have so many subdirectories to search that you want to have a separate path for each task). The plan of attack is the same for each of these problems. The steps are as follows:

1. Store the current path to a variable in the environment.
2. Replace the path with a new path or modify the existing path.
3. Restore the old path from the environment.

A batch file can store the current path to another environmental variable with the command:

```
SET OLDPATH=%PATH%
```

Of course, at this point, two versions of your path exist—one stored under OLDPATH and one stored under PATH—so you will need an expanded environment if you have a long path.

If you want to create a new path, it will be easier to either write a custom batch file for each alternative path or simply enter it from the command line. However, if you have two or three alternative paths that you use a lot, you might want to have a batch file that uses a replaceable parameter to let you select between them. For example,

```
@ECHO OFF
IF (%1)==(1) SET PATH=C:\;C:\DBASE
IF (%1)==(2) SET PATH=C:\;C:\WORD
IF (%1)==(3) SET PATH=C:\;C:\NORTON
```

would let you switch rapidly between three different paths. You could even use this same batch file to restore the original path with two modifications:

```
@ECHO OFF
IF (%1)==() SET PATH=%OLDPATH%
IF (%1)==() SET OLDPATH=
IF (%1)==(1) SET PATH=C:\;C:\DBASE
IF (%1)==(2) SET PATH=C:\;C:\WORD
IF (%1)==(3) SET PATH=C:\;C:\NORTON
```

A batch file can also remove subdirectories from your path, although the process is a little tricky. A batch file has access to the %PATH% environmental variable but has no way to strip it into its component parts. However, the different subdirectories in a path are separated by semicolons, which DR DOS treats as legal dividers for replaceable parameters. If you could issue the command

    BATCH %PATH%

and have DR DOS treat %PATH% as the environmental variable, then the first subdirectory in the path would be %1, the second would be %2, and so on. Unfortunately, you can't use environmental variables on the command line in this fashion. Luckily, batch files can, so if one batch file invokes another with this exact same command, the subdirectory components are passed as separate replaceable parameters—just as you would expect.

Putting all this together, we can come up with a very nice set of batch files for editing the path. The first is called EDITPATH.BAT. While it contains command line help and internal documentation, its single operation line is

    EDIT2 %PATH%

which calls EDIT2.BAT and passes it the path on the command line. This causes EDIT2.BAT, shown in Fig. 33-11, to be passed the entire path as a series of replaceable parameters.

EDIT2.BAT loops through the subdirectories one at a time and asks the users if they want to keep that subdirectory in the path. If they answer yes, it stores that subdirectory in an environmental variable. If they answer no, it does not store that subdirectory. When all of the subdirectories have been processed, EDIT2.BAT constructs the new path.

EDIT2.BAT is designed to store a maximum of twenty subdirectories. Users who are planning to retain more than twenty subdirectories in their path when running EDIT2.BAT will need to modify it before using it.

Batch File Line	Explanation
`@ECHO OFF`	Turn command-echoing off.

`REM NAME:      EDIT2.BAT`
`REM PURPOSE: Selectively Delete`
`REM             Path Subdirectories`
`REM VERSION: 2.00`
`REM DATE:      December 24, 1991`
	Documentation remarks.

33-11 EDIT2.BAT lets you decide whether or not to keep each subdirectory in your path.

318 *Batch file applications*

Batch File Line	Explanation
NEEDHELP %0 %1	Use the NeedHelp utility program to check and see if the user started the batch file with a /? switch.
IF ERRORLEVEL 1 GOTO HELP	If the user requested help, jump to a special section to display that information.
IF (%1)==() GOTO HELP	The batch file is not designed to run from the command line and it is always passed replaceable parameters when run by EDITPATH.BAT, so it knows that if it runs without replaceable parameters ,then it was run improperly, so it jumps to the help section.
SET MATH=0	Set a counter variable to 0.
:TOP	Top of the loop that processes the path.
IF (%1)==() GOTO ENDLOOP	One all the subdirectories have been processed, exit the loop.
BATCMD SL	Use the BATCMD SL utility to display a blank line.
BATCMD YN Keep %1 in PATH (Y/N)	Ask the user about keeping the subdirectory in %1 in the path. Because %1 is included in the Batcmd prompt, Batcmd displays its value.
IF NOT ERRORLEVEL 1 GOTO NOTSET	If the user answered no, skip over the processing to the bottom of the loop.
BATCMD AD	Use BATCMD AD to increase the value of the MATH environmental variable by 1.

33-11 Continued.

Batch File Line	Explanation
| ```
  IF %MATH%==1  SET A=%1
  IF %MATH%==2  SET B=%1
  IF %MATH%==3  SET C=%1
  IF %MATH%==4  SET D=%1
  IF %MATH%==5  SET E=%1
  IF %MATH%==6  SET F=%1
  IF %MATH%==7  SET G=%1
  IF %MATH%==8  SET H=%1
  IF %MATH%==9  SET I=%1
  IF %MATH%==10 SET J=%1
  IF %MATH%==11 SET K=%1
  IF %MATH%==12 SET L=%1
  IF %MATH%==13 SET M=%1
  IF %MATH%==14 SET N=%1
  IF %MATH%==15 SET O=%1
  IF %MATH%==16 SET P=%1
  IF %MATH%==17 SET Q=%1
  IF %MATH%==18 SET R=%1
  IF %MATH%==19 SET S=%1
  IF %MATH%==20 SET T=%1
``` | Store the subdirectory currently being processed in the next available replaceable parameter. |
| ```
:NOTSET
``` | Label used to skip storing the subdirectory when the user answers no. |
| ```
  SHIFT
``` | Move all the replaceable parameters down one level and make available another replaceable parameter as %9. |
| ```
  GOTO TOP
``` | Continue looping. |
| ```
:ENDLOOP
``` | Label used to mark the end of the loop. |
| ```
FOR %%J IN (1 2 3 4 5 6 7 8 9 10 11 12
   13 14 15 16 17 18 19 20) DO IF
   %MATH%==%%J GOTO %%J
``` | Loop through the twenty possible values for the MATH environmental variable and jump to a section to reset the path for that value. The text explains this in more detail. |

33-11 Continued.

Batch File Line	Explanation

`:1`
`PATH %A%`
`GOTO CLEAR`
	When only one subdirectory was retained, store it in the path and jump to the next section.

`:2`
`PATH %A%;%B%`
`GOTO CLEAR`
	Section to handle having two subdirectories in the new path.

`:3`
`PATH %A%;%B%;%C%`
`GOTO CLEAR`
	Section to handle having three subdirectories in the new path.

`:4`
`PATH %A%;%B%;%C%;%D%`
`GOTO CLEAR`
	Section to handle having four subdirectories in the new path.

`:5`
`PATH %A%;%B%;%C%;%D%;%E%`
`GOTO CLEAR`
	Section to handle having five subdirectories in the new path.

`:6`
`PATH %A%;%B%;%C%;%D%;%E%;%F%`
`GOTO CLEAR`
	Section to handle having six subdirectories in the new path.

`:7`
`PATH %A%;%B%;%C%;%D%;%E%;%F%;%G%`
`GOTO CLEAR`
	Section to handle having seven subdirectories in the new path.

`:8`
`PATH %A%;%B%;%C%;%D%;%E%;%F%;%G%;%H%`
`GOTO CLEAR`
	Section to handle having eight subdirectories in the new path.

`:9`
`PATH %A%;%B%;%C%;%D%;%E%;%F%;%G%;%H%;%I%`
`GOTO CLEAR`
	Section to handle having nine subdirectories in the new path.

`:10`
`PATH %A%;%B%;%C%;%D%;%E%;%F%;%G%;`
`    %H%;%I%;%J%`
`GOTO CLEAR`
	Section to handle having ten subdirectories in the new path. Of course, in the batch file the path line is all on one line, they just would not fit in the table.

`:11`
`PATH %A%;%B%;%C%;%D%;%E%;%F%;%G%;`
`    %H%;%I%;%J%;%K%`
`GOTO CLEAR`
	Section to handle having eleven subdirectories in the new path.

33-11 Continued.

Batch File Line	Explanation

`:12`
`PATH %A%;%B%;%C%;%D%;%E%;%F%;%G%;`
`    %H%;%I%;%J%;%K%;%L%`
`GOTO CLEAR`
	Section to handle having twelve subdirectories in the new path.

`:13`
`PATH %A%;%B%;%C%;%D%;%E%;%F%;%G%;`
`    %H%;%I%;%J%;%K%;%L%;%M%`
`GOTO CLEAR`
	Section to handle having thirteen subdirectories in the new path.

`:14`
`PATH %A%;%B%;%C%;%D%;%E%;%F%;%G%;`
`    %H%;%I%;%J%;%K%;%L%;%M%;%N%`
`GOTO CLEAR`
	Section to handle having fourteen subdirectories in the new path.

`:15`
`PATH %A%;%B%;%C%;%D%;%E%;%F%;%G%;`
`    %H%;%I%;%J%;%K%;%L%;%M%;%N%;%O%`
`GOTO CLEAR`
	Section to handle having fifteen subdirectories in the new path.

`:16`
`PATH %A%;%B%;%C%;%D%;%E%;%F%;%G%;`
`    %H%;%I%;%J%;%K%;%L%;%M%;%N%;%O%;%P%`
`GOTO CLEAR`
	Section to handle having sixteen subdirectories in the new path.

`:17`
`PATH %A%;%B%;%C%;%D%;%E%;%F%;%G%;`
`    %H%;%I%;%J%;%K%;%L%;%M%;%N%;`
`    %O%;%P%;%Q%`
`GOTO CLEAR`
	Section to handle having seventeen subdirectories in the new path.

`:18`
`PATH %A%;%B%;%C%;%D%;%E%;%F%;%G%;`
`    %H%;%I%;%J%;%K%;%L%;%M%;%N%;`
`    %O%;%P%;%Q%;%R%`
`GOTO CLEAR`
	Section to handle having eighteen subdirectories in the new path.

`:19`
`PATH %A%;%B%;%C%;%D%;%E%;%F%;%G%;`
`    %H%;%I%;%J%;%K%;%L%;%M%;%N%;`
`    %O%;%P%;%Q%;%R%;%S%`
`GOTO CLEAR`
	Section to handle having nineteen subdirectories in the new path.

`:20`
`PATH %A%;%B%;%C%;%D%;%E%;%F%;%G%;`
`    %H%;%I%;%J%;%K%;%L%;%M%;%N%;`
`    %O%;%P%;%Q%;%R%;%S%;%T%`
`GOTO CLEAR`
	Section to handle having twenty subdirectories in the new path.

33-11 Continued.

Batch File Line	Explanation
| ```
:CLEAR
    ECHO PATH Now Set To:
    PATH
    FOR %%J IN (A B C D E F G H I J K L M N
                O P Q R S T) DO SET %%J=
GOTO END
``` | Display the new path, reset the environmental variables used by the batch file and exit. |
| ```
:HELP
    ECHO This Batch File Is Used By
    ECHO EDITPAT2.BAT To Edit The Path
    ECHO *DO NOT RUN FROM COMMAND LINE**
GOTO END
``` | Display a help screen and exit the batch file when the user requests help. |
| ```
:END
``` | Label marking the end of the batch file. |

33-11 Continued.

You might be wondering why the batch file uses the roundabout approach of storing each subdirectory in a separate environmental variable and then uses a separate section to recombine them, depending on how many subdirectories were retained. The first problem is for the first subdirectory added; you do not want a leading semicolon, but you need it for all the rest of the subdirectories. When I first started writing this batch file, I tried to accomplish this with these two If-tests:

```
IF NOT (%PATH%)==( ) SET PATH=%PATH%;%1
IF (%PATH%)==( ) SET PATH=%1
```

This approach works well as long as your path is fairly short. However, the PATH environmental variable is expanded twice in this command, so even a moderately long path causes this statement to exceed the 127-character limit DR DOS places on the command line.

The command line where you enter the path is also restricted to 127 characters, and five of those are used up by the "PATH " that must precede the path. That means the path can be up to 122 characters long. As your path approaches that length, any If-test that used the %PATH% environmental variable exceeds the 127 character limit. I wanted to write a version of EDIT2.BAT that would work with a path of any length, especially because my own path is 120 characters. That meant avoiding any If-test that used the %PATH% variable. EDIT2.BAT accomplishes that so you can use it with a path of any length.

Repeating batch files

At one point, I was using a computer with two hard disks, and—strangely enough—the computer didn't recognize the D drive when it booted. When I rebooted, however, it did recognize the D drive. I spent several hours troubleshooting, but was unable to resolve the problem. Because the computer always recognized the D drive after rebooting once, or
```

occasionally twice, I decided that finding the problem just wasn't worth any more of my time. I created a 0-length file in the root directory of the D drive called TEST. I then formatted it as hidden and read-only so that no one would accidentally erase it. I then added these three lines at the top of the AUTOEXEC.BAT file:

```
IF EXIST D:\TEST GOTO SKIP
    BOOT
:SKIP
```

If DR DOS doesn't recognize the D drive, then D:\TEST won't exist and the AUTOEXEC.BAT file will run BOOT.COM, which reboots the computer. It will do this over and over until DR DOS recognizes the D drive. Of course, this kind of a problem can be indicative of additional problems and really should be fixed. Because I decided not to fix it, I did take the extra precaution to make very frequent backups.

This hint works under DR DOS 5 and 6 but has not been tested under earlier versions, so it might not work under all versions of DR DOS. In addition, it is known not to work under some versions of MS DOS. Some versions will fail to read the D drive and give you a "Not ready reading drive D, Abort, Ignore, or Fail?" error message. You then might have to respond to this error message several times, eliminating any time savings over simply rebooting the machine. Only experimentation can tell.

Similar to the problem accessing the D drive is when I purchased a new computer and faced a problem of occasional lockups. Right after I received my new Northgate 386/20, I was transferring files from old 360K disks to 1.44M disks. About every fifth disk, the computer would lock up completely, forcing me to reset the computer. Technical support was sure it wasn't the computer but rather a memory-resident program.

I wanted to test the system, so I wrote the batch file shown next:

```
@ECHO OFF
SET MATH=1
:TOP
    COPY A:*.* C:\TEMP
    DEL C:\TEMP\*.COM
    DEL C:\TEMP\*.EXE
    ECHO Copy Number %MATH%
    BATCMD AD
GOTO TOP
```

This batch file copies all the files on the floppy disk to a subdirectory. Then it deletes those files from the subdirectory and begins again. It also echoes a counter to the screen for each loop, so I'll know how many times it successfully completed the COPY command. I rebooted off a "clean" (e.g., no memory resident software) AUTOEXEC.BAT and CONFIG.SYS files with only the commands necessary for the system to run. With this clean system, I let this batch file run all night several times. It did that successfully, so I was sure nothing was wrong with the Northgate computer. I then began adding back commands to the CONFIG.SYS and AUTOEXEC.BAT files one at a time and letting the batch file run all night. When it finally locked up, I knew I had found the problem memory-resident program.

Controlling software access on a network

Consider a network administrator that I know. The network he manages has 50 users and over 25 software applications. He typically doesn't buy 50 versions of each package; rather, he buys the network version with permission to run 10 copies at once. Except for Lotus and Microsoft Word, 10 copies of most packages is enough, so users never have to wait too long for the software he wants to run. This administrator has no problems with the network programs. However, he has no way to control the non-network programs. For example, their art program runs only as a stand-alone program, but because it's on the network, everyone can load and run it at once. How can he make sure that no more than 10 copies are running at any one time?

This is a very good application for a batch file, and the approach is very simple. Simply maintain a counter that starts off with the number of authorized copies of the program you have. The batch file decreases the counter anytime someone begins to run a program and increases the counter when they exit. With a properly maintained counter, the batch file uses the counter to decide if a user can run the requested program.

Figure 33-12 shows just such a batch file. The batch file uses Batcmd to perform the necessary mathematics in order to keep track of the number of copies running. To use this on your network, you will need to modify NETWORK.BAT to run the application you use. If you will be using different versions of NETWORK.BAT to run different software, you will need to use a different environmental variable name in each version.

Batch File Line	Explanation
@ECHO OFF	Turn command-echoing off.
REM NAME: NETWORK.BAT REM PURPOSE: Restricts Art Program REM PURPOSE: To Five Users At Once REM VERSION: 2.00 REM DATE: June 6, 1992	Documentation remarks.
NEEDHELP %0 %1	Use the NeedHelp utility program to check and see if the user started the batch file with a /? switch.
IF ERRORLEVEL 1 GOTO HELP	If the user requested help, jump to a special section to display that information.
REM Assumes The Environmental Variable REM COUNTART Is Set To The Maximum REM Authorized Copies At The Beginning REM Of The Day	Documentation remarks.

33-12 NETWORK.BAT will restrict the number of users of an art package to the number stored in the environment.

Batch File Line	Explanation
`IF (%COUNTART%)==() GOTO INTERNAL`	If the counter environmental variable does not exist, jump to an error-handling section.
`IF %COUNTART%==0 GOTO SORRY`	If the counter environmental variable exists but equals 0, there are no available copies to run, so jump to an error-handling section.
`SET MATH=%COUNTART%`	Copy the value in the counter environmental variable to the MATH variable.
`BATCMD SU`	Use BATCMD to decrease the value of the MATH environmental variable by 1.
`IF (%MATH%)==(-1) GOTO INTERNAL`	If the MATH environmental variable has a value of -1, the counter variable did not contain a number, so jump to an error-handling routine.
`SET COUNTART=%MATH%`	Transfer the decreased counter value back to the counter variable.
`CALL ART`	Run the art program.

`SET MATH=%COUNTART%`
`BATCMD AD`
`SET COUNTART=%MATH%`
	Increase the counter variable by one now that this version is available to run.

`GOTO END`	Exit the batch file.

`:SORRY`
`    ECHO Sorry, But No More Versions`
`    ECHO Of This Software Are Available`
`    ECHO At This Time. Please Try Later.`
`    REM You Should Log This To Count How`
`    REM Often It Happens.`
`GOTO END`
	When no copies are available to run, display an error-message and exit the batch file.

`:HELP`
`    ECHO This Batch File Runs The Art`
`    ECHO Program While Tracking Usage`
`    ECHO So The Number Of Users Does`
`    ECHO Not Exceed The Maximum Allowed`
`    ECHO By The License`
`GOTO END`
	Display a help screen and exit the batch file when the user requests help.

33-12 Continued.

Batch File Line	Explanation

`:INTERNAL`
    `ECHO An Internal Error Has Occurred`
    `ECHO Contact System Administrator`
    `ECHO At Once!`
    `ECHO Her Name Is Nancy Smith`
    `ECHO Her Extension is 7038`
`GOTO END`
	When the batch file encounters an error, display a message to call the system administrator and exit the batch file.

`:END`	Label marking the end of the batch file.

33-12 Continued.

Of course, this approach is not without problems. The batch file won't prevent a user from running the art program directly and avoiding this check. Also, because you'll need a separate batch file and environmental variable for each application you want to track this way, you're going to need a fairly large environment if you deal with a lot of programs.

You can avoid the need for a larger environment by using 0-length files as the counter. However, this adds two other problems. First, when the network has to be rebooted because of a lockup, the startup files must delete all the counter files or the application programs will be assigned as being in use when they're not. Second, the user might need write privileges to the area where the counter is maintained in order for the batch file to rename the counter file. That could give the user the ability to accidentally or purposefully damage network-related files.

Modifying files during installation

It's not unusual for an installation program to want to modify the CONFIG.SYS or AUTOEXEC.BAT file during installation. You can sort of do this with batch files, but you're limited to adding text above or below the existing AUTOEXEC.BAT and CONFIG.SYS files and both locations have problems.

In the AUTOEXEC.BAT file, if you choose to add the commands at the top, you can't change the path because the user is probably going to have a path statement later on in the batch file that will overwrite it. Additionally, because the user has not set the path yet, no path will be in effect so you can't access external DR DOS commands. You cannot even specify the path to DR DOS commands because you cannot be sure where the user has them. C:\DRDOS is a good guess, but what's going to happen to your commands if the user used a different subdirectory name?

If you choose to add the commands at the bottom, it's possible that they'll never be run. If the last line in the existing AUTOEXEC.BAT file runs a menu program, that menu program might never turn control back over to the batch file, so your commands will never be executed.

The basic approach is to rename the AUTOEXEC.BAT file to something else and use the COPY command to combine a file containing the new text with the renamed AUTOEXEC.BAT file:

```
@ECHO OFF
REN AUTOEXEC.BAT AUTOEXEC.OLD
COPY AUTOEXEC.BAT + MYCHANGE.BAT AUTOEXEC.BAT
```

Notice that I've left out error checking. The batch files need to have error checking in order to make sure that it's in the root directory of the C drive, that an AUTOEXEC.BAT file exists, and that the filename the AUTOEXEC.BAT is being renamed to does not already exist. You should add these checks. To add the text to the top rather than the bottom, you should reverse the order of the COPY command.

If you want to add the text to the end, you could also use the dual greater-than sign appending pipe symbol:

```
ECHO PATH %PATH%;C:\MYCHANGE >> C:\AUTOEXEC.BAT
ECHO SET MYVARIABLE=MY _VALUE >> C:\AUTOEXEC.BAT
```

However, this will cause a problem if the last line of the AUTOEXEC.BAT file doesn't contain a Return because the pipe adds a Return only after the line, not before—and that could cause two commands to be on the same line.

Password protection

One way to keep casual users from accessing your hard disk is to add password protection. Password protections range from simple programs that require you to enter a password to complex systems that encrypt the file allocation table (FAT) and won't access the hard disk at all until the proper password is entered. DR DOS builds in password protection, while MS DOS users will have to buy an additional password program. If all you need is light protection, then you can put together a batch file password system that's very effective.

The password application we'll be looking at is simply a batch file that requires a password. Once the user enters a password, it terminates. You could add the commands to the batch file to run a specific application or you could add this code to the top of your AUTOEXEC.BAT file. Keep in mind that this system won't keep a user from booting off a floppy disk and then accessing your hard disk. In addition, because you can't encrypt the batch file, anyone with access to the hard disk can look at the batch file and figure out your password. They will have to have some experience to do this though, since the password is stored using its ASCII value. With that caveat in mind, let's construct the password system.

The password batch file, PASSWORD.BAT, is shown in Fig. 33-13. It uses Batcmd to get the first character of the password. If that character is correct, it uses Batcmd to get the second character. If the first character is incorrect, it increments a counter and asks again. It repeats this process for the second and third character. Any time an incorrect character is entered, the program begins prompting for the password from the beginning. Once the counter reaches three—which is after you've entered three incorrect passwords—the batch file will enter an endless loop and appear to lock up.

With any batch file, you have the problem of the user pressing Ctrl-Break to stop the batch file. PASSWORD.BAT avoids this problem almost completely by using the CTTY

Batch File Line	Explanation
`@ECHO OFF`	Turn command-echoing off.

`REM NAME:    PASSWORD.BAT`
`REM PURPOSE: Batch Password`
`REM VERSION: 1.51`
`REM DATE:    March 25, 1991`
	Documentation remarks.

`CLS`	Clear the screen.
`CTTY NUL`	Turn off the console. While this is in effect, the keyboard does not work and nothing shows up on the screen without piping.
`SET COUNTER=1`	Create a counter variable that will be used to count the number of password attempts.
`ECHO Enter Password > CON`	Tell the user to enter the password. This show up on the screen only because it is piped there.

`REM Enter Three Digit Password Here`
`REM A=ASCII Value Of First Digit`
`REM C=ASCII Value Of Second Digit`
`REM E=ASCII Value Of Third Digit`
`REM Run FINDPASS.BAT To Find These`
`REM If You Are Not Sure What To Use`
	Documentation remarks.

`REM -----------------------------`
`REM Change These Numbers`
`REM To Change Password`
`REM -----------------------------`
	Documentation remarks.

`SET A=82`
`SET C=79`
`SET E=78`
	Create the three variables that contain the ASCII values of the three digits of the password.

`REM -----------------------------`
`REM Need To Develop The Second Number`
`REM To Use In The Dual If-Tests`
	Documentation remarks.

33-13 PASSWORD.BAT requires the user to enter the correct password (which is RON at the moment, as currently set up) in three tries or less.

Batch File Line	Explanation

`SET MATH=%A%`
`BATCMD AD`
`SET B=%MATH%`
`SET MATH=%C%`
`BATCMD AD`
`SET D=%MATH%`
`SET MATH=%E%`
`BATCMD AD`
`SET F=%MATH%`
`SET MATH=`
	The dual If-tests need both the ASCII value of the password digit and the value one higher--for the *IF NOT ERRORLEVEL* portion of the test. Rather than having the user enter a value one higher, this section uses the addition abilities of BATCMD to calculate those values.

`:TOP`	Label marking the top of the section that gets the first digit of the password.
`    BATCMD GK<CON`	Use the BATCMD to obtain input from the user. This only works because the input is piped from the keyboard. This option obtains any character from the user and sets ERRORLEVEL to its ASCII value.
`    IF ERRORLEVEL %A% IF NOT` `    ERRORLEVEL %B% GOTO SECOND`	If the user entered this digit properly, jump to the section to get the second digit.

`    IF %COUNTER%==1 GOTO 1`
`    IF %COUNTER%==2 GOTO 2`
`    IF %COUNTER%==3 GOTO 3`
	Jump to a section to increment the counter. This section also automatically returns the user to the section to enter the first digit of the password.

`GOTO TOP`	The batch file never reaches this point; this line is just used to having a "closing" point for the loop.
`:SECOND`	Label marking the top of the section that gets the second digit of the password.
`    ECHO X>CON`	Display an X on the screen to represent the first digit of the password.
`    BATCMD GK<CON`	Use the BATCMD to obtain input from the user.

33-13 Continued.

Batch File Line	Explanation
`IF ERRORLEVEL %C% IF NOT` `    ERRORLEVEL %D% GOTO THIRD`	If the user entered this digit properly, jump to the section to get the third digit.

`IF %COUNTER%==1 GOTO 1`
`IF %COUNTER%==2 GOTO 2`
`IF %COUNTER%==3 GOTO 3`
	Jump to a section to increment the counter.

`GOTO SECOND`	The batch file never reaches this point, this line is just used to having a "closing" point for the loop.
`:THIRD`	Label marking the top of the section that gets the third digit of the password.
`    ECHO XX>CON`	Display an XX on the screen to represent the second digit of the password.
`    BATCMD GK<CON`	Use the BATCMD to obtain input from the user.
`IF ERRORLEVEL %E% IF NOT` `    ERRORLEVEL %F% GOTO CORRECT`	If the user entered this digit properly, jump to the section to leave the batch file.

`IF %COUNTER%==1 GOTO 1`
`IF %COUNTER%==2 GOTO 2`
`IF %COUNTER%==3 GOTO 3`
	Jump to a section to increment the counter.

`GOTO THIRD`	The batch file never reaches this point; this line is just used to having a "closing" point for the loop.

`:1`
`    ECHO Wrong Password, Start Over>CON`
`    SET COUNTER=2`
`GOTO TOP`
	Section to handle the first time the user enters the password wrong. Increments the counter by 1, tells the user about the mistake, and jumps to the top of the password routine.

`:2`
`    ECHO Wrong Password, Start Over>CON`
`    SET COUNTER=3`
`GOTO TOP`
	Section to handle the second time the user enters the password wrong. Increments the counter by 1, tells the user about the mistake, and jumps to the top of the password routine.

33-13 Continued.

Batch File Line	Explanation
`:3`	Label marking the top of the section used to lock up the computer for an invalid password.
`CLS > CON`	Clear the screen. The piping makes this work.
`BATCMD PC 12 38 > CON`	Position the cursor with BATCMD. Again, the piping makes this work.
`ECHO --DEATH-- > CON`	Pipe a message to the screen.
`:DEATH` `GOTO DEATH`	This endless loop locks up the computer. Because the keyboard is not working, the user cannot break out.
`:CORRECT`	Label marking the beginning of the section where the user entered the password properly.

`    FOR %%J IN (A B C D E F COUNTER)`
`        DO SET %%J=`
`    SET COUNTER=`
	Reset the environmental variables used by the batch file.

`    CTTY CON`	Turn the console back on.
`:END`	Label marking the end of the batch file.

33-13 Continued.

NUL command at the top. This turns off the console so that the computer won't accept most inputs from the keyboard, and won't write output to the screen. It's interesting to note that the batch file will still accept the Ctrl-Break, but won't accept the "y" in response to the Halt Batch Process (y/n) message—effectively locking the computer. Notice that, after the correct response is entered, the batch file restores the screen and keyboard with the CTTY CON command.

Because the keyboard and screen don't respond to the batch file under the CTTY NUL command, the batch file forces them to work by piping output to the screen with the >CON piping command and grabbing input from the keyboard with the <CON piping command.

If you add the password to the top of your AUTOEXEC.BAT file, anyone booting the computer from the hard disk will have to enter a password. It should be at the very top of the AUTOEXEC.BAT file so that the user won't have time to enter Ctrl-Break before the password part of the AUTOEXEC.BAT file takes over. You should also create a stand-alone batch file with a name like LOCK.BAT so you can lock your computer but leave it running when you have to leave it.

Determining codes to use
with the password batch file

One of the problems of using PASSWORD.BAT is you have to know the ASCII values of the three digits of the password in order to configure the batch file. You could use an ASCII chart, but a batch file can automate the process. FINDPASS.BAT in Fig. 33-14 will prompt you for the three characters you want to use as a password and tell you the values to enter into PASSWORD.BAT to configure it for the desired password.

Batch File Line	Explanation
@ECHO OFF	Turn command-echoing off.
REM NAME: FINDPASS.BAT REM PURPOSE: Find Password Errorlevel REM PURPOSE: Values For PASSWORD.BAT REM VERSION: 2.00 REM DATE: June 6, 1992	Documentation remarks.
NEEDHELP %0 %1	Use the NeedHelp utility program to check and see if the user started the batch file with a /? switch.
IF ERRORLEVEL 1 GOTO HELP	If the user requested help, jump to a special section to display that information.
ECHO Enter First Character Of Password	Tell the user what to do.
BATCMD GK	Use BATCMD to get the keystroke and set ERRORLEVEL accordingly.
CALL SAYERROR	Call SAYERROR.BAT to store the ERRORLEVEL in the environment.
SET A=%ERROR%	Store the ERRORLEVEL in another environmental variable.
ECHO Enter Second Character Of Password	Tell the user what to do.
BATCMD GK	Use BATCMD to get the keystroke and set ERRORLEVEL accordingly.
CALL SAYERROR	Call SAYERROR.BAT to store the ERRORLEVEL in the environment.

33-14 FINDPASS.BAT prompts you for the password you want to use in PASSWORD.BAT and then tells you the setting to use for the three environmental variables A, C, and E used in PASSWORD.BAT to store the three digits of the password.

Batch File Line	Explanation
`SET C=%ERROR%`	Store the ERRORLEVEL in another environmental variable.
`ECHO Enter Third Character Of Password`	Tell the user what to do.
`BATCMD GK`	Use BATCMD to get the keystroke and set ERRORLEVEL accordingly.
`CALL SAYERROR`	Call SAYERROR.BAT to store the ERRORLEVEL in the environment.
`SET E=%ERROR%`	Store the ERRORLEVEL in another environmental variable.

`ECHO In PASSWORD.BAT Set A=%A%`
`ECHO                Set C=%C%`
`ECHO                Set E=%E%`
`GOTO END`
	Tell the user what values to use in PASSWORD.BAT and exit the batch file.

`:HELP`
`   ECHO Tells You The Values For`
`   ECHO PASSWORD.BAT`
`GOTO END`
	Display a help screen and exit the batch file when the user requests help.

`:END`	Label marking the end of the batch file.

`SET A=`
`SET C=`
`SET E=`
`SET ERROR=`
	Before leaving the batch file, delete the environmental variable it used.

33-14 Continued.

Summary

One way to change subdirectories quickly is with a special utility like NCD in the Norton Utilities or QC from Steven Flores.

Another way to change to a single subdirectory quickly is with a custom batch file.

A batch file like RETURN.BAT can store the current subdirectory in a batch file for instant return.

A batch file like RETURN2.BAT can store a single subdirectory in the environment for quick changes.

A batch file like RCD.BAT can switch between a number of subdirectories quickly.

Programs that inflexibly store their configuration in a single file can be run in different configurations by making multiple copies of that configuration file and using batch files to activate different copies of the configuration file.

You can sometimes store printer configuration commands in a batch file and echo them to the printer to quickly configure your printer.

Combining the ATTRIB command with a batch file gives you a quick and powerful file location program.

Batch files can be used to quickly print labels on a dot matrix printer.

By having the AUTOEXEC.BAT "count" reboots by using the name of a 0-length file, you can run programs occasionally by running them only after a certain number of reboots.

A batch file like GETVOL.BAT can pipe the volume label into the environment, where you can perform If-tests on it to verify that the proper floppy disk has been inserted in the drive.

A batch file like CATALOG.BAT can be used to set up a quick-and-dirty floppy disk catalog.

A batch file like REMOVE.BAT can be used to help maintain this catalog by removing unwanted entries.

Passing the path between batch files as a replaceable parameter gives the second batch file access to the subdirectories in the path as individual replaceable parameters.

A batch file like EDITPATH.BAT can let you pick subdirectories individually to keep in the path or discard from the path.

A repeating batch file is a good way to test the hardware for malfunctions.

A batch file like NETWORK.BAT can be used to control the access to network software and even substitute for a counter to make sure the number of copies of the program in use does not exceed the allowable limit.

A batch file can modify the AUTOEXEC.BAT and CONFIG.SYS files during its operation; however, the process is very limited.

A batch file like PASSWORD.BAT can set up a surprisingly powerful password protection program using a batch file.

34

Applications and problems

Y ou have finished most of the book. All that remains is the section on configuration and the reference section. Because the upcoming reference section is so different from the topics we have been looking at, now is a good time to stop and review what we've learned. What follows are five quick problems; take a few moments and try to work them. It's important that you have the skills necessary to solve these problems before you go on. If you have difficulty with these problems, you might want to look back through the book before going on to the section on configuration.

Problem 10

A friend asks you if it's possible to put together a telephone database using batch files. She is looking for a system where she can run the batch file followed by a "nickname" of the person to call and have her modem dial the number for her. As she sees it, the command PHONE MOM should call her mother.

You decide to put together a "mock-up" first with just a few numbers like information and 911 first to make sure she likes the system. As you begin your research, you find out two pieces of critical information:

- A command like ECHO ATDT 911 > COM1 will dial the phone. The ATDT tells the modem to dial, the 911 is the phone number, and the COM1 pipes everything to the port to which the modem is connected.
- Once the modem has finished dialing and the user has picked up the receiver, the command ECHO ATH > COM1 will cause the modem to remove itself from the circuit without hanging up the connection.

Problem 11

A friend of yours recently bought his son a computer for his high school graduation. His son will use the computer in college to write term papers and do his homework. Your friend does not expect his son to create a lot of critical data, so he is not worried about performing backups too often. Just to be sure, though, he has asked you to write a batch file that will list the files that need to be backed up so that he can decide if it's time to perform a backup.

Problem 12

Your boss recently purchased a laptop computer. He likes the computer and keyboard but has trouble changing subdirectories because the backslash key is located in an awkward position. You have decided to try to win favor with the boss by writing a batch file to make it easier for him to change subdirectories without the need to use the backslash key.

You are looking for a system that will work with any subdirectory, mainly because you do not know how your boss has his hard disk structured. That lets out a system where your boss runs the batch file with a nickname for the most common subdirectories.

Problem 13

You have started trying to learn to use DR DOS piping. As you experiment, you find a lot of 0-length files appearing on your hard disk, so you have decided to write a batch file to automatically delete all the 0-length files in the current subdirectory.

Answers

You have a number of ways to tackle each of these problems. My solutions are shown in Appendix C in the back of the book. It is not important that you match my answers; if you've developed a working solution to the problem, your solution is just as good as mine and maybe even better.

PART SEVEN
Configuration

When you turn on your computer, after performing a few necessary tasks, DR DOS processes two user-created files, CONFIG.SYS and AUTOEXEC.BAT. To a great extent, these two files determine the configuration of your computing environment. The CONFIG-.SYS file is processed first, before even COMMAND.COM is loaded. For that reason, we will cover it first. The AUTOEXEC.BAT file is processed last, just before turning control over to you so we'll cover it last.

With batch files, the differences between MS and DR DOS are fairly minor—especially if you avoid the DR DOS 6 SWITCH and GOSUB commands. There is a fairly high chance that a batch file written for DR DOS will run under MS DOS and that one written for MS DOS will run under DR DOS. What minor differences that do crop up are due to differences in command syntax and operation. For example, the MS DOS FIND command is case-sensitive, although you must use FIND /u with DR DOS; and the MS DOS COPY command does not copy 0-length files, while the DR DOS COPY command does.

However, this comparability does not hold with the CONFIG.SYS file. Chances are very high that a CONFIG.SYS file written for MS DOS 5 will not run under DR DOS and one written for DR DOS will not run under MS DOS. Part of the reason for this difference is the use of different names for the commands to load items into high memory. DR DOS 6 uses the HIDEVICE to load device drivers into high memory, while MS DOS 5 uses the DEVICEHIGH command; and DR DOS 6 loads buffers into high memory using the HIBUFFERS command, while MS DOS 5 automatically loads them into high memory if MS DOS is loaded into high memory.

There are also significant differences between DR DOS 5 and 6. DR DOS 5 offers only a few specialized commands for the CONFIG.SYS file, while DR DOS 6 offers an entire batch-like programming language for the CONFIG.SYS files. For these reasons, I have broken the configuration section down into four chapters:

Chapter 35: CONFIG.SYS under MS DOS 3.3. This chapter covers the basics of configuration and introduces those commands that were available under MS DOS 3.3. As a general rule, these configuration commands will run under any version of MS or DR DOS. All readers will want to read this chapter—even if you never plan on using MS DOS—since the basic components of the CONFIG.SYS file—commands like FILES and BUFFERS—are covered here.

Chapter 36: CONFIG.SYS under DR DOS 5. DR DOS 5 introduced only a couple of advancements to the CONFIG.SYS file, but those few advancements were very powerful and extremely useful. DR DOS 6 users should also read this chapter because those advancements continue to be just as powerful and useful under DR DOS 6.

Chapter 37: CONFIG.SYS under DR DOS 6. DR DOS 6 expanded the CONFIG-.SYS file to have its own programming language that is every bit as powerful as the batch language. This gives the CONFIG.SYS file power and usefulness unheard of in the MS DOS world. This chapter explains how to use those enhancements.

Chapter 38: AUTOEXEC.BAT and shutdown files. The AUTOEXEC.BAT file is designed to set up your computing environment. However, if you write it like any other batch file, you are ignoring some of that power. This chapter shows you how to write your AUTOEXEC.BAT file for maximum power. Also, while neither DR or MS DOS offers a shutdown batch file that automatically runs when you turn the computer off, it would be a good idea to have one. This file could do things like park the heads on your computer. This chapter also explores this issue.

35

CONFIG.SYS file under MS DOS 3.3

In this chapter, I've used the word DOS to refer to both MS DOS and DR DOS in the generic sense.

Because this is a book on DR DOS batch file programming, the title for this chapter immediately suggests two major questions:

- Why am I covering the CONFIG.SYS file at all?
- Why am I covering the MS DOS version of the CONFIG.SYS file?

The answer to the first question is fairly simple. The batch file you use the most is your AUTOEXEC.BAT file, and you will end up spending a good bit of time fine-tuning your AUTOEXEC.BAT file to get the best performance out of your system. Because the AUTOEXEC.BAT file works hand-in-hand with the CONFIG.SYS file, it's important that you be able to fine tune both of them to get the exact performance you want out of your system. Plus, the CONFIG.SYS file is structured very much like a batch file—especially in DR DOS 6—so it makes good sense for this book to cover it.

The answer to the second question is more philosophical. The CONFIG.SYS commands in MS DOS 3.3 are not innovative or fancy. Rather, they represent a solid foundation. Most of these commands work under all versions of DR and MS DOS. They also represent the majority of the commands actually used to configure your system. Because many of you will have some contact with MS DOS systems, I have elected to separate out this common pool of knowledge into its own chapter. Once we have covered this basic information, we will spend the next two chapters covering commands specific to the two recent versions of DR DOS.

Getting started

The operating system is made up of three components:

- The Basic Input Output System or BIOS. This is made up of two parts: a hardware chip that comes with the computer, and a software portion that's read from the disk.

- The DOS kernel. This is the software portion of the operating system that provides the interface between your application programs and the hardware.
- COMMAND.COM. This is the command interpreter. It reads the commands you enter into the computer and takes appropriate action.

When you first turn on your computer, the BIOS goes through several steps to get the computer ready to use. The first thing it does is a power-on self test or POST. The POST checks the reliability of RAM (some clones skip this step—others let you skip it by pressing the Esc key) and initializes certain chips and disk drives and other standard equipment.

Problems booting

If something fails the POST test, the computer might freeze. The computer might also display a cryptic error message. A failure at this point might be something serious like a bad memory chip or something as simple as the keyboard connector being loose. Newer computers with setup information stored in a CMOS memory chip will fail at this point if the contents of that chip have been lost or don't agree with your current configuration. If your computer fails at this point, you can try a couple of things:

- If you've added memory, changed boards, or otherwise changed the configuration of your computer, boot off the setup disk or press the appropriate keystoke combination during booting to load the internal setup program and reconfigure the computer.
- If you haven't changed the configuration, you should still try booting off the setup disk. Your battery could have failed and the computer would have lost all setup information. Generally, if running the setup program will correct the problem, the error message will suggest running the setup program.
- If the problem isn't with the setup, try pushing the F1 key several times. An old Compaq I used to use always gave me an error message when it booted, and pressing F1 always cleared it. I was never able to identify the reason but it's never caused any other problems so I just lived with the annoyance until I replaced the computer.
- Try turning the computer off for thirty seconds or so and then turning it on again. Sometimes, random problems will crop up and turning the computer off for thirty seconds gives all the internal memory a chance to lose its contents.

If all these things fail, you'll need to either get your computer serviced or use the error message number to track down the problem yourself.

After the POST, the boot record is loaded into memory and executed. It doesn't know very much. In fact, all it knows is how to start DR DOS. This program is called a bootstrap program. The bootstrap routine isn't very smart; it could just as easily be loading different operating systems. In MS DOS, all it does is read the beginning of a disk; in DR DOS, it looks for the files IBMBIO.COM and IBMDOS.COM anywhere in the root directory. If there's a disk in the A drive, it will try to read DOS from that disk. If the A drive is empty, it will try to read DOS from the first hard disk—usually the C drive. If DOS isn't present or if the disk is defective, you'll get a non-system disk error message.

Recall Chapter 27. It was there that we first encountered the boot record. In Chapter 27, we saw how we could configure our computer to boot from either MS DOS 5 or DR DOS 6. One of the things we did was install each operating system and then save a copy of its boot record. We had to do that because the boot record for each operating system told the computer to load the operating system from different hidden files.

You might be wondering why the operating system isn't built into the computer. It is, in fact, built into some Tandy computers. The problem with building the operating system into hardware is that it makes upgrading to a newer operating system expensive and difficult. Over the past few years, there have been so many improvements to MS and DR DOS that I wouldn't want to still be locked into an older system because that was what was built into my machine. Additionally, having a built-in operating system would also prohibit you from running an alternative operating system.

Components of DOS

DR DOS is made up of three primary programs: IBMBIO.COM, IBMDOS.COM, and COMMAND.COM. IBMBIO.COM and IBMDOS.COM are hidden files; you don't see them when you perform a directory. IBMBIO.COM is a supplement to the internal ROM BIOS routines already in the computer. IBMDOS.COM handles input-output operations. COMMAND.COM is the command interpreter.

The bootstrap program in the boot sector loads IBMBIO.COM and IBMDOS.COM. Control is passed to IBMBIO.COM, which initializes all the hardware that's attached to the computer. That's why all the disk drive lights flash and the print head on your dot matrix printer moves to the left. Hardware initialization also moves the part of the operating system from its load position in memory to its final position in low memory and erases the IBMDOS.COM routines in memory that are no longer needed.

After initializing the hardware, IBMBIO.COM looks for and processes a file called CONFIG.SYS. This is short for CONFIGure the SYStem. If no CONFIG.SYS file is found, IBMBIO.COM continues with the boot process. Like the AUTOEXEC.BAT file, the CONFIG.SYS file must be in the root directory of the boot disk. Unlike the AUTOEXEC.BAT file, however, the CONFIG.SYS file contains unique commands. Most of these commands can't be used outside the CONFIG.SYS file. While these commands are unique, they're very similar to batch commands, which is why I've included them in this book.

After the CONFIG.SYS file is found and processed, control is passed to IBM-DOS.COM. This program loads routines that control the information flow to and from the computer and other hardware, like disk drives and printers. After IBMDOS.COM is finished, COMMAND.COM is loaded. When COMMAND.COM first begins operation, the last thing it does is look for a special file called the AUTOEXEC.BAT file, and it looks for this AUTOEXEC.BAT file only in the root directory of the boot disk. If it finds the AUTOEXEC.BAT file, it executes it just like any other batch file. This makes the AUTOEXEC.BAT file an excellent place to perform tasks that are performed only once, like setting the date and time and loading memory-resident software. This is explored in detail in Chapter 38.

Figure 35-1 illustrates the steps that take place when you switch your computer on. Figure 35-2 shows how the computer's memory is configured with the computer running a program.

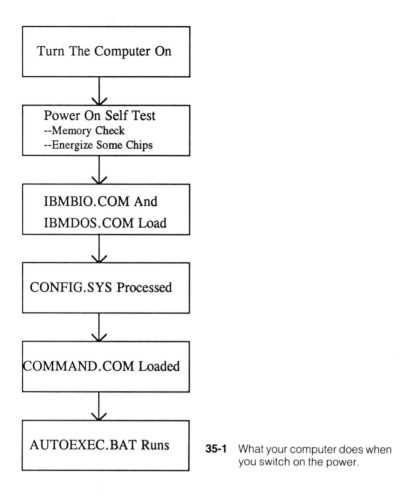

```
┌─────────────────────────────┐
│   Turn The Computer On      │
└─────────────────────────────┘
              │
              ↓
┌─────────────────────────────┐
│   Power On Self Test        │
│   --Memory Check            │
│   --Energize Some Chips     │
└─────────────────────────────┘
              │
              ↓
┌─────────────────────────────┐
│   IBMBIO.COM And            │
│   IBMDOS.COM Load           │
└─────────────────────────────┘
              │
              ↓
┌─────────────────────────────┐
│   CONFIG.SYS Processed      │
└─────────────────────────────┘
              │
              ↓
┌─────────────────────────────┐
│   COMMAND.COM Loaded        │
└─────────────────────────────┘
              │
              ↓
┌─────────────────────────────┐
│   AUTOEXEC.BAT Runs         │
└─────────────────────────────┘
```

35-1 What your computer does when you switch on the power.

The CONFIG.SYS file

The CONFIG.SYS file is an ASCII file that's very much like a batch file, with commands that control how much memory DOS allocates to certain tasks, and how it performs several other tasks. DOS uses it to control the configuration of the computer. In order to add a mouse or connect to a network, you enter commands into the CONFIG.SYS file. If there isn't a CONFIG.SYS file in the root directory, DOS skips this step and loads COMMAND-.COM.

The CONFIG.SYS file is structured just like a batch file and must be an ASCII file. It must have one command on each line. Unlike a batch file, however, most commands in the CONFIG.SYS file are unique to the CONFIG.SYS file and can't be used elsewhere. There's a reason for this. The CONFIG.SYS file runs before COMMAND.COM loads and configures certain aspects of memory usage. Once COMMAND.COM is loaded, there's no room to change the values set by the CONFIG.SYS file. Because the CONFIG.SYS file isn't a batch file, it can't contain batch file commands.

BIOS area
Device drivers loaded from **CONFIG.SYS** file
PSP of **COMMAND.COM** (program segment prefix)
Low-memory portion of **COMMAND.COM**
Master environment block (This is the copy of the environment accessed and modified by batch files.)
Memory-resident software (Along with a full copy of the environment for each program.)
Current program's copy of the environment
DOS memory control block (MCB) for the current program
Current program's PSP
Current program's code area
Current program's data area
Free memory

35-2 Configuration of a computer's memory when it's running a program, including space for memory resident software.

Nine commands can be used in a CONFIG.SYS file under MS DOS version 3.3, and most of the commands can be used under earlier versions of DOS. For the most part, they can be in any order. Keep in mind that, while there are nine commands you can use in your CONFIG.SYS file, only three are used a great deal: BUFFERS=, FILES=, and DEVICE=. The list of CONFIG.SYS commands is described next.

BREAK=on/off

Normally, DOS checks for a Ctrl-Break only during standard input, output, when printing, or when accessing the communications port. This is the default for setting of BREAK OFF. Setting BREAK ON causes DOS to check for a Ctrl-Break whenever a program requests any DOS function. Of course, because DOS has to spend time checking for a Ctrl-Break, DOS will run a little slower with BREAK turned on. The OFF setting is redundant because it's the default.

I recommend the ON setting. If a batch file you're working hangs when DOS performs some action where it's not checking the keyboard, then you're going to have to reboot to regain control.

The BREAK command is one of the few CONFIG.SYS commands that you can enter from the keyboard or in a batch file. The syntax is identical to the syntax in a CONFIG.SYS file. Entering BREAK alone (from the keyboard or batch file but not in the CONFIG.SYS file) will display the status of Break.

BUFFERS=n

DOS sets up a special place in memory, called a *buffer*, to hold information that's just been read from disk. If the program requests the same information again, DOS can supply it from very fast memory (the buffer) rather than the very slow disk—a process called *disk caching*. Up to a point, the larger the buffer, the faster the disk access system works. And the larger the buffer, the more memory it takes and the less you have available for other uses.

In addition to saving time on a disk read, the buffer saves time on a disk write because, before DOS can write a record to a sector, it must first read that sector. So a large buffer saves on both read and write time. The number *n* is between 1 and 99. The default value that DOS uses if there's no BUFFERS command is between 2 and 15, this depending on both the version of DOS you have and your machine's configuration. Each buffer causes DOS to allocate 512 bytes to the buffer. This exactly matches the 512-byte disk sectors that DOS uses. Due to internal overhead, each buffer reduces the amount of memory available to other applications by 528 bytes. So a BUFFERS value of 10 causes DOS to allocate 5280 bytes, or a little over 5K, to the buffer.

A higher buffers statement can dramatically speed up some operations. A program that reads the same information from disk over and over, like a database program, gains a great deal from either a higher level of buffers or a caching program. A program like Lotus, which reads its worksheet into memory and holds the entire set of data in memory, gains little or nothing. In order to load a file into memory, DOS must first load the proper directory. Therefore, systems with a large number of files in a directory or a complex subdirectory structure also gain from a higher buffer setting.

With all the memory-resident programs around, memory is already tight. Making your buffer too large might even slow down a program because it reduces the memory available to the program. Many commercial programs want you to set your buffer to 20. So unless you want to spend a lot of time experimenting to find the best setting or if you have a caching program, just set it to 20 and forget it. In fact, making your BUFFERS setting too high with some versions of DOS can dramatically slow DOS down, as opposed to having no buffers at all.

The DOS BUFFERS command is a very simple cache program. If you install a commercial caching program, like Super PC-Kwik, the installation instructions will probably tell you to set the buffer statement to a very low number—typically one or two. This avoids having two caching programs trying to cache your hard disk. You must have a statement in your CONFIG.SYS file setting BUFFERS to this value. Otherwise, it can default to a value as high as 15.

You might be wondering why you would want a separate caching program, because the BUFFERS setting is really a cache. The problem is that BUFFERS is a very simple cache. Before checking the hard disk for data, DOS first checks the buffers. Its search method is very simple; it starts with the first buffer and checks every single buffer sequentially until it either finds the information it's looking for or checks all the buffers. If

DOS is always reading new information from the disk but first has to sequentially check all the buffers, the buffers can actually slow down the computer! That's why the DOS manual warns about setting buffers too high.

On the other hand, a good caching program doesn't sequentially check its entire contents. In fact, most caching programs allow you to create multi-megabyte caches, way too large to check sequentially. Rather, they generate an index as data is being placed in the cache. All they do when DOS requests information is briefly check their index. That tells them right away if the cache has the data DOS is requesting and, if so, where to get it.

COUNTRY=n

COUNTRY=n controls how the date and time are displayed. It also affects the information DOS supplies to applications regarding currency symbols, decimal separator, sorting order and more. The n represents the country code. Table 35-1 shows all the COUNTRY codes, along with the corresponding default KEYB value. The default is USA if no value is entered.

**Table 35-1   Possible values for the
COUNTRY configuration command.**

Country	Abbreviation	Code pages	
Belgium	BE	437	850
Canada (French)	CF	863	850
Denmark	DK	865	850
Finland	SU	437	850
France	FR	437	850
Germany	GR	437	850
Italy	IT	437	850
Latin America	LA	437	850
Netherlands	NL	437	850
Norway	NO	865	850
Portugal	PO	860	850
Spain	SP	437	850
Sweden	SV	437	850
Swiss (French)	SF	437	850
Swiss (German)	SG	437	850
United Kingdom	UK	437	850
United States (default)	US	437	850

DEVICE=

A number of devices are attached to your computer, including disk drives, a hard disk, and printers. Some of these devices are unique and require a device driver in order to communicate with your computer. A *device driver* is a special program provided by the manufacturer to allow a special device to communicate with DOS. A device driver usually ends with the extension .SYS, although .EXE and .COM are also possible extensions. By using device drivers to control special types of equipment, DOS is device-independent. You can use almost any type of equipment with DOS as long as a device driver has been written for the equipment.

Device drivers are attached to DOS in the CONFIG.SYS file. For example, my current CONFIG.SYS file is shown here:

```
FCBS=1,1
DEVICE=C:\WINDOWS\HIMEM.SYS
DEVICE=C:\CDROM\SONY_CDU.SYS/D:MSCD210/U:1/B:340/M:H/Q:*/T:*
DEVICE=C:\MOUSE\MOUSE.SYS /Y
DEVICE=C:\SYSLIB\ANSI.SYS
DEVICE=C:\HARDCARD\ATDOSXL.SYS
DEVICE=C:\WINDOWS\SMARTDRV.EXE /DOUBLE_BUFFER
SHELL=C:\SYSLIB\COMMAND.COM C:\SYSLIB \ /E:800 /P
FILES=50
BUFFERS=20
BREAK=ON
LASTDRIVE=E
```

Note that the path isn't set when DOS reads the CONFIG.SYS file. Therefore, the device driver must be in the root directory or the command must supply the complete path to the driver, as my CONFIG.SYS does.

When DOS attaches a device driver, that driver becomes a part of DOS. As you can imagine, writing a device driver is complex and difficult. Most memory-resident software would function better if it were written as a device driver. However, the task of writing device drivers as complex as most memory-resident software is too difficult for even big software companies.

There are a couple of device drivers of particular note because they're included with DOS. They are listed as follows:

ANSI.SYS   ANSI.SYS was first included with DOS 2.0 and has been standard ever since. ANSI.SYS replaces the screen and keyboard handling of DOS with more powerful routines. See Chapter 21 for more information on ANSI.

VDISK.SYS   VDISK.SYS allows you to set aside part of your memory as an electronic floppy disk drive, called a RAM disk. The advantage of a RAM disk drive is speed: they're extremely fast. The disadvantage of a RAM disk is that all the data in them is lost when you turn the computer off or if you lock up the computer, and a RAM disk reduces the memory available to other applications.

DISPLAY.SYS, DRIVER.SYS, and PRINTER.SYS   DRIVER.SYS lets you define an external drive as a logical drive. The primary use for DRIVER.SYS is to define an external 5.25″ drive as a logical drive on a machine with only 3.5″ drives. The other two drivers, DISPLAY.SYS and PRINTER.SYS, are used for displaying and printing character sets from other countries.

FCBS=

This specifies the number of file control blocks (FCBs) that DOS can concurrently open. The format is

FCBS=*m,n*

where the *m* gives the total number of files that can be opened simultaneously by FCBs. The default is 4 and the range of possible values is 1–255. The *n* specifies the number of protected file openings—that is, the first *n* FCBs are protected against being closed if a program tries to open more than *m* files using FCBs. The default is 0 and the range of possible values is *m*–255.

MS DOS 5 only supports specifying one number for the FCBS command in the form

FCBS=*m*

where the *m* has the same meaning as it does above. DR DOS 5 and 6 support the two-number format. This setting is usually only required for very old programs that use the MS DOS 1.x data structure, although AutoCad 10.x users must have FCBS=48,4. Still, most DR DOS users can save memory by including a FCBS=1,1 statement in their CONFIG.SYS file.

FILES=#

The FILES=# command controls how many files the entire system can have open at any one time. The default value is 8, which is too few for many applications. The maximum number of files that a process can have open is 20. This twenty includes five predefined files: input, output, error, auxiliary, and printer files. Several major programs, like dBASE, require a FILES value of 20. Some programs offer the ability to shell to other programs, for example, /System in Lotus, Run a program in Wordstar, Shell in Basic, or Escape transfer run in Microsoft Word. The second application is called a child process. The shelling process can open twenty files, as can the second application, so it's possible, although unlikely, that you could require a FILES specification as high as 40. A very few programs require a value as high as 99.

If you don't specify a value, the default is 8. Each file above 8 requires about 60 bytes. The maximum value is 99. As a general rule, set your FILES value to 40. If you ever need more, you'll get an error message like "No free file handles." If that happens, you need to increase the value of the files statement in your CONFIG.SYS file and reboot. Of course, each file requires only a small amount of memory, so setting it too high won't affect your memory too much.

LASTDRIVE=n

This command controls how many disk drives DOS appears to have. The *n* represents the last drive in the system, which, on a typical XT, would be C. This number only sets an upper limit; DOS still tracks the correct number. Note there isn't a colon after the drive letter. Remember that LASTDRIVE must leave room for any non-disk drives you have. These include RAM disks, any unusual disk or tape drives added as device drivers, any hard disks that have been partitioned into more than one drive, and any "pseudo" drives set up with the SUBST command. Each drive letter to reserve beyond the C drive uses 88 bytes of memory.

If not specified, LASTDRIVE defaults to the E drive. However, certain software can overwrite the LASTDRIVE setting. Typically, network software will define several drive letters beyond the LASTDRIVE setting as network drives. For example, on a network computer I used to use, I had a LASTDRIVE=D setting. Once the Novell network software loads, however, it defines P, Q, R, S, Y, and Z as network drives.

SHELL=

The DOS command interpreter is called COMMAND.COM. You don't have to use COMMAND.COM in particular; you can use any other one, such as the NDOS program that comes with the Norton Utilities. You specify another command interpreter with the SHELL command in the CONFIG.SYS file. If, like device drivers, the command interpreter you want to use isn't in the root directory, you must specify the full path. The SHELL command is also used to expand the DOS environment.

The SHELL command can't be used at the DOS prompt. In addition, COMMAND-.COM doesn't show up in the environment under SHELL but under COMSPEC. You can change the location where DOS looks for COMMAND.COM at the DOS prompt with the COMSPEC (or optionally SET COMSPEC) command, like so:

    SET COMSPEC=C: COMMAND.COM

or

    COMSPEC=C: COMMAND.COM

In addition to pointing to COMMAND.COM, the SHELL command is used to expand the size of the DOS environment. This is explained back in Chapter 13.

STACKS=

Stacks controls the number and size of the stack frames. The command is

    STACKS=m,s

where m is the number of stack frames. The possible values are 0 or 8-64, and the default is 0. The m value increases memory usage by the size specified by s. The s value specifies the size of each stack frame. The possible values are 0 or 32-512, and the default is 0. The default for stacks is 0,0, which indicates that DOS shouldn't install STACKS support. This is acceptable for most systems. You'll get an error message from DOS if a program requires STACKS support and it isn't installed. A value of 6512 would tell DOS to install six stack frames of 512 bytes each.

DR DOS does not support the STACKS command. It already handles this function internally, so STACKS is unnecessary.

Summary

The operating system is made up of three components: the basic input output system or BIOS, the DOS kernel and COMMAND.COM.

When a computer begins to boot, it goes through a power-on self-test or POST to check the hardware for problems.

If the computer encounters problems during the POST, it might not boot or might require you to run the setup program.

After running the POST, the bootstrap program loads the boot record into memory and executes it.

DR DOS is made up of three primary programs: IBMBIO.COM, IBMDOS.COM and COMMAND.COM.

The bootstrap program loads IBMBIO.COM and then IBMDOS.COM.

IBMBIO.COM loads and processes the CONFIG.SYS file.

The BREAK command in the CONFIG.SYS file controls how often DOS checks to see if you have pressed Ctrl-Break.

The BUFFERS command in the CONFIG.SYS file controls how much memory DOS allocates for disk caching.

The COUNTRY command in the CONFIG.SYS file controls what format DOS uses for dates, time, currency symbols, decimal separators, sorting order and more.

The DEVICE command in the CONFIG.SYS file allows DOS to load device drivers to allow it to communicate with additional devices.

The FCBS command in the CONFIG.SYS file controls how many files DOS can open using the old MS DOS 1.x data structure.

The FILES command in the CONFIG.SYS file controls how many files DOS can have open at once, including predefined files like input, output, error, auxiliary and printer.

The LASTDRIVE command in the CONFIG.SYS file specifies the highest drive letter DOS is to allow.

The STACKS command in the CONFIG.SYS file controls the number and size of the stack frame. DR DOS does not support the STACKS command.

After it finishes, IBMBIO.COM loads COMMAND.COM.

COMMAND.COM loads and processes the AUTOEXEC.BAT file.

36

CONFIG.SYS file under
DR DOS 5

If you have not yet read Chapter 35, you should go back and read it now. This chapter explains the extensions to the CONFIG.SYS file added in DR DOS 5 with the assumption that you have read about the basics in Chapter 35.

The DR DOS 5 CONFIG.SYS commands

DR DOS 5 adds three commands (?, CHAIN, and ECHO) that add dramatic power to the CONFIG.SYS file, making it far more intelligent and useful than the CONFIG.SYS file under any version of MS DOS. We will take a brief look at the commands available under DR DOS 5, and then we will return to look at these three commands in more detail. Commands not explored in Chapter 35 are indicated with a New. Commands that do not have equivalent commands under MS DOS 5 are indicated with a Unique.

📢 **Notice** The question mark, CHAIN command, and ECHO command make the CONFIG.SYS file in DR DOS far more powerful than anything MS DOS offers.

? [New Unique]

When used at the beginning of a CONFIG.SYS statement, the question mark causes that statement to become conditional. When the CONFIG.SYS reaches that line, it stops and either displays the remark if one was used or the line itself if no remark was used and then waits. If the user presses the "y" key, the line is processed normally. If the user presses any other key, the line is skipped.

The format is as follows:

? "Remark" Command

📢 **Notice** Preceding a command with a question mark causes DR DOS to ask you before executing it.

BREAK

This controls how often DR DOS stops and checks to see if Ctrl-Break has been pressed. It was examined in more detail in Chapter 35.

    BREAK=On | Off

BUFFERS

This controls how much memory DR DOS allocates to disk caching. It was examined in more detail in Chapter 35.

    BUFFERS=n

CHAIN [New Unique]

CHAIN causes DR DOS to close the current configuration file and transfer control to the configuration file specified after this command. Control does not return to the original configuration command. CHAIN acts very much like running another batch file by using its name without the CALL command.

    CHAIN=[Drive:][Path]FileSpec

The new configuration file can have any name you like—you are not limited to an extension of .SYS or a name of CONFIG.

Notice   With the CHAIN command, the CONFIG.SYS file can load and process other files.

COUNTRY

This controls the format DR DOS uses for the date, time, currency and more. It was discussed in more detail in Chapter 35.

    COUNTRY=CountryCode,CodePage,[Drive:][Path]COUNTRY.SYS

DEVICE

This command allows DR DOS to load device drivers so it can communicate with devices—like a mouse—that are not normally supported. It was discussed in more detail in Chapter 35.

    DEVICE=[Drive:][Path]FileSpec

DRIVPARM [New]

This command lets you specify the physical characteristics for a drive. It is similar to DRIVER.SYS except it only works for a physical drive already recognized by DR DOS, while DRIVER.SYS is used to add a new logical drive. Some older computers do not expect to work with 3.5″ drives, so they do not configure the drive parameters properly. DRIVPARM lets you correct that.

DRIVPARM=/D:d [/C] [/F:f] [/H:h] [/N] [/S:s] [/T:t]

Command switches

/D:d   Specify the drive to use using a single digit, where A=0, B=1, C=2, and so on.

/C   Indicates that the drive is able to detect when a disk has been changed.

/F:f   Specify the drive type, where 0=360K, 1=1.2M, 2=720K and 7=1.44M. The default is 2.

/H:h   Specify the number of heads in the drive. Allowable values are 1 and 2.

/N   Indicate the drive has permanent media.

/S:s   Specify the number of sectors supported by the drive. Allowable values are 1-63.

/T:t   Specify the number of tracks supported by the drive. Allowable values are 40 and 80.

Unlike some of the other extensions supported by DR DOS 5, later versions of MS DOS support a DRIVPARM command in the CONFIG.SYS file.

ECHO [New Unique]

The ECHO command in the CONFIG.SYS file under DR DOS 5 works exactly like the ECHO command in a batch file. It allows the batch file to display messages to tell the user what is happening and—when using the question mark—to better explain the choices available to the user.

ECHO *[Message]*

✍ **Notice**   The ECHO command lets you display messages in the CONFIG.SYS file.

FASTOPEN [New]

Large hard disks have created a special problem for DR DOS. It has to weed through larger and larger hard disks to find the files you request. That takes time. The FASTOPEN command overcomes this. It stores the directory location of the files you've used recently in memory. This speeds up searching for files the second time you run a program or load a file. This is especially important because hard disks are becoming larger-and-larger. By storing the location of files in memory, when you access a file again, it knows right where to access the file and thus saves time looking for it.

FASTOPEN=*n*

FASTOPEN defaults to allocating space for 512 files. You can specify a value *n* between a minimum of 128 and a maximum of 32,768. Each table entry requires 2 bytes, and having a table larger than you need will not increase disk performance. Unlike some of the other extensions supported by DR DOS 5, later versions of MS DOS support a FASTOPEN command in the CONFIG.SYS file.

Under certain conditions, FASTOPEN can lead to a very disconcerting error message. When you run a disk optimizer, it changes the location of files on the hard disk. The optimizer does its work in such a way that FASTOPEN won't record the change. As a result, you can get a "File does not exist" error message when FASTOPEN tries to help DR DOS open a file you've run before. The file still exists, but not in the location FASTOPEN thinks it is. As a result, you should always reboot to clear out FASTOPEN after optimizing your hard disks. Most disk optimizers will warn you to reboot if you are running FASTOPEN.

☠ *Warning*   Under certain conditions, FASTOPEN can lead to a very disconcerting error message.

FCBS

This command controls how many files can be opened using an older MS DOS 1.x format. It was discussed in more detail in Chapter 35. The format is

FCBS=*m,n*

where *m* is the number of files that can be open at once (1-255) and *n* is the number that are protected from automatic closure (1-255).

FILES

This controls how many files can be opened at once. It was discussed in more detail in Chapter 35. The format is

FILES=*n*

where *n* is the number of files (20-255).

HIDEVICE [New]

The HIDEVICE command is identical to the DEVICE command except it attempts to load the device driver into high memory. If there is not enough room in high memory, the device driver is loaded into low memory. Prior to using this command, the CONFIG.SYS file must use a DEVICE command to load a device driver like EMM386.SYS that supports upper memory. This command is identical to the MS DOS 5 DEVICEHIGH command.

HIDEVICE=*[Drive:][Path]DeviceDriver*

HIDOS [New]

The HIDOS command tries to load much of DR DOS into upper memory. If it does not fit, it is loaded into lower memory. Prior to using this command, the CONFIG.SYS file must use a DEVICE command to load a device driver like EMM386.SYS that supports upper memory. This command is identical to the MS DOS 5 DOS=HIGH statement. The format is

HIDOS=On ┊ Off

HIINSTALL [New]

The HIINSTALL command is identical to the INSTALL command (covered later) only it tries to load a memory resident program into high memory. If it does not fit, it is loaded into low memory. Prior to using this command, the CONFIG.SYS file must use a DEVICE command to load a device driver like EMM386.SYS that supports upper memory. This command is identical to the MS DOS 5 LOADHIGH command. The format is

HIINSTALL=*[Drive:][Path]FileSpec*

The DR DOS 5 programs that can be loaded high with HIINSTALL are

CURSOR.EXE
KEYB.COM
NLSFUNC.EXE
GRAPHICS.COM
GRAFTABL.COM
PRINT.EXE
SHARE.EXE

HISTORY [New]

The HISTORY command is used to support extended command line editing. History sets off a portion of memory that is used to store prior commands. These can then be viewed, edited, and reused. While the CONFIG.SYS file in MS DOS 5 does not support a similar command, the memory resident Doskey program does. The format is

HISTORY=On[,*n*][,On | Off] | Off

where the *n* represents the amount of memory allocated to storing old commands and the On | Off determines if the command editor is in insert mode. The default memory allocation is 512 bytes, and allowable values are 128-4,096.

✍ *Notice*   With the HISTORY command, you can reuse your old commands.

INSTALL [New]

The INSTALL command allows you to load memory resident programs in the CONFIG-.SYS file. Few commercial programs support this option. The DR DOS 5 programs supporting this option are the same ones listed as supporting HIINSTALL earlier.

INSTALL=*[Drive:][Path]FileSpec*

The INSTALL command is identical to the INSTALL command in MS DOS 5.

LASTDRIVE

The LASTDRIVE specifies the last drive letter DR DOS is to allow. This just sets the upper limit; DR DOS still tracks the actual number of drives. This command was examined in more detail in Chapter 35. The format is

LASTDRIVE=*Drive*

REM [New]

The REM command lets you add a documentation remark to your CONFIG.SYS files. It's also useful to "commenting out" commands you want to skip but keep for later reference. Because any line beginning with a REM command is ignored, these commands are no longer executed. Its function is identical to the REM command in a batch file and the CONFIG.SYS REM command added in MS DOS 5. The format is

REM *[Comment]*

SHELL

The SHELL command is used to load an alternative command processor. It is also useful for loading COMMAND.COM if you want to load it from a location other than the root directory or if you need to expand the environment. It was examined in more detail in Chapter 35.

SHELL=*[Drive:][Path]CommandProcessor [Options]*

Device drivers

The device drivers supplied with DR DOS 5 are as follows:

ANSI.SYS   This device driver replaces the screen and keyboard handling of DR DOS with more powerful routines. See Chapter 21 for more information on ANSI.

CACHE.EXE   This device driver lets you set up a portion of memory as a disk cache to speed up disk reads and writes. It is dropped in DR DOS 6 in favor of the Super PC-Kwik program.

DISPLAY.SYS   This device driver supports code pages on EGA and VGA displays.

DRIVER.SYS   This device driver lets you define an external drive as a logical drive. The primary use for DRIVER.SYS is to define an external 5¼-inch drive as a logical drive on a machine with only 3½-inch drives.

EMM386.SYS   This device driver adds support for upper memory and will convert extended memory into expanded memory.

EMMXMA.SYS   This device driver enables LIM 4.0 memory support on 286 computers.

HIDOS.SYS   This device driver supports relocating the DR DOS kernel to high memory on some 286 computers.

PRINTER.SYS   This device driver supports code page switching on printers.

VDISK.SYS   VDISK.SYS allows you to set aside part of your memory as an electronic floppy disk drive, called a RAM disk.

Improved memory management

Several of the new commands and device drivers will give users with an 80386SX or better computer significantly more free conventional memory. If you have one of these machines, you might want to add the following lines to your CONFIG.SYS file:

```
DEVICE=C:\DRDOS5\EMM386.SYS
```

Of course, you'll want to modify this command to use the subdirectory where you have DR DOS 5 installed. This line loads the EMM386.SYS device driver to support upper memory.

Next, you'll want to load DR DOS into high memory with a

```
HIDOS=ON
```

command. You will also want to load any device drivers you use into high memory with a command like

```
HIDEVICE=C:\DRDOS5\ANSI.SYS
```

Finally, you will want to load any allowable DR DOS 5 programs into high memory with a command like:

```
HIINSTALL=C:\DRDOS5\SHARE.EXE
```

By the time you finish, you can end up with 600K or more of free conventional memory.

Notice EMM386.SYS, Hidos, Hiinstall and Hidevice let you save conventional memory by loading much of DR DOS and your device drivers into high memory—if you have a 386SX or better computer.

More power!

While the expanded memory management commands are nice, similar commands are available under MS DOS 5. Additionally, they don't really make your CONFIG.SYS file more powerful, they just free up a little more memory. However, the three commands labeled as Unique (?, CHAIN, and ECHO) significantly increase the power and flexibility of the CONFIG.SYS file.

Let me begin by describing a situation I faced in the last office I worked in. My computer was connected to a Novell network. Attaching the Novell network required both a device driver loaded in the CONFIG.SYS file and a memory resident program loaded in the AUTOEXEC.BAT file. Normally, I ran in this configuration. However, there were two occasions where I did not want to load the network software. The first time, I needed to work on a massive spreadsheet that the department used for analysis. Loading the network drivers did not leave me with enough memory to work on this spreadsheet comfortably. The second time was when I needed to run Ventura Publisher. I had a legal copy of Ventura Publisher but I did not have the network version. As a result, Ventura Publisher refused to run at all if it found a network driver loaded into memory. So, as dumb as it sounds, I had to run without the network to use Ventura Publisher.

In both of these situations, what I wanted to do was start my computer and skip over some of the lines in the CONFIG.SYS and AUTOEXEC.BAT files. Skipping the lines in the AUTOEXEC.BAT file is no problem—we have already seen how to do that. However, the MS DOS 5 I was running at the time has no facilities for skipping lines in the CONFIG.SYS file. If you want to run different versions of your CONFIG.SYS file under MS DOS, you must go through the cumbersome process of creating multiple versions of your CONFIG.SYS, copying the right one to the root directory, and then rebooting! This is not true with DR DOS 5. In fact, DR DOS 5 gives you two different approaches to the problem.

Approach 1: Ask about each line

In my situation, I just needed to skip over a line in my CONFIG.SYS file. For example, my CONFIG.SYS file might have looked like this:

```
FILES=40
BUFFERS=20
DEVICE=C:\DOS\ANSI.SYS
DEVICE=C:\NETWORK\NETWORK.SYS
```

Normally, I wanted to run the CONFIG.SYS file as written. However, when I needed to work on this massive spreadsheet or in Ventura Publisher, I wanted to run the following CONFIG.SYS file:

```
FILES=40
BUFFERS=20
DEVICE=C:\DOS\ANSI.SYS
```

Because these two versions are the same, except for the last line, what I really wanted to do, in pseudocode is

```
Set Files At 40
Set Buffers At 20
Load ANSI
Ask About Loading Network
      If Yes, Load Network Device Driver
      If No, Skip Loading Network Device Driver
```

This is exactly what the question mark does. When a command in the CONFIG.SYS file is preceded by a question mark and you boot the computer, DR DOS displays that line and waits for you to press a key. If you press the "y" key, the line is processed normally. If you press any other key, the line is skipped. Now my CONFIG.SYS could be rewritten as

```
FILES=40
BUFFERS=20
DEVICE=C:\DOS\ANSI.SYS
?DEVICE=C:\NETWORK\NETWORK.SYS
```

This approach is adequate for an experienced user but an inexperienced user might be confused by the message

```
DEVICE=C:\NETWORK\NETWORK.SYS (Y/N)?
```

appearing on the screen.

You can reduce that confusion in two ways. First, if you place a remark between the question mark and command and include it inside quote marks, DR DOS displays that message instead of the command line. Of course, the entire line must be 127 characters or less. If you need more room, you can precede the line with several ECHO commands. My CONFIG.SYS could be rewritten as

```
FILES=40
BUFFERS=20
DEVICE=C:\DOS\ANSI.SYS
ECHO YOU MUST NOW DECIDE IF YOU WANT TO LOAD THE NETWORK
ECHO PRESS Y TO LOAD NETWORK
ECHO PRESS N TO SKIP NETWORK
?"LOAD NETWORK (Y/N)?"DEVICE=C:\NETWORK\NETWORK.SYS
```

The messages are in all uppercase because DR DOS 5 converts your message to uppercase before displaying it.

Notice   With the question mark, you can ask about each line individually, although that can become burdensome if you have a lot of lines to ask about.

Approach 2: Select which file to run

The first approach of asking about each line works well when you simply want to sometimes skip a specific line. However, it does not work so well when your decision about one line impacts another line. For example, we used to use a network that required two device drivers in the CONFIG.SYS file so using the first approach to deciding about loading the network results in a CONFIG.SYS file that looks like this:

```
FILES=40
BUFFERS=20
DEVICE=C:\DOS\ANSI.SYS
?DEVICE=C:\NETWORK\NETWORK1.SYS
?DEVICE=C:\NETWORK\NETWORK2.SYS
```

This approach has two drawbacks. First, you must answer the network question twice when once should be enough. Second, with these particular device drivers, if you make a mistake and load the second without loading the first, the system immediately locks up.

The solution to this dilemma is easy. First, write a separate version of my CONFIG-.SYS file including everything needed to log onto the network and another one including everything needed when I do not work on the network. Then, ask a single question and use it to CHAIN to the proper configuration file. The resulting batch file might look like this:

```
?"LOAD NETWORK (Y/N)?"CHAIN CONFIG.NET
CHAIN CONFIG.NO
```

In this example, the CONFIG.SYS would CHAIN to the network configuration file—now called CONFIG.NET—if the user answered yes to the question and would chain to the non-network configuration file—now called CONFIG.NO—if the user answered no.

While this approach is nice, it has two drawbacks we can correct. First, if I now decide to install a disk caching program and I need to lower the BUFFERS statement, I have to remember to do it in two places. Second, if the user presses the wrong key, she has to reboot to rerun the CONFIG.SYS file because answering yes automatically processes the network file and answering no automatically processes the non-network file.

We can completely eliminate the first drawback and partially eliminate the second. The CONFIG.SYS file does not have to chain to a new configuration file first; it can perform other tasks before that. It is, in fact, a very good idea to perform all those tasks that will be common to all configurations first before chaining to another configuration file. That way, you only have to make modifications in one place when something changes. Using that, the new CONFIG.SYS file might look like this:

```
FILES=40
BUFFERS=20
DEVICE=C:\DOS\ANSI.SYS
?"LOAD NETWORK (Y/N)?"CHAIN CONFIG.NET
CHAIN CONFIG.NO
```

The drawback to this approach is still that it assumes the non-network configuration should be followed if you answer no to the network configuration. We cannot simply add a question to the non-network configuration because answering no to it too would mean that neither configuration file gets processed. However, if we do that and then have the CONFIG.SYS file CHAIN to itself, answering yes to one of these configurations represents the only way out of the loop. The resulting CONFIG.SYS file looks like this:

```
FILES=40
BUFFERS=20
?"LOAD NETWORK (Y/N)?"CHAIN CONFIG.NET
?"SKIP NETWORK (Y/N)?"CHAIN CONFIG.NO
CHAIN CONFIG.SYS
```

This CONFIG.SYS file sets the FILES and BUFFERS and then asks which configuration file to load. If you answer yes to either one, it loads that configuration file without control ever returning to the CONFIG.SYS file. If you answer no to both questions, the CONFIG.SYS file is reprocessed and you have a chance to answer the questions again.

Notice that the statement to load ANSI has been removed from the CONFIG.SYS file and would need to be added to each configuration file individually. That is because each time DR DOS loops through the CONFIG.SYS file, it loads another copy of ANSI if it is left in the loop. The FILES and BUFFERS are merely memory configurations so it does not hurt to reprocess them.

If you decide to use this approach, the best thing to do is to have a CONFIG.SYS file like this

```
FILES=40
BUFFERS=20
DEVICE=C:\DOS\ANSI.SYS
CHAIN ASK.SYS
```

where all the tasks that will be common to all configuration files are performed. As its last command, it CHAINS to another configuration file that questions the user about which configuration to load. This configuration can loop through itself as many times as needed for the user to select a configuration without using any additional memory. It might look like this:

```
REM ASK.SYS
?"LOAD NETWORK (Y/N)?"CHAIN CONFIG.NET
?"SKIP NETWORK (Y/N)?"CHAIN CONFIG.NO
CHAIN ASK.SYS
```

Because ASK.SYS does nothing but ask questions, it uses no additional memory to go through it more than once.

✍ *Notice*   By chaining to other files based on the user's response, you can reduce the number of questions you have to ask the user.

Other uses

My examples here have all been deciding between loading or not loading network software. However, you have some other uses for this approach. A few of them include

- Loading a mouse. When I use my notebook computer at home, I attach a mouse to it. However, when I'm traveling, I don't want to be bothered with the mouse. Instead of editing my CONFIG.SYS file all the time, I have it ask me if I want to load the mouse driver.
- Memory configuration. Some of my programs, like Windows and Lotus 3.1, work better with extended memory. Other programs, like Lotus 2.3, only work with expanded memory. By asking a question in the CONFIG.SYS file, I can CHAIN to a configuration file to set up the appropriate type of memory for the programs I will be working on this time.
- Running Windows. Windows wants different memory configuration and caching arrangements than I normally use. Rather than always running under the Windows configuration, I can load different configurations depending on if I will be running Windows.

These are just a few suggestions. As you think about it, I'm sure you will think of other uses to match your needs.

Communication with the AUTOEXEC.BAT file

As I stated earlier, my network software requires one device driver and one memory resident program in my AUTOEXEC.BAT file. It would be nice if the configuration file could tell the AUTOEXEC.BAT file which configuration was suggested so that it could branch automatically. DR DOS 6 adds this ability. However, it is not possible under DR DOS 5, so you either have to answer the questions again in the AUTOEXEC.BAT file or upgrade to DR DOS 6. It's a nice upgrade, so the latter would be my suggestion.

☠ *Warning*   If you want your CONFIG.SYS file to be able to communicate with your AUTOEXEC.BAT file, you will have to upgrade to DR DOS 6.

Summary

When a CONFIG.SYS file command is preceded by a question mark, DR DOS displays that line and only processes it if the user presses the "y" key.

The BREAK command in the CONFIG.SYS file controls how often DR DOS checks to see if you have pressed Ctrl-Break.

The BUFFERS command in the CONFIG.SYS file controls how much memory DR DOS allocates for disk caching.

A CHAIN command causes DR DOS to stop processing the current configuration file, close it and begin processing the specified configuration file. Control never returns to the original configuration file.

The COUNTRY command in the CONFIG.SYS file controls what format DR DOS uses for dates, time, currency symbols, decimal separators, sorting order, and more.

The DEVICE command in the CONFIG.SYS file allows DR DOS to load device drivers to allow it to communicate with additional devices.

The DRIVPARM command lets you specify the physical characteristic of a drive that DR DOS already recognizes.

The ECHO command displays a message in the CONFIG.SYS file similarly to the batch file ECHO command. However, all text is converted to uppercase before being displayed.

The FASTOPEN command sets aside a portion of memory to store the location of files on the hard disk so it can load them faster the next time it accesses them.

The FCBS command in the CONFIG.SYS file controls how many files DR DOS can open using the old MS DOS 1.x data structure.

The FILES command in the CONFIG.SYS file controls how many files DR DOS can have open at once, including predefined files like input, output, error, auxiliary, and printer.

The HIDEVICE command loads device drivers into upper memory, if enough upper memory is available. This requires that the CONFIG.SYS file first load a device driver that supports upper memory.

The HIDOS command loads much of DR DOS into upper memory. This requires that the CONFIG.SYS file first load a device driver that supports upper memory.

The HIINSTALL command loads memory resident software into upper memory. However, most programs do not support being loaded this way. This requires that the CONFIG.SYS file first load a device driver that supports upper memory.

The HISTORY command sets aside a portion of memory to store prior commands so they can be reused.

The INSTALL command loads memory resident software in the CONFIG.SYS file. However, most programs do not support being loaded this way.

The LASTDRIVE command in the CONFIG.SYS file specifies the highest drive letter DR DOS is to allow.

The REM command allows you to add documentation remarks to your CONFIG.SYS file as well as commenting out commands you want to save but not execute.

The SHELL command lets you load an alternative command processor, change the location of COMMAND.COM, and expand your environment.

The device drivers that come with DR DOS 5 are ANSI.SYS, CACHE.EXE, DISPLAY-.SYS, DRIVER.SYS, EMM386.SYS, EMMXMA.SYS, HIDOS.SYS, PRINTER.SYS, and VDISK.SYS.

The enhanced memory management commands in DR DOS 5 make it easy for users with a 386SX or better computer to free up a lot of additional conventional memory.

The question mark, CHAIN command, and ECHO command allow you to select your configuration each time the computer boots.

Under DR DOS 5, the CONFIG.SYS file cannot communicate with the AUTOEXEC.BAT file. This is corrected in DR DOS 6.

37

CONFIG.SYS file under DR DOS 6

If you have not yet read Chapters 35 and 36, you need to go back and read them now. This chapter examines the extensions to the CONFIG.SYS file added in DR DOS 6 with the assumption that you have read about the basics in the earlier chapters.

The DR DOS 6 CONFIG.SYS commands

DR DOS 5 added three commands (?, CHAIN, and ECHO) that add dramatic power to the CONFIG.SYS file, making it far more intelligent and useful than the CONFIG.SYS file under any version of MS DOS. After that, DR DOS 6 added almost the entire batch language to the CONFIG.SYS file. Commands not explored in Chapter 35 or Chapter 36 are indicated with a New, while commands that are not equivalent to any under MS DOS 5 are indicated with a Unique.

✍ *Notice* DR DOS 6 added almost the entire batch language to the CONFIG.SYS file!

? [Unique]

When used at the beginning of a CONFIG.SYS statement, the question mark causes that statement to become conditional. That statement is only executed if the user presses the "y" key. It was explored in more detail in Chapter 36.

> ?["Remark"]Command

:Label [New Unique]

DR DOS 6 supports the GOTO and GOSUB commands in configuration files identically to its support of the same commands in batch files. The colon followed by a name is used to name lines for these commands to jump to. The name should be eight characters or less and follow the same guidelines as labels in a batch file.

    :LABEL

BREAK

BREAK controls how often DR DOS stops and checks to see if Ctrl-Break has been pressed. It was examined in more detail in Chapter 35.

    BREAK=On | Off

BUFFERS

BUFFERS controls how much memory DR DOS allocates to disk caching. It was examined in more detail in Chapter 35.

    BUFFERS=*n*

CHAIN [Unique]

This causes DR DOS to close the current configuration file and transfer control to the configuration file specified after the CHAIN command. Control does not return to the original configuration command. It was examined in more detail in Chapter 36. The format is

    CHAIN=*[Drive:][Path]FileSpec*

CLS [New Unique]

The CLS command clears the screen, exactly as it does from the command line or in a batch file.

    CLS

COUNTRY

COUNTRY controls the format DR DOS uses for the date, time, currency, and more. It was examined in more detail in Chapter 35.

    COUNTRY=*CountryCode,CodePage,[Drive:][Path]*COUNTRY.SYS

CPOS [New Unique]

The CPOS command allows you to position the cursor at a specific row and column on the screen. This command is unique to configuration files, although a similar action can be performed in batch files using ANSI escape sequences if you load ANSI.SYS in the configuration file. The format is

```
CPOS r,c
```

where r is the row number (1-25) and c is the column number (1-80).

DEVICE

DEVICE allows DR DOS to load device drivers so it can communicate with devices—like a mouse—that are not normally supported. It was examined in more detail in Chapter 35. The format is

```
DEVICE=[Drive:][Path]FileSpec
```

DRIVPARM

This command lets you specify the physical characteristics for a drive. It is similar to DRIVER.SYS except that it only works for a physical drive already recognized by DR DOS while DRIVER.SYS is used to add a new logical drive. Some older computers do not expect to work with 3.5″ drives, so they don't configure the drive parameters properly. DRIV-PARM lets you correct that. It was examined in more detail in Chapter 36.

ECHO [Unique]

The ECHO command displays an uppercase comment for the user. It was examined in more detail in Chapter 36.

```
ECHO [Message]
```

✍ *Notice*   The ECHO command lets a CONFIG.SYS file display text just like a batch file.

EXIT [New Unique]

The EXIT command causes a configuration file to immediately stop processing. This could have been used in the CONFIG.SYS file in Chapter 36 to stop processing if the user did not want to load network drivers. The original CONFIG.SYS file looked like this:

```
FILES=40
BUFFERS=20
DEVICE=C:\DOS\ANSI.SYS
?DEVICE=C:\NETWORK\NETWORK1.SYS
?DEVICE=C:\NETWORK\NETWORK2.SYS
```

That could be rewritten as follows:

```
FILES=40
BUFFERS=20
DEVICE=C:\DOS\ANSI.SYS
?"STOP BEFORE LOADING NETWORK (Y/N)?"EXIT
```

```
DEVICE=C:\NETWORK\NETWORK1.SYS
DEVICE=C:\NETWORK\NETWORK2.SYS
```

If the user presses a "y" key, the EXIT command causes the CONFIG.SYS file to terminate before reaching the network device drivers. If the user presses any other key, the EXIT command is skipped and the network drivers loaded.

FASTOPEN

FASTOPEN uses a portion of memory to store the location of files that are accessed so they can be accessed faster next time. It was examined in more detail in Chapter 36.

    FASTOPEN=*n*

FCBS

This command controls how many files can be opened using an older MS DOS 1.x format. It was examined in more detail in Chapter 35. The format is

    FCBS=*m,n*

where *m* is the number of files that can be open at once (1-255) and *n* is the number that are protected from automatic closure (1-255).

FILES

This controls how many files can be opened at once. It was examined in more detail in Chapter 35. The format is

    FILES=*n*

when *n* is the number of files (20-255).

GOSUB [New Unique]

The GOSUB command works the same in a configuration file as it does in a batch file. It jumps to the label specified after the GOSUB command and continues processing until it hits a RETURN command. This causes processing to return to the line following the GOSUB command.

    GOSUB *Label*

✍ *Notice* The GOSUB command allows a section of code to be conditionally run as a subroutine with control returning to the original section of code when it's done.

HIBUFFERS [New]

The HIBUFFERS command is similar to the BUFFERS command, only the buffers are loaded into upper memory. If there is not enough upper memory for all the buffers, as many as possible are placed in upper memory with the remainder placed in conventional memory. Prior to using this command, the CONFIG.SYS file must use a DEVICE command to load a device driver like EMM386.SYS that supports upper memory. MS DOS 5 automatically loads as many buffers into upper memory as possible when it is loaded high, without the need for a special command. The format is

    HIBUFFERS=n

where n represents the number of desired buffers.

HIDEVICE

The HIDEVICE command is identical to the DEVICE command except it attempts to load the device driver into high memory. It was discussed in more detail in Chapter 36. The format is

    HIDEVICE=[Drive:][Path]DeviceDriver

HIDOS

The HIDOS command tries to load much of DR DOS into upper memory. It was examined in more detail in Chapter 36. The format is

    Format: HIDOS=On|Off

HIINSTALL

The HIINSTALL command is identical to the INSTALL command, only it tries to load a memory resident program into high memory. It was examined in more detail in Chapter 36. The format is

    HIINSTALL=[Drive:][Path]FileSpec

HISTORY

The HISTORY command is used to support extended command line editing. It was examined in more detail in Chapter 36. The format is

    HISTORY=On[,n][,On|Off]|Off

INSTALL

The INSTALL command allows you to load memory resident programs in the CONFIG-.SYS file. It was examined in more detail in Chapter 36. The format is

    INSTALL=[Drive:][Path]FileSpec

LASTDRIVE

The LASTDRIVE specifies the last drive letter DR DOS is to allow. This just sets the upper limit; DR DOS still tracks the actual number of drives. This was examined in more detail in

Chapter 35. The format is

LASTDRIVE=*Drive*

REM

The REM command lets you add a documentation remark to your CONFIG.SYS files. It was examined in more detail in Chapter 36. The format is

REM *[Comment]*

RETURN [New Unique]

The RETURN command is used in conjunction with the GOSUB or SWITCH command. After a GOSUB or SWITCH command is issued, a RETURN causes control to return to the line following the GOSUB or SWITCH command. The format is

RETURN

SET [New]

The SET command is used in the configuration file to store values to an environmental variable, exactly as it is used in batch files. The format is

SET *Variable=Value*

✍ *Notice*   The SET command allows the CONFIG.SYS file to communicate with the AUTOEXEC.BAT file to tell it what selections the user made.

SHELL

The SHELL command is used to load an alternative command processor. It is also useful for loading COMMAND.COM if you want to load it from a location other than the root directory or if you need to expand the environment. It was examined in more detail in Chapter 35. The format is

SHELL=*[Drive:][Path]CommandProcessor [Options]*

SWITCH [New Unique]

The SWITCH command in a configuration file works identically to a SWITCH command in a batch file. It is followed by up to nine labels and the user enters a number corresponding to the option she wishes to select. The SWITCH command then jumps to that label as though a GOTO LABEL command had been issued. A RETURN causes control to return to the line following the SWITCH command.

SWITCH *Label1, Label2 [, Label3..., Label9]*

✍ *Notice*   The SWITCH command allows you set up a menu of configuration options in your CONFIG.SYS file—especially when combined with the ECHO command.

TIMEOUT [New Unique]

One problem with booting with some of your commands preceded with a question mark or using a SWITCH command is if you walk away without answering the question, your computer will not finish booting until you return and answer the question. The TIMEOUT command avoids this problem by allowing you to specify the maximum amount of time to wait for an answer. If a line with a question mark is not answered in that period of time, DR DOS assumes the user responded with a no. If a SWITCH command is not answered in that period of time, DR DOS assumes the user selected the first option. The format is

TIMEOUT=*n*

where *n* is the number of sections to wait for a response.

📣 *Notice*   The TIMEOUT command allows you specify how long the CONFIG.SYS file waits for the user to respond.

Device drivers

The device drivers supplied with DR DOS 6 are as follows:

ANSI.SYS   This device driver replaces the screen and keyboard handling of DR DOS with more powerful routines. See Chapter 21 for more information on ANSI.

DEVSWAP.COM   This device driver changes the drive assignments for Super-Stor compressed drives.

DISPLAY.SYS   This device driver supports code pages on EGA and VGA displays.

DRIVER.SYS   This device driver lets you define an external drive as a logical drive. The primary use for DRIVER.SYS is to define an external 5.25″ drive as a logical drive on a machine with only 3.5″ drives.

EMM386.SYS   This device driver adds support for upper memory and will convert extended memory into expanded memory.

EMMXMA.SYS   This device driver enables LIM 4.0 memory support on 286 computers.

HIDOS.SYS   This device driver supports relocating the DR DOS kernel to high memory on some 286 computers.

PRINTER.SYS   This device driver supports code page switching on printers.

SSTORDRV.SYS   This device driver attaches the SuperStor partitions and lets it allocate drive letters.

VDISK.SYS   VDISK.SYS allows you to set aside part of your memory as an electronic floppy disk drive, called a RAM disk.

Some of these device drivers have specific loading requirements. These requirements are examined in your DR DOS 6 manual.

Improved memory management

The memory improvements in DR DOS 6 are the same as those introduced in DR DOS 5. See Chapter 36 for details. However, the improved configuration language makes it easier to load just the configuration of memory you need each time the computer boots.

More power!

The question mark, ECHO command, and CHAIN command make it easy to write configuration files that let the user select between different configurations as the computer is booting. This is examined in detail in Chapter 36. However, using these commands along means you end up with several different configuration files and a convoluted chain of logic to load the proper file. All that goes away with DR DOS 6!

DR DOS 6 introduces subroutines to configuration files using the same GOSUB, RETURN, and SWITCH commands used in the batch language. Because MS DOS offers no form of user query or subroutines in the CONFIG.SYS file, we might as well use all these commands to customize the CONFIG.SYS file.

To see this, let's look back to the situation that caused so many problems in Chapter 36: a network that requires two device drivers to load, and we only want to ask the user about it once. Our first attempt was the following CONFIG.SYS file:

```
FILES=40
BUFFERS=20
DEVICE=C:\DOS\ANSI.SYS
?DEVICE=C:\NETWORK\NETWORK1.SYS
?DEVICE=C:\NETWORK\NETWORK2.SYS
```

However, this requires asking the user about the network twice, which is what we want to avoid. Our next attempt was the following CONFIG.SYS file:

```
FILES=40
BUFFERS=20
DEVICE=C:\DOS\ANSI.SYS
?"LOAD NETWORK (Y/N)?"CHAIN CONFIG.NET
CHAIN CONFIG.NO
```

This has some problems that are examined in Chapter 36. However, the problem of interest now is it requires three files—CONFIG.SYS, CONFIG.NET and CONFIG.NO. This can be a problem if we are running short of hard disk space. It can also be a problem remembering what all the files do and remembering to send all the files if we decide to share this with other users.

Luckily, both the GOSUB and SWITCH command can be used to correct this problem. First, the solution using the GOSUB command:

```
FILES=40
BUFFERS=20
DEVICE=C:\DOS\ANSI.SYS
```

```
?"LOAD NETWORK (Y/N)?"GOSUB NETWORK
EXIT

:NETWORK
    DEVICE=C:\NETWORK\NETWORK1.SYS
    DEVICE=C:\NETWORK\NETWORK2.SYS
RETURN
```

If the user answers yes to the load network prompt, everything in the Network subroutine is processed. Otherwise, that step is skipped and the next line terminates the CONFIG.SYS file.

While a prompt and subroutine is an excellent way to handle loading a single set of drivers, it becomes cumbersome when trying to select between several different configurations. If you have that need, the SELECT command is a better alternative. Figure 37-1 shows a CONFIG.SYS file that uses the SELECT command to pick between three unique sets of configurations. It does this cleanly where each question is answered once and without the need for any supporting files to CHAIN to.

✍ *Notice*   Subroutines make it easier to specify multiple configurations within a single CONFIG.SYS file.

Communication with the AUTOEXEC.BAT file

Naturally, after you are finished selecting a configuration in the CONFIG.SYS file, your selection is going to affect the things you want do in the AUTOEXEC.BAT file. Prior to DR DOS 6, your only choice was to ask the questions again in the AUTOEXEC.BAT file. However, the addition of the SET command to the available commands in the configuration file eliminates this problem.

Using the SET command, the CONFIG.SYS file can create an environmental variable with a different value depending on the selected configuration. The AUTOEXEC.BAT file can then vary its processing using If-tests depending on the value of that environmental variable. That way, the AUTOEXEC.BAT file can easily respond to choices made in the CONFIG.SYS file.

✍ *Notice*   Subroutines combined with the SWITCH command make it easier still to specify multiple configurations within a single CONFIG.SYS file.

Summary

When a configuration file command is preceded by a question mark, DR DOS displays that line and only processes it if the user presses the "y" key.

A line in a configuration file is given a name by a colon followed directly by a label. The GOTO and GOSUB commands can then jump to this line.

The BREAK command in the configuration file controls how often DR DOS checks to see if you have pressed Ctrl-Break.

CONFIG.SYS Line	Explanation
REM NAME: CONFIG.SYS REM PURPOSE: Custom Configuration File REM VERSION: 1.00 REM DATE: June 13, 1992	Documentation remarks.
CLS	Clear the screen.
CPOS 24,01	Position the cursor at the bottom left corner.
ECHO Copyright (c) 1992 Tab Books	Display a message.
CPOS 01,01	Position the cursor at the top left corner.
ECHO 1=Normal Configuration ECHO 2=Network Configuration ECHO 3=386 Maximum Memory Configuration	Display a menu.
SWITCH NORMAL, NETWORK, MAXIMUM	Use the SWITCH command to have the user select from the menu options. The SELECT command will not allow an invalid selection.
GOSUB USUAL	After running the subroutine selected via the SWITCH command, run the USUAL subroutine.
EXIT	After returning from the USUAL subroutine, exit the configuration file.

:USUAL
   FILES=20
   HISTORY=ON,2000,OFF
RETURN
	In the USUAL subroutine, set values for FILES and HISTORY, then return.

:NORMAL
   BUFFERS=20
   DEVICE=C:\DRDOS\ANSI.SYS
   SET CONFIGURATION=NORMAL
RETURN
	In the NORMAL subroutine, set a value for BUFFERS, load ANSI and create an environmental variable to specify the configuration used.

:NETWORK
   BUFFERS=20
   DEVICE=C:\DRDOS\ANSI.SYS
   DEVICE=C:\NETWORK\NETWORK.SYS
   SET CONFIGURATION=NETWORK
RETURN
	In the NETWORK subroutine, set a value for BUFFERS, load ANSI, load the network driver, and create an environmental variable to specify the configuration used.

37-1 A sample DR DOS 6 CONFIG.SYS file.

CONFIG.SYS Line	Explanation

`:MAXIMUM`
  `DEVICE=C:\DRDOS\EMM386.SYS`
  `HIDOS=ON`
  `HIBUFFERS=99`
  `HIDEVICE=C:\DRDOS\ANSI.SYS`
  `SET CONFIGURATION=MAXIMUM`
`RETURN`
	In the MAXIMUM subroutine, load the EMM386.SYS device driver to support upper memory, load DR DOS into upper memory, load buffers and ANSI into upper memory, and create an environmental variable to specify the configuration used.

37-1 Continued.

The BUFFERS command in the configuration file controls how much memory DR DOS allocates for disk caching.

A CHAIN command causes DR DOS to stop processing the current configuration file, close it and begin processing the specified configuration file. Control never returns to the original configuration file.

The CLS command in a configuration file clears the screen.

The COUNTRY command in the configuration file controls what format DR DOS uses for dates, time, currency symbols, decimal separators, sorting order, and more.

The CPOS command allows you to position the cursor in a configuration file.

The DEVICE command in the configuration file allows DR DOS to load device drivers to allow it to communicate with additional devices.

The DRIVPARM command lets you specify the physical characteristic of a drive that DR DOS already recognizes.

The ECHO command displays a message in the configuration file similarly to the batch file ECHO command. However, all text is converted to uppercase before being displayed.

The EXIT command causes a configuration file to immediately terminate.

The FASTOPEN command sets aside a portion of memory to store the location of files on the hard disk so it can load them faster the next time it accesses them.

The FCBS command in the configuration file controls how many files DR DOS can open using the old MS DOS 1.x data structure.

The FILES command in the configuration file controls how many files DR DOS can have open at once, including predefined files like input, output, error, auxiliary, and printer.

The GOSUB command causes the configuration file to jump to the line specified after the GOSUB command and continue processing until a RETURN command is reached. The RETURN command causes control to return to the line following the GOSUB command.

The GOTO command causes the configuration file to jump to the line specified after the GOTO command. Control never returns to the original location.

The HIBUFFERS loads buffers into upper memory. If they do not all fit, the remainder are loaded into conventional memory.

The HIDEVICE command loads device drivers into upper memory, if enough upper memory is available. This requires that the configuration file first load a device driver that supports upper memory.

The HIDOS command loads much of DR DOS into upper memory. This requires that the configuration file first load a device driver that supports upper memory.

The HIINSTALL command loads memory resident software into upper memory. However, most programs do not support being loaded this way. This requires that the configuration file first load a device driver that supports upper memory.

The HISTORY command sets aside a portion of memory to store prior commands so they can be reused.

The INSTALL command loads memory resident software in the configuration file. However, most programs do not support being loaded this way.

The LASTDRIVE command in the configuration file specifies the highest drive letter DR DOS is to allow.

The REM command allows you to add documentation remarks to your configuration file as well as commenting out commands you want to save but not execute.

The RETURN command causes control to return to the line following a GOSUB or SWITCH command.

The SET command is used to create environmental variable.

The SHELL command lets you load an alternative command processor, change the location of COMMAND.COM, and expand your environment.

The SWITCH command lets the user select between up to nine options, which are then run as subroutines.

The device drivers that come with DR DOS 6 are ANSI.SYS, DEVSWAP.COM, DISPLAY.SYS, DRIVER.SYS, EMM386.SYS, EMMXMA.SYS, HIDOS.SYS, PRINTER.SYS, SSTORDRV.SYS, and VDISK.SYS.

The enhanced memory management commands in DR DOS 6 make it easy for users with a 386SX or better computer to free up a lot of additional conventional memory.

The question mark, CHAIN command, and ECHO command allows you to select your configuration each time the computer boots.

Subroutines and the SELECT command make it easy to pick between multiple configurations without the need for any supporting files.

Using the SET command in the CONFIG.SYS file to create an environmental variable allows the CONFIG.SYS file to communicate the choices made there to the AUTOEXEC-.BAT file.

38

The AUTOEXEC.BAT and LEAVING.BAT files

The last step the computer performs when it boots is checking for the AUTOEXEC.BAT file in the root directory. If it finds this file, it runs it automatically—hence the name AUTOmatically EXECuted BATch file. Because it runs automatically when you boot or reboot, the AUTOEXEC.BAT file is the perfect place to do those things you only do once, like setting the path and loading memory-resident software. With one very minor exception, the AUTOEXEC.BAT file is just like any other batch file. There are no special AUTOEXEC.BAT commands. The only commands you can use in an AUTOEXEC.BAT file are the same commands you would use in any other batch file.

One minor difference

One unusual but very minor difference of the AUTOEXEC.BAT is that if no AUTOEXEC.BAT file exists, the last thing DR DOS will do is prompt you for the date and time. If an AUTOEXEC.BAT file does exist, DR DOS will turn control over to it and never prompt for the date and time.

Older computers didn't come with a built-in clock. They required a DATE and TIME command in the AUTOEXEC.BAT file so that the user could set the clock manually. Later, vendors began selling boards containing a clock. These required running a program in the AUTOEXEC.BAT (some used a device driver in the CONFIG.SYS file) to transfer the date and time from the clock to DR DOS. Almost all newer computers have a clock built in that automatically communicates with DR DOS, so most users can ignore the clock.

✔ *Remember* With an AUTOEXEC.BAT file, DR DOS does not ask you for the date and time. Without one, it asks you automatically.

System configuration

As I explained in Chapter 36 and Chapter 37, most system configuration is performed by the CONFIG.SYS file. However, several configuration commands belong in the AUTOEXEC.BAT file. They are as follows.

PATH

DR DOS will accept four types of commands: internal commands, .EXE program names, .COM program names, and .BAT filenames. Every time DR DOS receives a command, it first checks to see if that command is an internal command, like ERASE. If so, it executes that command. If the command isn't an internal command, DR DOS next checks the current subdirectory for a .COM file by that name, then an .EXE file, and finally a .BAT file. If DR DOS finds a program with the correct name, it executes that program. If DR DOS doesn't find a file in the current directory, it searches the path for a .COM, .EXE, or .BAT file. If it finds a program in the path with the correct name, it executes that program. Otherwise, DR DOS returns the "Command or filename not recognized" error message. See Table 38-1.

Table 38-1 Hierarchy of DR DOS commands when the path is C: FIRST;C: SECOND;C: THIRD.

When the path is C:\FIRST;C:\SECOND;C:\THIRD

1. An internal command.
2. A .COM file in the current subdirectory.
3. A .EXE file in the current subdirectory.
4. A .BAT file in the current subdirectory.
5. A .COM file in the C:\FIRST subdirectory.
6. A .EXE file in the C:\FIRST subdirectory.
7. A .BAT file in the C:\FIRST subdirectory.
8. A .COM file in the C:\SECOND subdirectory.
9. A .EXE file in the C:\SECOND subdirectory.
10. A .BAT file in the C:\SECOND subdirectory.
11. A .COM file in the C:\THIRD subdirectory.
12. A .EXE file in the C:\THIRD subdirectory.
13. A .BAT file in the C:\THIRD subdirectory.

So the path is nothing more than a list of subdirectories for DR DOS to search when a program isn't in the current subdirectory. The syntax for the PATH command is:

PATH=C:\;Subdirectory1;Subdirectory2;...;SubdirectoryLast

If your path is

PATH=C:\;\DRDOS;\DATABASE;\WP

then DR DOS will search the following subdirectories in this order:

1. The current subdirectory
2. C:\
3. \DRDOS
4. \DATABASE
5. \WP

This is normally what you want. However, if you're working on the A Drive, then the path is really

```
PATH=C:\;A:\DRDOS;A:\DATABASE;A:\WP
```

because A is the default drive. So you're better off to specify the full path, like this:

```
PATH=C:\;C:\DRDOS;C:\DATABASE;C:\WP
```

A second problem is that the PATH command can contain only the same 127 characters, just like any other DR DOS commands. Because "PATH=" itself takes five characters, 122 characters are left over for the path itself. A solution to this problem is the SUBST command. The SUBST command allows you to substitute a drive letter for a subdirectory, so

```
SUBST D: C:\DRDOS
SUBST E: C:\DATABASE
SUBST F: C:\WP
```

allows you to use D: anywhere you would have used C:\DRDOS. Your PATH command can now be

```
PATH=C:\;D:\;E:\;F:\
```

This makes the PATH command shorter, as well as easier to read. Generally speaking, you won't have set a path before using the SUBST command. Therefore, SUBST.EXE must be in the root directory, you must change to the directory containing the path before you issue the SUBST command, or you must specify the full path to the SUBST program. Here's an example of having SUBST.EXE in the C:\DRDOS directory:

```
CD\DRDOS
SUBST D: C:\DRDOS
```

or

```
\DRDOS\SUBST D: C:\DRDOS
```

Warning If you use the SUBST command in your AUTOEXEC.BAT file to shorten your path, it is unlikely that you have a path set at the time. Therefore, you must change to the subdirectory containing SUBST.EXE, have a copy of SUBST.EXE in the root directory, or specify the full path to SUBST.EXE.

Keep in mind that if you do not specify a last drive in your CONFIG.SYS file with a LASTDRIVE command, DR DOS defaults to using the E drive as the last drive. If you plan on using the SUBST command to define several substitute drives, you will need to specify a higher LASTDRIVE value in the CONFIG.SYS file.

If you enter the PATH command with nothing after it, DR DOS displays the current path. If you enter the path followed by a semicolon, then DR DOS resets the path to nothing. This causes DR DOS to search only the default directory for programs and batch files. If you specify a path incorrectly, DR DOS will not find the error until it needs to search the path. If you enter an invalid directory in the path, DR DOS ignores that entry.

The PATH command is really an environmental variable. The difference is that you don't have to start the command with a SET command, although you could. Like other environmental variables, the path is accessible to a batch file with its name surrounded by percent signs. A batch file could add the E drive to the path with the command:

```
PATH=%PATH%;E:\
```

This won't work from the command line, only from a batch file.

PROMPT

The default DR DOS prompt is a C>, which tells you that C is the default drive. You can use the PROMPT command to make the DR DOS prompt display a wide range of information. When used by itself, PROMPT resets the prompt to C>.

Any printable character string can be included in the PROMPT command. Some characters require special coding. They're shown in Table 38-2. It's important to remember that any prompt you develop is stored in the environmental space, along with the path and environmental variables. A long prompt combined with a long path and several environmental variables might require you to expand your environmental space, as explained in Chapter 13.

Table 38-2   Prompt metacharacters.

Command	Action
$$	Display a dollar sign.
$_	Include a carriage return and line feed.
$b	Display a vertical bar.
$d	Display the date.
$e	Include an escape. This is useful for sending ANSI escape sequences via the prompt command.
$g	Display a greater-than sign.
$h	Display a backspace--thus deleting the prior character.
$l	Display a less-than sign.
$n	Display the current drive.
$p	Display the current subdirectory.
$q	Display an equal sign.
$t	Display the time.
$v	Display the DOS version.

There's an additional drawback to using an expanded prompt. The most common prompt is pg, which causes DR DOS to display both the drive and the current subdirectory. However, to display the current subdirectory, DR DOS must be able to read the disk. That means trouble if you try to switch to an empty floppy disk drive. DR DOS will try to read the disk to get the information it needs for your prompt. When it fails, you'll get the familiar "Abort, Retry, Fail?" error message. Either abort or retry will get you back to the C drive.

VERIFY

From the name, you would expect that setting VERIFY to "on" causes DR DOS to check data it writes to a disk to make sure that it was written properly. You would expect DR DOS to read back the data as it writes it and compare what it reads back to what it wrote. When they match, it would go on to new data. When they didn't match, it would either retry or signal an error.

This isn't what DR DOS does, however. When DR DOS writes information to disk, it also includes a special checksum, called a Cyclical Redundancy Check, or CRC. The CRC is a number calculated mathematically and based on the data on the disk. Writing the same data to disk will always cause DR DOS to write the same CRC to disk. By including the data and the CRC on the disk, DR DOS has two versions of the data.

When DR DOS reads data from disk, it computes the CRC and compares it to the one already read from the disk. If they don't match, DR DOS knows it's read the data incorrectly. When the two CRCs don't match, DR DOS tries several more times. If it can't read the data where the CRCs match, it responds with an error message.

When VERIFY is on, DR DOS does more than write data to disk. After writing the data, it reads the data and computes a new CRC. If the new CRC matches the CRC stored with the data on the disk, DR DOS assumes the data was written properly. Note that DR DOS doesn't compare the data on the disk with the data in memory, which would be the better test. All it does is compare checksums.

So having VERIFY on causes DR DOS to perform a partial test of the data on the disk after a write operation. This partial test will catch some, but not all, errors. One thing VERIFY=ON will always do is slow down disk operations. After writing data to disk, DR DOS must wait for that data area of the disk to rotate back under the head, read in the data, compute a new CRC, and compare it to the existing CRC. All that takes time. So having verify on catches some disk errors but slows down all disk write operations.

You must decide whether or not to have this tradeoff. My recommendation is to leave VERIFY on (VERIFY=ON). Entering VERIFY alone displays it current status.

Mode

The program MODE.COM is used to configure the serial ports on a PC. For example, in order to use my modem at 2400 baud, I have to issue the command:

```
MODE COM1: 2400,,,,,
```

Because I always use my modem at 2400 baud, I have this command in my AUTOEXEC.BAT file. Serial printers and plotters typically require a similar command or set of commands. You would also place these in the AUTOEXEC.BAT file. Note that MODE.COM must be in your path statement, and you must have already issued the PATH command or you need to specify the full path to MODE.COM, like this:

```
C:\DRDOS\MODE COM1: 2400,,,,,
```

Memory-resident software

Memory-resident software (also called TSR for terminate and stay resident) is software that stays in memory until you reboot or specifically remove it. There are special problems associated with loading memory-resident software. Generally, the software is only loaded once. Trying to load it a second time when it's already in memory can cause problems. If you load more than one memory-resident software program, there's usually only one loading order that will work.

The problems associated with memory-resident software make the AUTOEXEC.BAT file an excellent way to load it. With the AUTOEXEC.BAT file, you can specify a specific order so that you don't have to worry about loading in the wrong order. Because the AUTOEXEC.BAT file automatically loads the programs into memory when the computer is booted, they're always available without you having to remember to load them.

AUTOEXEC.BAT arrangements

As you have seen, the AUTOEXEC.BAT file has several important tasks:

- Perform some final configuration tasks not performed in the CONFIG.SYS file.
- Define a path.
- Create any other environmental variables required by the system. Some environmental variables, like COMSPEC, are created automatically. Others might be created in the CONFIG.SYS file.
- Define a prompt.
- Load any memory resident software.

There are two general approaches to performing these tasks, and both have advantages and disadvantages. One approach is to just perform everything in the AUTOEXEC.BAT file, while the other is to run other batch files to perform some or all of these tasks.

All-in-one approach

With the all-in-one approach to writing an AUTOEXEC.BAT file, you write one AUTOEXEC.BAT file to perform all the startup tasks you need performed. Using this approach, your AUTOEXEC.BAT file might look something like the one shown next:

```
@ECHO OFF
REM NAME:     AUTOEXEC.BAT
REM PURPOSE: Perform System Configuration All-In-One
REM VERSION:  4.01
REM DATE:     May 23, 1992
ECHO Setting Prompt and Environment
PROMPT=$e[s$e[1;1H$e[K$e[1B$e[K$e[1A$e[47m$e[34m$d  $t$h$h
PROMPT=%PROMPT%$h$h$h$h  $e[1m$p$e[u$e[44m$e[37m$p$g
SET DOSONLY=1
SET 4100=P:300,I:3,D:1
```

```
SET DMCONFIG=C: PCLINK
SET TEMP=D:\
SET GIFDESK=VGA
SET HARD=D:
SET FLOPPY=B:
PATH=C:\;..;C:\NORTON;C:\SYSLIB;C:\UTILITY;C:\BAT;C:\WORD
PATH=%PATH%;C:\123;C:\VPIC;C:\ZIP;C:\LHA;D:\TODO;C:\BLDLITE
PATH=%PATH%;C:\NE;C:\DBASE
PATH=%PATH%
REM Delete .Tmp Files That Keep Appearing In Word Subdirectory
IF EXIST C:\WORD\*.TMP DEL C:\WORD\*.TMP
REM Run Utility To Reduce Printer Retries From 20 To 1
NOWAIT-1     Uses LPT1
NOWAIT-2     Uses LPT2
REM Run Utility To Turn Off Screen Print
NOPRTSCR
REM Loading CD ROM Driver
C:\CDROM\MSCDEX /D:MSCD210 /M:4 /L:E /V
C:\CDROM\MSCDINFO
ECHO Saving Hard Disk Information
ECHO Making Final Configurations
IMAGE C: /SAVE
IMAGE D: /SAVE
LOCKEYS N:OFF
CD\
FASTCONS
IF EXIST \WINDOWS\*.SWP DEL \WINDOWS\*.SWP > NUL
C:\WINDOWS\SMARTDRV
SCREEN1
```

This is not a made-up AUTOEXEC.BAT file. Rather, it is a slightly modified version of my own AUTOEXEC.BAT file. Only one modification was made, and I'll describe that in a moment.

The advantage of an all-in-one AUTOEXEC.BAT is that everything is collected into one location for easy maintenance. Plus, using a single file saves space and makes it easier to share a copy with someone else.

☑ Remember The all-in-one AUTOEXEC.BAT file saves disk space and keeps everything together.

The first disadvantage of an all-in-one AUTOEXEC.BAT is easy to see. The AUTOEXEC.BAT file tends to become long, hard to follow, and hard to maintain. Another disadvantage crops up when you use your CONFIG.SYS file to select between multiple configurations. Usually, that means you want to do different things in the AUTOEXEC-.BAT file, depending on the configuration selected in the CONFIG.SYS file.

For example, if you select a network configuration, you might want to include some network drives in your path; however, you would want to leave them out of the path if you selected the non-network configuration. Or selecting the network configuration might require you to load some memory resident programs in the AUTOEXEC.BAT file that are not needed if you skip the network. Or selecting a maximum memory configuration might lead you to skipping the memory resident software you normally load in the AUTOEXEC-.BAT file.

As you can see, just selecting between three different configurations can lead to a very confusing configuration. Now, what if you have installed the Dual Boot Utility examined in Chapter 27. You now have two different AUTOEXEC.BAT files with both of them performing very similar tasks. They both set a path: one uses your DR DOS subdirectory, while the other uses your MS DOS subdirectory. They both create the same prompt and load mostly the same memory resident software and create the same environmental variables.

With this arrangement, if you buy a copy of the Norton Utilities—for example—and decide you want to include their subdirectory in the path, you have to remember to change the path in two locations. If the Norton Utilities requires any environmental variables, you must remember to create them in two locations.

☠ *Warning*   The all-in-one AUTOEXEC.BAT file makes it more difficult to maintain multiple configurations and leads to a more complex AUTOEXEC.BAT file.

One-per-task approach

As you can see, when you boot with multiple configurations, multiple operating systems or just have a lot of things to do in the AUTOEXEC.BAT file, it quickly becomes very confused. If you can spare the space for multiple batch files, the task of writing an AUTOEXEC.BAT file for all these conditions can be greatly simplified.

I mentioned earlier that my AUTOEXEC.BAT file shown earlier had one slight modification. My real AUTOEXEC.BAT file is much shorter and calls several other batch files to perform much of the work. In order to illustrate an all-in-one AUTOEXEC.BAT file, I simply merged all these together. My actual working AUTOEXEC.BAT file is shown next:

```
@ECHO OFF
REM NAME:     START.BAT
REM PURPOSE: Perform System Configuration All-In-One
REM VERSION: 4.01
REM DATE:     May 23, 1992

ECHO Setting Prompt and Environment
CALL C:\BAT\NICEPROM

CALL C:\BAT\SETS
CALL C:\BAT\SETPATH

REM Delete .Tmp Files That Keep Appearing In Word Subdirectory
IF EXIST C:\WORD\*.TMP DEL C:\WORD\*.TMP

REM Run utility to reduce printer retries from 20 to 1
NOWAIT-1     Uses LPT1
NOWAIT-2     Uses LPT2
```

```
REM Run Utility To Turn Off Screen Print
NOPRTSCR

REM Loading CD ROM Driver
CALL C:\BAT\CDROM

ECHO Saving Hard Disk Information
ECHO Making Final Configurations

IMAGE C: /SAVE
IMAGE D: /SAVE
LOCKEYS N:OFF
CD\
FASTCONS
IF EXIST \WINDOWS\*.SWP DEL \ WINDOWS\*.SWP > NUL
C:\WINDOWS\SMARTDRV
SCREEN1
```

While this version is still not short or simple, it is much simpler than the all-in-one version shown previously.

☑ Remember With a one-per-task AUTOEXEC.BAT file, the AUTOEXEC.BAT file calls other batch files to perform a number of tasks.

This approach makes it much easier to deal with multiple configurations. For example, suppose we are developing an AUTOEXEC.BAT file to work with a CONFIG.SYS file that lets us choose between loading or not loading network drivers. The CONFIG.SYS creates an environmental variable called NETWORK with a value of YES when the user elects to log onto the network and a value of NO otherwise. The AUTOEXEC.BAT needs to load a memory resident program and add some of the network subdirectories to the path when the user elects to load the network. An AUTOEXEC.BAT segment to deal with this might look like this:

```
CALL C:\BAT\SETPATH
IF (%NETWORK%)==(YES) PATH=%PATH;%Q:\;R:\
CALL C:\BAT\LOAD-TSR
IF (%NETWORK%)==(YES) NET-TSR
```

The first line creates the normal path. If you add a utility or do anything else that requires a change to the path, you make one change here and it works both when the user selects the network and skips the network. The AUTOEXEC.BAT appends the network subdirectories onto the path in the second line only when the user selects the network configuration. The third line of this segment loads the normal memory resident programs. If you want to change your memory resident software, you make the change here and it affects all configurations. The last line loads the memory resident software for the network but only when the user selects the network configuration.

☑ Remember The one-per-task AUTOEXEC.BAT file makes it easier to deal with multiple configurations.

One note about this segment is important. If your non-network path is over 92 characters long, the second line above expands to longer than the allowable 127-character limit when the %PATH% environmental variable is expanded by DR DOS. If you anticipate a path this long, you can rewrite this segment to avoid problems when the %PATH% environmental variable is expanded, as shown next:

```
CALL C:\BAT\SETPATH
IF (%NETWORK%)==(YES) GOTO SKIP
PATH=%PATH;%Q:\;R:\
:SKIP
CALL C:\BAT\LOAD-TSR
IF (%NETWORK%)==(YES) NET-TSR
```

In this new arrangement, the path can reach 114 characters before a problem arises. The problem that arises at the 115-character mark is the 122-character limit on the path (127-character limit on command lines, less 5 characters for the "PATH=") no longer leaves room for the ";Q:\;R:\" to be added to the path. At this point, you must shorten your path.

Besides making the AUTOEXEC.BAT shorter and easier to understand, this one-per-task approach has another advantage. Your AUTOEXEC.BAT performs two different types of tasks:

- Tasks you would never want to perform again until you reboot, like loading memory resident software.
- Tasks you might need to perform again, like setting the path or prompt.

When all these tasks are performed in a single AUTOEXEC.BAT file, it can be difficult to refresh the path if you've made changes to it because running your AUTOEXEC.BAT file again will load your memory resident software again—at least unless you have some clever programming in your AUTOEXEC.BAT.

However, if you use the one-per-task approach, it's easy to refresh your path or return the prompt to its default value. These activities are performed by stand-alone batch files that the AUTOEXEC.BAT file calls as needed. Because they are stand-alone batch files, you can run them from the command line.

This is especially easy if you write these stand-alone batch files to facilitate this. My SETPATH.BAT batch file is shown next:

```
@ECHO OFF
REM NAME:     SETPATH.BAT
REM PURPOSE: Set The Path
REM VERSION: 2.00
REM DATE:     May 31, 1992
ECHO SETTING PATH
PATH;
PATH=C:\
PATH=%PATH%;..
PATH=%PATH%;C:\NORTON
PATH=%PATH%;C:\SYSLIB
```

```
PATH=%PATH%;C:\UTILITY
PATH=%PATH%;C:\BAT
PATH=%PATH%;C:\WORD
PATH=%PATH%;C:\123
PATH=%PATH%;C:\VPIC
PATH=%PATH%;C:\ZIP
PATH=%PATH%;C:\LHA
PATH=%PATH%;D:\TODO
PATH=%PATH%;C:\BLDLITE
PATH=%PATH%;C:\NE
PATH=%PATH%;C:\DBASE
```

It begins by resetting the path to NUL. That way, any existing path will not interfere with the new path it's creating. Thus, it resets the path to the default even if I'm running it from the command line and a path already exists.

This approach works well with the Dual Boot Utility [DBU] explored in Chapter 27. As you recall, DBU allows you to have a copy of DR DOS 6 and MS DOS 5 on your hard disk and boot from either one. Each operating system has its own CONFIG.SYS and AUTOEXEC.BAT file. Rather than maintaining the path in both versions of the AUTOEXEC.BAT file, I can have each copy call a batch file like SETPATH.BAT to create all of the path except the subdirectory that contains the operating system. The individual AUTOEXEC.BAT files can add that. So a segment for the one for DR DOS might look like this:

```
CALL C:\BAT\SETPATH
PATH=C:\DRDOS;%PATH%
```

That way, the path only has to be maintained in one location. Notice that the operating system subdirectory—which is likely to be accessed a lot—is appended to the front of the path rather than the end. That will make running operating system programs faster.

Leaving.BAT

DR DOS automatically runs AUTOEXEC.BAT when you turn the computer on and that gives you a place to perform those tasks you need to perform when the computer is first turned on. Wouldn't it be nice if there was a batch file called something like LEAVING-.BAT that would run automatically when you turned the computer off? That would give you a place to perform those tasks that need to be performed prior to turning off the computer—tasks like

- saving the contents of any RAM disks back to the hard disk.
- making an incremental backup.
- parking the hard disk heads.

Of course, the specific tasks that need to be performed on your system will be different. For example, on my system I don't use a RAM disk, so I can skip the first one; and the heads on my hard drive automatically park when the power is turned off, so I can skip the third step. However, I do need to eject any disk in my CD ROM drive, so LEAVING.BAT for my system might look like this:

```
XCOPY D:\*.* A: /S /M
C:\CDROM\EJECT
```

You will need to add the commands your system uses to park the heads. The manual that comes with your computer will tell you how to do this. Also, if you save data files to a RAM disk, you will need to add commands to copy them back to the hard disk. If you put working files on the RAM disk, like the Windows swap file, you can skip this.

Because DR DOS will not automatically run LEAVING.BAT before shutting off power to the computer, you must remember to do this. However, if you get into the habit, copying RAM disk information to the hard disk and performing an incremental backup will protect your data; and parking the heads on your hard disk will save wear and tear on your system.

☑ *Remember*   A batch file like LEAVING.BAT will protect your data and save wear and tear on your system.

Summary

If an AUTOEXEC.BAT file exists in the root directory of the drive you boot from, DR DOS runs it as the last step when booting.

If there is an AUTOEXEC.BAT file to run, DR DOS does not prompt you for the date and time.

The AUTOEXEC.BAT file is a good place to create a path.

The AUTOEXEC.BAT file is a good place to create a prompt.

The AUTOEXEC.BAT file is a good place to set VERIFY=ON, issue any required MODE commands, and perform any other configuration tasks that cannot be performed in the CONFIG.SYS file.

The AUTOEXEC.BAT file is a good place to load memory resident software.

The AUTOEXEC.BAT file can be written as one large all-in-one batch file or a one-per-task batch file that calls other batch files to perform specific tasks.

The all-in-one arrangement saves disk space but leads to a more complex AUTOEXEC-.BAT file.

The one-per-task AUTOEXEC.BAT file makes it easier to deal with multiple configurations.

A batch file like LEAVING.BAT allows you to perform all those tasks you really should perform before turning off the computer.

Appendices

The appendices in this section are designed to give you quick access to a large amount of information. Often, this information is presented in the very briefest of fashions. For more information, refer back to earlier sections of this book or to your DR DOS manual.

Appendix A: Program documentation. This appendix provides brief documentation on the programs that are included on the disk that comes with this book.

Appendix B: Batch file documentation. This appendix provides brief documentation on the batch files that are included on the disk that comes with this book.

Appendix C: Solutions to problems. This appendix presents a solution to each of the problems in the book. These are not the only solutions, and your solution might even be better than the one given!

A

Program documentation

ASCII.EXE   [Chapter 7]

Syntax   ASCII

Displays a screen showing all the ASCII characters 30-255 and their associated ASCII codes. Characters below 30 are generally control characters that cannot be displayed on the screen. This makes a handy reference while designing fancy batch file screens.

BATCMD.COM   [Chapter 25]

Syntax   BATCMD *Command Prompt*

Batch Commands (BATCMD for short) is a full-function batch file utility. BATCMD adds many of the functions batch files need to be much more powerful. The features of BATCMD and the proper syntax are explained in detail in Chapter 25.

BatScreen   [Chapter 20]

Syntax   BS

BatScreen was written by Doug Amaral—the maker of Builder—of hyperkinetix, especially for my batch books. The BatScreen screen compiler combines the ease of creating an ASCII file with much of the power of writing a program.

   BatScreen takes an ASCII text file and converts it to a small .COM file. When you enter the name of the .COM file, the screen will flash up on the screen almost instantaneously. To run BatScreen from DR DOS, simply enter BS at the command line.

   BatScreen first presents a screen showing all the non-blinking color choices with a box around the currently selected color combination. You use the cursor to move the box to where it surrounds the color combination you want. If you want the text to blank, press PgDn and select from the blinking text in the same fashion.

   Next, BatScreen prompts you for the name of an ASCII file. To completely fill the screen, the ASCII file should contain 80 columns and 24 rows. If the file is larger, BatScreen ignores the excess. Finally, BatScreen asks you if you want to clear the screen when the program displays. Answer yes and the .COM file clears the entire screen, sets it to the colors you selected and displays the contents of the ASCII file. Answer no and the .COM file clears off only enough lines to display the message. The original ASCII file is not modified and does not have to be present for the .COM file to operate, so you can modify and recompile it if you even need to change the screen.

BatScreen makes excellent menus. You can also use BatScreen to reset the cursor, change the screen colors, and generate attractive colorful messages for your batch files. After trying BatScreen, I'm sure you'll agree that Doug has produced an excellent tool for screens for batch files. In fact, I use it almost exclusively for my screens.

CAPITAL.EXE [Chapter 18]

Syntax   CAPITAL *Word*

CAPITAL takes a single word as input, converts it to uppercase, and stores the resulting word in the environment under the variable name RONNY. Its common use is to convert a batch file replaceable parameter prior to performing logic testing on the replaceable parameter. If CAPITAL is passed more than one word, it aborts without making the conversion and sets ERRORLEVEL to 1.

Dual Boot Utility [Chapter 27]

This package allows you to have both DR DOS 6 and MS DOS 5 on your computer and boot from either one. See Chapter 27 for details.

ISITZERO.EXE [Chapter 30]

Syntax   ISITZERO *File*

IsItZero is used to test to see if a single file is a 0-length file. It returns one of five different ERRORLEVELs:

0   The user requested command line help so IsItZero performs no testing.
1   The file you requested IsItZero to test does not exist.
2   No file to test was specified on the command line.
3   The file size is greater than 0.
4   The file is a 0-length file. Because this is the highest ERRORLEVEL that IsItZero returns, testing for a 0-length file can involve the single IF ERROR LEVEL 0 rather than a nested If-test or even several tests.

Wildcards are not allowed in the file specification because IsItZero has no way of returning values for more than one file.

NEEDHELP.EXE   [Chapter 18]

Syntax   NEEDHELP %0 %1

If you enter the name of a batch file and a "/?" without a space, DR DOS treats the /? as %1, while MS DOS treats it as part of %0. In order to allow you to write batch files with command line help that will run under either operating system, I wrote NeedHelp. You pass it %0 and %1 near the top of the batch file. It sets ERRORLEVEL to 1 if the user requested help via the /? switch and a 0 otherwise. The batch file can then jump to a help routine based on the value of ERRORLEVEL. This allows the same batch file to work identically under either operating system.

B
Batch file documentation

The following appendix is a quick reference to the sample batch files included on your disk. For more detailed information on these scripts, refer to the appropriate chapter.

Many of the batch files included in this book and on the disk are teaching batch files. In other words, the batch files were designed to teach concepts and not perform useful tasks. As a result, many of them will require modifications in order to be useful to you on a daily basis. In many cases, these modifications are quite minor.

You might find these batch files useful right away, without any modification:

A.BAT
ANSIKEY1.BAT
ANSIKEY2.BAT
BLANK.BAT
CATALOG.BAT
CL.BAT
COPYTHEM.BAT
COPYTHE2.BAT
EDITPATH.BAT
EDIT2.BAT[1]
FASTFIND.BAT
HELPBAT.BAT
HELPBAT3.BAT
KILLZERO.BAT
LISTFILE.BAT
MACRO.BAT
MULTI.BAT
NICEPROM.BAT
QCD.BAT
REMOVE.BAT

---

[1]This batch file is called by EDITPATH.BAT to perform the work; you cannot run it from the command line.

RETURN.BAT
RETURNTO.BAT
RETURN3.BAT
RONNYMD.BAT
SAYERROR.BAT
SENDANSI.BAT
SENDANS2.BAT
TEMPLATE.BAT
TESTCOMM.BAT
TOA.BAT
UNBLANK.BAT
USEOVER.BAT

1.BAT through 6.BAT [Chapter 29]

Syntax   1
            2
            :
            6

These batch files are used to run the menu options used by the demonstration non-resident and hybrid menu systems on the disk in the subdirectories \MENU1 and \MENU2. They are designed to simulate applications without really running them.

A.BAT [Chapter 1]

Syntax   A

A.BAT performs a directory of the A drive.

ACCTHELP.BAT [Chapter 9]

Syntax   ACCTHELP

ACCTHELP.BAT is a demonstration batch file that displays imaginary help for three accounting problems. This is a solution to Problem 3 in the book.

ANSIDEMO.BAT [Chapter 21]

Syntax   ANSIDEMO

ANSIDEMO.BAT is a demonstration batch file. While you might find it useful to include similar code in other batch files, ANSIDEMO.BAT performs no useful function beyond demonstrating how to include ANSI escape sequences in a batch file. Readers wanting to run ANSIDEMO.BAT must load ANSI.SYS in their CONFIG.SYS file.

ANSIHIDE.BAT   [Chapter 21]

Syntax   ANSIHIDE

ANSIHIDE.BAT is a demonstration that shows how ANSI escape sequences can change the foreground and background colors to black, effectively hiding messages that are displayed through DR DOS. While you might find it useful to include similar code in other batch files, ANSIHIDE.BAT performs no useful function beyond demonstrating how to hide DR DOS messages in a batch file.

ANSIKEY1.BAT   [Chapter 21]

Syntax   ANSIKEY1 91 40 93 41 40 91 41 93

ANSIKEY1.BAT is used to reassign pairs of keys using their ASCII values. The first number is the key to reassign and the second number is the ASCII value to assign to that key. As many pairs of numbers can be specified after the batch file name as will fit on the command line. The keyboard reassignment is performed using Ansi, so reassignments will not work in programs that bypass DR DOS to read the keyboard. ANSIKEY1.BAT is designed for experimentation. Users wishing to make the same reassignments on a regular basis should modify this batch file to issue those commands automatically without having to enter them on the command line.

ANSIKEY2.BAT   [Chapter 21]

Syntax   ANSIKEY2 ([ )] [( ]

ANSIKEY2.BAT is used to reassign pairs of keys using their actual values. The first value is the key to reassign, and the second value is the value to assign to that key. The sample command shown here reassigns the parentheses key to square brackets and the square brackets to parentheses. As many values can be specified after the batch file name as will fit on the command line. The keyboard reassignment is performed using ANSI, so reassignments will not work in programs that bypass DR DOS to read the keyboard. ANSIKEY2.BAT is designed for experimentation. Users wanting to make the same reassignments on a regular basis should modify this batch file to issue those commands automatically without having to enter them on the command line.

AUTO-1.BAT   [Chapter 9]

Do not run AUTO-1.BAT from the command line. AUTO-1.BAT is a sample AUTOEXEC.BAT file that is the solution to Problem 2 in the book. Of course, before being used, it must be renamed to AUTOEXEC.BAT.

BLANK.BAT [Chapter 30]

Syntax   BLANK

BLANK.BAT changes the foreground and background colors to black, effectively blanking the screen. Only programs that display their text through DR DOS will be blanked. Users wanting to run BLANK.BAT must load ANSI.SYS in their CONFIG.SYS file. UN-BLANK.BAT can be run to restore the screen colors.

BOOT-4-D.BAT [Chapter 17]

Do not run BOOT-4-D from the command line. BOOT-4-D.BAT continually reboots the computer until the D drive is available. This is a solution to Problem 5 in the book. It must be called by the AUTOEXEC.BAT file in order to run properly.

CATALOG.BAT [Chapter 33]

Syntax   CATALOG *[Diskette Name]*

CATALOG.BAT creates a catalog of the files on multiple floppy disks by echoing the name of the diskette entered on the command line and a directory of the floppy disk in the A drive to a file called C:\CATALOG\CATALOG.TXT. A name must be entered on the command line. If the name is longer than nine words, everything after the ninth word is ignored. REMOVE.BAT is used to remove entries.

CHECKERR.BAT [Chapter 16]

Syntax   CHECKERR

CHECKERR.BAT is a demonstration batch file that displays the current errorlevel. CHECKERR.BAT is a large batch file that takes the brute-force approach of simply testing for all 256 possible ERRORLEVEL values.

CHECKER1.BAT [Chapter 18]

Syntax   CHECKER1

CHECKER1.BAT is a demonstration batch file that displays the current errorlevel. It uses nested If-tests to produce a batch file much shorter than CHECKERR.BAT.

CL.BAT [Chapter 32]

Syntax   CL *Command*
         CL D
         CL *n*

CL.BAT is used to store long command lines, display the saved contents of command lines, and execute saved command lines. CL.BAT saves commands in the C:\CL subdirectories using the batch files 0.BAT through 9.BAT. It uses the first available batch file. If all of them are in use, it deletes 0.BAT, moves the other batch files down one level, and saves the command line in 9.BAT. After saving the command line, CL.BAT executes that command line. The CL D command is used to display the saved command lines. The CL n command is used to run an existing command line where n is the number of the saved command line to run.

CL.BAT is useful even if you have HISTORY=ON. Because CL.BAT only saves those command lines you run using CL.BAT, you can use it only on your long command lines. As a result, you do not have to wade through all the shorter command lines saved by HISTORY to find a long one to reuse. Additionally, CL.BAT is able to store command lines between sessions, something HISTORY and other similar programs cannot do.

CONFIG.SYS [Chapter 37]

Syntax   NA

CONFIG.SYS is a sample CONFIG.SYS file for DR DOS 6 that uses the SWITCH command to run one of several configurations depending on which one the user selects. It also illustrates several other CONFIG.SYS configuration commands. Before experimenting with this CONFIG.SYS file, readers should make certain to save their existing CONFIG.SYS file under another name so its contents are not overwritten.

COPYBACK.BAT [Chapter 31]

Syntax   COPYBACK *Source Target*

COPYBACK.BAT is used as part of the document archival system in Chapter 31. Copies an important file to a backup file name in the C:\OLD subdirectory. It checks first to make sure the Target filename does not already exist in the C:\OLD subdirectory.

COPYTHEM.BAT [Appendix C]

Syntax   COPYTHEM *File1 File2 ... FileLast*

COPYTHEM.BAT copies the files you specify on the command line to the A drive without writing over any files. This is the solution to Problem 7 in the book.

COPYTHE2.BAT [Appendix C]

Syntax   COPYTHE2 *File1 File2 ... FileLast*

COPYTHE2.BAT copies the files you specify on the command line to the A drive without writing over any files. Unlike COPYTHEM.BAT, COPYTHE2.BAT gives you the option of overwriting files when they exist on the A drive. This is the solution to Problem 9 in the book.

DELOLD.BAT   [Chapter 31]

Syntax   DELOLD

DELOLD.BAT is used as part of the document archival system in Chapter 31. After copying files to the A drive from the \DISCARD subdirectory, DELOLD.BAT deletes the files in the C:\DISCARD that exist on the A drive.

DISCARD.BAT   [Chapter 31]

Syntax   DISCARD *File1 File2 ... FileLast*

DISCARD.BAT is used as part of the document archival system in Chapter 31. It copies all the files listed on the command line to the C:\DISCARD subdirectory. Prior to copying, it checks to make sure that a file doesn't already exist in the C:\DISCARD subdirectory with the same name. After successfully copying the file, it erases the original.

DOBATCMD.BAT   [Chapter 25]

Syntax   DOBATCMD

DOBATCMD.BAT is a demonstration batch file that illustrates most of the commands in Batch Commands (Batcmd) not involved in getting information from the user. SHOWGETS.BAT is a second demonstration batch file that illustrates using Batcmd to get information from the user.

DOXCOPY.BAT   [Chapter 16]

Syntax   DOXCOPY *Source Target Switches*

DOXCOPY.BAT runs XCOPY and reports any error conditions it encounters by testing on the errorlevel. The information entered after the Doxcopy command should be identical to the information you would supply the Xcopy command.

EDITPATH.BAT   [Chapter 33]

Syntax   EDITPATH

EDITPATH.BAT calls EDIT2.BAT and passes it the path as a series of replaceable parameters. EDIT2.BAT loops through each subdirectory in your path and asks you if you want to keep that subdirectory in your path. After processing all the subdirectories, it constructs a new path containing just the subdirectories you elected to keep. Run EDITPATH.BAT and not EDIT2.BAT, as EDIT2.BAT will not run properly from the command line.

EDIT2.BAT   [Chapter 33]

EDIT2.BAT loops through each subdirectory in your path and asks you if you want to keep that subdirectory in your path. After processing all the subdirectories, it constructs a new path containing just the subdirectories you elected to keep. EDIT2.BAT is designed to be called by EDITPATH.BAT and should not be run from the command line. Doing so will reset your path to nul.

ENDLESS.BAT   [Chapter 12]

Syntax   ENDLESS

ENDLESS.BAT is a demonstration batch file that illustrates the GOTO command with a loop that continues until you press Ctrl-Break and stop it.

FASTFIND.BAT   [Chapter 33]

Syntax   FASTFIND *FileSpec*

FASTFIND.BAT searches the current hard disk for the file name specified on the command line. Wildcards are allowed.

FINDPASS.BAT   [Chapter 33]

Syntax   FINDPASS

Chapter 33 shows how to add password protection to a batch file using PASSWORD.BAT as an example. PASSWORD.BAT has you enter a three-digit password by entering the ASCII values of the three digits. Rather than having you use an ASCII chart, FINDPASS-.BAT prompts you for the password you want to use and displays the appropriate ASCII values on the screen.

FORMAT.BAT   [Chapter 9]

Syntax   FORMAT

FORMAT.BAT automatically formats the A drive even if the user fails to specify a drive. It also explains the command to the user. This is a solution to Problem 1 in the book.

HELP.BAT   [Chapter 28]

Syntax   HELP

HELP.BAT is a demonstration batch file that displays summary information about the function of several other batch files.

HELP1.BAT   [Chapter 28]

Syntax   HELP1 *Category*

HELP1.BAT is a modified version of HELP.BAT that uses the category entered on the command line to jump to a specific category of batch file. This allows it to provide limited context-sensitive help.

HELPBAT.BAT   [Chapter 28]

Syntax   HELPBAT

HELPBAT.BAT uses the documentation information built into batch files—as described in this book—to display custom help about each batch file. It loops through each batch file in the C:\BAT subdirectory. For each batch file, it first displays the name of the batch file and underlines it. After displaying the name, it displays only the line containing PURPOSE:. This allows the user to scroll through all her batch files easily, and review their function.

HELPBAT2.BAT   [Chapter 28]

Syntax   HELPBAT2 *[Topic Of Interest]*

HELPBAT2.BAT is a modified version of HELPBAT.BAT. It displays the name of all the batch files but only displays the purpose line for those batch files containing the words entered on the command line in the purpose line. The words must be in the same order and match exactly.

HELPBAT3.BAT   [Chapter 28]

Syntax   HELPBAT3 *[Topic Of Interest]*

HELPBAT3.BAT is a modified version of HELPBAT2.BAT that still searches for text but only displays the names of the batch files matching the purpose—along with the purpose line displays just line HELPBAT2.BAT. This makes it much easier to find a batch file that performs a specific function because you don't have to see all the batch file names as part of the search—just the ones that match your search criteria. The words must be in the same order and match exactly.

HI-ASCII.BAT   [Chapter 7]

Syntax   HI-ASCII

HI-ASCII.BAT is a demonstration batch file that displays two types of boxes that can be created using high-ordered ASCII characters as well as a single type of box that can be created without using high-ordered ASCII characters.

INDEX.BAT   [Chapter 31]

Syntax   INDEX *Number*

INDEX.BAT is a demonstration batch file that uses the ZyIndex program to index all the text files on the A drive. A number for the diskette must be specified after the INDEX command.

KILLZERO.BAT   [Appendix C]

Syntax   KILLZERO

KILLZERO.BAT erases all the 0-length files in the current subdirectory. This is the solution to Problem 13 in the book.

LISTFILE.BAT   [Chapter 31]

Syntax   LISTFILE

LISTFILE.BAT creates a list of all the files on the C drive and stores it in C:\CHANGED.TXT file. This is useful as a record of the current file names just prior to making an incremental backup.

MACRO.BAT   [Chapter 32]

Syntax   MACRO *n Command*
MACRO D
MACRO *n*

MACRO.BAT is used to store keyboard macros, display the contents of the keyboard macros and execute the saved keyboard macros. MACRO.BAT saves commands in the C:\MACRO subdirectories using the batch files 0.BAT through 9.BAT. It saves the macro under the name *n* specified on the command line. After saving the macro, MACRO.BAT does not execute that macro. The MACRO D command is used to display the saved macros. The MACRO *n* command is used to run a macro where *n* is the number of the saved macro to run. Additionally, MACRO.BAT is able to store macros between sessions, something other keyboard macro programs cannot do.

MENU1.BAT   [Chapter 29]

Syntax   MENU1

MENU1.BAT drives the non-resident non-nested demonstration menu system stored in the \MENU1 subdirectory on the disk that comes with this book.

MENU2.BAT   [Chapter 29]

Syntax   MENU2

MENU2.BAT drives the hybrid non-nested demonstration menu system stored in the \MENU2 subdirectory on the disk that comes with this book.

MENU3.BAT   [Chapter 29]

Syntax   MENU3

MENU3.BAT drives the resident non-nested demonstration menu system stored in the \MENU3 subdirectory on the disk that comes with this book. MENU3.BAT simulates applications rather than running actual applications.

MSDRSUB.BAT   [Chapter 22]

Syntax   MSDRSUB

MSDRSUB.BAT is a demonstration batch file that shows how to create GOSUB and RETURN environmental variables to simulate the DR DOS 6 batch file subroutine structure under MS DOS.

MULTI.BAT   [Chapter 32]

Syntax   MULTI *Command1* ^ *Command2* ^ ... ^ *Last Command* ·

MULTI.BAT allows you to enter multiple commands on one command line and have them executed in turn. The commands must be separated by a caret (^) with a space on both sides of it. You can enter as many commands as will fit on a command line, and each command may have as many terms as necessary.

NETWORK.BAT   [Chapter 33]

Syntax   NETWORK

NETWORK.BAT is a demonstration batch file that shows how environmental variables can be used to track the number of copies of a software package that are running on a network to make sure the authorized limit is not exceeded.

NICEPROM.BAT   [Chapter 21]

Syntax   NICEPROM

NICEPROM.BAT creates a very nice prompt. It displays the date, time, and current subdirectory at the top of the screen along with the drive and subdirectory in the usual prompt position. It also sets the screen colors to bright-white on blue. Users wanting to run NICEPROM.BAT must load ANSI.SYS in their CONFIG.SYS file.

OCCASION.BAT [Chapter 33]

OCCASION.BAT is designed to be called by the AUTOEXEC.BAT file and should not be run from the command line. Every tenth time the AUTOEXEC.BAT file calls it, OCCASION.BAT performs a backup. It tracks the number of times it runs by a series of If-tests that simply try all possible values for the name of the 0-length file used as a counter. Note that the batch file counts reboots and not days.

OCCASIN2.BAT [Chapter 33]

OCCASIN2.BAT is designed to be called by the AUTOEXEC.BAT file and should not be run from the command line. Every tenth time the AUTOEXEC.BAT file calls it, OCCASIN2.BAT performs a backup. Unlike OCCASION.BAT, OCCASIN2.BAT uses the mathematical abilities of Batcmd to track the number of times it is run—although this information is still stored in a 0-length file. Since it uses math rather than a series of If-tests for each possible value, OCCASIN2.BAT is better suited for longer periods. Note that the batch file counts reboots and not days.

PASSWORD.BAT [Chapter 33]

Syntax   PASSWORD

Chapter 33 shows how to add password protection to a batch file using PASSWORD.BAT as an example. PASSWORD.BAT has you enter a three-digit password by entering the ASCII values of the three digits. It is then impossible to exit PASSWORD.BAT without entering the proper password. It gives you three attempts and then locks up the computer. If you press Ctrl-Break, it locks up the computer. As configured, the password is RON and the password is case-sensitive.

PHONE.BAT [Appendix C]

Syntax   PHONE *Nickname*

PHONE.BAT uses a GOTO *Nickname* to jump to the section containing the phone number of interest. From there, it dials the phone for you. PHONE.BAT will abort if an invalid nickname is entered. Users will need to modify the batch file to use the phone numbers and nicknames they want to call before using it. This is the solution to problem 10 in the book.

PHONE1.BAT [Appendix C]

Syntax   PHONE1 *Nickname*

PHONE1.BAT uses a GOTO *Nickname* to jump to the section containing the phone number of interest. From there, it dials the phone for you. Unlike PHONE.BAT, PHONE1.BAT verifies that the nickname exists before issuing the GOTO Nickname command, so it is able to handle invalid nicknames gracefully. Users will need to modify the batch file to use the phone numbers and nicknames they want to call before using it. This is an alternative solution to Problem 10 in the book.

QCD.BAT   [Appendix C]

Syntax   QCD *Drive Subdirectory1 ... Last Subdirectory*

QCD.BAT is useful for laptop computers, which generally have the colon and backslash keys in awkward positions. QCD.BAT allows you to enter the drive and/or subdirectory path without colons or backslashes and it still changes to the appropriate location. This is the solution to Problem 12 in the book.

RCD.BAT   [Chapter 33]

Syntax   RCD *Nickname*

RCD.BAT uses a GOTO %1 command to jump to the specified nickname and then changes to the appropriate subdirectory and exits. It lacks error-checking to validate that the specified subdirectory exists. Users will need to add their own subdirectories and nicknames before using the batch file.

READFILE.BAT   [Chapter 17]

Syntax   READFILE *ASCII-File*

Displays an ASCII file on the screen. This is a solution to Problem 6 in the book.

REMOVE.BAT   [Chapter 33]

Syntax   REMOVE *[Text To Search For]*

REMOVE.BAT searches through the floppy disk catalog created by CATALOG.BAT and removes all the entries containing the text entered on the command line. It first creates a backup copy of the catalog in case there is a problem.

RETURN.BAT   [Chapter 33]

Syntax   RETURN

RETURN.BAT pipes as CD *command* followed by the current subdirectory to a file called RETURNTO.BAT. RETURNTO.BAT will then return you to the current subdirectory when run. By running RETURN.BAT prior to transferring out of a subdirectory, you can quickly return to that subdirectory.

RETURNTO.BAT   [Chapter 33]

Syntax   RETURNTO

RETURNTO.BAT is the batch file created by RETURN.BAT that returns you to the subdirectory from which RETURN.BAT was last run.

RETURN2.BAT   [Chapter 33]

Syntax   RETURN2

If you store a home subdirectory in the environment under the environmental variable name HOME, issuing the RETURN2 command will return you to that home subdirectory.

RETURN3.BAT   [Chapter 33]

Syntax   RETURN3
            RETURN3 *Path*

When the RETURN3 command is followed by a subdirectory specification, RETURN3.BAT changes to that subdirectory and stores that subdirectory in the environment under the environmental variable named HOME. When the RETURN3 command is issued by itself, RETURN3.BAT changes to the subdirectory stored in the environment under the environmental variable named Home.

RONNYMD.BAT   [Chapters 10 and 16]

Syntax   RONNYMD *Subdirectory*

RONNYMD.BAT creates a subdirectory branching off the current subdirectory and then changes to that subdirectory.

RUNCHECK.BAT   [Chapter 17]

Syntax   RUNCHECK

RUNCHECK.BAT is a demonstration batch file that continually runs a diagnostic program to check out a disk drive. This is a solution to Problem 4 in the book.

SAYERROR.BAT   [Chapter 18]

Syntax   SAYERROR

SAYERROR.BAT displays the current ERRORLEVEL value and saves it to the environmental variable ERROR. It uses a For-loop to keep the batch file small and quick.

SENDANSI.BAT [Chapter 21]

Syntax   SENDANSI *ANSI command*

SENDANSI.BAT is a batch file that will send a single ANSI escape sequence from the command line without the user needing to enter the Escape that precedes the command. Users wanting to use SENDANSI.BAT must load ANSI.SYS in their CONFIG.SYS file. ANSI commands containing a semicolon cannot be sent with this batch file because DR DOS treats the semicolon as a replaceable parameter separator and does not pass it on to the batch file.

SENDANS2.BAT [Chapter 21]

Syntax   SENDANS2 *ANSI commands*

SENDANS2.BAT is a batch file that will send up to fifty ANSI escape sequences from the command line without the user needing to enter the Escape that precedes each command. Users wanting to use SENDANS2.BAT must load ANSI.SYS in their CONFIG.SYS file. ANSI commands containing a semicolon cannot be sent with this batch file because DR DOS treats the semicolon as a replaceable parameter separator and does not pass it on to the batch file.

SHOWBACK.BAT [Appendix C]

Syntax   SHOWBACK

SHOWBACK.BAT lists the files on the C drive that have been modified since the last backup, allowing you to decide if you need to perform a backup. SHOWBACK.BAT will not run under MS DOS. This is the solution to Problem 11 in the book.

SHOWGETS.BAT [Chapter 19]

Syntax   SHOWGETS

SHOWGETS.BAT is a demonstration batch file that illustrates using Batcmd commands in a batch file to get information from the user. DOBATCMD.BAT is a second demonstration batch file that illustrates using Batcmd to perform other functions.

SHOWREPL.BAT [Chapter 10]

Syntax   SHOWREPL *Parameter1 Parameter2...Parameter9*

SHOWREPL.BAT is a demonstration batch file that displays the first nine replaceable parameters entered on the command line.

SHOWSHIF.BAT   [Chapter 11]

Syntax   SHOWSHIF *Parameter1 Parameter2...Parameter15*

SHOWSHIF.BAT is a demonstration batch file that shows the first nine replaceable parameters entered on the command line and then shows the available replaceable parameters after several SHIFT commands.

STARTDAT.BAT   [Chapter 33]

Syntax   STARTDAT *Name*

STARTDAT.BAT is a demonstration batch file that runs a custom database program using different configuration files depending on the name of the user.

STARTWOR.BAT   [Chapter 33]

Syntax   STARTWOR *Name*

STARTWOR.BAT is a demonstration batch file that runs Microsoft Word using different configuration files depending on the name of the user.

SWITCH-M.BAT   [Chapter 33]

Syntax   SWITCH-M

SWITCH-M.BAT is a demonstration batch file that illustrates the SWITCH command with a working batch file. One interesting note about SWITCH-M.BAT is it is completely self-contained. It needs no utility to key a keystroke from the user, it needs no other batch files to run, and it handles all text display itself.

TEMPLATE.BAT   [All Chapters]

Syntax   TEMPLATE

TEMPLATE.BAT is a template batch file that has the first seven lines that most batch files begin with. It contains the following:

```
@ECHO OFF
REM NAME:
REM PURPOSE:
REM VERSION:
REM DATE:

NEEDHELP %0 %1
IF ERRORLEVEL 1 GOTO HELP
```

To start a new batch file, copy TEMPLATE.BAT to the name you want to use and fill out the information on lines 2 through 5.

TESTCOMM.BAT [Chapter 30]

Syntax   TESTCOMM

TESTCOMM.BAT tests to see if COMMAND.COM has been modified. TESTCOMM-.BAT requires some special preparation before it can be used. See Chapter 30 for details.

TOA.BAT [Chapters 10-16]

Syntax   TOA *File1 File2...FileN*

For the files specified on the command line, TOA.BAT copies the .DOC and .CMP files to the A drive while deleting the associated .BAK file.

TOA-2.BAT [Chapter 22]

Syntax   TOA *File1 File2...FileN*

TOA-2.BAT is a modified version of TOA.BAT that calls a subroutine called TOA-2SUB.BAT to perform the actual copying and file deleting.

TOA-2SUB.BAT [Chapter 22]

TOA-2SUB.BAT is the subroutine called by TOA-2.BAT to perform the actual copying and deleting. It is not designed to be run from the command line.

TOA-3.BAT [Chapter 22]

Syntax   TOA-3 *File1 File2...FileN*

TOA-3.BAT is a modified version of TOA-2.BAT that calls itself as a subroutine rather than calling an external batch file. The call is made in such a way that it is compatible with MS DOS and batch file compilers.

TOA-4.BAT [Chapter 22]

Syntax   TOA-4 *File1 File2...FileN*

TOA-4.BAT is a modified version of TOA-2.BAT that calls itself as a subroutine rather than calling an external batch file. The subroutine is constructed using DR DOS 6 subroutine batch sub-commands, so the batch file only runs under DR DOS 6.

UNBLANK.BAT   [Chapter 21]

Syntax   UNBLANK

UNBLANK.BAT sets the foreground color to bright-white and the background color to blue, undoing the screen blanking of BLANK.BAT. Note that this color assignment is permanent and will not change with a CLS command. Users wanting to use UNBLANK-.BAT must load ANSI.SYS in their CONFIG.SYS file.

USEOVER.BAT   [Appendix C]

Syntax   USEOVER *Command*
       USEOVER

When the USEOVER command is followed by a command, that command is stored in the environment and then executed. When the USEOVER command is used alone, it reruns the command stored in the environment previously. This is the solution to Problem 8 in the book.

VOLUME.BAT   [Chapter 33]

VOLUME.BAT is designed to be run by STOREVOL.BAT and should not be run from the command line. VOLUME.BAT processes the information passed to it as replaceable parameters by STOREVOL.BAT and stores the volume label in the environment under the environmental variable named VOLUME.

C

Solutions to problems

Batch File Line	Explanation
`@ECHO OFF`	Turn command-echoing off.

`REM NAME:    FORMAT.COM`
`REM PURPOSE: Format Diskette In A Drive`
`REM VERSION: 1.00`
`REM DATE:    May 12, 1992`
	Documentation remarks.

`CLS`	Clear the screen.

`ECHO PURPOSE`
`ECHO`
`ECHO    You Are About To Format A Disk.`
`ECHO This Prepares The Disk To Be Used`
`ECHO By The Computer But It Also Erases`
`ECHO Any Information Already On The Disk.`
`ECHO`
	Explain the purpose to the user. Note that the lines that appear to be an ECHO command by itself also contain the invisible Alt-255 character.

`ECHO What To Do`
`ECHO`
`ECHO    Place The Disk To Be Formatted`
`ECHO In The A drive (The One On Top) And`
`ECHO Press Any Key. If You Are Not Sure`
`ECHO You Want To Erase This Disk, Press`
`ECHO Ctrl-Break And Answer Yes To Stop`
`ECHO This Batch File.`
`ECHO`
	Tell the user what to do.

C-1 Answer to Problem 1. FORMAT.BAT gives some general information on formatting a disk and then pauses before the actual formatting in case the user wants to press Ctrl-Break.

Batch File Line	Explanation
ECHO Safety Check ECHO ECHO If You Break Out Of This Batch ECHO File, You Can Check The Disk To See ECHO If It Has Any Files With The DIR A: ECHO Command From The DR DOS Prompt. ECHO	Tell the user what to do if he encounters a problem.
PAUSE	Pause the batch file prior to running the formatting program to give the user a chance to read the screen and abort the process if desired.
XYZ A:	Perform the formatting using the renamed XYZ.COM.
C: CD\	Change to the root directory of the C drive. (This could also have been performed at the top of the batch file.)
MENU	Start the menu program.

C-1 Continued.

Batch File Line	Explanation
@ECHO OFF	Turn command-echoing off.
REM NAME: AUTO-1.BAT REM Of Course, To Run REM Properly, Would Need REM To Be Renamed To REM AUTOEXEC.BAT REM PURPOSE: Solution To Problem #2 REM VERSION: 1.00 REM DATE: May 12, 1992	Documentation remarks.
REM Set Path REM ========	Documentation remarks for this section.
ECHO Creating Path	Tell the user what will happen next.
PATH=C:\;C:\DRDOS;C:\BAT;C:\NORTON; C:\123;C:\WP;C:\UTILITY;C:\MENU	Set the path using a DR DOS command. Of course, in the batch file, this is all on one line.

C-2 Answer to Problem 2. AUTO-1.BAT is a sample AUTOEXEC.BAT file that performs the four tasks outlined in the book. In order for this file to work properly, you would have to rename it AUTOEXEC.BAT and store it in the root directory of the boot drive.

Batch File Line	Explanation
`REM Create Environmental Variables` `REM ===============================`	Documentation remarks for this section.
`ECHO Creating Environmental Variables`	Tell the user what will happen next.

`SET TEMP=C:\TEMP`
`SET DOSONLY=YES`
`SET LIB=D:\BLDLITE`
`SET OBJ=D:\BLDLITE`
	Create four environmental variables and store values to them.

`REM Turn Off Screen Prints` `REM =======================`	Documentation remarks for this section.
`ECHO Turning Off Screen Prints`	Tell the user what will happen next.
`NOPRTSCR`	Run a utility program to turn off screen printing. Many such programs are available on networks such as CompuServe and PC-Link.
`REM Starting Menu` `REM =============`	Documentation remarks for this section.
`ECHO Starting Menu`	Tell the user what will happen next.
`MENU`	Run the menu program.

C-2 Continued.

Batch File Line	Explanation
`@ECHO OFF`	Turn command-echoing off.

`REM NAME:     ACCTHELP.BAT`
`REM PURPOSE: Provide Accounting Help`
`REM VERSION: 1.00`
`REM DATE:    May 12, 1992`
	Documentation remarks.

`CLS`	Clear the screen.

C-3 Answer to Problem 3. ACCTHELP.BAT explains how to use three accounting programs stored on the computer.

Get More Tips and Tricks from "Dr. Batch File"

Ronny Richardson can help you:

"Richardson includes many advanced considerations, but many of his explanations can be understood by beginners with relatively little computer experience, and they're much better that many introductory titles could offer."
—The Midwest Book Review

"Programmer's will relish [Ronny Richardson's Batch Files to Go] . . . . supplies a variety of time-saving batch files."—BOOKWATCH

"Now, "The .BAT book" will set me free!!! The book goes straight into batch files . . . will recommend this one."—Computer Shopper on
MS-DOS Batch File Programming

"By the end of this book, readers will be able to implement even the most difficult batch files, and will thoroughly understand the whole process."
—Computer Monthly on
MS-DOS Batch File Programming

Batch File Line	Explanation
ECHO Introduction ECHO ECHO This Accounting System Uses Three ECHO Different Programs To Manage Customer ECHO Accounts. They Are: ECHO 1. DAILY.EXE ECHO 2. WEEKLY.EXE ECHO 3. ANNUAL.EXE ECHO	Display the first section of information. Note that the lines containing just an Echo command are followed by an Alt-255 character to display a blank line.
ECHO Daily ECHO ECHO This Program Performs The Closing That ECHO Is Required Each Day. It Can Be Run By ECHO Any Clerk Using The General Clerical ECHO Password. Note That It Must Be Run ECHO After 4PM And Not Before. ECHO	Display the next section of information.
PAUSE	Pause the program until the user presses a key. This gives the user time to read the screen.
CLS	Once the user presses a key, clear the screen.
ECHO Weekly ECHO ECHO This Program Performs The Closing That ECHO Is Required Each Week. It Can Only Be ECHO Run By A Senior Clerk Or Above And ECHO Requires A Management-1 Password. It ECHO Must Be Run On The Last Working Day Of ECHO The Month And Must Be Run After ECHO Running The Daily Closing Program. ECHO	Display the next section of information.

C-3 Continued.

Batch File Line	Explanation
ECHO Annual ECHO ECHO This Programs Performs The Annual ECHO Closing Required At The End Of Each ECHO Year. It Can Only Be Run By A Branch ECHO Manager And Requires A Management-4 ECHO Password. It Must Be Run On The Last ECHO Day Of The Year After Running The Daily ECHO Closing Program. ECHO	Display the next section of information.
PAUSE	Pause the program until the user presses a key. This gives the user time to read the screen.
CLS	Once the user presses a key, clear the screen.
ECHO Backups ECHO ECHO Corporate Policy Require Two Backups ECHO To Be Performed After A Weekly Closing. ECHO One Backup Must Be Sent To The IS ECHO Department At Headquarters (24/185) ECHO And The Other Retained Locally. ECHO Three Backups Are Required After An ECHO Annual Closing. In Addition To The IS ECHO And Local Copies, A Copy Is To Be ECHO Sent To The Legal Department (28/185). ECHO	Display the next section of information.
ECHO More Help ECHO ECHO If You Need More Help, Contact: ECHO ECHO Mark Williams ECHO 24/185 ECHO Extension 256 ECHO	Display the last section of information.
PAUSE	Pause the program until the user presses a key.

C-3 Continued.

Batch File Line	Explanation
@ECHO OFF	Turn command-echoing off.
REM NAME: RUNCHECK.BAT REM PURPOSE: Run Check-It-Out Program REM And Report Errors REM Solution To Problem #4 REM VERSION: 1.00 REM DATE: May 17, 1992	Documentation remarks.
IF (%1)==(/?) ECHO Continually Runs CHKITOUT IF (%1)==(/?) GOTO END	Display help and exit when the user requests help with /? as the first replaceable parameter.
CLS	Clear the screen.
:TOP	Label marking the top of a loop.
CHKITOUT	Run the Check-It-Out program.
IF ERRORLEVEL 1 ECHO Check-It-Out Had Problems IF ERRORLEVEL 1 GOTO TOP	If it had a problem, display a message and continue looping.
ECHO Check-It-Out Ran Fine GOTO TOP	If it did not have a problem, it reaches this point, so display a message and continue looping.
:END	Label marking the end of the batch file.

C-4 Answer to Problem 4. RUNCHECK.BAT continually runs a program called Check-It-Out and displays the results on the screen.

Batch File Line	Explanation
`@ECHO OFF`	Turn command-echoing off.

`REM NAME:      BOOT-4-D.BAT`
`REM PURPOSE: Reboot Until D Drive Works`
`REM          Solution To Problem #5`
`REM VERSION: 1.00`
`REM DATE:     May 17, 1992`
	Documentation remarks.

`IF (%1)==(/?) ECHO Reboots If D Drive`
`IF (%1)==(/?) ECHO Not Working`
`IF (%1)==(/?) GOTO END`
	Display help and exit when the user requests help with /? as the first replaceable parameter.

`IF EXIST D:\*.* GOTO END`	If any file on the D drive exists, then the batch file does not need to do anything, so jump to the end.
`BOOT`	Run a program to reboot the computer. Of course, this halts the execution of this batch file.
`:END`	Label marking the end of the batch file.

C-5 Answer to Problem 5. BOOT-4-D.BAT is called by the AUTOEXEC.BAT file and reboots the computer if the D drive is not working.

Batch File Line	Explanation
`@ECHO OFF`	Turn command-echoing off.

`REM NAME:      READFILE.BAT`
`REM PURPOSE: Display ASCII Files`
`REM VERSION: 1.00`
`REM DATE:     May 17, 1992`
	Documentation remarks.

`IF (%1)==(/?) ECHO Display ASCII Files` `IF (%1)==(/?) GOTO END`	Display help and exit when the user requests help with /? as the first replaceable parameter.
`:TOP`	Label marking the top of a loop.
`   CLS`	Clear the screen.
`   IF (%1)==() GOTO END`	If there are no more replaceable parameters, jump to the end of the batch file.

C-6 Answer to Problem 6. READFILE.BAT displays the files entered on the command line one at a time by typing them to the screen and using the MORE filter to display them one screen at a time.

Batch File Line	Explanation
`ECHO Displaying %1`	Display the name of the next file to be displayed.
`TYPE %1 | MORE`	Type the file and use the MORE filter to display it one screen at a time.
`SHIFT`	Move all the replaceable parameters down one level and make available another replaceable parameter as %9.
`PAUSE`	Pause the program until the user presses a key.
`GOTO TOP`	Continue looping.
`:END`	Label marking the end of the batch file.

C-6 Continued.

Batch File Line	Explanation
`@ECHO OFF`	Turn command-echoing off.

`REM NAME:    COPYTHEM.BAT`
`REM PURPOSE: Copy Files To A Drive`
`REM VERSION: 1.00`
`REM DATE:    May 26, 1992`
	Documentation remarks.

`NEEDHELP %0 %1`	Use the NeedHelp utility program to check and see if the user started the batch file with a /? switch.
`IF ERRORLEVEL 1 GOTO HELP`	If the user requested help, jump to a special section to display that information.
`IF (%1)==() GOTO ERROR`	If the user did not request help and did not specify files to copy, jump to an error-handling section. This must come after running the NeedHelp routine because *COPYTHEM/?* will not have a %1 under MS DOS.

C-7 Answer to Problem 7. COPYTHEM.BAT copies all the files specified on the command line to the A drive only if that file does not already exist on the A drive.

Batch File Line	Explanation
IF (%1)==(XYZ123ABC) GOTO SUB	If the batch file is running as a subroutine, jump to the subroutine section.
:TOP	Label marking the top of the main loop.
IF ERRORLEVEL 1 GOTO END	If XCOPY reported an error via ERRORLEVEL in the subroutine, exit the batch file.
IF (%1)==() GOTO END	Once the batch file runs out of replaceable parameters, exit the batch file.
FOR %%J in (%1) DO CALL COPYTHEM XYZ123ABC %%J	Loop through all the files matching the current %1 replaceable parameter and call this batch file as a subroutine for each one. This is required to handle files individually when the user specifies a wildcard.
SHIFT	Move all the replaceable parameters down one level and make available another replaceable parameter as %9.
GOTO TOP	Continue looping.
:SUB	Label marking the top of the subroutine portion of the batch file.
IF EXIST A:%2 ECHO %2 Already On A Drive	If the file is already on the A drive, warn the user.
IF EXIST A:%2 GOTO END	If the file is already on the A drive, exit the subroutine without copying the file.
XCOPY %2 A:	If the subroutine reaches this point, the file does not exist on the A drive so copy it with XCOPY in order to use the errorlevel.

C-7 Continued.

Batch File Line	Explanation
`    IF ERRORLEVEL 1 ECHO Problem Copying %2`	If XCOPY reports an error via ERRORLEVEL, display a warning message.
`GOTO END`	This is the end of the subroutine so exit the batch file so that control will return to the calling version of this batch file.

`:ERROR`
`    ECHO Must Speficy The Files To`
`    ECHO Copy On The Command Line`
`GOTO END`
	Display an error message and exit when the user does not enter any replaceable parameters.

`:HELP`
`    ECHO Copies The Files You Specify`
`    ECHO On The Command Line To The`
`    ECHO A Drive Without Writing`
`    ECHO Over Any Files`
`GOTO END`
	Display help and exit when requested by the user.

`:END`	Label marking the end of the batch file.

C-7 Continued.

Batch File Line	Explanation
`@ECHO OFF`	Turn command-echoing off.

`REM NAME:     USEOVER.BAT`
`REM PURPOSE: Use A Command Over And Over`
`REM VERSION: 1.02`
`REM DATE:    August 3, 1991`
	Documentation remarks.

`NEEDHELP %0 %1`	Use the NeedHelp utility program to check and see if the user started the batch file with a /? switch.
`IF ERRORLEVEL 1 GOTO HELP`	If the user requested help, jump to a special section to display that information.
`IF (%1)==() GOTO JUSTCMD`	If the user did not enter a new command, rerun the one already in the environment.

C-8 Answer to Problem 8. When run with a command following its name, USEOVER.BAT stores that command to an environmental variable and then runs the command. When run alone, USEOVER.BAT runs the command stored in the environment.

Batch File Line	Explanation
`REM Construct Command in` `REM Environmental Variable`	Documentation remarks.
`SET COMMAND=`	If the batch file reaches this point, then the user has entered a new command so delete the old one. This command has no effect if an old value does not exist.
`:TOP`	Label marking the top of the loop to define the command.
`   SET COMMAND=%COMMAND% %1`	Replace the contents of the COMMAND environmental variable with its current value plus %1 added to the end. Building the final variable in this fashion avoids having to limit the command to nine components.
`   SHIFT`	Move all the replaceable parameters down one level and make available another replaceable parameter as %9.
`   IF (%1)==() GOTO JUSTCMD`	If no more portions of the command exist, jump to a section to run the command.
`GOTO TOP`	If more portions of the command exist, loop through again and add them.
`:JUSTCMD`	Beginning of the section to run the command.
`   %COMMAND%`	Run the command.
`GOTO END`	Exit the batch file.

`:HELP`
`   ECHO JUSTCMD Runs Stored Command`
`   ECHO JUSTCMD Part1 Part2 ... PartN`
`   ECHO Stores And Runs The New Command`
`GOTO END`
	Display a help screen and exit the batch file when the user requests help.

`:END`	Label marking the end of the batch file.

C-8 Continued.

Batch File Line	Explanation
`@ECHO OFF`	Turn command-echoing off.

`REM NAME:    COPYTHE2.BAT`
`REM          Modified For Problem 9`
`REM          And Stored As COPYTHE2.BAT`
`REM PURPOSE: Copy Files To A Drive`
`REM VERSION: 2.00`
`REM DATE:    May 26, 1992`
	Documentation remarks.

`NEEDHELP %0 %1`	Use the NeedHelp utility program to check and see if the user started the batch file with a /? switch.
`IF ERRORLEVEL 1 GOTO HELP`	If the user requested help, jump to a special section to display that information.
`IF (%1)==() GOTO ERROR`	If the user did not request help and did not specify files to copy, jump to an error-handling section. This must come after running the NeedHelp routine since *COPYTHEM/?* will not have a %1 under MS DOS.
`IF (%1)==(XYZ123ABC) GOTO SUB`	If the batch file is running as a subroutine, jump to the subroutine section.
`:TOP`	Label marking the top of the main loop.
`IF ERRORLEVEL 1 GOTO END`	If XCOPY reported an error via errorlevel in the subroutine, exit the batch file.
`IF (%1)==() GOTO END`	Once the batch file runs out of replaceable parameters, exit the batch file.

C-9 Answer to Problem 9. COPYTHE2.BAT copies all the files specified on the command line to the A drive. Unlike COPYTHEM.BAT, COPYTHE2.BAT will ask the user what to do if there is already a version of the file on the A drive.

Batch File Line	Explanation
`FOR %%J in (%1) DO` `    CALL COPYTHE2 XYZ123ABC %%J`	Loop through all the files matching the current %1 replaceable parameter and call this batch file as a subroutine for each one. This is required to handle files individually when the user specifies a wildcard.
`SHIFT`	Move all the replaceable parameters down one level and make available another replaceable parameter as %9.
`GOTO TOP`	Continue looping.
`:SUB`	Label marking the top of the subroutine portion of the batch file.
`IF EXIST A:%2 GOTO DUP`	If the file is already on the A drive, jump to the subroutine to handle this.
`XCOPY %2 A:`	If the subroutine reaches this point, the file does not exist on the A drive, so copy it with XCOPY in order to use the errorlevel.
`IF ERRORLEVEL 1 ECHO Problem Copying %2`	If Xcopy reports an error via errorlevel, display a warning message.
`GOTO END`	This is the end of the subroutine, so exit the batch file and return control to the calling version of this batch file.
`:DUP`	Beginning of the subroutine to deal with the file already existing on the A drive.
`ECHO %2 Already Exists On A Drive`	Tell the user about the duplicate file.

`ECHO A Drive`
`ECHO --------`
`DIR A:%2`
	Show the user the file on the A drive.

C-9 Continued.

Batch File Line	Explanation
| ```
ECHO Current Drive
ECHO ------------
DIR %2
``` | Show the user the file on the current drive. |
| ```
BATCMD YN Overwrite %2 On A Drive (Y/N)?
``` | Ask the user if the batch file should overwrite the file on the A drive. |
| ```
IF NOT ERRORLEVEL 1 GOTO END
``` | If the user answers no, exit the subroutine. |
| ```
XCOPY %2 A:
``` | The subroutine only reaches this point if the user answers yes, so copy the file. |
| ```
IF ERRORLEVEL 1 ECHO Problem Copying %2
``` | If XCOPY reports an error via ERRORLEVEL, display a warning message. |
| ```
GOTO END
``` | This is the end of the subroutine, so exit the batch file and return control to the calling version of this batch file. |
| ```
:ERROR
   ECHO Must Speficy The Files To
   ECHO Copy On The Command Line
GOTO END
``` | Display an error message and exit when the user does not enter any replaceable parameters. |
| ```
:HELP
   ECHO Copies The Files You Specify
   ECHO On The Command Line To The
   ECHO A Drive Without Writing
   ECHO Over Any Files
GOTO END
``` | Display help and exit when requested by the user. |
| ```
:END
``` | Label marking the end of the batch file. |

C-9 Continued.
```

Batch File Line	Explanation
`@ECHO OFF`	Turn command-echoing off.

`REM NAME:      PHONE.BAT`
`REM PURPOSE: Telephone Database`
`REM VERSION: 1.00`
`REM DATE:     June 11, 1992`
	Documentation remarks.

`NEEDHELP %0 %1`	Use the NeedHelp utility program to check and see if the user started the batch file with a /? switch.
`IF ERRORLEVEL 1 GOTO HELP`	If the user requested help, jump to a special section to display that information.
`IF (%1)==() GOTO NONE`	If the user did not enter a nickname, jump to an error-handling section.
`GOTO %1`	Jump to the section for the nickname the user entered. If the nickname entered by the user does not exist as a label, the batch file will abort on this line.

`REM --------------------------`
`REM The GOTO %1 Line Above Will`
`REM Cause The Batch File To`
`REM Abort If The Label Does`
`REM Exist`
`REM --------------------------`
	Documentation remarks.

`:HELP`
`   ECHO Dials Phone`
`   ECHO The Syntax Is`
`   ECHO PHONE Nickname`
`GOTO END`
	Display a help screen and exit the batch file when the user requests help.

`:NONE`
`   ECHO You Did Not Enter A`
`   ECHO Nickname To Dial`
`   ECHO The Syntax Is`
`   ECHO PHONE Nickname`
`GOTO END`
	Error section that handles the situation when the user does not enter a nickname.

C-10A Answer to Problem 10. PHONE.BAT dials the phone number for the nickname entered on the command line. You will have to enter your own nicknames and phone numbers before using PHONE.BAT.

Batch File Line	Explanation

``
:DIRECTORY
:INFORMATION
    ECHO ATDT 411 > COM1
    ECHO Dial Information
    ECHO Press Any Key When Ringing
    PAUSE
    ECHO ATH > COM1
GOTO END
``
	Section that handles dialing information. Notice the use of multiple labels. The echoing of ATDT and ATH is explained in the text.

``
:TAB
:TABBOOKS
    ECHO ATDT 1 (800) 233-1128 > COM1
    ECHO Dialing TAB Books
    ECHO Press Any Key When Ringing
    PAUSE
    ECHO ATH > COM1
GOTO END
``
	Section that handles dialing TAB Books.

``
:911
    ECHO ATDT 911 > COM1
    ECHO 911
    ECHO Press Any Key When Ringing
    PAUSE
    ECHO ATH > COM1
GOTO END
``
	Section that handles dialing 911.

``` :END ```	Label marking the end of the batch file.

C-10A Continued.

Batch File Line	Explanation
``` @ECHO OFF ```	Turn command-echoing off.
``` REM NAME: PHONE1.BAT REM PURPOSE: Telephone Database REM Modified Version Of REM PHONE.BAT That Checks REM For Valid Label First REM VERSION: 1.00 REM DATE: June 11, 1992 ```	Documentation remarks.

C-10B Alternate answer to Problem 10. PHONE1.BAT does everything PHONE.BAT does plus built-in error-checking. Before issuing a *GOTO %1* command, it searches PHONE1.BAT to ensure that the specified batch file exists. While slower and more complex, this check prevents the batch file from aborting with the "Label not found" error message.

Solutions to problems **427**

Batch File Line	Explanation
NEEDHELP %0 %1	Use the NeedHelp utility program to check and see if the user started the batch file with a /? switch.
IF ERRORLEVEL 1 GOTO HELP	If the user requested help, jump to a special section to display that information.
IF (%1)==() GOTO NONE	If the user did not enter a nickname, jump to an error-handling section.
REM Type The Batch File And Search REM For A Valid Label	Documentation remarks.
TYPE C:\BAT\PHONE1.BAT|FIND ":%1">JUNK	Type the batch file and use the FIND filter to search for the specified label. Notice that the full path to the batch file is specified. This is required because you never know from which subdirectory it will be run. Also note the colon before the %1; this makes sure the matching text is a label.
ISITZERO JUNK	Check to see if the resulting file is a 0-length file.
IF NOT ERRORLEVEL 4 GOTO %1	IsItZero sets ERRORLEVEL to 4 for a 0-length file, which indicates that the label was not found. For any other ERRORLEVEL value, jump to the appropriate section.
GOTO MISSING	Jump to an error-handling section that handles the problem of the user entering an invalid label.

:MISSING
    ECHO The Label You Specified (%1)
    ECHO Does Not Exist As A Nickname
    ECHO PHONE1.BAT Aborting
GOTO END
	When the label is not found, explain the problem to the user and exit the batch file.

:HELP
    ECHO Dials Phone
    ECHO The Syntax Is
    ECHO PHONE Nickname
GOTO END
	Display a help screen and exit the batch file when the user requests help. From here on down, PHONE1.BAT is identical to PHONE.BAT.

C-10B Continued.

Batch File Line	Explanation

`:NONE`
    `ECHO You Did Not Enter A`
    `ECHO Nickname To Dial`
    `ECHO The Syntax Is`
    `ECHO PHONE Nickname`
`GOTO END`
	Error section that handles the situation when the user does not enter a nickname.

`:DIRECTORY`
`:INFORMATION`
    `ECHO ATDT 411 > COM1`
    `ECHO Dial Information`
    `ECHO Press Any Key When Ringing`
    `PAUSE`
    `ECHO ATH > COM1`
`GOTO END`
	Section that handles dialing information. Notice the use of multiple labels. The echoing of ATDT and ATH is explained in the text.

`:TAB`
`:TABBOOKS`
    `ECHO ATDT 1 (800) 233-1128 > COM1`
    `ECHO Dialing TAB Books`
    `ECHO Press Any Key When Ringing`
    `PAUSE`
    `ECHO ATH > COM1`
`GOTO END`
	Section that handles dialing TAB Books.

`:911`
    `ECHO ATDT 911 > COM1`
    `ECHO 911`
    `ECHO Press Any Key When Ringing`
    `PAUSE`
    `ECHO ATH > COM1`
`GOTO END`
	Section that handles dialing 911.

`:END`	Label marking the end of the batch file.

C-10B Continued.

Solutions to problems **429**

Batch File Line	Explanation
@ECHO OFF	Turn command-echoing off.
REM NAME: SHOWBACK.BAT REM PURPOSE: Show Files Needing Backup REM VERSION: 1.00 REM DATE: June 11, 1992	Documentation remarks.
NEEDHELP %0 %1	Use the NeedHelp utility program to check and see if the user started the batch file with a /? switch.
IF ERRORLEVEL 1 GOTO HELP	If the user requested help, jump to a special section to display that information.
XDIR C:*.* +A /S	Use the XDIR command to show all the files on the C drive that need to be backed up.
GOTO END	Exit the batch file.

:HELP
   ECHO Shows Files Needing Backup
   ECHO Will Not Work Under MS DOS
GOTO END
	Display a help screen and exit the batch file when the user requests help.

:END	Label marking the end of the batch file.

C-11 Answer to Problem 11. SHOWBACK.BAT uses the XDIR command to list every file on the C drive that has been modified since the last backup.

Batch File Line	Explanation
@ECHO OFF	Turn command-echoing off.
REM NAME: QCD.BAT REM PURPOSE: Speed Directory Changes REM VERSION: 1.00 REM DATE: December 20, 1991	Documentation remarks.
NEEDHELP %0 %1	Use the NeedHelp utility program to check and see if the user started the batch file with a /? switch.
IF ERRORLEVEL 1 GOTO HELP	If the user requested help, jump to a special section to display that information.

C-12 Answer to Problem 12. QCD.BAT allows the user to enter a drive and subdirectories after the batch file name without a colon or backslash, and it still changes to the proper subdirectory.

Batch File Line	Explanation
`IF (%1)==() GOTO ERROR1`	If the user did not enter a subdirectory to change to, jump to an error-handling routine.
`SET DIR=NO`	Store a default value to this environmental variable.
`FOR %%J IN (a A b B c C d D) DO` `    IF (%1)==(%%J) SET DIR=YES`	Loop through the more common values to see if the user entered a drive as the first replaceable parameter. Users without a B drive or D drive might want to delete those letters.
`IF %DIR%==NO GOTO SKIP`	If the user did not enter a drive as the first replaceable parameter, skip over the section to change drive letters.
`%1:`	Add the colon and change drives.
`SHIFT`	Move all the replaceable parameters down one level and make available another replaceable parameter as %9.
`IF (%1)==() GOTO END`	If there are no more replaceable parameters, exit the batch file.
`:SKIP`	Label used to skip over the drive changing routine.
`SET DIR=`	Reset the environmental variable.
`:TOPLOOP`	Label marking the top of the loop to construct the environmental variable containing the final subdirectory to change to.
`SET DIR=%DIR%\%1`	Append a backslash and the next subdirectory onto the environmental variable.
`SHIFT`	Move all the replaceable parameters down one level and make available another replaceable parameter as %9.

C-12 Continued.

Batch File Line	Explanation
`    IF NOT (%1)==() GOTO TOPLOOP`	If there are more replaceable parameters, continue looping.
`    CD %DIR%`	Change to the subdirectory stored in the environment.
`GOTO END`	Exit the batch file.

`:ERROR`
`    ECHO No Drive / Subdirectory Specified`
`    ECHO Use QCD Drive Sub1 Sub2 So On`
`    ECHO Without A Colon Or Backslash`
`GOTO END`
	Section to display an error-message when the user does not enter a replaceable parameter.

`:HELP`
`    ECHO QCD.BAT Will Change Drives And`
`    ECHO Subdirectories Without Entering`
`    ECHO The Colon After The Drive Or The`
`    ECHO Backslash Between The`
`    ECHO Subdirectories`
`    BATCMD SL`
`    ECHO Enter: QCD Drive Sub1 Sub2 So On`
`GOTO END`
	Display a help screen and exit the batch file when the user requests help.

`:END`	Label marking the end of the batch file.
`SET DIR=`	Reset this environmental variable before exiting.

C-12 Continued.

Batch File Line	Explanation
`@ECHO OFF`	Turn command-echoing off.

`REM NAME:    KILLZERO.BAT`
`REM PURPOSE: Erase 0-Length Files`
`REM VERSION: 1.00`
`REM DATE:    June 11, 1992`
	Documentation remarks.

`IF (%1)==(ABC123XYZ) GOTO SUB1` `IF (%1)==(XYZ123ABC) GOTO SUB2`	If KILLZERO.BAT is being called as a subroutine, jump to the appropriate subroutine section.

C-13 Answer to Problem 13. KILLZERO.BAT will list the 0-length files on the screen and give you the option to delete them. If you select "Yes," it automatically deletes them all.

Batch File Line	Explanation
`NEEDHELP %0 %1`	Use the NeedHelp utility program to check and see if the user started the batch file with a /? switch.
`IF ERRORLEVEL 1 GOTO HELP`	If the user requested help, jump to a special section to display that information.
`SET KILL=NO`	Create an environmental variable to act as a flag indicating if any 0-length files are found.
`FOR %%J IN (*.*) DO` `        CALL KILLZERO ABC123XYZ %%J`	Loop through the files once and call KILL-ZERO.BAT as a subroutine to list the 0-length files.

`IF (%KILL%)==(NO) ECHO No 0-Length`
`      Files To Erase`
`IF (%KILL%)==(NO) GOTO END1`
	If no 0-length files were found, display a message and jump to an exiting section.

`BATCMD YN Erase These Files? (Y/N)`	If the batch file reaches this point, 0-length files were found. Ask the user about deleting them.
`IF NOT ERRORLEVEL 1 GOTO END1`	If the user answers no, jump to an exiting section.

C-13 Continued.

Index

435

Other Bestsellers of Related Interest

BUILD YOUR OWN 386/386SX COMPATIBLE AND SAVE A BUNDLE—2nd Edition
Aubrey Pilgrim

Assemble an 80386 microcomputer at home using mail-order parts that cost a lot less today than they did several years ago. Absolutely no special technical know-how is required—only a pair of pliers, a couple of screwdrivers, and this detailed, easy-to-follow guide. 248 pages, 79 illustrations. **Book No. 4089, $18.95 paperback, $29.95 hardcover**

BIT-MAPPED GRAPHICS
Steve Rimmer

This is one of the first books to cover the specific graphic file formats used by popular paint and desktop publishing packages. It shows you how to pack and unpack bit-map image files so you can import and export them to other applications. And, it helps you spot through available file formats, standards, patches, and revision levels, using commercial-quality C code to explore bit-mapped graphics and effectively deal with image files. 504 pages, 131 illustrations. **Book No. 3558, $26.95 paperback, $38.95 hardcover**

MACINTOSH SYSTEM 7:
The Complete Sourcebook
Gordon M. Campbell

Campbell shows off some of the exciting new features of System 7 and offers tips for upgrading your hardware and software. This is your best guide to the first major development in the Macintosh since its introduction in 1984. With this book by your keyboard, you can count on clear skies and smooth sailing, for either upgrade or installation. 320 pages, illustrated. Includes 3.5″ disk. **Book No. 4074, $32.95 paperback only**

THE CONCISE PC NOTEBOOK AND LAPTOP USER'S GUIDE
Dan Gookin

Here, you'll find complete information on computers designed to leave the office and follow you on the road. Useful tips are furnished throughout to help make laptop computing easier and more productive for you, no matter what your technical skill. With this book in hand, your initiation to laptop computing will be virtually painless! 304 pages, 40 illustrations. Includes 3^1/2″ disk. **Book No. 3921, $22.95 paperback only**

MS-DOS® BATCH FILE PROGRAMMING—3rd Edition
Ronny Richardson

Now updated to cover DOS 5.0, this book explores the power of .BAT—the PC user's key to total system control. Richardson shows how to boost productivity dramatically with simple step-saving programs. He discusses two of the most often customized system batch files, AUTOEXEC.BAT and CONFIG.SYS and then shows you how to create your own batch files. 440 pages, 186 illustrations. 5.25″ disk included. **Book No. 3916, $26.95 paperback, $36.95 hardcover**

MS-DOS® BATCH FILE UTILITIES
Ronny Richardson

Featuring more than 200 of the best batch file programs available for the PC, this is the most complete source of documentation available for batch file utilities currently offered as shareware or in the public domain. Arranged alphabetically and meticulously cross-referenced by category, this valuable reference features detailed descriptions and instructions for ALL commercial batch files on the DOS market today. 368 pages, 275 illustrations. 5.25″ disk included. **Book No. 3915, $29.95 paperback, $36.95 hardcover**

FOXPRO®: The Master Reference—2nd Edition
Robin Stark and Shelley Satonin

Design and run powerful, customized databases in no time using all the exciting new features of FoxPro. This alphabetical guide to every FoxPro command and function covers all versions through 2.0—more than 350 entries in all. Its innovative three-part indexing system leads you quickly to all commands, functions, and examples found in the book. 512 pages, 135 illustrations. **Book No. 4056, $24.95 paperback only**

NORTON UTILITIES® 6.0: An Illustrated Tutorial
Richard Evans

Richard Evans shows you how to painlessly perform the most dazzling Norton functions using the all-new features of Norton Utilities 6.0. He also reviews the best from previous releases, providing clear, easy-to-follow instructions and screen illustrations reflecting Norton's new developments. You'll also learn about NDOS, a new configuration and shell program that replaces COMMAND.COM. 464 pages, 277 illustrations. **Book No. 4132, $19.95 paperback, $29.95 hardcover**

101+ FOXPRO® AND dBASE®
IVUSER-DEFINED FUNCTIONS
Philip Steele

Whether you've already written many lines of database code and just want to improve your code or you want to develop more complex applications for distribution in the corporate marketplace, this book's for you. It contains professional guidelines for developing and writing UDFs that will eliminate repetitive database programming tasks. A companion disk, offered on an order form at the end of the book, contains all the UDFs used in the book. 368 pages, 159 illustrations. **Book No. 3951, $22.95 paperback only**

COMPUTER SECURITY
HANDBOOK—2nd Edition
Richard H. Baker

This edition emphasizes practical, affordable measures that protect networks and database servers, featuring all-new coverage of virus control methods, the 1986 Computer Fraud and Abuse Act, and recent case studies of security problems. You'll find complete information on prevention and cure of viruses, electronic eavesdropping, personnel controls, identifying your most vulnerable points, password perils, security planning, and how a computer can protect itself. 432 pages, 70 illustrations. **Book No. 3592, $24.95 paperback, $34.95 hardcover**

GRAPHICAL USER
INTERFACE PROGRAMMING
Steve Rimmer

Graphical user interfaces are one of the hottest topics in PC software technology today. Creating and using GUIs requires a delicate combination of graphics programming skill and an ability to organize multiple graphic objects. This book shows you how to combine these skills to create images through bit-mapping graphics. Rimmer shows you how to write tight code menus, screen fonts, mouse interfaces, icons, and more. 440 pages, 176 illustrations. **Book No. 3875, $24.95 paperback, $36.95 hardcover**

THE RELATIONAL DATABASE ADVISOR:
Elements of PC Database Design
Kimberly Maughan Saunders

Kimberly Saunders gives you easy-to-follow guidelines for every phase in the database design process, providing specific suggestions for building databases that fit a variety of business needs and software environments. You'll soon create sophisticated libraries of database files with common informational links. 248 pages, 128 illustrations. **Book No. 3944, $16.95 paperback only**

SQL: Structured Query Language—2nd Edition
Dr. Carolyn J. Hursch and Dr. Jack L. Hursch

Carolyn J. Hursch and Jack L. Hursch present a complete overview of SQL, tracing its mathematical structure from its basis in first-order logic to its present-day role and the efforts of the American National Standards Institute (ANSI) to develop a standard SQL language. They cover all the components of conventional SQL language; SQL commands, keywords, and data types; and value expressions supported by SQL. 216 pages, illustrated. **Book No. 3803, 21.95 paperback, $32.95 hardcover**

DOS 5 DEMYSTIFIED
James S. Forney

This book provides a frank appraisal of the strengths, weaknesses, and peculiarities of this new release, offering insider tips to help you get the most from DOS 5's new features. It emphasizes compatibility and productivity to help you take full advantage of the power of DOS 5. Some of the new and enhanced features covered include: HIMEM.SYS, DISK SERVICES, QBASIC, and EDIT. 440 pages, illustrated. **Book No. 3860, $24.95 paperback, $34.95 hardcover**

THE ENTREPRENEURIAL PC
Bernard J. David

Put that expensive home PC to work for you. You will learn about the profit-making potential of computers in typing, word processing, desktop publishing, database programming, hardware installation, electronic mail, and much more. David uses detailed, real-life examples to describe some of the more popular avenues of entrepreneurship for the home PC owner. 336 pages, 50 illustrations. **Book No. 3823, $19.95 paperback, $29.95 hardcover**

UPGRADE YOUR IBM® COMPATIBLE
AND SAVE A BUNDLE—2nd Edition
Aubrey Pilgrim

Praise for the first edition . . .
"Every aspect is covered . . . liberally and clearly illustrated . . . invaluable."

—*PC Magazine*

Find valuable advice on adding the newest high-quality, low-cost hardware to your PC with this book. It offers informative how-to's for replacing motherboards with 80286, 80386, and 08486 boards; adding new floppy and hard disks drives; replacing old BIOS chips, installing chips and memory boards; and plugging in internal modems and VGA, fax, and network boards. 264 pages, 60 illustrations. **Book No. 3828, $19.95 paperback, $29.95 hardcover**

Prices Subject to Change Without Notice.

Look for These and Other TAB Books at Your Local Bookstore

To Order Call Toll Free 1-800-822-8158
(24-hour telephone service available.)

or write to TAB Books, Blue Ridge Summit, PA 17294-0840.

Title	Product No.	Quantity	Price

☐ Check or money order made payable to TAB Books

Charge my ☐ VISA ☐ MasterCard ☐ American Express

Acct. No. _____ Exp. _____

Signature: _____

Name: _____

Address: _____

City: _____

State: _____ Zip: _____

Subtotal $ _____

Postage and Handling
($3.00 in U.S., $5.00 outside U.S.) $ _____

Add applicable state and local
sales tax $ _____

TOTAL $ _____

TAB Books catalog free with purchase; otherwise send $1.00 in check or money order and receive $1.00 credit on your next purchase.

Orders outside U.S. must pay with international money order in U.S. dollars drawn on a U.S. bank.

TAB Guarantee: If for any reason you are not satisfied with the book(s) you order, simply return it (them) within 15 days and receive a full refund. **BC**

If you need help

The disk included here contains programs and batch files described in *Writing DR DOS®*
Batch Files (Book #4289), (C) 1993 by Windcrest Books. Contents of this disk include six
subdirectories and two files:

BAT	DUALBOOT
MENU1	MENU2
MENU3	PROGRAM
README.BLD	README.EXE

You might find it more convenient to keep all of these files on your hard drive instead
of having to access them from the floppy disk. To create a hard drive directory to store
these files and subdirectories in, simply type

MD *dname*

at your hard drive prompt (most likely C: \ ), where *dname* is what you want to name the
directory. (Possible suggestions are "4289" or "DRDOS".)

Now change into this directory by typing

CD *dname*

at the prompt. You should now be inside your newly created directory called *dname*.

Now, to copy all your files, you must make six more subdirectories named after the
ones on the disk, using the MD command like before. Do this first.

Then use the COPY command to actually transfer the files:

COPY A: \ *sdname* \ *.* C: \ *dname* \ *sdname*

where *dname* is the name of the directory you previously created and *sdname* is the name
of the subdirectory you are copying from and into. For example, to copy all the files form
the BAT subdirectory on the disk, make a subdirectory called BAT on your hard drive and
then type COPY A: \ BAT \ *.* C: \ *dname* \ BAT. To copy the last two files, simply
type

COPY A: \ *.* C: \ *dname*

For more help and for information about the contents of the disk type

README

at the DOS prompt with your disk in Drive A or run it from your hard drive after copying.

Order Form for Readers
Requiring a Single 5.25″ Disk

This Windcrest/McGraw-Hill software product is also available on a 5.25″/1.2Mb disk. If you need the software in 5.25″ format, simply follow these instructions:

- Complete the order form below. Be sure to include the exact title of the Windcrest/McGraw-Hill book for which you are requesting a replacement disk.

- Make check or money order made payable to *Glossbrenner's Choice*. The cost is **$5.00** (**$8.00** for shipments outside the U.S.) to cover media, postage, and handling. Pennsylvania residents, please add 6% sales tax.

- Foreign orders: please send an international money order or a check drawn on a bank with a U.S. clearing branch. We cannot accept foreign checks.

- Mail order form and payment to:

    Glossbrenner's Choice
    Attn: Windcrest/McGraw-Hill Disk Replacement
    699 River Road
    Yardley, PA 19067-1965

Your disk will be shipped via First Class Mail. Please allow one to two weeks for delivery.

Windcrest/McGraw-Hill Disk Replacement

Please send me a replacement disk in 5.25″/1.2Mb format for the following Windcrest/McGraw-Hill book:

Book Title _____

Name _____

Address _____

City/State/ZIP _____